THE HISTORY OF MARXISM

The History of Marxism

Edited by: Eric J. Hobsbawm, Georges Haupt, Franz Marek, Ernesto Ragionieri, Vittorio Strada and Corrado Vivanti

Volume 1: Marxism in Marx's Day

Volume 2: Marxism in the Age of the Second International

Volume 3: The Marxism of the Third International

Volume 4: Contemporary Marxism

THE
HISTORY OF
MARXISM

Volume One:
Marxism in Marx's Day

EDITED BY
ERIC J. HOBSBAWM

Professor of Social History,
Birkbeck College, University of London

Indiana University Press
Bloomington

Copyright this edition © 1982 by the Harvester Press
preface and chapters 1, 8 and 11 © 1982 by E.J. Hobsbawm

First published in Italy as
Storia del marxismo, volume primo:
Il marxismo ai tempi di Marx
© 1978 by Giulio Einaudi editore s.p.a., Torino

Manufactured in Great Britain

Library of Congress Cataloging in Publication Data
Main entry under title:
Marxism in Marx's day.
(The History of Marxism; v. 1)
Translation of: Il Marxismo ai tempi di Marx, v. 1 of Storia del Marxismo.
    1. Socialism–History–Addresses, essays, lectures. 2. Communism–
History–Addresses, essays, lectures. I. Hobsbawm, Eric J. II. Series: Storia
del Marxismo. English; v. 1.
HX15.S8513 vol. [HX39.5] 335'.009s 81-6473
[335.4] AACR2
1 2 3 4 5 85 84 83 82 81

ISBN 0-253-32812-8

CONTENTS

PREFACE

When the *History of Marxism* of which this is the first volume began to be planned some years ago, no large-scale and comprehensive historical and analytical survey of the development of Marxism existed. And indeed, though a number of authors have attempted single-handed surveys of this kind, and there have also been collections of studies by various contributors, a survey such as was in the mind of the group which conceived the present *History*, still does not exist, at all events in the West. The nearest thing to it remains G.D.H. Cole's *History of Socialist Thought*, but its range is wider than Marxism, its analytical interest is limited, and much of the history of Marxism has taken place since its completion.[1]

On the other hand, the past twenty years have produced, in addition to much worthless polemicising and mediocre sub-scholarship, a remarkable body of work on special aspects of Marxist theory and history, ranging from vast projects, like E.H. Carr's *History of the Bolshevik Revolution*, through monographs on important individual Marxists, schools of thought, social democratic and communist parties during some or all of their histories, to such detailed surveys of highly specialised problems of theory, as G. Sofri's survey of the problem of Marx's 'asiatic mode of production'. This period, which has probably seen a greater quantity, variety — and perhaps quality — of Marxist writing and serious studies of Marxism than any other, with the possible exception of the years from 1890 to 1914, has thus provided, in a widely scattered and unco-ordinated form, a mass of material which can today be synthesised. It has also provided a sufficiently large body of serious students prepared to contribute to such a synthesis. The object of the present history is to construct it. Our work will no doubt express the point of view of the 1970s, but it is hoped that nevertheless it will retain its value substantially for a period of 10–20 years.

'The philosophers have hitherto only interpreted the world: the point, however is to change it'. Marxism, the most practically influential (and practically rooted) school of theory in the history of the modern world, is both a method of interpreting and of changing it, and its history must be written accordingly. It cannot only be the history of what Marxists, beginning with Marx, have thought, written and discussed, whether in the form of a traditional tracing of the genealogical tree of descent of ideas, or even by the Marxist method of investigating the relation of 'consciousness' to the 'social being' from which it springs. It must also deal with the movements inspired, or claiming to be inspired by the ideas of Marx, and with the revolutions in which Marxists have played a part, and with the attempts to construct socialist societies by Marxists who have been in a position to make such attempts. Moreover, since both the theoretical scope of the Marxist analyses and the practical influence of Marxism have left virtually no field of human thought and activity and no part of the world untouched; the scope of such a history must be extremely wide. Marxism has been of political significance in the shores of the Arctic Sea and in Patagonia, from China westwards to Peru. Marxist thinkers have expressed opinions on mathematics, painting and sexual relations, with or without the incursions of administrative and state power into these subjects.

How to give the history of so vast and apparently limitless a subject form and organisation, is a crucial problem. It may be useful for prospective readers of this history to set out the principles upon which we have tried to organise it.

We begin with the self-evident propositions that the history of Marxism is not concluded, that Marxism is a living body of thought and that its continuity since the days of Marx and Engels has been substantially unbroken. We therefore assume that a good many readers will open the present work not only with the academic curiosity with which they might approach a history of astrology or medieval scholasticism, but with a powerful desire to discover what, if anything, Marxist thought contributes to the solution of present problems. Marxists are engaged in writing about such problems at the present time, and this activity belongs to the history of Marxism. In doing so, they almost invariably attempt to express their thought in terms of specific writings by Marx and various subsequent Marxists, or at least to link their thought to such texts. In this sense the continuity of Marxism is much more direct and obvious than that of other living but eponymous schools of thought, such as Darwinism. No scientist working in the field of evolution fails to pay his respects to Darwin, but none would today read the *Origin of species* except for purpose of history, *pietas* or private interest. The works of

Marx, even those of his youth, continue to be read as valid contributions to present discussion, and so (at least by some) are those of particular subsequent Marxists.

Second, we do not make the assumption that the subject of this history is a single specific Marxism, let alone 'true' Marxism as opposed to the false or deviant. All bodies of thought claiming to be derived from Marx or influenced by his writings are in principle part of its history, including even the remoter influences which take us outside the range of thinkers, movements and institutions describing themselves as Marxist. Insofar as ideas taken from Marx have become, like some from Freud or Darwin, part of the common stock of intellectual discourse, or insofar as academic and political discussion deals consciously with problems raised by Marxists (if only for the purpose of polemics), they cannot be excluded, though they must occupy a marginal position in this work.

Such an all-inclusive programme does not imply agnosticism about what is Marxist and what is not, and certainly not about what Marx himself meant, or whether his views have been correctly interpreted by later Marxists. However, even demonstrably incorrect interpretations belong to the history of Marxism. Marxism possesses a unity, deriving both from the coherent body of theory which Marx claimed to hold, the specifiable practical problems he hoped to solve with its aid (for example, those of revolution and the transition to a socialist society) and from the historic continuity of the major organised bodies of Marxists, all of whom can be, as it were, 'placed' on a family tree whose original trunk consists of the social democratic organisations of the last years of Engels' life. But it is a unity in diversity. It is based not on theoretical and political agreement, but on common objectives (for example, 'socialism') and above all on a common adherence, in principle, to a body of doctrine derived from the writings of Marx and Engels, however added to or modified. The 'legal Marxists' of Tsarist Russia are outside it (as distinct from, say, the Bund), when they ceased *de facto* and *de jure* to maintain the common objective, though — at least initially — maintaining the theory. The Fabians are outside it (as distinct from the politically very similar Bernstein, who had been directly influenced by them), because they rejected the entire doctrine, whereas the 'revisionists' did not.

Beyond this there is not one Marxism, but many Marxisms, often, as is well known, engaged in bitter internecine polemics and denying one another's right to the name. It is not the task of this history to decide on their respective claims, except in a purely technical or factual sense. It is the historian's business to show that Marx, at least at one important stage of his thinking, believed in an 'asiatic mode of production', to observe the political considerations which, among others, led to the elimination of this concept from most communist Marxism in the 1930s and to observe the attempts to reinstate the concept since the 1950s. It is not his task to decide whether those who refuse to accept an 'asiatic mode of production' are worse or better Marxists than those who do. It is the historian's business to show that, among the numerous organisations of Bolshevik inspiration, the orthodox (Stalinist) communist parties were, at least between the early 1920s and the late 1950s, overwhelmingly the largest and most significant, and that, with a few local or at most regional exceptions, dissident Leninist theorists and groups attracted insignificant numerical support. But this statement implies no judgement about the relative contributions of the various organisations, large or tiny, to the development of Marxist analysis. The historian ought to refrain from such judgement, except insofar as it is beyond rational dispute. He may record the self-evident fact that while orthodox communists were virtually precluded from applying any analysis to, say, the political and economic developments of the USSR, dissident Leninists, for obvious reasons, spent much of their energy on such an analysis. On the other hand, he will merely take note of the divergences in these analyses (for example, on the question whether the USSR should be regarded as a degenerate proletarian state or a form of state capitalism) without attempting to conclude a discussion which is still in progress. Conversely, he can and ought to state that the dogmatic and hieratic orthodoxy, which came to characterise Russian Marxism after the death of Lenin, differs from anything of which Marx himself would have approved, so far as we can tell. But even if, as is extremely likely, he will personally disagree with it, he will be obliged to treat it as a development within Marxism, one which demonstrably forms one of the major branches of the family tree of Marxist descent, and was indeed, by the criteria of practical politics, dominant within the development of Marxism for several decades.

The third assumption follows from the second. It is evident that a collective history of Marxism will be written by authors whose views differ, both on the theoretical aspects of Marxist analysis and on its political consequences. For various reasons authors holding some extreme views will hardly take part in this project.

Those who reject both the theory and the objects of Marx entirely, or who can see no merit whatever in either, are not likely to make a significant contribution to its historiography, any more than those who believe the French revolution to have been entirely unnecessary and undesirable are likely to possess that minimum of *Verstehen*, of emotional and intellectual empathy, without which its history cannot profitably be written. On the other hand those for whom Marxism is a dogmatic theology must find it difficult, even if permitted by official authority, to question rather than to defend positions to which they are committed. This still leaves a wide range of interpretation and opinion. Twenty years ago this might have made a collective project such as this impossible. It is still difficult, but experience has demonstrated that there is sufficient common ground between students of Marxism of varying opinions to make it practicable. There is or can be, agreement about facts verifiable by evidence. There is already a substantial consensus about the merits of much of the secondary literature. Whatever their political or ideological commitments, hardly any serious students of the subject will fail to hold a high opinion of works (themselves written from different points of view) like Carr's *History of the Bolshevik Revolution*, Isaac Deutscher's biography of Trotsky, J.P. Nettl's *Rosa Luxemburg*, or Carl Schorske's *German Social Democracy 1905-1917*, or to assent to many of their findings. The 1970s are perhaps the first time since shortly before 1914 when it is possible for Marxists of various persuasions and serious students of the subject uncommitted to Marxism, to write a co-operative history of Marxism which is more than a record of divergences (that is, to treat contributions of writers with a different orientation as valid, though sometimes open to discussion, rather than as unacceptable).

No attempt will be made in this project to establish agreement where none exists, let alone to impose on contributors interpretations which they do not accept. However, while chapters and paragraphs of the work will undoubtedly disagree sometimes, and may occasionally contradict one another, we feel confident that on the whole it will demonstrate a considerable consensus about the history of Marxism, though not about its future developments.

So much for the assumptions. So far as the treatment of the subject is concerned, we shall try to apply the following principles:

1 Both the thought and practice of Marx and subsequent Marxists are the product of their times, whatever their permanent intellectual validity or practical achievement. They must therefore be analysed in terms of the historic conditions in which they were formulated (that is, both the situation in which Marxists found themselves and the problems arising from it, and the specific combination of intellectual materials from which they constructed their ideas). In the most general sense, Marx derived a general analysis of the 'law of motion' of capitalism from the phase of capitalism through which he lived in the mid-nineteenth century, more especially from its British version; and he did so as a nineteenth-century thinker (that is, as one who had undergone a certain type of education, was nourished on a historically specific body of information and experience, shared certain current assumptions, etc.). This is also true of subsequent Marxists, for whom of course the writings of previous Marxists and the experience and traditions of Marxist movements were a decisive element in the formation of their ideas and actions. (For this reason our history will attempt to establish not only what the different schools of Marxism were at various times — schools not only in the metaphoric sense, but in the literal sense of the organisations, groups, etc., in which men learned to be Marxists — but also what writings of Marx and other 'authoritative' Marxists were available at a given time, and, if possible, how widely they were diffused).

2 Being the product of a specific historic situation, Marxism was inevitably developed and modified in the light of its changes (that is, of the larger transformations of history, of changing circumstances, of the discovery of new facts, the lessons of experience, not to mention change in the surrounding intellectual climate). This is true both of Marxist theory and of Marxist strategy. It does not necessarily imply any fundamental change in either, though at times some Marxists suggested that it did (for example, the Bernsteinian revisionists). Marx's own thought developed in this way (for example, between the 1840s and the 1850s), and the subsequent developments in Marxism are largely due to the attempts to come to terms with the problems, theoretical and practical, arising out of new historic situations, or out of situations to which the writings of Marx and Engels provided no specific guidance, or only the most general guidance. Apart from changes which affected not so much the development of the general theories of Marxists as of their ideas of strategy and tactics, the following types of changes are of particular significance:

(a) The development of world capitalism, which modified the system to the point where, from time to time, a 'new phase' of capitalism had to be recognised (for example, at the end of the nineteenth century, 'Imperialism').

(b) The geographical diffusion of Marxism and Marxist movements, which brought them into regions quite unlike the countries of central and western Europe, which formed the basis of most of Marx's concrete analysis and of the earlier Marxist working class movements (for example, China).

(c) The victory of revolutions, which faced Marxists with unprecedented problems of state organisation and the construction of socialism, for which earlier Marxist theory provided hardly any concrete guidance (for example, typically, Russia after the October Revolution).

(d) Arising out of the last, the subsequent developments within that part of the world where Marxist movements (parties) held state power, and for which Marx's own writings provided, for practical purposes, no concrete guidance at all (for example, the relations between socialist states).

(e) The pattern of uneven, divergent (and perhaps convergent) development on a world scale, which embodies the changes listed above.

Fortunately most of these changes cluster together chronologically, so that a suitable periodisation enables us, with certain reservations, to present them not only separately, but in their interaction.

3 The major chronological divisions we suggest are the following:

(a) *Before 1848–1850*. This was the period of the origin of socialism and the formation of Marx's thought. It coincided with the first major crisis of growth of early industrial capitaliam (1830s–1840s), which was at the same time the crisis of transition to industrial capitalism in some countries; and with the revolutionary crisis which culminated in 1848. Though Marx and Engels participated actively and prominently in politics, we have for practical purposes no Marxist movements yet.

(b) *1850–1875/83*.[2] This was the classic period of nineteenth-century capitalist development: the rapid growth of a world system of liberal capitalism, centred in Britain, the first stages of major industrial development in the major 'developed' countries of the West and the concomitant construction of an international system of national capitalist states — USA, Germany, etc. —; the emergence of a working-class movement

on the European continent — the First International —; the
first 'crisis of the underdeveloped countries' — a Russian
revolutionary movement; the Paris Commune, at once the last
of the jacobin and the first of the proletarian revolutions —.
This period coincided with the mature development of Marx's
thought, and saw his second major intervention in political
affairs (in the First International period). However, with the
partial exception of Germany, no Marxist movement of
significance as yet existed, and Marx's influence was
negligible.

(c) *1883-1914*. This was the period of the Marxism of the
Second International. Its immediate background was the
second crisis of world capitalist development, the period of
crisis and tension 1873–96, out of which there emerged a new
phase of capitalism ('Imperialism'), with new technological,
economic, social and political characteristics, and consequently new strategic perspectives, with which Marxists
attempted to come to terms from the end of the 1890s ('crisis of
Marxism'). However, it is not our intention to introduce major
sub-periodisations in our presentation. Mass working-class
parties, increasingly under the hegemony or leadership of
Marxism, as formulated in the German social democratic
party, and revolutionary Marxist movements in the agrarian
underdeveloped countries of East and South Europe
developed rapidly, grouped in the Second International. This
expansion produced important divergences, for example: (i) in
general between the national movements ('the national
question'); (ii) between the 'developed' countries, in which
these movements operated under conditions of a stable
capitalism and, in varying degrees, bourgeois-democratic
politics (among which in turn we must now distinguish
countries where the labour movements were under Marxist
leadership — the European continent — and those where they
were not — the Anglo-Saxon countries); and (iii) the
underdeveloped countries and regions of Europe. There we
find both conditions of revolutionary crisis (Romanian
jacquerie, Russian Revolution of 1905) and revolutionary
movements largely under the ideological influence of the
western proletarian movements (Russian social democracy),
though confronting quite different problems; (iv) the early
stages of the movements for national liberation in the colonial
and semicolonial countries of the 'Third World', as yet hardly
touched — with some exceptions: Indonesia, Russian narod-

nik influences in India — by western socialist theory and practice. At the same time the revolution of 1905 introduced a series of new problems — the 'models' of 1789, or even 1848 were no longer an adequate or even plausible guide — and the discussions arising out of them anticipate the later problems of proletarian power.

(d) *1914–1949*.[3] With one or two major subperiods, divided by the 'great crisis' of 1929–33 and World War II, this was the period of the Marxism of the Third International, which runs, broadly speaking from the October Revolution to the Chinese Revolution. This was the period of capitalist 'general crisis' (war, revolutions, economic breakdown, fascism, war) of the October Revolution and the creation of the first socialist country, and of the spread of Marxist movements into the colonial and semi-colonial world as part of the Third World revolution.

The divergence of development was now such that three main sectors have to be considered separately, though in interaction: (i) The developed countries, in which, after the failure of the hopes of world revolution in 1918–23, the revolutionary (that is, overwhelmingly communist) sector of the Marxist movement remained in the minority — at least until World War II — and reformist labour movements (including those maintaining an increasingly attenuated Marxism) prevailed, so long as the conditions of bourgeois democracy subsisted. (ii) The underdeveloped countries of East and South Europe and the Third World, where the centre of gravity of the international revolutionary perspectives were obvious. (iii) The USSR, where post-revolutionary problems arose. These three sectors were linked together by common global developments affecting all simultaneously (war, post-war revolutionary crisis, slump, fascism, war) or by a chronological parallelism into the exact nature of which we need not for the moment enquire (for example, capitalist stabilisation of the 1920s/Nep; industrialisation-collectivisation/slump); but also by the overwhelming domination over the revolutionary Marxist movements of the October Revolution, the USSR, and the increasingly Russian-dominated monocentric 'international party', the Comintern.

(e) *Since 1949*. This is the period of *de facto*, and later *de jure* polycentric Marxism. It is the period of the first general and long-term stabilisation of international capitalism since 1914. It is also the period of the triumph of the anti-imperialist revolution in the Third World, in the form of a general political decolonisation and a partial victory of social revolution, of which the establishment of communist states marks the most advanced point. Among these, in turn, the triumph of communism in China is by far the most significated development. Thirdly, it is the period when the USSR extended its type of socialist system to a number of European countries and developed into the second great power in what is, during these years, an international system based on bilateral rivalry. The variety and complexity of these developments, and the disintegration of the dominant Marxist force of period 1914–49, USSR-centric communism, is such that a coherent treatment of this period is exceptionally difficult. It is probably best seen as a period of major expansion, but at the same time of major secular crisis for Marxism, in which both the analyses and the perspectives of the period 1914–49 have to be extensively reviewed in the light of developments in all three sectors of the world.

For practical purposes it has proved to be more convenient to treat periods (d) and (e) together, since world Marxism, both in theory and in practice, was dominated between 1917 and 1956 by the fact of a single global communist movement which accepted the USSR as its core and the Soviet Communist Party as its head. Consequently the fourth and last part of this *History* will survey the situation of Marxism since 1956, which marks a major caesura in the history of the international communist movement. No clear date for the conclusion of this essentially open-ended survey is suggested. However, it should be borne in mind that the mid-1970s mark a major change in international capitalism, namely the end of long-term stability and unprecedented prosperity and global economic expansion, and the onset of a period of lengthy crisis.

4   The major chronological divisions define not merely the narrative, or '*événementiel*' framework of our historical exposition, but also the analytical framework. For the value of the projected work lies less in the accumulation or synthesis of information, but in the formulation and answering of questions. Where the answer to the questions must be left open, or where disagreement among the contributors produces alternative answers, we hope that the formulation and the ordering of the material will be such as to clarify the problems at issue.

There are clearly three principal groups of questions which will be asked by prospective readers of this history. They can be grouped under the following headings:

1   How has Marxism interpreted the complex and changing world?
2   How has it evolved strategies, forms of organisations, etc., to bring about the revolutionary transformation which was Marx's object; or such other objectives as Marxists may have substituted for it?
3   Where revolution has been victorious, how has it set about the construction of new socialist systems of society?

These questions may be, without substantial change of the historical treatment of the subject, reformulated in other ways (for example, how far have Marxists adequately interpreted the world?, how far have they succeeded in constructing socialist systems or society?, etc.). Except in the most general and abstract terms, the analytical and political problems which Marxists have posed themselves, therefore arise only in the context of concrete historical situations, and are solved in terms of these situations. The record of their formulation and solution in an earlier situation remains as the basis of new (perhaps modified) formulations and new (perhaps modified) solutions in new situations. Alternatively, new concrete situations allow Marxists to fill in the outlines of problem and solution suggested or adumbrated in the relevant part of the earlier general analysis [by Marx or some other Marxist theorist(s)], but not discussed in concrete terms there. Marxist analysis thus consists of a constant interplay between past doctrine and experience and present situation, each influencing the other.

The process is familiar, but some examples may nevertheless clarify it. The problems of modern automation, which could hardly arise concretely before the middle of the twentieth century, will be confronted by Marxists in the light of the relevant prophetic passages in the *Grundrisse* of 1857–8. Indeed, in a sense the discovery of the significance of these passages by Marxists is due to the emergence of automation as a concrete problem in our era. The problem of interpreting the character of post-war capitalism arose, for practical purposes only during the 1950s, and implied a reconsideration of a whole accumulation of earlier analyses — of capitalism in general, of the successive phases of its development recognised by Marxists (the 'classical' phases of Marx's day, the imperialism/monopoly capitalism, whose analyses were formulated between, say 1900 and 1929, of the 'general crisis of capitalism', etc.). These in turn have significant implications for strategy and tactics. How far ought revolutionary trade unions to adapt their policy to the conditions of a new, and for long periods stable and prosperous, structure of the capitalist economy, as the French CGT and the Italian CGIL did, *de jure* or *de facto*, though with some delay, after the expectation of a post-war crisis were disappointed? How far does (or did) such an adaptation lead inevitably to a reformism of the social democratic type, as the new extreme left argued in from the 1960s? The answers to such questions must in turn imply an analysis of the situation which gave rise to them and the social-political forces determining formulation and answer, or providing support for each of the possible strategies and tactics.

As for the relation of the new answers to the accumulated body of past Marxist doctrine, opinions among Marxists have always been divided between those who believed that they did, and those who believed that they did not require a formal 'revision' of that doctrine, and among the former, between those who were prepared to push their formal 'revision' to the point of abandoning the doctrine, and those who chose to remain 'Marxists'. These differences are of importance only for the doctrinal history of Marxism. In practice, every form of Marxist movement that has been of any practical significance, and every version of Marxist analysis that has exercised any influence, has, at least at some stages of its development, modified the doctrines of the past in the light of changed conditions. The task of the historian is to record and analyse these modifications, whether they are labelled revisions or not.[4]

The treatment of the major problems of Marxism cannot be mechanically fitted into, or broken up according to, a chronological scheme. There are three possibilities, all of which will be utilised according to convenience and the requirements of lucid and systematic exposition:

1   To single out a theme and treat it as a whole, apart from the chronological scheme.
2(a) To confine the treatment of a theme entirely to the chronological period within which it arose historically (for example, the treatment of Marx's general analysis of capitalism to period 1850–75/83). We also propose to use the device of 'portraits' of significant Marxists, normally inserted at a suitable point of the relevant period, but which will discuss the theoretical

issues arising out of the activities of their subject. Thus the 'portrait' of Rosa Luxemburg will be inserted in period 1883–1914. It should, however, so far as possible define and discuss the entire complex of problems and debates associated then and since with Luxemburg.

2(b) Insofar as this is not implied in 2(a), to extend the discussion of certain problems beyond the chronological limits of the period in which they arise (that is, it may be convenient, within period 1883–1914, to discuss not only the Marxist analysis of imperialism as it developed before 1914 — Kautsky, Hobsonian influences, Hilferding, Luxemburg — but also later developments such as Lenin, Sternberg) perhaps even with brief anticipations of the post-war discussion on the transformations of imperialism or the continued validity of the analysis — Sweezy, Barratt Brown, Jalée, Kidron, etc.

3 To divide the treatment of a theme chronologically, returning to it in each successive period (for example, the theme of the nature of proletarian revolution, the perspectives for the ending — collapse, transformation — of capitalism, are likely to recur in each period, in the context of the changed conditions of that period).

Since we are concerned with the history and development of Marxism, other matters are treated only insofar as they are relevant to this subject; or insofar as the absolute minimum of information must be given about the historical background to readers who would otherwise find the subject incomprehensible. The problem of finding the right balance can best be illustrated by examples. Thus it is not our intention to write a history, however brief, of the October Revolution or Lenin's part in it, but to assess the contribution of the October Revolution to the development of Marxism and its significance within that development. This will mean that our history will say very little about Kerensky, Kornilov and the cruiser *Aurora*, but much about such problems as the problem of the nature of the Bolshevik party and the role of such a party in a revolution, the problem of the transition from bourgeois-democratic to proletarian revolution, the problem of forecasting the nature, structure and programme of proletarian power (*State and revolution*), the problem of taking power in a country in which some crucial conditions for the building of socialism are lacking ('Moscow or Berlin?'), the attitudes of different kinds of Marxists to the October Revolution, the effects of the October Revolution on the different labour and socialist movements (attraction of Bolshevism and the Russian model), etc. This list is merely for the purpose of illustration.

A history of Marxism is inevitably also, in part, a history of the critique of Marxism, at least inasmuch as Marxist discussion itself attempts to refute or come to terms with such critiques (for example, in economics, with the Böhm–Bawerkian arguments). Anti-Marxist critiques are also worth brief treatment insofar as the attempt to provide an alternative to the Marxist analysis has made a permanent contribution to the development of general (non-Marxist) science, for example, Max Weber. In general, however, no systematic treatment of the development of anti-Marxism will be provided, or probably required.

In conclusion, some remarks about the present and first volume of this *History of Marxism*. There is a natural difference between it and subsequent volumes, since it deals with developments in the lifetime of Marx and Engels and, above all, with the activities and writings of the founders of Marxism (that is, with its point of departure). For later Marxists, Marx and Engels were and are a point of permanent reference and, since the death of Engels, a corpus of texts and data which can no longer be added to by the 'classics' themselves. At most hitherto unpublished writings can be discovered and published, or hitherto unknown facts about their activities brought to light. These writings and activities can be, and have been, analysed, interpreted and glossed. What would no doubt have been more to Marx's and Engels' taste, their methods of thought and action, derived from the study of both, can be, and has been, used to interpret and change a world which clearly, in many respects, did not remain the same as it had been in the lifetime of the founders. The earliest generation of Marxists were still able to consult Marx himself occasionally and Engels much more frequently, but evidently after 1895 this possibility also disappeared.

Inevitably, therefore, the work of the founders must be analysed differently from that of their followers. Let us take one example. We know that Marx saw himself as advancing from a position on the left of the Young Hegelians *via* Feuerbach to what we can, unless very pedantic, describe as a 'Marxian' position, though this was only the starting-point of a very considerable process of further theoretical elaboration and evolution. The question of what date in his career he thus became the 'Marxian' Marx has been hotly debated among Marxists and others, particularly since the publication of the *Frühschriften* in 1932, chiefly because there are far-reaching disagreements among them about the extent to which it marks a rejection of, and a rupture with, Marx's earlier thinking. These debates were or are believed by some to have considerable political implications. But it is evident that for Marx himself the problem, if it arose at all, presented itself quite differently. If he thought about the relation between his Paris Manuscripts of 1843 and, say, *Capital* at all, it cannot have been in terms of the debates since 1932. It must be assumed that he simply considered these early manuscripts as a stage in this theoretical development, including some views he had abandoned and others he still maintained. No question of systematically confronting the Marx of 1843 with the Marx of 1867 was likely to arise in his mind, since he knew quite well how much continuity or discontinuity there was between the two positions. At most he might feel impelled (as in the postscript to the second edition of *Capital*) to clarify his position (for example, in relation to Hegel in the light of criticism and current intellectual fashion). But his own *ad hoc* remarks cannot be considered in the same light as later discussions of the problem of the continuity of his thought.

Another example may be apposite. The relation between the thought of Marx and Engels has also become a matter of considerable debate since their lifetime. Some writers have gone so far as to discover not merely a difference between the two thinkers but a virtual incompatibility between their thought, or at least the implications of their thought. Now it is obvious that Marx and Engels were not identical thinkers, being different individuals. Engels himself was deeply aware of Marx's greater genius, though no surviving writings of Marx record any sense of Engels' inferiority. There was also, evidently, a division of labour between the two, certain topics being left to one or the other (for example, military subjects to Engels). There is also no doubt that the two sometimes disagreed, and that each sometimes accepted the other's criticisms.

Moreover, it is evident that their styles of thought and work differed. Marx, except perhaps when working against the clock, appears to have found it extremely difficult, indeed in most cases impossible, to complete the plans for his larger theoretical works. Even when he appeared to succeed, he could not resist modifying and developing the finished text, as witness the very substantial changes which *Capital* vol. I underwent between the first (1867) edition and the posthumous editions (1884, 1891) edited by Engels. On the other hand Engels wrote rapidly, lucidly, and perhaps with a more constant concern, particularly after Marx's death, for the systematic popular presentation of Marx's and his own ideas rather than for the further development of the theory. Finally, there is no denying that their thoughts did not always run along the same lines. It seems to be established that the work Marx hoped to write under the stimulus of L.H. Morgan would — to judge by his preliminary notes — have been somewhat different from the book Engels, seeking to carry out his comrade's wishes, actually wrote under the title *The Origin of the Family, Private Property and the State*.

It is therefore legitimate and necessary to abandon the practice of treating Marx–Engels as a single two-headed thinker, rather than as two separate thinkers. Nevertheless, the basic fact about both is their lifelong and intellectually undisturbed partnership. This was so close that Marx not only respected and acknowledged Engels' contributions to his own thought, but even asked him to write articles to be published over his own name (or to be considered as written by him). There is no evidence whatever that Marx expressed or felt any reservations about such works as Engels' *Anti-Dühring*, which is today often considered to embody specifically Engelsian positions. In short, the analysis of the possible divergences between the thought and activities of Marx and Engels belongs to the subsequent history of Marxism, but not to that of Marx's and Engels' own development.

The present volume has to consider both the problems of Marx's and Engels' own development and those later to arise out of the conversion of their lives and works into Marxism. From the perspective of the history of Marxism the second set of problems are fundamental, and contributors have attempted to bear in mind the developments and debates to which the work of the classics has subsequently given rise, and to draw attention to them. How far the term 'Marxism' was itself used, and is applicable, in the lifetime of Marx and Engels is also specifically considered, notably in Georges Haupt's chapter, but also elsewhere. We have assumed that Engels' systematic efforts after Marx's death to publish a corpus of his own and Marx's writings, to establish what was of permanent value in them, to produce a coherent body of theory and interpretation, and to clarify uncertain questions, constitute the first stage in the formation of the main tradition of Marxism. However, though the present volume necessarily looks forward, it has deliberately set out to avoid writing the history of the classics in the light of later developments. It deals with the period up to 1895, though keeping an eye on the future. The only chapter which specifically links Marx and Engels with our own times is that which sketches the fortunes of Marx's and Engels' writings from their original publication to the present. Such a chapter is, of course, necessary, since the bulk of subsequent Marxist development, at least in matters of theory, takes the corpus of classic texts available at any time as its point of departure, and consists to a very large extent of a commentary on and a critical development of these texts. The object of this chapter is naturally not to compete with the valuable and voluminous studies in the bibliography of Marx and Engels which are already in existence.

As for the development of Marx's and Engels' thought (one chapter seeks to distinguish Engels' specific contributions to it), the literature about this subject is already enormous. We have not attempted to compete directly with it. In the main we have, as already suggested, attempted to provide a background for the study of later developments in Marxism. Our object has been to situate Marx and Engels in the context of their times, and especially that of the socialist tradition which they transformed. A chapter on the young Marx — the early and transitional period which ended in the middle and later 1840s — was indispensable. For the rest we have attempted to survey three aspects of the mature Marx and Engels as theorists, which have been persistently debated since his death: as economist, philosopher and historian. It is perhaps worth mentioning that the chapter on Marx as economist is the last work ever written by the late Maurice Dobb. It was actually being typed at the time of his death. Another chapter deals with the complex question of Marx's and Engels' thought on what may broadly be called politics — including the state, revolution and the class struggle. Since this is inseparable from the actual political activities and analyses of the classics, a more chronological approach has been thought suitable for this chapter.

It is not the intention of this volume to engage in polemics, although it is impossible to write about any aspect of Marx's and Engels' lives and works without agreeing and/or disagreeing with some positions taken in the Marxist and anti-Marxist literature of the past century. The interpretations of the authors are their own. Where they conflict no attempt has been made to arrive at a consensus. Nor has it been the object of this volume to add to the body of knowledge about Marx, Engels and the socialist movement in their lifetime. The enormous quantity of erudition which has been devoted to both men for several generations, would make it almost impossible to do so. The purpose of the present volume is mainly to establish the foundations on which later volumes in this *History of Marxism* can be built.

It is in every sense a co-operative work. So this preface may fitly be concluded with a note in memory of three members of the group of friends and colleagues who planned it together, but who are now dead: Ernesto Ragionieri, historian of socialism and communism as well as of his native Sesto Fiorentino; Georges Haupt, historian of socialism, whose life took him from his native Romania via Auschwitz, the USSR and Romania to France; and Franz Marek of Vienna who, in a long career as a political intellectual, survived a German sentence of death in the Paris of 1944. All, in their way, united theory and practice. Their separate publications survive them, but this history is also their memorial.

E.J. Hobsbawm

Notes

1 The following introduction is a slightly modified version of the memorandum circulated to all contributors to the *History of Marxism*. It will therefore help readers to understand the nature of the task we have set ourselves, and to judge the degree to which we have succeeded. The parts dealing with technical editorial problems have been omitted. On the other hand a section dealing more specifically with the present (first) volume of the *History* has been added.

2 In terms of historic change some date in the 1870s is more logical (economic crisis and turning-point 1873, Paris Commune 1871, end of the First International 1872, unification of German social democratic party 1875): but it is probably more convenient to take the date of Marx's death. There is little practical difference, since Marx did little theoretical or practical work after the early 1870s.

3 The start of this period is clear enough: the collapse of the Second International in 1914, which also forms a useful point from which to survey the earlier development of the revolutionary currents which later flow together to form Bolshevism, and the development of the 1917 revolution. The end is more problematic, since world development is now so uneven that no date is entirely satisfactory for the whole globe. However, the Chinese revolution has the advantage: (a) of stressing the increasing significance of colonial liberation; and (b) coinciding with the stabilisation of post-war capitalism.

4 Genuine Marxist 'fundamentalism' (to use a theological analogy) is rare, and when it occurs — as in the tiny Socialist Party of Great Britain, which has preached the same gospel since 1905 — is without theoretical or practical interest. Most of what purports to be the literal adherence to Marxist doctrine, is the selection of a group of 'texts' from past doctrine suitable to the requirements of the selectors, or the maintenance of established doctrine as a body of dogma, by the side of which another *de facto* but unacknowledged theory is applied.

1 MARX, ENGELS AND PRE-MARXIAN SOCIALISM

Eric J. Hobsbawm

Part I

Marx and Engels were relative late-comers to communism. Engels declared himself a communist late in 1842, Marx probably not until the latter part of 1843, after a more prolonged and complex settling of accounts with liberalism and Hegel's philosophy. Even in Germany, a political backwater, they were not the first. German journeymen (*Handwerksgesellen*) working abroad had already made contact with organised communist movements, and produced the first native German communist theorist, the tailor Wilhelm Weitling, whose first work had been published in 1838 (*'Die Menschheit, wie sie ist und wie sie sein sollte'*). Among the intellectuals Moses Hess preceded — and indeed claimed to have converted — the young Frederick Engels. However, the question of priority in German communism is unimportant. By the early 1840s a flourishing socialist and communist movement, both theoretical and practical, had existed for some time in France, Britain and the USA. How much did the young Marx and Engels know about these movements? What did they owe to them? In what relation does their own socialism stand to their predecessors' and contemporaries? These questions will be discussed in the present chapter.

Before doing so we may briefly dismiss the pre-historic figures of communist theory, though historians of socialism usually pay their respects to them, since even revolutionaries like to have ancestors. Modern socialism does not derive from Plato or Thomas More, or even from Campanella, though the young Marx was sufficiently impressed with his 'City of the Sun' to plan its inclusion in an abortive 'Library of the best foreign socialist writers' he projected with Engels and Hess in 1845[1]. Such works had some interest for nineteenth-century readers, since one of the main difficulties of communist theory for urban intellectuals was that the actual operations of communist society appeared to have no precedent and were difficult to make plausible. The name of More's book, indeed, became the term used to describe any attempt to sketch the ideal society of the future, which in the nineteenth century meant primarily a communist one: Utopia.

1

Inasmuch as at least one utopian communist E. Cabet (1788–1856) was an admirer of More, the name was not ill-chosen. Nevertheless, the normal procedure of the pioneer socialists and communists of the early nineteenth century, if sufficiently given to study, was not to derive their ideas from some remote author, but to discover, or have their attention drawn to, the relevance of some earlier theoretical architect of ideal commonwealths — when about to construct their own critique of society or Utopia — and then to use and praise him. The fashion for utopian — not necessarily communist — literature in the eighteenth century, had made such works familiar enough.

Nor, in spite of varying degrees of familiarity with them, were the numerous historical examples of Christian communist establishments among the inspirers of modern socialist and communist ideas. How far the older ones (like the descendants of the sixteenth-century Anabaptists) were widely known at all, is unclear. Certainly the young Engels, who cited various such communities as proof that communism was practicable, confined himself to relatively recent examples: Shakers, (whom he regarded as 'the first people to set up a society on the basis of community of goods... in the whole world'),[2] Rappites and Separatists. Insofar as they were known, they also primarily confirmed an already existing desire for communism more than they inspired it.

It is not possible to dismiss quite so summarily the ancient religious and philosophical traditions which, with the rise of modern capitalism, acquired or revealed a new potential for social criticism, or confirmed an established one, because the revolutionary model of a liberal-economic society of unrestrained individualism conflicted with the social values of virtually every hitherto known community of men and women. For the educated minority, to whom practically all socialist, as indeed any other social, theorists belonged, they were embodied in a chain or network of philosophical thinkers, and most notably in a tradition of Natural Law stretching back to classical antiquity. Though some eighteenth-century philosophers were engaged in modifying such traditions to fit in with the new aspirations of a liberal-individualist society, philosophy carried with it from the past a strong heritage of communalism, or even, in several cases, the belief that a society without private property was in some sense more 'natural' or at any rate historically prior to one with private property. This was even more marked in Christian ideology. Nothing is easier than to see the Christ of the Sermon

on the Mount as 'the first socialist' or communist, and though the
majority of early socialist theorists were not Christians, many
later members of socialist movements have found this reflection
useful. Insofar as these ideas were embodied in a succession of
texts, commenting upon, adding to and criticising their predecessors, which were part of the formal or informal education of
social theorists, the idea of a 'good society', and specifically a
society not based on private property was at least a marginal part
of their intellectual heritage. It is easy to laugh at Cabet, who lists
a huge array of thinkers from Confucius to Sismondi, and passing
through Lycurgus, Pythagoras, Socrates, Plato, Plutarch,
Bossuet, Locke, Helvétius, Raynal and Benjamin Franklin as
recognising in his communism the realisation of their fundamental
ideas — and indeed Marx and Engels made fun of such
intellectual genealogy in the *German Ideology*.[3] Nevertheless, it
represents a genuine element of continuity between the
traditional critique of what was wrong in society and the new
critique of what was wrong in *bourgeois* society; at least for the
literate.

Insofar as such older texts and traditions embodied communal
concepts, they actually reflected something of the powerful
elements in European — mainly rural — pre-industrial societies,
and the even more obvious communal elements in the exotic
societies with which Europeans came into contact from the
sixteenth century. The study of such exotic and 'primitive'
societies played a notable role in the formation of western social
criticism, particularly in the eighteenth century, as witness the
tendency to idealise them as against 'civilised' society, whether in
the form of the 'noble savage', the free Swiss or Corsican
peasant, or otherwise. At the very least, as in Rousseau and other
eighteenth-century thinkers, it suggested that civilisation also
implied the corruption of some prior and in some ways more just,
equal and benevolent human state. It might even suggest that
such societies before private property ('primitive communism')
provided models of what future societies should once again aspire
to, and proof that it was not impracticable. This line of thought is
certainly present in nineteenth-century socialism, and not least in
Marxism, but, paradoxically, it emerges much more strongly
towards the end of the century than in its early decades —
probably in connection with Marx's and Engels' increasing
acquaintance and preoccupation with primitive communal
institutions.[4] With the exception of Fourier, the early socialists
and communists show no tendency to look back, even out of the

corner of their eye, towards a 'primitive happiness' which could
in some sense serve as a model for the future felicity of mankind;
and this in spite of the fact that the most familiar model for the
speculative construction of perfect societies, throughout the
sixteenth to eighteenth centuries, was the utopian novel,
purporting to recount what the traveller had encountered in the
course of some journey to remote areas of the Earth. In the
struggle between tradition and progress, the primitive and the
civilised, they were firmly committed on one side. Even Fourier,
who identified the primitive state of man with Eden, believed in
the ineluctability of progress.

The word 'progress' brings us to what was clearly the main
intellectual matrix of early modern socialist and communist
critiques of society, namely the eighteenth-century and in
particular the French Englightenment. At least this was Friedrich
Engels' firm opinion.[5] What he stressed above all was its
systematic rationalism. Reason provided the basis of all human
action and the formation of society, and the standard against
which 'all previous forms of society and government, all the old
ideas handed down by tradition' were to be rejected: 'Henceforth
superstition, injustice, privilege and oppression were to be
superseded by eternal truth, eternal justice, equality grounded in
Nature and the inalienable rights of man.'[6] The rationalism of the
Enlightenment implied a fundamentally critical approach to
society, logically including bourgeois society. Yet the various
schools and currents of the Enlightenment provided more than
merely a charter for social criticism and revolutionary change.
They provided the belief in the capacity of man to improve his
conditions, perhaps even — as with Turgot and Condorcet — in
his perfectibility, the belief in human history as human progress
towards what must eventually be the best possible society, and
social criteria by which to judge societies more concrete than
reason in general. The natural rights of man were not merely life
and liberty, but also 'the pursuit of happiness', which
revolutionaries, rightly recognising its historical novelty (Saint-
Just), transformed into the conviction that 'happiness is the only
object of society'.[7] Even in its most bourgeois and individualist
form, such revolutionary approaches contributed to encourage a
socialist critique of society when the time was propitious. We are
unlikely to regard Jeremy Bentham as any kind of socialist. Yet
the young Marx and Engels (perhaps more the latter than the
former) saw Bentham as a link between the materialism of
Helvétius and Robert Owen who 'proceeded from Bentham's

system to found English communism', while 'only the proletariat and the Socialists... have succeeded in developing his teachings a step forward'.[8] Indeed, both went so far as to propose Bentham's inclusion — if only as a consequence of that of William Godwin's *Political Justice* — in their projected 'Library of the best foreign socialist writers'.[9]

The specific debt of Marx to schools of thought produced within the Enlightenment (for example, in the field of political economy and philosophy) need not be discussed in this connection. The fact remains that they rightly saw their predecessors, the 'utopian' socialists and communists, as belonging to illuminism. Insofar as they traced the socialist tradition back beyond the French Revolution, it was to the philosophical materialists Holbach and Helvétius, and to the illuminist communists Morelly and Mably — the only names from this early period (with the exception of Campanella) to figure in their projected Library of Foreign Socialists.

Nevertheless, though he appears to have had no great direct influence on Marx and Engels, the role of one particular thinker in the formation of later socialist theory must be briefly considered: J-J. Rousseau. Rousseau can hardly be called a socialist; for though he developed what was to be the most popular version of the argument that private property is the source of all social inequality, he did not argue that the good society must socialise property, but only that it must ensure its equal distribution. Though he agreed with it, he did not even develop in any detail the theoretical concept that 'property is theft', which was later popularised by Proudhon — but, as witness its elaboration by the Girondin Brissot — did not in itself imply socialism either.[10] Yet two observations must be made about him. First, the view that social equality must rest on common ownership of wealth and central regulation of all productive labour is a natural extension of Rousseau's argument. Second, and more important, the political influence of Rousseau's egalitarianism on the Jacobin left, out of which the first modern communist movements emerged, is undeniable. In his defence Babeuf appealed to Rousseau.[11] The communism whose acquaintance Marx and Engels first made, had *equality* as its central slogan;[12] and Rousseau was its most influential theorist. Inasmuch as socialism and communism in the early 1840s were French — as they largely were — a Rousseauist egalitarianism was one of the original components. The Rousseauist influence on classical German philosophy should not be forgotten either.

Part II

As already suggested, the unbroken history of communism as a modern social movement begins on the left wing of the French Revolution. A direct line of descent links Babeuf's Conspiracy of the Equals through Buonarroti with Blanqui's revolutionary societies of the 1830s; and these in turn, through the 'League of the Just' — later, the 'Communist League' — of the German exiles which they inspired, with Marx and Engels, who drafted the *Communist Manifesto* on its behalf. It is natural that Marx and Engels' projected 'Library' of 1845 was to have begun with two branches of 'socialist' literature: with Babeuf and Buonarroti (following upon Morelly and Mably) who represent the openly communist wing, and with the left-wing critics of the formal equality of the French Revolution and the *Enragés* (the '*Cercle Social*', Hébert, Jacques Roux, Leclerc). Yet the theoretical interest of what Engels was to call 'an ascetic communism, deriving from Sparta' (*Werke* 20, p.18) was not great. Even the communist writers of the 1830s and 1840s, do not seem to have impressed Marx and Engels as theorists. Indeed Marx argued that it was the crudeness and one-sidedness of this early communism which 'allowed other socialist doctrines such as those of Fourier, Proudhon etc. to appear in distinction from it, not by accident but by necessity'.[13] Though Marx read their writings — even such relatively minor figures as Lahautière (1813–82) and Pillot (1809–77) — he clearly owed little to their social analysis, which was chiefly significant in formulating the class struggle as one between 'proletarians' and their exploiters.

However babouvist and neo-babouvist communism was significant in two ways. In the first place, unlike most of the utopian socialist theory, it was profoundly embedded in politics, and therefore embodied not only a theory of revolution but a doctrine of political praxis, of organisation, strategy and tactics, however limited. Its chief representatives, in the 1830s — Laponneraye (1808–49), Lahautière, Dézamy, Pillot and above all Blanqui were active revolutionaries. This, as well as their organic connection with the history of the French Revolution, which Marx studied intensively, made them highly relevant to the development of his thought. In the second place, though the communist writers were mainly marginal intellectuals, the communist movement of the 1830s visibly attracted the workers. This fact noted by Lorenz von Stein clearly impressed Marx and Engels, who later recalled the proletarian character of the communist movement of the 1840s, as distinct from the middle class character of most utopian socialism.[14] Moreover, it was from this French movement, which adopted the name 'communist' around 1840,[15] that German communists, including Marx and Engels, took the name of their views.

The communism which emerged in the 1830s from the neo-babouvist, and essentially political and revolutionary tradition of France, fused with the new experience of the proletariat in the capitalist society of the early industrial revolution. That is what made it into a 'proletarian' movement, however small. Insofar as communist ideas rested directly upon such experience, they were clearly likely to be influenced by the country in which an industrial working class already existed as a mass phenomenon — Great Britain. It is thus no accident that the most prominent of the French communist theorists of the time, Etienne Cabet (1788–1856) was inspired not by neo-babouvism, but by his experiences in England during the 1830s, and especially by Robert Owen, and therefore belongs rather to the utopian socialist current. Yet insofar as the new industrial and bourgeois society could be analysed by any thinker within the regions directly transformed by one or the other aspect of the 'dual revolution' of the bourgeoisie — the French Revolution and the (British) Industrial Revolution, such analysis was not so directly linked with the actual experience of industrialisation. It was, in fact, simultaneously and independently undertaken in both Britain and France. This analysis forms a major basis for the subsequent development of Marx's and Engels' thought. It may be observed, incidentally, that, thanks to Engels' British connection, Marxian communism was from the outset under British as well as French intellectual influence, whereas the remainder of the German socialist and communist left was acquainted with little more than French developments.[16]

Unlike the word 'communist', which always signified a programme, the word 'socialist' was primarily analytical and critical. It was used to describe those who held a particular view of human nature (for example, the fundamental importance of 'sociability' or the 'social instincts' in it), which implied a particular view of human society, or those who believed in the possibility or necessity of a particular mode of social action, notably in public affairs (for example, intervention in the operations of the free market). It was soon realised that such views were likely to be developed by or to attract those who favoured equality, such as the disciples of Rousseau, and to lead to interference with property rights — the point is already made by eighteenth-century Italian opponents of the Enlightenment and of 'socialists'[17] — but it was not entirely identified with a society based on the fully collective ownership and management of the means of production. Indeed, it did not become completely so identified in general usage until the emergence of socialist political parties in the late nineteenth century, and some may argue that it is not completely identified even today. Hence evident non-socialists (in the modern sense) could, even in the late nineteenth century describe themselves or be described as 'socialists', like the *Kathedersozialisten* of Germany or the British Liberal politician who declared 'we are all socialists now'. This programmatic ambiguity extended even to movements regarded as socialist by socialists. It should not be forgotten that one of the major schools of what Marx and Engels called 'utopian socialism', the Saint-Simonians, was 'more concerned with collective regulation of industry than with co-operative own-ership of wealth'.[18] The Owenites who first used the word in England (1826) — but only described themselves as 'socialists' several years later — described the society they aspired to as one of 'co-operation'.

Yet in a society in which the antonym of 'socialism', 'individualism'[19] itself implied a specific liberal-capitalist model of the competitive unrestricted market economy, it was natural that 'socialism' should also have a programmatic connotation as the general name for all aspirations to organise society on an associationist or co-operative model (that is, based on co-operative rather than private property). The word continued to be imprecise though from the 1830s on associated primarily with the more or less fundamental reshaping of society in this sense. Its adherents ranged from social reformers to freaks.

Two aspects of early socialism must therefore be distinguished: the critical and the programmatic. The critical consisted of two elements, a theory of human nature and society, mainly derived from various currents of eighteenth-century thought, and an analysis of the society produced by the 'dual revolution', sometimes in the framework of a view of historical development or 'progress'. The first of these was of no great interest to Marx and Engels, except insofar as it led (in British rather than French thought) to political economy. We shall consider this below. The second evidently influenced them very much. The programmatic aspect also consisted of two elements: a variety of proposals to create a new economy on the basis of co-operation, in extreme cases by the foundation of communist communities; and an attempt to reflect on the nature and the characteristics of the ideal society which was thus to be brought about. Here again, Marx and Engels were uninterested in the first. Utopian community-building they rightly regarded as politically negligible, as indeed it was. It never became a movement of any practical significance outside the USA, where it was rather popular in both a secular and a religious form. At best it served as an illustration of the practicability of communism. The politically more influential forms of associationism and co-operation, which exercised a substantial appeal to both British and French artisans and skilled workers they either knew little about at the time (for example, the Owenite 'labour exchanges' of the 1830s), or distrusted. Retrospectively, Engels compared Owen's 'labour bazaars' with Proudhon's proposals.[20] Louis Blanc's remarkably successful *Organisation du Travail* (ten editions 1839–48), they clearly did not consider significant and insofar as it was, they opposed it.

On the other hand the utopian reflections on the nature of communist society influenced Marx and Engels very substantially, though their hostility to the drafting of such prospectuses for the communist future has led many subsequent commentators to underestimate this influence. Very nearly everything that Marx and Engels said about the concrete shape of communist society is based on earlier utopian writings (for example, the abolition of the distinction between town and country — derived, according to Engels from Fourier and Owen[21] — and the abolition of the state — from Saint-Simon[22]) or it is based on a critical discussion of utopian themes.

Pre-Marxian socialism is therefore embedded in the later work of Marx and Engels, but in a doubly distorted form. They made a highly selective use of their predecessors, and also, their mature and late writings do not necessarily mirror the impact which the early socialists made upon them in their formative period. Thus the youthful Engels was clearly much less impressed with the Saint-Simonians than the later Engels,[23] while Cabet, who does not figure in *Anti-Dühring* at all is not infrequently referred to in the writings before 1846.

However, almost from the start Marx and Engels singled out three 'utopian' thinkers as specially significant — Saint-Simon, Fourier and Robert Owen. In this respect the late Engels maintains the judgement of the early 1840s.[24] Owen stands slightly apart from the other two, and not only because he was clearly introduced to Marx (who can hardly have known him, since his works were as yet untranslated) by Engels, who was in close contact with the Owenite movement in England. Unlike Saint-Simon and Fourier, Owen is usually described by the Marx and Engels of the early 1840s as a 'communist'. Engels then, as later, was specially impressed by the practical common sense and businesslike manner with which he designed his utopian communities ('from an expert's standpoint, there is little to be said against the actual detailed arrangements' *Werke* 20, p245). Owen's single-minded hostility to the three great obstacles to social reform, 'private property, religion and marriage in its present form' (*ibid.*) also clearly appealed to him. Moreover, the fact that Owen, himself a capitalist entrepreneur and factory-owner, criticised the actual bourgeois society of the Industrial Revolution, gave his critique a specificity which the French socialists lacked. (That he had also, in the 1820s and 1830s, attracted substantial working-class support, does not seem to have been appreciated by Engels, who only knew the Owenite socialists of the 1840s).[25] Nevertheless, Marx had no doubt that theoretically Owen was notably inferior to the French.[26] The major theoretical interest of his writings, as of those of the other British socialists whom he later studied, lay in their economic analysis of capitalism (that is, in the manner in which they derived socialist conclusions from the premises and arguments of bourgeois political economy).

In Saint-Simon we find the breadth of view of genius, thanks to which almost all ideas of later socialists, which are not strictly economic, are contained in his work in embryo.[27] There is no doubt that Engels' later judgement reflects the very considerable debt which Marxism owes to Saint-Simonism, though, curiously enough, there is not much reference to the Saint-Simonian school (Bazard, Enfantin etc.) which actually turned the ambiguous, if brilliant, intuitions of their master into something like a socialist system. The extraordinary influence of Saint-Simon (1759–1825) on a variety of significant and often brilliant talents, not only in France but abroad (Carlyle, J.S. Mill, Heine, Liszt) is a fact of European cultural history in the era of Romanticism which is not always easy to appreciate today by those who read his actual writings. If these contain a consistent doctrine, it is the central importance of productive industry which must make the genuinely productive elements in society into its social and political controllers and shape the future of society: a theory of industrial revolution. The 'industrialists' (a Saint-Simonian coinage) form the majority of the population and include both the productive entrepreneurs — including notably the bankers — the scientists, technological innovators and other intellectuals, and the labouring people. Insofar as they contain the latter, who incidentally function as the reservoir from which the former are recruited, Saint-Simon's doctrines attack poverty and social inequality, while he totally rejects the French Revolution's principles of liberty and equality as individualist and leading to competition and economic anarchy. The object of social institutions is to 'faire concourir les principales institutions à l'accroissement du bien-être des proletaires', defined simply as 'la classe la plus nombreuse' (*Organisation Sociale*, 1825). On the other hand, insofar as the 'industrialists' are entrepreneurs and technocratic planners, they oppose not only the idle and parasitic ruling classes, but also the anarchy of bourgeois-liberal capitalism, of which he provides an early critique. Implicit in him is the recognition that industrialisation is fundamentally incompatible with an unplanned society.

The emergence of the 'industrial class' is the result of history. How much of Saint-Simon's views were his own, how much influenced by his secretary (1814–17), the historian Augustin Thierry, need not concern us. At all events social systems are determined by the mode of organisation of property, historic evolution on the development of the productive system, and the power of the bourgeoisie on its possession of the means of production. He appears to hold a rather simple view of French history as class struggle, dating back to the conquest of the Gauls by the Franks, which was elaborated by his followers into a more specific history of the exploited classes which anticipates Marx: slaves are succeeded by serfs, and these by nominally free but propertyless proletarians. However, for the history of his own times, Saint-Simon was more specific. As Engels later noted with admiration, he saw the French Revolution as a class struggle between nobility, bourgeois and propertyless masses. (His followers extended this by arguing that the Revolution had liberated the bourgeois, but the time had now come to liberate the proletarian.)

Apart from history, Engels was to stress two other major insights: the subordination, indeed eventually the absorption, of politics into economics and consequently the abolition of the state in the society of the future: the 'administration of things' replacing the 'government of men'. Whether or not this Saint-Simonian phrase is to be found in the writings of the founder, the concept is clearly there. Yet a number of concepts which have become part of Marxian, as of all subsequent socialism, can also be traced back to the Saint-Simonian school, though not perhaps explicitly to Saint-Simon himself. 'The exploitation of man by man' is a Saint-Simonian phrase; so is the formula slightly altered by Marx to describe the distributive principle of the first phase of communism: 'From each according to his abilities, to each ability according to its work'. So is the phrase, singled out by Marx in the *German Ideology* that 'all men must be assured the free development of their natural capacities'. In short, Marxism was evidently much indebted to Saint-Simon, though the exact nature of the debt is not easy to define, since the Saint-Simonian contribution cannot always be distinguished from other contemporary ones. Thus the discovery of the class struggle in history was likely to be made by anyone who studied, or even who had lived through, the French Revolution. It was indeed ascribed by Marx to the bourgeois historians of the French Restoration. At the same time the most important of these (from Marx's point of view), Augustin Thierry had, as we have seen, been closely linked with Saint-Simon at one period of his life. Still, however we define the influence, it is not in doubt. The uniformly favourable treatment of Saint-Simon by Engels, who noted that 'he positively suffered from a plethora of ideas' and whom he actually compared with Hegel as 'the most ency-clopedic mind of his age', speak for themselves.[28]

The mature Engels praised Charles Fourier (1770–1837) mainly on three grounds: as a brilliant, witty and savage critic of bourgeois society, or rather of bourgeois behaviour,[29] for his advocacy of women's liberation and for his essentially dialectical conception of history. (The last point seems to belong more to Engels than to Fourier.) Yet the first impact which Fourier's thought made on him, and that which has perhaps left the most profound traces in Marxian socialism, was his analysis of labour. Fourier's contribution to the socialist tradition was idiosyncratic. Unlike other socialists, he was suspicious of progress, and shared a Rousseauist belief that humanity had somehow taken the wrong turning in adopting civilisation. He was suspicious of industry and technical advance, though prepared to accept and use it, and convinced that the wheel of history could not be turned back. He was also — in this respect like several other utopians — suspicious of Jacobin popular sovereignty and democracy. Philosophically he was an ultra-individualist whose supreme aim for humanity was the satisfaction of all individuals' psychological urges, and the attainment of maximum enjoyment by the individual. Since — to quote Engels' first recorded impressions of him[30] — 'each individual has an inclination or preference for a particular kind of work, the sum of all individual inclinations must, by and large, constitute a sufficient force to satisfy the needs of all. From this principle there follows: if all individuals are allowed to do and not to do whatever corresponds to their personal inclinations, the needs of all will be satisfied', and he demonstrated 'that . . . *absolute inactivity* is nonsense, and has never existed nor can it ever exist... . He further demonstrates that labour and enjoyment are identical, and it is the irrationality of the present social order which separates the two.' Fourier's insistence on the emancipation of women, with the explicit corollary of radical sexual liberation, is a logical extension — indeed perhaps the core — of his Utopia of the liberation of all personal instincts and impulses. Fourier was certainly not the only feminist among the early socialists, but his passionate commitment made him perhaps the most powerful, and his influence may be detected in the radical turn of the Saint-Simonians in this direction.

Marx himself was perhaps more aware than Engels of the possible conflict between Fourier's view of labour as the essential satisfaction of a human instinct, identical with play, and the full development of all human capacities which both he and Engels believed communism would ensure, though the abolition of the division of labour (that is, of permanent functional specialisation) might well produce results which could be interpreted on Fourierist lines ('to hunt in the morning, to fish in the afternoon, to rear cattle in the evening, and criticise after dinner').[31] Indeed, later he specifically rejected Fourier's conception of labour as 'mere fun, mere amusement'[32] and in doing so implicitly rejected the Fourierist equation between self-realisation and instinctual liberation. Fourier's communist humans were men and women as nature had made them, liberated from all repression; Marx's communist men and women were more than this. Nevertheless, the fact that the mature Marx specifically reconsiders Fourier in his most serious discussion of labour as human activity, suggests the significance of this writer for him. As for Engels, his continuing laudatory references to Fourier (for example, in the *Origin of the Family*) attest to a permanent influence, and to his permanent sympathy for the only utopian socialist writer who can still be read today with the same sense of pleasure, illumination — and exasperation — as in the early 1840s.

The utopian socialists thus provided a critique of bourgeois society, the outlines of a historical theory, the confidence that socialism was not only realisable but called for at this historical moment, and a great deal of thinking about what the human arrangements in such a society would be like (including individual human behaviour). Yet they had striking theoretical and practical deficiencies. They had both a minor and a major practical weakness. They were mixed up, to put it mildly, with various kinds of romantic eccentricity ranging from the penetratingly visionary to the psychically unhinged, from mental confusion, not always to be excused by the overflow of ideas to curious cults and exalted quasi-religious sects. In short, their followers tended to make themselves ridiculous and, as the young Engels observed of the Saint-Simonians, 'once something has been made ridiculous, it is hopelessly lost in France'.[33]

Marx and Engels, while regarding the fantastic elements in the great utopians as the necessary price for their genius or originality, could hardly envisage much of a practical role in the socialist transformation of the world for increasingly odd and often increasingly isolated groups of cranks. Second, and more to the point, they were essentially apolitical, and thus, even in theory, provided no effective means by which such a trans- formation could be achieved. The exodus into communist communities was no more likely to produce the desired results than the earlier appeals of a Saint-Simon to Napoleon, Tsar Alexander, or the great Paris bankers. The utopians (with the exception of the Saint-Simonians, whose chosen instrument, the dynamic capitalist entrepreneurs, drew them away from social- ism) did not recognise any special class or group as the vehicle of their ideas, and even when (as Engels later recognised in the case of Owen) they appealed to the workers, the proletarian movement played no distinctive part in their plans, which were addressed to all who ought to — but generally failed to — recognise the obvious truth they alone had discovered. Yet doctrinal propaganda and education, especially in the abstract form which the young Engels criticised in the British Owenites, would never succeed by themselves. In short, as he saw clearly from his British experience, 'socialism, which goes far beyond French communism in its basis, in its development lags behind it. It will have for a moment to revert to the French point-of-view, in order subsequently to go beyond it.'[34] The French point of view was that of the revolutionary — and political — class struggle of the proletariat. As we shall see, Marx and Engels were even more critical of the non-utopian developments of early socialism into various kinds of co-operation and mutualism.

Among the numerous theoretical weaknesses of utopian socialism, one stood out dramatically: its lack of an economic analysis of *private property* which 'the French socialists and communists . . . had not only criticised in various ways but also "transcended" [*aufgehoben*] in a utopian manner',[35] but which they had not systematically analysed as the basis of the capitalist system and of exploitation. Marx himself, stimulated by Engels' early *Outline of a Critique of Political Economy* (1843–4),[36] had come to the conclusion that such an analysis must be the core of communist theory. As he later put it, when describing his own process of intellectual development, political economy was 'the anatomy of civil society' (Preface to the *Critique of Political Economy*). It was not to be found in the French 'utopian' socialists. Hence his admiration and (in the *Holy Family*, 1845) extended defence of P-J. Proudhon (1809–65), whose *What is Property?* (1840) he read towards the end of 1842, and whom he immediately went out of his way to praise as 'the most consistent and acute socialist writer'.[37] To say that Proudhon 'influenced' Marx or contributed to the formation of his thought, is an exaggeration. Even in 1844 he compared him in some respects unfavourably as a theorist with the German tailor-communist Wilhelm Weitling,[38] whose only real significance was that (like Proudhon himself) he was an actual worker.

Yet, though he regarded Proudhon as an inferior mind to Saint-Simon and Fourier, he nevertheless appreciated the advance he made upon them, which he later compared to that of Feuerbach over Hegel, and, in spite of his subsequent and increasingly bitter hostility to Proudhon and his followers, never modified his view.[39] This was not so much because of the economic merits of the work, for 'in a strictly scientific history of political economy the work would be hardly worth a mention'. Indeed, Proudhon was not and never became a serious economist. He praised Proudhon, not because he had anything to learn from him, but because he saw him as pioneering that very 'critique of political economy' which he himself recognised as the central theoretical task, and he did so all the more generously because Proudhon was both an actual worker and unquestionably an original mind. Marx did not have to advance far in his economic studies before the deficiencies of Proudhon's theory struck him more forcibly than its merits: they are flayed in the *Poverty of Philosophy* (1847).

None of the other French socialists exercised any significant influence on the formation of Marxian thought.

Part III

The triple origin of Marxian socialism in French socialism, German philosophy, and British political economy, is well-known: as early as 1844 Marx observed something like this international division of intellectual labour in 'the European proletariat'[40] This chapter is concerned with the origins of Marxian thought only insofar as it is to be found in pre-Marxian socialist or labour thought, and consequently it deals with Marxian economic ideas only insofar as these were originally derived from, or mediated through, such thought, or insofar as Marx discovered anticipations of his analysis in it. Now British socialism was in fact intellectually derived from classical British political economy in two ways: through Owen from Benthamite utilitarianism, but above all through the so-called 'Ricardian socialists' (some of them originally utilitarians), notably William Thompson (1783–1833), John Gray (1799–?1850), John Francis Bray (1809–95) and Thomas Hodgskin (1787–1869). These writers are significant, not only for using Ricardo's labour theory of value to devise a theory of economic exploitation of the workers, but also for their active connection with socialist (Owenite) and working-class movements. There is in fact no evidence that even Engels knew many of these writings in the early 1840s, and Marx certainly did not read Hodgskin, 'the most cogent socialist among pre-Marxian writers'[41] until 1851; after which he expressed his appreciation with his usual scholarly conscientiousness.[42] That these writers were eventually to make a contribution to Marx's economic studies is perhaps better known than the British contribution — radical rather than socialist — to the Marxian theory of economic crisis. As early as 1843–4 Engels acquired — it would seem from John Wade's *History of the Middle and Working Classes* (1835)[43] the view that crises with a regular periodicity were an integral aspect of the operations of the capitalist economy, using the fact to criticise Say's Law.

Compared with these links with British left-wing economists, Marx's debt to continental ones is slighter. Insofar as French socialism had an economic theory, it developed in connection with the Saint-Simonians, possibly under the influence of the heterodox Swiss economist Sismondi (1773–1842), especially through Constantin Pecqueur (1801–87), who has been described as 'a link between Saint-Simonism and Marxism' (Lichtheim). Both were among the first economists to be seriously studied by Marx (1844). Sismondi is frequently quoted, Pecqueur discussed in *Capital* vol. III. Neither, however, is included in the *Theories on Surplus Value*, though Marx at one point wondered whether to include Sismondi. On the other hand the British Ricardian socialists are: Marx was, after all, the last and overwhelmingly the greatest of Ricardian socialists himself.

Yet if we can pass briefly over what he approved or developed in the left-wing economics of his day, we must also briefly consider what he rejected. He rejected what he saw as 'bourgeois' (*Communist Manifesto*) and later 'petty-bourgeois' or otherwise misguided attempts to deal with the problems of capitalism by such means as credit reform, currency manipulation, rent reform, measures to inhibit capitalist concentration by the abolition of inheritance or other means, even if they were intended to benefit not small individual proprietors but associations of workers operating within, and eventually designed to replace, capitalism. Such proposals were widespread on the left, including parts of the socialist movement. Marx's hostility to Sismondi, whom he respected as an economist, to Proudhon, whom he did not, as well as his criticism of John Gray, derives from this view. At the time when he and Engels formed their own communist views, these weaknesses in the contemporary left-wing theory did not detain them much. However, from the mid-1840s on they increasingly found themselves obliged to pay greater critical attentions to them in their political practice, and consequently in theory.

Part IV
What of the German contribution to the formation of their thought? Economically and politically backward, the Germany of Marx's youth possessed no socialists from whom he could learn anything of importance. Indeed, until almost the moment of Marx's and Engels' conversion to communism — and indeed in some ways until after 1848 — it is misleading to speak of a socialist or communist left distinct from the democratic and Jacobin tendencies which formed the radical opposition to reaction and princely absolutism in the country. As the *Communist Manifesto* pointed out, in Germany (unlike France and Britain) the communists had no option other than to march in common with the bourgeoisie against absolute monarchy, feudal landed property and petty bourgeois conditions (*die Kleinbürgerei*), while encouraging the workers to become clearly conscious of their opposition to the bourgeois. Politically, and ideologically, the German radical left looked westwards. Ever since the

German Jacobins of the 1790s France provided the model, the place of refuge for political and intellectual refugees, the source of information about progressive tendencies: in the early 1840s even Lorenz von Stein's survey of socialism and communism there served chiefly as such, in spite of the author's intention, which was to criticise these doctrines. In the meanwhile a group, mainly consisting of travelling German journeymen craftsmen working in Paris, had separated from the post-1830 liberal refugees in France to adapt French working class communism for their own purposes. The first clear German version of communism was therefore revolutionary and proletarian in a primitive way.[44]

Whether the radical young intellectuals of the Hegelian left wished to stop at democracy or advance politically and socially beyond it, France provided the intellectual models and catalyst of their ideas. Among them Moses Hess (1812–75) was significant, not so much for his intellectual merits — for he was far from a clear thinker — but because he became a socialist before the rest and succeeded in converting a whole generation of young intellectual rebels. His influence on Marx and Engels was crucial in 1842–5, though very soon both ceased to take him very seriously. His own brand of 'True Socialism' (mainly a sort of Saint-Simonism translated into Feuerbachian jargon) was not destined to be of much significance. It is chiefly remembered because it has been embalmed in Marx's and Engels' polemics against it (in the *Communist Manifesto*), which were mainly directed against the otherwise forgotten and forgettable Karl Grün (1813–87). Hess, whose intellectual development converged for a while with Marx's, to the point where in 1848 he may well have regarded himself as Marx's follower, suffered from his inadequacies both as a thinker and as a politician, and must be content with the role of the eternal precursor: of Marxism, of the German labour movement and finally of Zionism.

However, if German pre-Marxian socialism is not very important in the genesis of Marxian ideas, except, as it were, biographically, a word must be said of the German non-socialist critique of liberalism, which struck notes potentially classifiable as 'socialist' in the ambiguous nineteenth-century sense of the word. The German intellectual tradition contained a powerful component hostile to any form of eighteenth-century Enlightenment (and therefore to liberalism, individualism, rationalism and abstraction — for example, any form of the Benthamite or Ricardian arguments), one devoted to an organicist conception of history and society, which found expression in German romanticism, initially a militantly reactionary movement, though in some ways Hegelian philosophy provided a sort of synthesis of the Enlightenment and the romantic view. German political practice, and consequently German applied social theory, was dominated by the activities of an all-embracing state administration. The German bourgeoisie — a late developer as an entrepreneurial class — did not, on the whole, demand either political supremacy or unrestricted economic liberalism, and a large part of its vocal members consisted in any case of servants of the state in one form or another. Neither as civil servants (including professors) nor as entrepreneurs did German liberals tend to have an unqualified belief in the unrestricted free market. Unlike France and Britain the country bred writers who hoped that the complete development of a capitalist economy, such as was already visible in Britain, could be avoided, and with it the problems of mass poverty, by a combination of state planning and social reform. The theories of such men might actually come quite close to a kind of socialism, as in J.K. Rodbertus-Jagetzow (1805–75), a conservative monarchist (he was briefly Prussian minister in 1848) who in the 1840s elaborated an under-consumptionist critique of capitalism and a doctrine of 'state socialism' based on a labour theory of value. For propagandist purposes this was to be used in the Bismarckian era as a proof that imperial Germany was as 'socialist' as any Social Democrat, not to mention as a proof that Marx himself had plagiarised an upstanding conservative thinker. The accusation was absurd, for Marx only read Rodbertus around 1860 when his views were fully formed, and Rodbertus could at best have taught Marx how not to go about his task and how to avoid the grossest errors'.[45] The controversy has long been forgotten. On the other hand it may well be argued that the type of attitude and argument exemplified by Rodbertus was influential in the formation of Lassalle's kind of state socialism. (The two men were associated for a while.)

It need hardly be said that these non-socialist versions of anti-capitalism not only played no role in the formation of Marxian socialism,[46] but were actively combated by the young German left on account of their obvious conservative associations. What may be called 'romantic' theory belongs to the pre-history of Marxism only in its least political form (for example, that of 'natural philosophy' for which Engels always kept a slight fondness; cf. his Preface to *Anti-Dühring*, 1885), and insofar as it had been absorbed into classical German philosophy in its Hegelian form. The conservative and liberal tradition of state intervention in the economy — including state ownership and management of industries — merely confirmed them in the view that the nationalisation of industry by itself was not socialist.

Thus neither the German economic, social or political experience, nor the writings designed specifically to deal with its problems, contributed anything of great significance to Marxian thought. And indeed it could hardly have been otherwise. As has been often observed, not least by Marx and Engels, the issues which in France and England appeared concretely in political and economic form, in the Germany of their youth appeared only in the costume of abstract philosophical enquiry. Conversely, and no doubt for this reason, the development of German philosophy at this period was considerably more impressive than that of philosophy in other countries. If this deprived it of contact with the concrete realities of society — there is no actual reference in Marx to the 'propertyless class' whose problems 'cry out to heaven in Manchester, Paris and Lyons' before the autumn of 1842[47] — it provided a powerful capacity of generalise, to penetrate beyond the immediate facts. To realise its full potential, however, philosophical reflection had to be transformed into a means of acting upon the world, and speculative philosophical generalisation had to be married to the concrete study and analysis of the actual world of bourgeois society. Without this marriage the German socialism sprung from a political radical-isation of philosophic development, mainly Hegelian, was likely to produce at best that 'German or "true" socialism' which Marx and Engels lampooned in the *Communist Manifesto*.

The initial steps of this philosophical radicalisation took the form of a critique of religion and later (since the topic was more politically sensitive) the state, these being the two chief 'political' issues with which philosophy was directly concerned as such. The two great pre-Marxian landmarks of this radicalisation were Strauss' *Life of Jesus* (1835) and particularly Feuerbach's by now clearly materialist *Wesen des Christenthums* (1841). The crucial significance of Feuerbach as a stage between Hegel and Marx is familiar, though the continued central role of the critique of religion in the mature thought of Marx and Engels is not always so clearly appreciated. However, at this vital stage of their radicalisation, the young German politico-philosophical rebels could draw directly upon the radical and even socialist tradition, since the most familiar and consistent school of philosophical materialism, that of eighteenth-century France, was linked not only with the French Revolution, but even with early French communism — Holbach and Helvétius, Morelly and Mably. To this extent French philosophic development contributed to, or at least encouraged, the development of Marxist thought, as the British philosophical tradition did through its seventeenth- and eighteenth-century thinkers, directly or via political economy. However, fundamentally the process by which the young Marx 'turned Hegel the right way up' took place within classical German philosophy, and owed little to the pre-Marxian revolutionary and socialist traditions except a sense of the direction it was to move in.

Part V
Politics, economics and philosophy, the French, British and German experience, 'utopian' socialism and communism, were fused, transformed and transcended in the Marxian synthesis during the 1840s. It is surely no accident that this transformation should have taken place at this historical moment.

Sometime around 1840 European history acquired a new dimension: the 'social problem' or (seen from another point of view) potential social revolution, both expressed typically in the phenomenon of the 'proletariat'. Bourgeois writers became systematically conscious of the proletariat as an empirical and political problem, a class, a movement — in the last analysis a power for overturning society. At one end this consciousness found expression in systematic enquiries, often comparative, on the conditions of this class (Villermé for France in 1840, Buret for France and Britain in 1840, Ducpétiaux for various countries in 1843), at the other in historical generalisations already reminiscent of the Marxian argument:

But this is the content of history: no major historical antagonism disappears or dies out unless there emerges a new antagonism. Thus the general antagonism between the rich and the poor has been recently polarised into the tension between capitalists and the hirers of labour on the one hand and the industrial workers of all kinds on the other; out of this tension there emerges an opposition whose dimensions become more and more menacing with the proportional growth of the industrial population.[48]

We have already seen that a revolutionary and consciously proletarian communist movement emerged at this time in France, and indeed that the very words 'communist' and 'communism' came into currency around 1840 to describe it. Simultaneously a massive proletarian class movement, closely observed by Engels, reached its peak in Britain: Chartism. Before it, earlier forms of 'utopian' socialism in western Europe retreated to the margins of public life, with the exception of Fourierism which flourished modestly, but persistently, in the proletarian soil.[49]

A new and more formidable fusion of the Jacobin-revolutionary-communist and the socialist-associationist experience and theories became possible on the basis of a visibly growing and mobilising working class. Marx, the Hegelian, seeking for the force which would transform society by its negation of existing society, found it in the proletariat, and though he had no concrete acquaintance with it (except through Engels) and had not given the operations of capitalism and political economy much thought, immediately began to study both. It is an error to suppose that he did not seriously concentrate his mind on economics before the early 1850s. He began his serious studies not later than 1844.

What precipitated this fusion of social theory and social movement was the combination of triumph and crisis in the developed, and apparently paradigmatic, bourgeois societies of France and Britain during this period. Politically the revolutions of 1830 and the corresponding British reforms of 1832–5 established regimes which evidently served the interests of the predominant part of the liberal bourgeoisie, but fell spectacularly short of political democracy. Economically, industrialisation, already dominant in Britain, was visibly advancing on parts of the continent — but in an atmosphere of crisis and uncertainty which appeared to many to put in question the entire future of capitalism as a system. As Lorenz von Stein, the first systematic surveyor of Socialism and Communism (1842) put it:

There is no longer any doubt that for the most important part of Europe political reform and revolution are at an end; social revolution has taken their place and towers over all movements of the peoples with its terrible power and serious doubts. Only a few years ago, what now confronts us seemed but an empty shadow. Now it faces all Law as an enemy, and all efforts to compress it into its former nothingness are vain.[50]

Or as Marx and Engels put it 'A spectre is haunting Europe — the spectre of communism'.

The Marxian transformation of socialism would therefore hardly have been historically possible before the 1840s. Nor, perhaps, would it have been possible within the main bourgeois countries themselves, where both the radical political and working-class movements, and radical social and political theory, were deeply embedded in a long history tradition and practice from which they found it hard to emancipate themselves. As subsequent history was to show, the French left was long resistant to Marxism, in spite of — indeed because of — the strength of the autochthonous revolutionary and associationist tradition, the British labour movement remained unreceptive to Marxism for even longer, in spite of — indeed because of — its home-grown success in developing a conscious class movement and a critique of exploitation. Without the French and British contribution, the Marxian synthesis would have been quite impossible, and, as has been suggested, the biographical fact that Marx established a lifelong partnership with Engels, with his unique experience of Britain (not least as a practising Manchester capitalist), was undoubtedly important. Nevertheless, it was perhaps more likely that the new phase of socialism should be developed not at the centre of bourgeois society, but on its German margin, and by means of a reconstruction of the all-embracing speculative architecture of German philosophy.

The actual development of Marxian socialism will be the subject of later chapters. Here we need merely recall that it differed from its predecessors in three respects. First, it replaced a partial critique of capitalist society with a comprehensive critique, based on an analysis of the fundamental (in this instance economic) relation determining that society. The fact that analytically it penetrated deeper than the superficial phenomena accessible to empirical criticism, implied an analysis of the 'false consciousness' which stood in the way, and of the (historical) reasons for it. Second, it set socialism in the framework of an evolutionary historical analysis, which explained both why it emerged as a theory and a movement when it did, and why the historic development of capitalism must in the end generate a socialist society. Incidentally, unlike the earlier socialists, for whom the new society was a finished thing, which had only to be instituted in a final form, according to whatever the preferred model was, at the suitable moment, Marx's future society itself continues to evolve historically, so that only its very general principles and outlines can be predicted, let alone designed. Third, it clarified the mode of the transition from the old to the new society: the proletariat would be its carrier, through a class movement engaged in a class struggle which would achieve its object only through revolution, 'the expropriation of the expropriators'. Socialism had ceased to be 'utopian' and become 'scientific'.

In fact, the Marxian transformation had not only replaced but

also absorbed its predecessors. In Hegelian terms, it had
'sublated' them (*aufgehoben*). For most purposes other than the
writing of academic theses, they have either been forgotten, form
part of the pre-history of Marxism, or (as in the case of some
Saint-Simonian strains) developed in ideological directions which
have nothing to do with socialism. At most, like Owen and
Fourier, they survive among educational theorists. The only
socialist writer of the pre-Marxist period who still maintains some
significance as a theorist within the general area of socialist
movements is Proudhon, who continues to be cited by the
anarchists, (not to mention, from time to time, the French
ultra-right and various other anti-Marxists.) This is in some ways
unfair to men who, even when below the illuminations of the best
utopians, were original thinkers with ideas which, if proposed
today, would often be taken quite seriously. Yet the fact remains
that, as socialists, they are today of interest chiefly to the
historian.

This should not mislead us into supposing that pre-Marxian
socialism died immediately Marx developed his characteristic
views. Even nominally, Marxism did not become influential in
labour movements until the 1880s, or at the earliest, the 1870s.
The history of Marx's own thought and his political and
ideological controversies cannot be understood unless we recall
that, for the remainder of his life, the tendencies he criticised,
combated or had to come to terms with within the labour
movement, were primarily those of the pre-Marxian radical left,
or those deriving from it. They belonged to the progeny of the
French Revolution, whether in the form of radical democracy,
Jacobin republicanism, or the neo-babouvist revolutionary
proletarian communism surviving under the leadership of
Blanqui. (This last was a tendency with which, on political
grounds, Marx found himself allied from time to time.)
Occasionally they sprung from, or at least had been precipitated
by, that same left Hegelianism or Feuerbachianism through
which Marx himself had passed; as in the case of several Russian
revolutionaries and notably Bakunin. But in the main they were
the offspring, indeed the continuation of, pre-Marxian socialism.

It is true that the original utopians did not survive the 1840s; but
then, as doctrines and movements they had already been
moribund in the early 1840s, with the exception of Fourierism
which, in a modest way, flourished until the revolution of 1848 in
which its leader Victor Considérant therefore found himself
playing an unexpected and unsuccessful role. On the other hand

various kinds of associationism and co-operative theories, partly derived from utopian sources (Owen, Buchez) partly developed on a less messianic basis in the 1840s (Louis Blanc, Proudhon) continued to flourish. They even maintained the aspiration to transform the whole of society on co-operative lines, from which they had originally been derived. If this was so even in Britain, where the dream of a co-operative Utopia which would emancipate labour from capitalist exploitation was diluted into co-operative shopkeeping, it was even more alive in other countries, where the co-operation of producers remained dominant. For most workers in Marx's lifetime this *was* socialism; or rather the socialism which gained working class support, even in the 1860s, was one which envisaged independent groups of producers without capitalists but supplied by society with enough capital to make them viable, protected and encouraged by public authority but in turn with collective duties to the public. Hence the political significance of Proudhonism and Lassalleanism. This was natural in a working class whose politically conscious members consisted largely of artisans or those close to the artisan experience. Moreover, the dream of the independent productive unit controlling its own affairs did not merely belong to men (and much more rarely women) who were not yet fully proletarian. In some ways this primitive 'syndicalist' vision also reflected the experience of proletarians in the workshops of the mid-nineteenth century.

It would thus be a mistake to say that pre-Marxian socialism died out in Marx's time. It survived among Proudhonians, Bakuninite anarchists, among later revolutionary syndicalists and others, even when these later learned, for want of any adequate theory of their own, to adopt much of the Marxian analysis for their own purposes. Yet from the middle 1840s on it can no longer be said that Marx derived anything from the pre-Marxist tradition of socialism. After his extended dissection of Proudhon (*The Poverty of Philosophy*, 1847), it can no longer even be said that the critique of pre-Marxian socialism played a major part in the formation of his own thought. By and large, it formed part of his political polemics rather than of his theoretical development. Perhaps the only major exception is the *Critique of the Gotha Programme* (1875), in which his shocked protests against the German Social-Democratic Party's unjustified concessions to the Lassalleans provoked him into a theoretical statement which, if probably not new, had at any rate not been publicly formulated by him before. It is also possible that the development of his ideas on credit and finance owed something to the need to criticise the belief in various currency and credit nostrums which remained popular in labour movements of the Proudhonist type. However, by the mid-1840s Marx and Engels had, on the whole, learned all they could from pre-Marxian socialism. The foundations of 'scientific socialism' had been laid.

Notes

1 See K. Marx and F. Engels, *Collected Works*, vol.4, note 242, p. 719.
2 Engels, Beschreibung der in der neueren Zeit entstandenen und noch bestehenden kommunistischen Ansiedlungen, *Werke* 2, pp. 521, 522.
3 *Werke* 3, pp. 508 ff.
4 Though for Marx the original form of property is 'tribal', there is no suggestion that this represents a phase of 'primitive communism' in the early writings. The well-known footnote about it in the *Communist Manifesto* was added in the 1880s.
5 F. Engels, *Anti-Dühring* (first draft) begins with the following sentence (*Werke* 20, 16 footnote):

However much *modern socialism* originated in substance (der Sache nach) with the contemplation of the class contradictions found in existing society, between those owning property and the propertyless, workers and exploiters, in its theoretical form it appears in the first instance as a more consistent continuation and development of the principles propounded by the great French spokesmen of the 18th century Enlightenment. Its first representatives, Morelly and Mably, belonged to this group.

6 *Werke* 20, p. 17.
7 V. Advielle, *Histoire de Gracchus Babeuf* (Paris, 1884), II, 34.
8 K. Marx and F. Engels, *The Holy Family (Coll. Works* IV, 131; F. Engels Condition of the Working Class, *ibid*. 528).
9 K. Marx and F. Engels, *Coll. Works* IV, 666; Engels to Marx 17.3.45 (*Werke* 27 p 25). However, very soon Marx's attitude to this thinker became distinctly less favourable, though the judgement in *The German Ideology* is still positive.
10 J.P. Brissot de Warville, *Recherches philosophiques sur le droit de propriété et le vol* (1780); cf. J. Schumpeter, *History of Economic Analysis*, (N.Y., 1954), pp. 139–140.
11 V. Advielle, *op. cit.* II, pp. 45, 47.
12 Cf. F. Engels, *Anti-Dühring, op. cit.* p. 116.
13 For Engels' view, see 'Progress of social reform on the continent' (*Werke* I, pp. 484-5), written for the Owenite *New Moral World* (1843); for Marx's view (1843), see *Werke* I, p. 344.
14 Cf. F. Engels (1888), Preface to the *Communist Manifesto* (*Werke* 21, p. 354 f.).
15 The *Premier banquet communiste* was held in 1840, Cabet's *Comment je suis communiste'* and *Mon crédo communiste'* dates from 1841. By 1842 Lorenz von Stein, *Der Socialismus und Communismus des heutigen Frankreichs* — widely read in Germany — first attempted a clear distinction between the two phenomena.
16 Cf. *German Ideology* (*Werke* 3, p. 448) for a proud display — presumably by

Engels — of his knowledge of 'English communists' as against the ignorance of the German 'true socialists'. The list — 'More, the Levellers, Owen, Thompson, Watts, Holyoake, Harney, Morgan, Southwell, J.G. Barmby, Greaves, Edmonds, Hobson, Spence' — is interesting not only for what it contains but for what it does not. It makes no reference to several of the 'labour economists' familiar to the mature Marx, notably J.F. Bray and Thomas Hodgskin. Conversely, it includes now-forgotten figures familiar to those who, like Engels, frequented the radical left of the 1840s, such as John Goodwyn Barmby (1820–1881) who claimed to have introduced the word 'communism', James Pierrepont Greaves (1777–1842) 'the Sacred Socialist', Charles Southwell (1814–60), and Owenite 'social missionary' like John Watts (1818–87) and G.J. Holyoake (1817–1906) — a much less obscure figure — and Joshua Hobson (1810–76), an Owenite-activist and publisher of the *New Moral World* and the *Northern Star*. Owen, William Thompson, John Minter Morgan, T.R. Edmonds and Thomas Spence are still to be found in any history of socialist thought in Britain.

17 F. Venturi, 'Le mot "socialista" ' (*Second Internat. Conference of Econ. Hist., Aix 1962*, (The Hague, 1965), vol. II, p. 825–7).
18 G. Lichtheim, *The Origins of Socialism*, (N.Y., 1969), p. 219.
19 The first article on the subject, by the Saint-Simonian Pierre Leroux, bracketed the two terms: 'De l'individualisme et du socialisme' (1835).
20 F. Engels, *Anti-Dühring*, *Werke* 20, p. 246.
21 F. Engels, *Anti-Dühring*, *Werke* 20, p. 272–3.
22 For the general debt to the utopians, *Communist Manifesto* (*Werke*, 4, p. 491) where the 'positive propositions about the future society' are listed.
23 F. Engels, 'Progress of Social Reform', *Werke* I, p. 482; Cabet is defended at length against Grün's misrepresentations in the *German Ideology*.
24 Cf. the projected 'Library' in which they already appear together.
25 F. Engels 'Condition of the Working Class', *Werke* 2, p. 451–2.
26 K. Marx, 'Peuchet on suicide' (1846) *Coll. Works*, vol. IV, p. 597.
27 K. Engels, *Anti-Dühring*, *Werke* 20, p. 242.
28 F. Engels to F. Toennies 24.1.95 (*Werke* 39, pp. 394–5); *Anti-Dühring*, *Werke* 20, p. 23.
29 The young Engels noted that Fourier did not actually write much about the workers and their conditions until very late ('A Fragment of Fourier's on Trade' *Werke* 2, p. 608).
30 F. Engels 'Progress of social reform' (1843), *Werke* 1, p. 483.
31 K. Marx and F. Engels, *German Ideology*, *Werke* 3, p. 33.
32 K. Marx, *Grundrisse* (1953 Berlin edition), p. 505, 599.
33 F. Engels, *Werke* I, p. 482.
34 F. Engels, Condition of the Working Class, *Werke* 2, pp. 452–3.
35 K. Marx, On P-J. Proudhon (1865) *Werke* 16, p. 25.
36 F. Engels, *Werke* 1, pp. 499–524.
37 K. Marx, Communism and the Augsburger Allgemeine Zeitung (*Rheinische Zeitung*, 1842), *Werke* 1, p. 108. *Rheinische Zeitung*, 4 January 1843 (*New MEGA*, I, 1 p. 417).
38 K. Marx, Kritische Randglossen zu dem Artikel eines Preussen, *Werke* 1, pp. 404–5.
39 K. Marx, On P-J. Proudhon, *Werke* 16, pp. 25 ff.
40 K. Marx, *Kritische Randglossen*, *Werke* 1, p. 405.
41 E. Roll, *A History of Economic Thought* (London, 1948), p. 249.

42 Cf. Theorien über den Mehrwert III, *Werke* 26, iii, pp. 261–316 and the references to Hodgskin in *Capital* I, where Bray, Gray and Thompson are also cited.
43 F. Engels, Umrisse einer Kritik *Werke* 1, p. 514. Marx also read this author, together with Bray and Thompson, in Manchester in 1845 *Grundrisse*, 1953 edn. pp. 1069, 1070.
44 Wilhelm Weitling (1808–71) lived in Paris 1835–6 and 1837–41 where he read Pillot and various communist journals.
45 Schumpeter, *History of Economic Analysis*, p. 506.
46 The section on 'feudal socialism' in the *Communist Manifesto*, which discusses comparable tendencies, makes no reference whatever to Germany but only to French legitimists and Disraeli's 'Young England'.
47 *Rheinische Zeitung*, 16 October 1842 *Werke* 1, p. 106. Cf. S. Avineri, *The Social and Political Thought of Karl Marx* (Cambridge, 1968, p. 54).
48 'Revolution' in Rotteck and Welcker, *Lexicon der Staatswissenschaften* XIII (1842) quoted in Avineri *op. cit.*, p. 55. For similar quotations, cf. J. Kuczynski, *Geschichte der Lage der Arbeiter under dem Kapitalismus*, vol. 9 (Berlin, 1960) and C. Jandtke and D. Hilger (eds) *Die Eigentumslosen* (Munich, 1965).
49 This left traces in the later Marxist labour movement (for example, through the devoted Fourierist Eugène Pottier, author of the words of the Internationale, and even through August Bebel, who published a work on *Charles Fourier, His Life and Theories* as late as 1890).
50 Cited in W. Hofmann, *Ideengeschichte der sozialen Bewegung des 19. u.20. Jahrhunderts* (Berlin, 1968), p. 90.

2 THE MATERIALISTIC CONCEPT OF HISTORY
David McLellan

It was not until the composition of *The German Ideology* — in Brussels in 1845–6 — that Marx arrived at the materialistic conception of history that was to be the 'guiding thread' for the rest of his studies. During the previous decade Marx's writings show a development through the successive stages of idealism — romantic and then Hegelian — to liberal rationalism and an extended criticism of Hegel's philosophy that yielded many of the major themes of Marxian socialism. Engels said that Marx's ideas were based on a synthesis of German idealist philosophy, French political theory, and English classical economics: the early writings (up to, and including, the *Economic and Philosophical Manuscripts* of 1844) show Marx assimilating all three influences — though not, as yet, integrating them. These early writings are pre-Marxist in the sense that they contain neither any theory of history in terms of classes, modes of production, and so on, nor, more specifically, the economic concepts of labour power, surplus value etc. which are basic to many of Marx's later works. Thus, although it is undeniable that his early works are important in order to understand the genesis of Marx's thought, their status in the overall context of his thought has been (and still is) a matter of considerable controversy. And this controversy — for Marxists who are interested in some sort of unity of theory and practice — has obvious implications beyond the purely academic.

The intellectual background of Marx's home and school was the rationalism of the Enlightenment, a pale Protestantism incorporating the virtues of reason, moderation, and hard work. A radically different perspective was opened up by Marx's father-in-law, Baron von Westphalen. Marx's daughter Eleanor wrote that the Baron 'filled Karl Marx with enthusiasm for the romantic school and, whereas his father read Voltaire and Racine with him, the Baron read him Homer and Shakespeare — who remained his favourite authors all his life'.[1] During his early student days in Bonn, therefore, Marx gave himself up to the current romanticism, though his move to Berlin in 1836 brought about a decisive change: previously, Hegel's conceptual rationalism had been rejected by Marx, the follower of Kant and

Fichte, the romantic subjectivist who considered the highest being to be separate from earthly reality. Now, however, it began to appear as though the idea was immanent in the real. Previously, Marx had 'read fragments of Hegel's philosophy, but I did not care for its grotesque and rocky melody'.[2] Now he embraced Hegelianism in a conversion that was as profound as it was sudden. It was probably the most important intellectual step of his whole life. For however much he was to criticise Hegel, accuse him of idealism, and try to stand his dialectic 'on its feet', Marx was the first to admit that his method stemmed directly from that of his master of the 1830s.

Hegel started from the belief that, as he said of the French Revolution, 'man's existence has its centre in his head, i.e., in Reason, under whose inspiration he builds up the world of reality'.[3] In his greatest work, *The Phenomenology of Spirit*, Hegel traced the development of Mind, or Spirit, reintroducing historical movement into philosophy and asserting that the human mind can attain to absolute knowledge. He analysed the development of human consciousness from its immediate perception of the here and now to the stage of self-consciousness, the understanding that allowed man to analyse the world and order his own actions accordingly. Following this was the stage of reason itself, understanding of the real, after which spirit, by means of religion and art, attained to absolute knowledge, the level at which man recognised in the world the stages of his own reason. These stages Hegel called 'alienations', insofar as they were creations of the human mind yet thought of as independent and superior to the human mind. This absolute knowledge was at the same time a sort of recapitulation of the human spirit, for each successive stage retained elements of the previous ones at the same time as it went beyond them. This movement that suppressed and yet conserved Hegel called *Aufhebung*, a word that has this double sense in German. Hegel also talked of 'the power of the negative', thinking that there was always a tension between any present state of affairs and what it was becoming. For any present state of affairs was in the process of being negated, changed into something else. This process was what Hegel meant by dialectic.

Hegel's philosophy was ambivalent: although he himself preferred to talk of philosophy painting grey with grey and the owl of Minerva only rising at dusk, emphasis on its negative and dialectical side could obviously give it a radical bent — a development associated with a group of intellectuals known as the Young Hegelians. They embarked on a process of secularisation, progressing from a critique of religion to one of politics and society. It is important to note that Marx in his early writings worked out his ideas in interaction with the other members of this close-knit movement. His doctoral thesis clearly reflected the Young Hegelian climate: its field-post-Aristotelian Greek philosophy — was one of general interest to the Young Hegelians and Marx's proclamation in the Preface that 'Philosophy makes no secret of it. Prometheus' confession "in a word, I detest all Gods"', is its own confession, its own slogan against all Gods in heaven and earth who do not recognise man's self-consciousness as the highest divinity,'[4] was typical of the Young Hegelians' anti-religious idealism. Thus the way forward for Marx lay in an application to the 'real' world of the principles that Hegel had discovered.

But Marx did not immediately have the leisure to work on this line of thought: deprived of the possibility of an academic career, his contact with the real world came through his work as a journalist for the *Rheinische Zeitung*. In his seven major articles for the paper, he seldom made his own ideas explicit, since he gave his articles the form of critical exegeses by exposing the absurdities in his opponents' ideas. For this he used any weapon to hand, usually combining a radical Hegelianism with the simple rationalism of the Enlightenment. In October 1842, now editor of the paper, Marx had to reply to the accusation that his paper was flirting with communist ideas. 'The *Rheinische Zeitung*,' he wrote, 'does not even concede theoretical validity to communist ideas in their present form let alone desires their practical realisation'[5] and he promised a fundamental criticism of such ideas. Soon, however, Marx had to write on such sociopolitical matters as the law on the thefts of wood and the poverty of the Moselle Winegrowers — subjects, as he said later, which 'provided the first occasions for occupying myself with economic questions'[6] and impressed on him how closely the laws were formed by the interests of those who were in power.

The eighteen months following the suppression of the *Rheinische Zeitung* were to be decisive for Marx's ideas: in his assault on the metaphysical fog that engulfed not only Hegel but also Young Hegelian writing, Marx was helped by two things. First, he was reading a lot of politics and history: he read French socialism even before he went to Paris and his reading on the French Revolution was extensive. Indeed, his writing of this period can be viewed as an extended meditation on the question of why the French Revolution, which started out with such excellent principles, had yet failed to solve the fundamental problem of the redistribution of social wealth. Second, there was the influence of his Young Hegelian colleague Ludwig Feuerbach. Although Engels exaggerated when he said later that 'we all become Feuerbachians',[7] this influence was profound. Feuerbach was fundamentally interested in religion, and his main thesis was that God was merely a projection of human attributes, desires and potentialities. If men once realised this, they would be in a position to appropriate these attributes for themselves by realising that they had created God, not God them, and thus be in a position to restore to themselves their alienated 'species-being' or communal essence. What interested Marx was the application of this approach to Hegel's philosophy, which Feuerbach regarded as the last bulwark of theology in that Hegel still started from the ideal instead of the real. Feuerbach wrote: 'The true relationship of thought to being is this: being is the subject, thought the predicate. Thought arises from being — being does not arise from thought'.[8]

This view of Feuerbach was incorporated into a long manuscript that Marx composed in the summer of 1843. Here, by means of a critique of Hegel, Marx's views on democracy and the abolition of the State began to take shape. According to Hegel's political philosophy, human consciousness manifested itself objectively in man's juridical, social, and political institutions which alone permitted man to attain to full liberty. Only the highest level of social organisation — the State — was capable of uniting particular rights and universal reason. Hegel thus rejected the view that man was free by nature: on the contrary, for him the State was the only means of making man's freedom real. In other words, Hegel was aware of the social problems created by a competitive society in which there was an economic war of all against all — a state of affairs which he summed up under the term 'Civil Society'; but he considered that these conflicts could be harmonised by the organs of the State into some 'higher' unity. Following Feuerbach, Marx's fundamental criticism of Hegel was that as in religion men had imagined God to be the Creator and man to be dependent on Him, so Hegel mistakenly started from the Idea of the State and made everything else — the family and various social groups — dependent on this Idea. Applying this general approach to particular issues, Marx declared himself in favour of democracy: 'Just as religion does not create man, but man creates religion, so the constitution does not create the people but the people the constitution'.[9] Marx was especially concerned, in a few pages of brilliant analysis, to reject Hegel's view that the bureaucracy performed a mediating function between different social groups and this acted as a 'universal class' in the interests of all. Marx considered that bureaucracy encouraged the political divisions that were essential to its own existence and thus pursued its own ends to the detriment of the community at large. Towards the end of his manuscript, Marx described how he expected universal suffrage to inaugurate the reform of civil society. Marx saw two possibilities: if the state and civil society continued to be separate, then all as individuals would not be able to participate in the legislature except through deputies, the 'expression of the separation and merely a dualistic unity'. Secondly, if civil society became political society, then the significance of legislative power as representative disappeared, for it depended on a theological kind of separation of the state from civil society. Hence, what the people should aim for was not legislative power but governmental power. Marx ended his discussion with a passage which makes clear how, in the summer of 1843, he envisaged future political developments:

Only in unlimited voting, active as well as passive, does civil society actually rise to an abstraction of itself, to political existence as its true universal and essential existence. But the realisation of this abstraction is also the transcendence of the abstraction. By making its political existence actual as its true existence, civil society also makes its civil existence unessential in contrast to its political existence. And with the one thing separated, the other, its opposite, falls. Within the abstract political state the reform of voting is a dissolution of the state, but likewise the dissolution of civil society.[10]

Thus Marx arrives here at the same conclusion as in his discussion of 'true democracy'. Democracy implied universal suffrage, and universal suffrage would lead to the dissolution of the state.

It is clear from this manuscript that Marx was adopting the fundamental humanism of Feuerbach and with it Feuerbach's reversal of subject and predicate in the Hegelian dialectic. Marx considered it evident that any future development was going to involve a recovery by man of the social dimension that had been lost ever since the French Revolution levelled all citizens in the political state and thus accentuated the individualism of bourgeois society. He was explicit that private property must cease to be the basis of social organisation, but it is not obvious that he was arguing for its abolition, nor did he make clear the various roles of classes in social evolution.

The manuscript on Hegel was never published, but the embryonic ideas it contained received a clearer formulation when Marx got to Paris. During the winter of 1843–4 Marx wrote two essays for the *Deutsch-Französische Jahrbücher* — both as clear and sparkling as the Hegel manuscript had been involved and obscure. In the first, entitled 'On the Jewish Question', Marx reviewed the opinions of his old mentor Bruno Bauer on Jewish emancipation. According to Bauer, for Jewish emancipation to be effective, the state had to cease to be Christian — otherwise discrimination against the Jews was inevitable. But for Marx, Bauer had not gone far enough: the mere secularisation of politics did not entail the emancipation of men as human beings. The USA had no established religion, yet was notorious for the religiosity of its inhabitants:

But since the existence of religion [Marx continued,] is the existence of a defect, the source of this defect can only be sought in the nature of the state itself. Religion for us no longer has the force of a basis for secular deficiencies but only that of a phenomenon. We do not change secular questions into theological ones. We change theological questions into secular ones. History has for long enough been resolved into superstition: we now resolve superstition into history. The question of the relationship between political emancipation and religion becomes for us a question of the relationship of political emancipation to human emancipation.[11]

In Marx's view this problem arose because 'man has a life both in the political community, where he is valued as a communal being, and in civil society, where he is active as a private individual, treats other men as means, degrades himself to a means, and becomes the plaything of alien powers'.[12]

Bauer had argued for a state based exclusively on the universal rights of man as proclaimed by the French Revolution and the American Declaration of Independence. For Marx, however, the rights of man were only the rights of the atomised, mutually hostile individuals of civil society. Thus:

the right of man to freedom is not based on the union of man with man, but on the separation of man from man . . . . The right of man to property is the right to enjoy his possessions and dispose of the same arbitrarily, without regard for other men, independently of society, the right of selfishness. It is the former individual freedom together with its latter application that forms the basis of civil society. It leads man to see in other men not the realisation but the limitation of his own freedom.'[13]

After pointing out that the society inaugurated by the French Revolution had forfeited many of the social and communal dimensions present in feudal society, Marx drew on Rousseau in order to sketch his goal of bridging the gap between the individual viewed as a citizen member of a community and as an isolated egoistic member of civil society:

Human emancipation will only be complete when the real, individual man has absorbed into himself the abstract citizen; when as an individual man, in his everyday life, in his work, and in his individual relationships, he has become a species-being; and when he has recognised and organised his own powers [*forces propres*] as social powers so that he no longer separates this social power from himself as political power'.[14]

The article 'On the Jewish Question' had set the goal of full human emancipation; in his second article for the *Jahrbücher* Marx identified the means to achieve it. This article was intended as an introduction to his critique of Hegel which was to be written up for publication. The article began with Marx's famous epigrams on religion:

The foundation of irreligious criticism is this: man makes religion, religion does not make man. But man is no abstract being, squatting outside the world. Man is the world of man, the state, society. This state, this society, produces religion's inverted attitude to the world, because they are an inverted world themselves. Thus the struggle against religion is indirectly the struggle against that world whose spiritual aroma is religion . . . . Religion is the sigh of the oppressed creature, the feeling of a heartless world, and the soul of soulless circumstances. It is the opium of the people . . . .[15]

But the role of religion having been exposed, the duty of philosophers was now to direct their attention to politics, a particularly appropriate activity in a Germany which was, according to Marx, still pre-1789. The one hope for Germany lay in her political philosophy, which was very progressive: the Germans had thought what other nations had done.

Therefore, to criticise this philosophy and progress beyond it would show, at least theoretically, what the future of society was to be. And although Marx was clear that 'the criticism of religion ends with the doctrine that man is the highest being for man, that is, with the categorical imperative to overthrow all circumstances in which man is humiliated, enslaved, abandoned, and despised,'[16] the difficulty obviously lay in finding 'a passive element, a material basis' necessary to revolution. He proclaimed the solution in a passage that has given much support to the view of Marx as a messianic, prophetic figure. The solution lay:

in the formation of a class with radical chains, a class in civil society that is not a class of civil society, of a social group that is the dissolution of all social groups, of a sphere that has a universal character because of its universal sufferings and lays claim to no particular right, because it is the object of no particular injustice but of injustice in general. This class can no longer lay claim to a historical status, but only to a human one. It is, finally, a sphere that cannot emancipate itself without emancipating these other spheres themselves. In a word, it is the complete loss of humanity and thus can only recover itself by a complete redemption of humanity. This dissolution of society, as a particular class, is the proletariat. . . .[17]

Thus the vehicle of revolution was clear to Marx: the proletariat was destined to assume the universal role that Hegel had misleadingly assigned to the bureaucracy. And there is also adumbrated here the idea that it is precisely the backwardness of Germany that offered her the opportunity to come to the forefront of the European revolutionary movement — an idea that was destined to reappear continually in less 'orthodox' variants of Marxism. But hitherto Marx's writings had been almost exclusively political, although he had come to realise that politics was not enough: his interest in the essential economic dimension was sparked by an essay published in the *Deutsch-Französische Jahrbücher* alongside his own two. It was by Engels and entitled 'Outlines of a Critique of Political Economy'. In it, Engels indicted private property and its concomitant spirit of competition. Growing capitalist accumulation necessarily entailed a lowering of salaries and accentuated the class struggle. Uncurtailed growth of the economy meant recurrent crises, and the progress of science only served to increase the misery of the workers. This 'sketch of genius'[18] (as he later called it) made a great impression on Marx, and his notebooks during the summer of 1844 begin with extracts from it. These notes (unpublished by Marx) were entitled by their first editors 'Economic and Philosophical Manuscripts' (*EPM*) and represent a radical critique of capitalism based partly on Engels, partly on the anti-industrial ideas of such German romantics as Schiller, and partly on Feuerbach's humanism. On their first full publication in 1932 they were hailed by some as Marx's most important single piece of work.

The fact that a manuscript of such obvious importance was not published by Marx prompts a short comment on Marx's mode of writing. Since his day as a student he had been in the habit of copying down lengthy extracts from his reading in notebooks[19] — which means that his sources are peculiarly easy to trace. He was also quick to sketch out in these same notebooks plans and drafts of future works. A combination of anxiety to make his ideas accessible to the public and the need for financial support made him over-ready to sign contracts with publishers. Although Marx did in fact complete and publish more works before 1848 than in any subsequent period of comparable length, his difficulty in actually delivering anything for publication was apparent even in the 1840s and pre-figured the long travail that was to preceed *Capital*, vol. I. This congenital reluctance to publish was prompted largely by Marx's fanatical attachment both to accuracy of expression and presentation and to a complete mastery of an ever-growing volume of primary material. It is ironical that the drafts of the *Critique of Hegel's Philosophy of Right* (1843), *EPM* (1844) and *The German Ideology* (1845) came to exercise far more influence than Marx's published work of this period. In his later works there have, similarly, been those who have wished to accord the unpublished *Grundrisse* an importance equivalent to that of *Capital*, vol. I. Obviously, the status of unpublished manuscripts as representative of an author's considered intentions is inherently problematic.

The *EPM* consist of three main sections: a critique of the classical economists culminating with a section on alienated labour; a description of communism; and a critique of Hegel's dialectic.

The first section contains lengthy quotations from the classical economists — in particular Adam Smith and David Ricardo — to demonstrate the increasing polarisation of classes and the deleterious effects of private property. Although he considered that the economists faithfully reported the workings of capitalist society, Marx criticised their approach on three main grounds: first, while admitting that labour was fundamental to the working of the economy, they acquiesced in assigning to it an increasingly poverty-stricken role; second, they did not view the economic system as one of interacting forces, that is, they took the laws of capitalism to be immutable and could not explain the origins of the system they were describing; and third, they took a one-sided view of man simply as a cog in the economic wheel and did not consider him 'in his free time, as a human being'.[20]

At this point Marx began a new section headed 'alienated labour' and containing a description of the general impoverishment and dehumanisation of the worker in capitalist society. Alienated labour had four aspects to it. First, the worker was related to the product of his labour as to an alien object; it stood over and above him, opposed to him as an independent power.

Second, the worker became alienated from himself in the very act of production; the worker did not view his work as part of his real life and did not feel at home in it. Third, man's 'species-life' his social essence, was taken away from him in his work which did not represent the harmonious efforts of man as a 'species-being'. Fourth, man found himself alienated from other men.

In an extended note on James Mill written about this time (unfortunately not included in most editions of the *EPM*), Marx attacked the notion of credit, which he called 'the economic judgement on the morality of a man. In credit, man himself, instead of metal or paper, has become the mediator of exchange but not as man, but as the existence of capital and interest.'[21] In contemporary society, according to Marx, men were increasingly producing with the sole object of exchanging and thus 'you have no relation to my object as a human being because I myself have no human relation to it . . . our mutual value is the value of our objects or us.'[22] The passage toward the end of the note constitutes a sort of positive counterpart to the description of alienated labour and deserves quoting in full:

Supposing that we had produced in a human manner; each of us would in his production have doubly affirmed himself and his fellow men. I would have: (1) objectified in my production my individuality and its peculiarity and thus both in my activity enjoyed an individual expression of my life and also in looking at the object have had the individual pleasure of realising that my personality was objective, visible to the senses and thus a power raised beyond all doubt. (2) In your enjoyment or use of my product I would have had direct enjoyment of realising that I had both satisfied a human need by my work and also objectified the human essence and therefore fashioned for another human being the object that met his need. (3) I would have been for you the mediator between you and the species and thus been acknowledged and felt by you as a completion of your own essence and a necessary part of yourself and have thus realised that I am confirmed both in your thought and in your love. (4) In my expression of my life I would have fashioned your expression of your life, and thus in my own activity have realised my own essence, my communal essence.[23]

The second main section of the *EPM* contained Marx's solution to the problem of alienation: communism. Although while still in Germany he had rejected communism as a 'dogmatic and one-sided abstraction,'[24] the impact of Paris with its socialist salons and workers' clubs had made him a swift convert. But Marx's communism was not the 'crude' kind, inspired by 'universal envy', that aimed to negate all culture in a levelling-down process. He summarised his ideas in an almost mystical passage:

. . . communism as the positive abolition of private property and thus of human self-alienation and therefore the real reappropriation of the human essence by and for man. This is communism as the complete and conscious return of man himself as a social, i.e. human, being. Communism as completed naturalism is humanism and as completed humanism is naturalism. It is the genuine solution of the antagonism between man and nature and between man and man. It is the true solution of the struggle between existence and essence, between objectification and self-affirmation, between freedom and necessity, between individual and species. It is the solution to the riddle of history and knows itself to be this solution.[25]

In the following sections (in many ways the key passage of the *EPM*), Marx expanded on three particular aspects of his conception of communism. First, he stressed that communism was a historical phenomenon whose genesis was 'the entire movement of history'. At the present stage, the essential problem was an economic one — in particular, the abolition of private property: 'the positive abolition of private property and the appropriation of human life is the positive abolition of all alienation, thus the return of man from religion, family, state, etc., to his human, that is, social being.'[26] Second, Marx stressed that everything about man — starting with his language — was social. Even man's relationship to nature was included in this social dimension:

thus society completes the essential unity of man with nature, it is the genuine resurrection of nature, the fulfilled naturalism of man and humanism of nature. . . . For not only the five senses but also the so-called spiritual and moral senses (will, love, etc.), in a word, human love and the humanity of the senses come into being only through the existence of their object, through nature humanised. The development of the five senses is a labour of the whole previous history of the world.[27]

Nevertheless, Marx emphasised, thirdly, that the stress on man's social aspects only served to enhance the individuality of communist, unalienated man, whom he described as 'total' or 'all sided'. For just as the state of alienation vitiated all human faculties, so the supersession of this alienation would be a total liberation. It would not just be limited to the possession and enjoyment of material objects: all human faculties would, in their different ways, become means of appropriating reality. This was difficult to imagine for alienated man, since private property has so blunted men's sensibility that they could only imagine an object to be theirs when they actually possessed it: all physical and intellectual senses had been replaced by the single alienation of having. And, finally, the reciprocal relationship between man and nature would be reflected in a single all-embracing science: 'natural science will in time comprise the science of man, as the science of man will embrace natural science: there will be one single science'.[28]

The third and final section of the *EPM* was devoted to a critique of Hegel's dialectic as found in his most famous work, *The Phenomenology of Spirit*. Marx began by praising Feuerbach for having shown that Hegel's philosophy was no more than a rationalised theology and discovering the true materialist approach by starting from the social relationship of man to man. But Marx's attitude to Hegel was far from being wholly negative:

The greatness of Hegel's *Phenomenology* and its final product, the dialectic of negativity as the moving and creating principle is on the one hand that Hegel conceives of the self-creation of man as a process, objectification as loss of the object as externalisation and the transcendence of this externalisation. This means, therefore, that he grasps the nature of labour and understands objective man, true because real man, as the result of his own labour.[29]

On the other hand, this whole dialectic was viewed from an idealist standpoint in that the appropriation of man's objectified and alienated faculties was first only an appropriation that occurred in the mind, in pure thought (that is, in abstraction). Marx, however, started from the 'real man of flesh and blood, standing on the solid round earth and breathing in and out all the powers of nature'[30] and defined his position as a consistent naturalism or humanism that avoided both idealism and materialism. Hegel saw man as a disembodied consciousness and the world as necessarily inimical to man's fulfilment, but Marx considered that it was only man's present relationship to the world that was askew: man needed to interact with external objects in order to develop or 'objectify' himself. For Hegel, all objectification was alienation; for Marx, man could overcome alienation only if he objectified himself by using nature in co-operation with his fellow men.

It is not difficult to see why — on their publication in 1932 — the *EPM* should have aroused so much controversy. Intellectually, there had been a revival of interest in Hegel with the publication of some of *his* early writings in the early 1900s. And since the early writings of Marx were those which most directly showed the influence of Hegel, the ground was well prepared. There was also a contemporary political factor: in the early twentieth century the Social Democratic and Communist parties had been concerned to claim that they had a totally different *Weltanschauung* from that of bourgeois parties. And, since Hegel was held to be a bourgeois thinker, the influence of Hegel on Marx — mostly in the early writings — had to be minimised. However, with the menace of Fascism, Marxists in general were concerned to emphasise the affinities between Marx's humanism and the humanism of the liberal bourgeoisie in contrast to the barbarities of fascist ideology viewed as a rejection of the Western European tradition. More immediately, during the 1920s there was an increasing feeling among Marxists that the eclipse of Hegel and the rise of Darwin as an influence on the theorists of the Second International (for example, Kautsky) was in part responsible for the debacle of German Social Democracy. Although the Bolsheviks' debt to Hegel was not an evident one (Lenin's *Philosophical Notebooks* were not published until 1929–30), writers with Communist Party affiliations such as Lukacs, Korsch and, to a lesser extent, Gramsci attempted a Hegelian reading of Marx which obviously implied an interest in such works as the *EPM*.

The orthodox Stalinist position considered these early works to be so many *juvenilia* rendered superfluous by Marx's later works — they were not even included in the original *Werke* published in East Germany in the late 1950s. In Eastern Europe, where Marxism, instead of being the creed of the under-dog, had been enthroned as the ruling ideology, there was obviously room to point out that Marx's communist man did not seem to have much in common with the products of state bureaucracies of the Stalinist type and the cautious thesis was put forward that alienation could exist even under socialism. Study of the early writings was seen as a return to the original source of communist thought much as the Reformers used the New Testament to show up abuses rife in the later medieval Church. Schaff in Poland, the theorists of the Prague Spring or the *Praxis* group in Yugoslavia would be examples of this tendency. In post-war Western Europe and the USA, those seeking a non-Stalinist version of Marxism eagerly seized on the early Marx who was read by some as simply the best of the humanists or even as an existentialist. For such thinkers, the notion of alienation — much more to the four in the *EPM* than in *Capital* — was the central one. Inevitably, the vagueness and lack of political direction in the early Marx lead to a reaction from thinkers such as Althusser who wished to classify the Feuerbachian problematic of the early Marx as ideological as opposed to the scientific foundations of his later work.

Indeed, it is undeniable that with his move to Brussels in 1845, Marx's writings take on a systematic form — albeit as an open-ended system — that is not present in his early writings. These early writings document Marx's struggle to conclude, from very idealistic beginnings, that the fundamental activity of man was one of productive interchange with nature; that this activity was vitiated by the class divisions of capitalist society with its institutions of private property and the division of labour; and that this present alienation could be overcome by a proletarian revolution inaugurating communism.

What Marx's writings up to 1844 failed to deal with was the nature of historical change: although a communist by the beginning of 1844, by its end he was not yet a Marxist. It would not, of course, be fair to say that the *EPM* had no developmental view of society: but it was only of the vaguest sort and although Marx had used Hegel against Feuerbach to demonstrate the importance of man's self-creation through labour, this still remained very abstract. Marx, now working in close co-operation with Engels, devoted himself to clarifying his materialist view of history by 'setting accounts with our erstwhile philosophical consciousness.'[31] (*The Holy Family*, published early in 1845, is merely a forerunner of *The German Ideology* in its attacks on the Young Hegelians and only of interest for its brief account of the materialist origins of socialism).

Engels said later that when he moved to Brussels at the beginning of April Marx 'had already advanced from these principles [that is "that politics and its history have to be explained from the economic conditions and their evolution and not vice versa"] to the main aspects of his materialist theory of history';[32] and in the Preface to the English edition of the *Communist Manifesto* he wrote that Marx had already worked out his theory in the spring of 1845 'and put it before me in terms almost as clear as those in which I have stated it here'.[33] The only writings of Marx's surviving from this period are the famous eleven *Theses on Feuerbach* rightly called by Engels 'the first document in which the brilliant kernel of the new world view is revealed'.[34] From his first reading of Feuerbach in the early 1840s Marx had never been entirely uncritical; but both in the 'Paris Manuscripts' and in the *Holy Family* Marx had nothing but praise for Feuerbach's 'real humanism'. Marx was now becoming identified too closely as a mere disciple of Feuerbach from whose static and unhistorical views Marx was bound to diverge owing to the growing attention he was paying to economics. In the *Theses on Feuerbach* Marx gave a very brief sketch of the ideas that he and Engels elaborated a few months later in *The German*

Ideology. By any standard *The German Ideology* is one of Marx's major works. In it by criticising Feuerbach, the most 'secular' of the Young Hegelians, he and Engels completed the 'settling of accounts with our erstwhile philosophical consciousness',[35] a process which had lasted since the Doctoral Thesis of 1841.

It was in Brussels in late 1845 that Marx and Engels first set down what Marx termed in 1859 the 'guiding thread' of his studies. They wrote:

The way in which man produces his food depends first of all on the nature of the means of subsistence that he finds and has to reproduce. This mode of production must not be viewed simply as reproduction of the physical existence of individuals. Rather it is a definite form of their activity, *a* definite way of expressing their life, *a* definite mode of life. As individuals express their life, so they are. What they are, therefore, *coincides* with what they produce, and how they produce. The nature of individuals thus depends on the material conditions which determine their production.[36]

They went on to state that 'how far the productive forces of a nation are developed is shown most evidently by the degree to which the division of labour has been developed'.[37] They showed how the division of labour led to the separation of town and country and then to the separation of industrial from commercial labour and so on. Next they summarised the different stages of ownership that had corresponded to the stages in the division of labour: tribal ownership, communal and state ownership, feudal or estate ownership. Marx and Engels summarised their conclusions so far as follows:

The fact is, then that definite individuals who are productively active in a specific way enter into these definite social and political relations. The social structure and the state continually evolve out of the life-process of definite individuals, but individuals not as they may appear in their own or other people's imagination but rather as they really are, that is, as they work, produce materially, and act under definite material limitations, presuppositions, and conditions independent of their will.[38]

They then reiterated their general approach, stating that 'consciousness does not determine life, but life determines consciousness', and showed how the division of labour, leading to private property, created social inequality, class struggle and the erection of political structures.

Having acquired a coherent view of the world, Marx and Engels immediately set about actively propagating their views. They began at the end of 1845 by the creation of Correspondence

Committees which were designed to help spread their views both in Germany and in the main centres of German emigré workers in Paris, Brussels and London. The most important result of these Correspondence Committees was to create close ties between Marx and Engels and the London communists who were at that time the largest and best organised colony of German workers. London was the centre of the most active of the emigré socialist organisations known as the League of the Just. It was clear that the London communists, in terms of numbers and organisation, represented for Marx and Engels by far the most promising entrée into working class politics, particularly because their Cor- respondence Committees never really got off the ground. And, in their turn, the leaders of the League felt their activities hampered by the absence of any coherent doctrine. By 1847, the successful negotiations between Brussels and London culminated in Marx and Engels being commissioned to write a *Manifesto* for the renamed Communist League.

Marx's entry into active politics was marked by two controversies. The first, with the tailors' leader Weitling, was the political counterpart of *The German Ideology*. Weitling con- trasted the picture of human nature that he got from Feuerbach with the current evils of capitalist society and called in messianic terms for an immediate revolution. Marx, by contrast, emphas- ised the historical nature of progress and declared that 'the bourgeoisie must first come to the helm'. The second controversy was more substantial in that it gave rise to Marx's *Poverty of Philosophy* which contained the first public and systematic statement of the materialist conception of history and which Marx himself recommended as an introduction to *Capital*. It was a critique of the French socialist Proudhon and, like Marx's critique of Hegel, combated the mystification of 'eternal' categories such as Reason and Justice to which Proudhon constantly had recourse. The book also contained a systematic exposition of Marx's economics, although the concepts of labour power and surplus value were yet to appear. In the *EPM* Marx had rejected the labour theory of value. Following Engels in his Outlines, Marx had, in the summer of 1844, equated value and price and criticised Ricardo for taking demand into account in the determination of value. In other words, Marx rejected the labour theory of value for its neglect of competition which he saw as the basis of the real economic world. However, on moving to Brussels, and particularly during the course of his visit to Manchester in the summer of 1845, Marx discovered the socialist interpretation of Ricardo in the works of William Thompson, Francis Bray and (later) writers such as Hodgskin and Ravenstone. There were favourable, though peripheral, references to the labour theory of value in *The German Ideology* whose conception of man as essentially a producer of his material means of subsistence obviously reinforced this view. But it was in the *Poverty of Philosophy* that this basic Marxian concept received its first exposition.

Thus the materialist conception of history outlined in *The German Ideology* and the economics of *The Poverty of Philosophy* formed the theoretical basis for Marx's political activities in the late 1840s and particularly his work in the Communist League. Large sections of the *Communist Manifesto* are simply trenchant summaries of *The German Ideology*. With the failure of the 1848 revolutions, Marx concentrated more on the study of economics, and, in his work on the production process of capitalist society — *Capital*, brought to a partial conclusion the research he had begun in Paris in 1844.

Notes

1 Eleanor Marx, on Karl Marx, *Die Neue Zeit*, 1883, p. 441.
2 K. Marx, Letter to his Father, *MEGA*, I, i (2), p. 218.
3 G.W.F. Hegel, *Werke*, Berlin, 1832 ff., vol. 9, p. 441.
4 K. Marx, Doctoral Thesis, *MEGA*, I, i (i), p. 10.
5 K. Marx, Communism and the *Augsburger Allgemaine Zeitung*, *MEGA*, I, i, (2), p. 263.
6 K. Marx, *Preface to a Critique of Political Economy, Werke*, vol. 13, p. 8.
7 F. Engels, *Ludwig Feuerbach and the End of Classical German Philosophy* (Moscow, 1946), p. 20.
8 L. Feuerbach, *Anthropologischer Materialismus: Ausgewählte Schriften* (Frankfurt, 1967), vol. I, p. 84.
9 K. Marx, Critique of Hegel's Philosophy of Right, *MEGA*, I, i (i), p. 434.
10 K. Marx, Critique of Hegel's Philosophy of Right, *MEGA*, I, i (i), pp. 543f.
11 K. Marx, On the Jewish Question, *MEGA*, I, i (i), pp. 581f.
12 K. Marx, *op. cit. MEGA*, I, i (i), p. 584.
13 K. Marx, *op. cit. MEGA*, I, i (i), p. 594.
14 K. Marx, *op. cit. MEGA*, I, i (i), p. 599.
15 K. Marx, Introduction to a critique of Hegel's Philosophy of Right, *MEGA*, I, i (i), p. 607.
16 K. Marx, *op. cit. MEGA*, I, i (i), p. 614f.
17 K. Marx, *op. cit. MEGA*, I, i (i), pp. 619f.
18 K. Marx, *Preface to a Critique of Political Economy, Werke*, vol. 13, p. 10.
19 See further: M. Rubel, Les Cahiers d'Etude de Karl Marx (1840–1853), *International Review of Social History*, 1957.
20 K. Marx, *Economic and Philosophical Manuscripts, MEGA*, I (3), p. 45.
21 K. Marx, *Oekonomische Studien (Exzerpthefte), MEGA*, I (3), p. 534.
22 K. Marx, *op. cit. MEGA*, I (3), p. 544.

23 K. Marx, *op. cit. MEGA*, I (3), pp. 546f.
24 K. Marx, Letter to Ruge, *MEGA*, I, i (i), p. 573.
25 K. Marx, *Economic and Philosophical Manuscripts, MEGA*, I (3), p. 114.
26 K. Marx, *op. cit. MEGA*, I (3), p. 115.
27 K. Marx, *op. cit. MEGA*, pp. 116, 120.
28 K. Marx, *op. cit. MEGA*, I (3), p. 123.
29 K. Marx, *op. cit. MEGA*, I (3), p. 156.
30 K. Marx, *op. cit. MEGA*, I (3), p. 160.
31 K. Marx, *Preface to a Critique of Political Economy, Werke*, vol. 13, p. 10.
32 K. Marx and F. Engels, *Werke*, vol. 21, p. 212.
33 K. Marx and F. Engels, *Werke*, vol. 21, p. 357.
34 F. Engels, Ludwig Feuerbach und der Ausgang der klassischen Deutschen Philosophie, *Werke*, vol. 21, p. 264.
35 K. Marx, Preface to *A Critique of Political Economy, Werke*, vol. 13, p. 10.
36 K. Marx and F. Engels, *The German Ideology, Werke*, pp. 21f.
37 K. Marx and F. Engels, *op. cit. Werke*, pp. 21f.
38 K. Marx and F. Engels, *op. cit. Werke*, vol. 3, p. 25.

3 MARX AND THE CONCEPT OF HISTORY

Pierre Vilar

I have often envisaged a study written in two parts, the second of which, *Marx in History*, would be closely related to the first: *History in Marx*.

The major difficulty is to determine whether Marxism's remarkable development in little more than a century, as a factor in history, is due to the capacity for analysis and intervention, which Marx's scientific discovery, as opposed to his historical material, has placed at man's disposal. In this paper which is concerned for the most part with Marx in history, I shall devote no more than a few pages to the examination of history in Marx. That is little enough, and will only allow us to take a few 'compass bearings'. May they inspire further research at a less superficial level!

We would do well to realise from the moment the problem is set that there are peculiar difficulties. The word 'history' — and this is not true of the natural sciences — covers both the knowledge of material and the material of that knowledge. 'History in Marx' is the transformation of one of the most ancient needs of the human spirit so as to comply with the exigencies of science. 'Marx in history' is both the examination of man's role in the march of events and the evolution of societies. This dual meaning of a single phrase, which accounts for its richness and justifies its prestige — but which also gives rise to ambiguity — explains why it has been said that Marx opens up the 'continent of history' to science but also why the 'concept of history' has remained unformulated.

Surely it would be a simple matter, from Marx's immense output, to discover many instances not only of his use of the word 'history' in its commonly accepted meaning; but also of new uses. To try and discover if, amidst this apparent chaos, there exists an order, a chronology, any editing, any 'thresholds' linked to refinements or to discoveries, would be a rewarding and enthralling task, requiring an exhaustive catalogue of these different uses, and a careful analysis of each. It goes without saying that this cannot be undertaken here. But the problem is not only in the use of words; there are also theoretical propositions,

47

some of which are extensively cited, while others are far less well known. Above all — and in history this is crucial — there are the examples of use and the method in practice. If Marx, in opening up the 'continent of history', had refrained from treading on this ground, his work would definitely have lost its dimension. It is therefore good to know *how* he trod there, even how he approached it. Is there anything more exciting than the first discovery of a thought, however incomplete it may be, when, on shattering the previous understanding, it paves the way for a significant *volte-face*? And is the 'investigative process' less important than the setting forth of ideas? According to Marx, it is a question of defining certain material, and the task of the investigation is to make this one's own.

'To make something one's own': history, then, besides being discovery, is also conquest. Every historian worthy of the name, provided he follows step-by-step the conquest which Marx achieved, will therein quickly recognise his own problems, his own progress; and often the initial stages to a solution, too.

One must begin with Marx the student. The atmosphere of the university was steeped in Hegelianism, even though Hegel already belonged to the past. No one has completely determined what the young Marx rejected, or assimilated, from lessons which were less indirectly learned — Ritter's, for example, or Savigny's. Those who see Marx predominantly as a 'determinist' have suggested that Ritter's 'geographical determinism' played a part in his development. But it hardly needs saying that there is no more 'geographical determinism' in Marx than 'economic determinism'. Nothing is further from his line of thought than the recent attempts, by means of mathematical play, to reduce human grafting to spatial conditions. It is true, however, that Marx never forgets 'the geological, orological, hydrographic, climatic and other conditions' which are at the root of all history and all economics. This is something that Hegel had already done, explaining that 'all history [*Geschichtsschreibung*] inevitably springs from such natural sources, and from their modification by man's action in the course of history [*Geschichte*]'.

Before man can 'make history [*um "Geschichte machen" zu können*]' he concerns himself with certain conditions. This recourse to the evidence will often recur within the framework of a comprehensive theory in which man's grip upon nature is the ultimate criterion. *Nature* cannot be said to impose, because sooner or later technology conquers it. However, as each level is reached, nature, within specified limits, *pro-poses* or *op-poses*.

In the complexity of history and in every concrete case, the assessment of nature's helping and hindering hand is the historian's first task. There is no history in geography, no geography in history. History, according to Marx, is a man–nature dialectic. (Though it goes beyond that, that is what it is in the first instance.) It is the first encounter between Marx and the best methods of modern historiography.

Just as the historian faces the problem of relationships between Earth and man, history and geography, so too he faces those relationships which men establish among themselves: institutions, legislation, the principles and practice of law, which he all too often takes as a *datum*.

When Marx was at university he 'read law'. But, as he himself tells us, he instinctively relegated this discipline to a subordinate role, after philosophy and history. To be sure, law and history were discussed by Savigny, whose lectures he is known to have attended; and it is tempting to ask if 'the Historical School of Positive Law', which countered the concept of 'natural' or 'rational' law with a concrete law which was the product of history, is not closer to Marx's final conception (that is, to an historically determined law of 'superstructure'), than were Kant or even Hegel.

On the other hand, in one of his very first works, and even before he took issue with Hegel on the subject of law, the young Marx unleashed a fierce attack on 'the Historical School' on the occasion of the jubilee anniversary of its founder, Hugo. Although in actual fact, his real butt was Savigny.

Does this mean that Savigny's lessons had had no influence on Marx? No, because it was characteristic of Marx's intellectual progress that he should always read (or listen to) other men with passion, and if he often came to reject them with an equal passion, it was not without putting them to use in his own philosophy.

In actual fact, in the *Rheinische Zeitung*, 1842, his refusal to consider law as a product of history was never presented as a rejection of Hugo or Savigny. Basically Marx reproached them for:

(a) having ascribed to themselves the role of legislators (Savigny had declared this in the title of one of his works, and was eventually appointed Minister of Law);
(b) having admitted 'that all existence was the basis of an authority, and all authority was the basis of law'; and
(c) having let the School flounder in the whimsies of romanticism.

From the '*positiv, dass heisst unkritisch*' the article leads on to a denunciation of the '*unhistorische Einbildungen*'. The defence of reason turns to a defence of history — of real history.

Moreover, in this same series of *Rheinische Zeitung* articles (1842–3), another opportunity was almost immediately given him — invariably a political opportunity, that is to say that action prompted thought, practice prompted theory — to penetrate still further into self-determining history. He went on to observe a law of gestation: the Rhineland Diet had decreed that the gathering of dead wood, which tradition had allowed as helpful to the poor, was now 'wood stealing', and therefore an offence, in the name of an ownership, which, to be 'modern', had to be made absolute. Thus it was by reading these debates that the young Marx reached the first insight into some of the basic precepts of his future theory, by which we understand theory of history, his 'materialist concept of history', which Engels was to describe as the fundamental discovery, of equal relevance/weight as his central economic theory: surplus value:

(a) Law categorises the divergences between individual action and the principle of society, and determines relative role. But this principle is not immutable. Before the Diet met, dead wood was 'gathered'; thereafter it was 'stolen'; an act which (according to one deputy) 'popular opinion' would not consider a theft was declared to be theft. The concept of ownership altered. Does this lead to a more perfect rationality, to greater 'justice'? Marx, still a liberal at that time, and an advocate of the French Republic, and still sufficiently Hegelian to believe that the State embodies the Idea, suddenly grasped that the legislator does not legislate in the abstract, because
(b) The judicial definition of property is entrusted to property-owners. The article exposes this and repeats it in a variety of ways: 'The forest owner has silenced the legislator... .' 'When the individual property-owner is unable to raise himself to the State's point of view, it is the State that has to descend to measures that are contrary to right and reason, those of private property. Such is the reasoning of the "practical" property-owner . . . the good is what is in my own interest . . . .'

Observe the hesitancy in his use of those words, the regrets of the complaisant legislator at the manner in which the facts constitute a negation of the ideal State! But the question has been asked: is it not for civil society to determine the role of the State, and not the State that of civil society? From the reply to this question the whole concept of history will be drawn.

(c) Why does the new civil society impose so absolute a view of property? The answer will not only be found in dead wood, but next in the picking of wild berries, which grow uncultivated and which will be forbidden, now that they have become commercial goods and are exported to Holland in exchange for money. Natural goods are appropriated when they become merchandise: 'The nature of the object demands the monopoly, because private property has invented it.'

These terms may cause surprise. The identifying of 'monopoly' with 'property' is a pre-capitalist idea, frequently used in earlier peasant revolts. But it touches on the same delusion of economic liberty: against those who have nothing, the free disposal of appropriated goods has all the effects of a monopoly; in the fundamental hypotheses of the capitalist economy one always forgets to pin-point the basics: in order to become 'merchandise', goods must become absolute property; before capitalism, not all goods were such. These are the lessons which can be drawn from parliamentary debates.

(d) Marx then turns his attention to society before the French Revolution, which he calls, in keeping with the unquestioned terminology of his day, 'feudal' society. (He did not coin the term.) Such a society, he concluded, was 'irrational'; he perceived that it had its own rationality, and functional logic; it was particularly characterised by:

a dual private right, the private right of the property-owner and the private right of the non-property-owner . . . . a marriage of public and private rights, such as we shall encounter in all the institutions of the Middle Ages. . . .

To be sure, 'legislative reason' (the young Marx was still occasionally writing 'reason' without qualification) has simplified and unified the principles of social functioning, and rendered them more logical. But the 'concessions of time-honoured custom to the utterly deprived masses', being considered as 'accidental', were mercilessly eliminated, while precautions were taken to preserve the shaky privileges of the old ruling classes. Thus the wealth of the monastries was sequestered by the State, 'and that was all to the good', Marx categorically declares; but while there was much talk of compensating the Church, no one dreamed of compensating the poor for the loss of their traditional rights which had been preserved through the monasteries. This analysis does not imply for one moment that Marx was in favour of the old order and regretted its passing. But the analysis of the 'transition',

whose characteristics are satisfactorily delineated by the play of
the respective interests and forces of each class, was outlined for
the first time.

(e) The analysis is a particularly remarkable one as far as the
relations between society and the State are concerned. Not only
is it a class (and not an abstract State) which dictates and
legislates, but the class that comes to power is assured of all the
resources of the State and its organisation, and the subordinate
class will thereafter be subordinated.

The logic that transforms the economy of the property-owner into State
authority renders the authorities of that State servants of the property-owners.
All the organs of the State become the eyes, ears, arms and legs with which the
interests of the property-owners listen, spy, evaluate, protect, seize and
run. . . .

On the other hand:

The form of the unwritten law was consistent with nature to the extent that the
very existence of the poor was nothing more than what custom demanded: they
had not yet found their position as a class within the conscious organisation of
the State. The actual debates of the time, however, reveal the attitude adopted
towards these traditional rights, and indeed exemplify how method and the spirit
of the change were pushed to their logical extreme.

In other words, under the old order, the political exclusion of
the poor left room for a form of compensation through social
custom; with the arrival of 'modern' society — in 1842 it was
still politically collective and economically individualist — 'the
poor' were to suffer greater deprivation.

It could be argued that the articles written during 1842–3 were
witness to a humanist sensibility, even an anarchical tendency, in
the very germ of Marx's thought. It could be demonstrated that
the Marx of this period was not Marx. And in 1859 Marx himself
alluded to these early works, with decided modesty, as mere
stammerings. Nonetheless, it was here that he first came to grips
with the problems of 'material interests', and 'economic
questions'. In the most frequently quoted passages he would
seem to go further, for they herald, intuitively but distinctly,
Marx's concern with his historical questions. We shall be told
that this interpretation projects a mature Marxism upon these
early, clumsy texts, that it shifts the history of a thought 'into the
future perfect'. And yet it seems to me even less admissible to
view these texts as a mere juvenile dread of the authorities, or as
the banal assertion of a 'democratic' sensibility when confronted

with the 'abuses' of property-owners. No, these are the relationships between property and the State; and it is the nature of both which is brought into question, from 1842 onwards, before 'the self-producing phenomenon'. Many Marxists, if they questioned their own beliefs, would rediscover, at the root of their conviction, revelations of this kind, as naïve as they are powerful, offered by historical experience. It is not only by reading Marx that one becomes a Marxist. It is by looking about one, following debates, and judging actions — *critically*. In the same way one becomes an historian; and this is how Marx became one.

It is true that in his intellectual biography, as in anybody else's, one episode will be followed by a totally dissimilar one, because no biography is purely 'intellectual'. After the taxing experience of active journalism, Marx settled in Kreuznach. It was his honeymoon, a time in his life of unaccustomed calm meditation, as well as of copious reading. This ranged from Hegel's *Philosophy of Law*, which he vehemently criticised, to numerous works on a wide range of topics. I venture to think, *pace* Maximilien Rubel, that this episode, as far as Marx's development is concerned, marks a back-sliding from 1842; for it is as a philosopher (that is to say, without changing his ground) that the denouncer of Hegel judges the *Philosophy of Law*. Formalism in 'the negation of negation', idealism (in which the analysis of *class* utterly disappears) in the definitions of 'bureaucracy' and 'democracy', the transposition of the Hegelian critique of the State to Feuerbach's religious critique, attacks on the Hegelian concept of property which could be (in the case of primogeniture) a bourgeois critique. As for his 'historical' reading at Kreuznach, in which Rousseau, Montesquieu and Machiavelli jostle with the classical historians, it bears witness above all to Marx's need for historical knowledge, in the banal sense of the word. For it was now that he compiled extensive chronologies and for ancient history, moreover.

In his 1859 reminiscences he will only say — and Maximilien Rubel telescopes this a bit — that the 'conductor' which guided his subsequent studies was discovered at Kreuznach. He places this discovery after the Paris episode when he immersed himself in political economy, grew better acquainted with certain French socialists, and joined forces decisively with Engels.

Admittedly, from the beginning of 1844, in his *Introduction to the Critique of Hegel's 'Philosophy of Law'*, and here and there in *The Jewish Question*, he had rediscovered — and with greater clarity — the concepts of 1842 concerning the *anteriority* of civil society *vis-à-vis* the State, a concept in which Engels saw the true breakthrough. Nevertheless, in the same issue of the *Franco-German Annals*, Engels, for his part, had published a 'Sketch for a Critique of Political Economy', which Marx, fifteen years later, was still calling 'a work of genius'. But it is certainly this which is significant — not that I want 'a decisive turning-point' — for I believe that every conquest in the realm of thought is progressive. Even so, it is pertinent to note that the two friends believed they had arrived at the same result 'by different routes' (for Engels, via the English *inductive* method, working from the facts; for Marx, the *deductive* method, through the critique of Hegel) this no longer strikes me as fundamental; for Engels had not escaped from the Hegelian atmosphere, and Marx, as we have seen, had also drawn from the facts. The 'link', in both their cases, had at first been an interior one. This became clear to them when they met, and that is why the meeting was so fruitful.

When in 1845 they decided to collaborate on a day-to-day basis, they had two certainties to go on:

1 In the attempt at justifying modern societies, political economy is the only theory whose starting-point is scientific, so the critique of it — and its re-ordering — became the pressing subject of their enquiry. From Engels' *Sketch* to Marx's *Capital*, the words 'critique of political economy' never ceased to figure in their projects and their works.
2 On the other hand, philosophy had to be abandoned, particularly the unhealthy territory of post-Hegelian pretensions.

But there was something of which they were still unaware: that a lifetime would not suffice to complete even the first project. In 1844 they had illusions as to their knowledge of economics. However, from now on they would publish nothing till they were sure of themselves. Their 'enquiry into philosophical awareness' was soon to be laid aside, and finally, as is well known, exposed to 'gnawing criticism'.

Nevertheless, between the kernel of economics, 'the final instance that so easily eludes the grasp', and the philosophers' unsubstantial wrappings of interpretation, lies the nebula of facts, whether social, political, judicial or ideological, the assemblage of material to organise and submit to scientific enquiry. Such material cannot be treated in isolation. For Marx and Engels it is this assemblage of material which constitutes *the* new aim of science. Shall we call it *History*?

We recognise one science, and one only, the science of history. [*Wir kennen nur eine einzige Wissenschaft, die Wissenschaft der Geschichte.*]

The Marxist historian would love to be able to brandish such august credentials in support of his life's work. Unfortunately it is a crossed-out sentence in an unpublished book. So some may feel a sense of scruple at this. The problem of history as science, however, is genuinely tackled in *The German Ideology*.

Even the hesitations are instructive: crossed-out sentences, the repeated use of the word '*Geschichte*' in the margin, and its use in a variety of meanings. The same word had been used — and abused — by Hegel and his disciples. But were the professional historians any better? In 1845 Marx entered their territory. First of all he read their works. Then, unlike all too many so-called Marxists, who would rather spare themselves the trouble, he went to the sources, to the original texts and documents at first hand. He once planned to write the history of the Convention. Eventually, however, he gave up the idea.

In so doing, did he give up the profession of historian? I tend to believe that the opposite was true. He felt that by dedicating himself to a single aspect (political, that is to say) of a single episode (however important, however profoundly investigated) he was conforming to the traditional definition of history — the pursuit of the particular fact — when what he, in fact, needed was to carve out the principles of a systematic scientific approach, not those of a 'philosophy'.

These principles or '*Voraussetzungen*' (and Marx reproached the German ideologues for having failed to realise their necessity) appear in *The German Ideology*, but less clearly, less instructively, than in the Preface to the 'Contribution' of 1859, because *The German Ideology*, a polemical, unfinished work, had not yet completely freed itself from the very forms of expression — and hence of thought — with which it meant to do battle. However, some striking phrases are to be found; here and there are pages that develop the essentials of what one day will guide the work of history. His obsession with the core of economics would later prevent Marx from returning for any length of time to historical materialism, considered as an entity; so it's not a bad thing if, rather that repeat the *dicta* of 1859 we acknowledge how he erected the scaffolding of premises and reasonings from 1845 onwards, albeit in an incomplete form, which were to subtend the entire historical structure worthy of that name for all who wished to see.

First, do men 'make history'? Here we touch on that notorious 'little sentence', 'Men make their own history...', destined to be discovered by a host of para-Marxists or pseudo-Marxists, rediscovered, repeated, dismembered and reinterpreted according to need, so that idealism and voluntarism could be reintroduced into Marx's materialism. Now, in *The German Ideology* the words *Geschichte machen* are written in inverted commas, implying irony and doubt. Not that Marx wanted to exclude men's actions from history, for he distinguished between a 'history of nature' external to that action, and a 'history of men', in which man interacts with nature. But the irony implied by the inverted commas was aimed not only at Hegel and the German ideologues, but additionally at the overwhelming illusion of quasi-inclusivity which had pervaded the works of historians from earliest times.

It is significant that Marx seems to have arrived at this point in passing and apparently by chance, as a result of some youthful controversy. In such a manner he came to refute one of man's great weaknesses *vis-à-vis* his past. Traditionally speaking, history begins with writing (that is, when man, by writing, can attribute responsibility to himself). Before that, there was pre-history. Thus, there can be no history without theology, politics, literature. But inversely, where there is only pre-history for want of evidence and 'raw material' (that is to say events), the door is open to speculation and a thousand hypotheses, each destined to be refuted before very long.

Marx and Engels held all this against 'the Germans'; the young polemicists laid their charge against the immediate national enemy. But surely we too have fallen into the same trap? Our pre-historians, faced with a vast mass of material and apparently less susceptible to ideological temptations, cut a more convincingly 'scholarly' figure than *the historians* do. But are they not constantly involved in confrontations that are devoid of general meaning, and mixed with hypotheses that are at best nebulous? And as soon as the first inscriptions, chronicles, or monuments appear, the grandiose realities fade away, and we are reduced to historiography, where the stage is dominated by individuals, minorities and myths. The great problem is that the dearth of factual information concerning the pre-historic habitat, tools and productions tends to leave us in the dark, while the human evidence, from its first appearance, is deceptive. In future, however, historical science will consist of objective information, which is both extensive and independent, combined with the reading of subjective documents which have been subjected to a critique in depth. Let us freely admit that at present we are still no more than groping blindly to achieve this difficult task.

How easily one understands the violent reaction of two demanding minds when faced with the pride of a Hegel in the Germany of more than a century ago — not to mention his critics' 'revolutionary' claims, and the learned pedantry of the 'historical school' in the making. It is only to be expected, that with this reaction more than one judgement should border on the unfair. Here was a Germany considered 'underdeveloped'. (The word itself, needless to say, does not occur, though it is continually suggested.) Marx and Engels were going through the process of discovering the French historians of the Revolution, and British economic and para-economic literature. Here they found an articulation of their own concerns. But they were determined to go further, to reach the theory of history. And if *The German Ideology* contains passages of polemics, philosophy or even revolutionary speculation, which now seem partially outdated, if we no longer feel the full force of the *Manifesto* or the profundity of *Capital*, at least we can observe:

1   new formulae, crucial to the future of all human science; and
2   plans that are capable of guiding the research historian through the most pressing current problems.

First, there is the primacy of production. This is not to be confused with the arbitrary hypotheses concerning the origin of societies, for if it is a piece of evidence, this is imposed in spite of traditional history which has always forgotten it: 'The first historical act of individuals, whereby they are distinguished from beasts, is not that they think, but that they apply themselves to producing their means of existence'.

But the word 'production' is no magic key. Production must be considered in terms of population and men's relationships one to another. Marx uses the word *Verkehr*, a term that he translates into French as 'commerce', but clearly in the old sense of the word: intercourse of *all* kinds. Within these relationships, population and production, there is a continual interaction: 'This production only comes about with an increase in population. In itself it pre-supposes the intercourse between individuals. The form that this intercourse takes is conditioned in turn by production'.

Thus a vital activity arises, without which history is unthinkable: 'As soon as these processes of vital activity are depicted anew, history ceases to be a collection of dead facts, as with the empiricists, who are themselves abstract, or to be the imaginary action of imaginary subjects, as with the idealists.'

Let us keep in mind this just accusation against the empirical historian, who likes to imagine himself as 'concrete', when he presses the concept of the 'fact in itself' to the extreme of abstraction, an inoperative abstraction.

This does not mean for one moment that 'empirical observation' is to be overlooked. What is necessary is that the hypothesis (starting with the hypothesis of the rationality of the real) should organise observation, which confirms it, invalidates it, or corrects it:

Here, then, are the facts: specific individuals, who engage in a productive activity in accordance with a specific mode, enter specific political and social relationships. Hence it is in the facts — and this must apply to all cases — that the empirical observation must demonstrate, without any speculation or mystification, the link between the political and social structure and production.

Marx does not yet use *Struktur* — a Latin word and a formal, architectural image. He uses '*Gliederung*', an anatomical and functional image, which introduces the useful idea of 'articulation'.

The crossings-out in the manuscript of *The German Ideology* only confirm how this work cannot disguise the extent of the difficulty in 'constructing' history without being lost in philosophical idealism while using abstraction:

All autonomous philosophy loses the basis of its existence with the representation of reality. In its place is offered a synthesis of the most general results which may be abstracted from an examination of man's historical development. Cut off from real history, these abstractions have no intrinsic value. They can only serve to facilitate the classification of historical matter, to mark the succession of its various layers. But they in no way provide, in the manner of philosophy, a recipe or a blueprint to determine the boundaries of historical eras. On the contrary, the difficulty begins precisely when one begins to examine, and classify the material, to offer a real picture of it, no matter whether one is dealing with the past or the present. The elimination of these difficulties depends on premises which can only emerge from the study of the processes of life itself, and from the action of individuals of each age.

A deleted phrase (why?) pinpointed what the examination and classification of the material of history must consist of: '. . . enquire into the real, practical interdependence of its various stratifications.'

This strikes me as important. Did Marx want to reject the word 'stratification'? In any event, by resorting to different words, he sidesteps this danger that I repeatedly find in the present-day language of sociology. Neither history nor society presents 'layers' that are statically placed as in an archaeological site. The vestiges of the past in a present reality, or the social classes within the framework of a mode of production, are active elements, in a position of reaction or progress, defence or attack, and are never fixed or distinct. Their 'practical, real interdependence' is the aim of research and the exposé of history. For the Marxist historian, at any rate, this should be a major concern. The phrase we have just quoted provides no 'proof' of this, of course. But it marks how Marx and Engels evolved a concept of history that was both profound and original, in full awareness of its pitfalls and difficulties, when it comes to mapping a route between empirical description, stripped of meaning, and abstraction, and 'divorced from real history'.

We may add that the still philosophical character of *The German Ideology* ensures that its lessons, as far as the idea of 'history' is concerned, are not only technical, scientific, and useful to the historian, but are often considerations to be classified in the immense list of the discussions *on* history — on the necessity (or indeed the noxiousness) of 'the historical spirit' in general, if not of a systematic 'historicism'. Could it not be that to think in a way that is historically correct before even having constructed the concept of history is at once a possibility and a requirement of the spirit? Marx and Engels blame Feuerbach for:

seeing, in Manchester for example, only factories and machines, where, only a century ago, there were spinning-wheels and weaving trades; and he only sees pastures and swamps in the Roman campagna, where in the time of Augustus he would have found vineyards and the villas of Roman capitalists.

This incapacity to think beyond the present, outside the static — and this alone impedes a true historical culture — leads Feuerbach (and others) ceaselessly to distinguish between 'history' and 'nature', a 'nature' which, in our own day, 'no longer exists anywhere, except perhaps in a few recently formed Australian atolls'; as if — and here the objection is against Bruno Bauer — 'man did not always find himself confronted by a nature that is historical and by a history that is natural'. The result is that Feuerbach 'insofar as he is a materialist never allows history to intervene, and insofar as he allows history to intervene . . . is not a materialist'.

For if he sees in man a conscious object, he does not see a

conscious activity; and if he invokes a real, individual man of flesh and blood, it is a man of passion and sentiment, not a being who is tied to daily, material necessities. Half a century later, this criticism seems directed at Miguel de Unamuno, also a lawyer, by some flesh-and-blood historians, but in fine contempt of real necessities.

Let us not pour too much scorn on these objections to literary philosophies though, even if they are banal. The brilliant formulae round history produce more echoes than the serious treatment of realities. After all, it is more important that Marx and Engels in their 'examination of philosophical awareness' should have laid some of the positive foundations of historical materialism, even if they did so imperfectly:

1 There are close links between the productive forces at society's disposal (to which the productivity of labour bears witness) and the division of labour, which orders the forms of social relationships (a grouping still described as 'civil society'), and between the functioning of this 'civil society' and the movement of political history, with its 'events':

...the entire internal structure [of a nation] . . . depends on the level of development of its production and its internal and external exchanges . . . all new productive force has as its effect a new development of the division of labour.

The various stages of development in the division of labour represent as many distinct forms of property; in other words, every new stage in the division of labour also determines the relationships of individuals with one another, with regard to materials, tools, and the products of labour... .

This vocabulary is not yet 'Marxist'. The 'division of labour', dear to classical economists, here plays a part which later analyses will simultaneously clarify and destroy. But some remarks are already to be found here, which too many historians, even Marxist ones, tend to forget; one must not confuse the increase in productive forces and 'the simple quantitative extension of already known productive forces (land reclamation, for instance)', the great extension of uncultivated lands conditioning the primitive forms of property. Let us note this against the unwarranted application of modern economic law to societies which they do not govern. Let us bear in mind that if Marx and Engels, who are concerned with the future and with immediate action, referred so often to the most primitive modes of production, it is because these modes of production in space and time have taken up more room than the forms of economy which dominate us. The great law emerges: that of the correspondence between productive forces and the social relationships of production.

2 Between these realities and the representations that men make of them, the relationship does not arise in the direction representation→reality, but in the direction reality→ representation:

It is men who produce their own representations, their ideas etc., the real, active men, such as are conditioned by a development which is determined by their productive forces and the intercourse [*Verkehr*] which correspond to them, including the broadest forms that these can take.

Hence, morality, religion, metaphysics and all other ideologies, as well as the forms of consciousness which correspond to them, lose all appearance of autonomy. They have no history, no development. On the contrary, it is men who, by developing their material production and their material relationships, do the transforming, with this reality which is their own and their thoughts and the products of their thoughts. It is not consciousness that determines life, but life that determines consciousness.

The anti-idealist struggle of 1845 lends this point its particular clarity. Let us recall, as a lesson for the historian, the necessity of struggle, particularly urgent at the present time, between all history 'of ideas', 'mentalities', indeed, of 'sciences', founded on exclusively internal, formal coherences or filiations, and not on solidarity between 'the production of thoughts' (of whatever order they may be) and changes in the conditions and relationships of social and material existence. Evey moment the threat reappears, in its historical (and especially philosophical) application, of an autonomous treatment of the facts of thought; under guises that are sometimes completely new, it is the return to the traditional facilities.

3 Less clear perhaps, but present nonetheless, is the following theme in *The German Ideology*: that the relationships of productive forces are in contradiction with its revolutionary effects:

In the development of productive forces, the moment comes when there arise productive forces and means of circulation which can only be harmful within the framework of existing relationships, and hence are no longer productive forces but destructive ones. Related to this is the further fact that there is born a class that bears all the burden of society without enjoying its advantages. Society's outcast, this class thereupon finds itself in the most overt opposition to all other classes.

Here is the germ of the 'communist conscience', which,

according to Marx and Engels, reveals an incipient contradiction, and, with great precocity, foresees the future. But the historical repetition of these revolutionary transitions shows that it is a question of the past as much as the future:

The conditions under which certain productive forces can be utilised are those of domination by a certain class in society; the social power of this class derives from what it possesses, and finds its practical expression, in its ideal form, in the type of State that is peculiar to each age; that is why every revolutionary struggle is directed against the class that has hitherto been dominant.

4   Curiously enough, Marx and Engels observe that traditional history — and doubtless the economists more than anyone else — admit that the levels of unequal material development dominate the relationships and determine the struggles between the 'nations'. And it is true that often bourgeois ideology, which systematically obscures internal realities, justifies conquests and colonisation by considerations of material and intellectual 'superiority': 'Relationships between different nations depend on the stage of development each has reached, judged from the point of view of its productive forces, the division of labour and internal trade. This principle is universally allowed.'

The German Ideology even suggests, in relation to Germany and her 'tormented national conscience', that the contradiction between productive relations and the forces of production can arise (or, better, manifests itself) not within the national sphere, but in this national consciousness and the experience of other nations. The present-day problems of 'underdevelopment' justify, in some of their aspects, this precocious intuition.

5   Nevertheless, if the Marxist innovation does not disregard, as we have just seen, the division of mankind into organised groups — into 'States', the concept of the 'nation' remaining problematical — its essential feature is the supplanting of classical opposition between 'individual' interests and 'collective' ones by the opposition between the interests of classes with power and those in subjection:

It follows that all struggles within the State, the struggle between democracy, aristocracy and monarchy, the struggle for the right to vote, etc. are only illusory forms behind which are conducted the real struggles of one class against another.

It equally follows that every class that aspires to domination, even if this domination requires the abolition of every former social order and domination, as is the case for the proletariat, must first gain political power, in order to portray its own interest as in the universal interest.

Thus the historian is forewarned: beneath the illusion he must look for the real; beneath the political, the social; beneath 'the general interest', the class interest; beneath the forms of the State, the structures of 'civil society':

It is therefore evident that this civil society is the true hearth, the genuine stage, of all history. The earlier concept of history can be seen as nonsense, for it disregarded the real relationships, and limited itself to great historical and political events.

We here find Marx and Engels tending to caricature the existing historiography to suit the exigencies of their 'fight for history'. Febvre, Bloch, Simiand were to do the same. There has never been a dearth of biassed attempts to illuminate the background to the great stage of history. But when economics, finance, law and language were considered to be the concern of 'specialists', the title of 'historian' was reserved for official praters and philosophers.

After Marx, in the second half of the nineteenth century, learned positivist history was to multiply still further the 'specialised' fields, including political history, aimed at the 'little fact', but always cut off from the social, while the imagery of 'the great events' and moral judgements took over from the King's historian in the textbooks. This time, it was in reaction to half-aware Marx, and barely formulated, preferring silence to attempts at refutation, the struggle against a history that led to revolutionary conclusions.

And so the rediscovery in the twentieth century of a history that went beyond 'the event' in order to search for the 'real relationship' could be made without reference to Marx, and consequently, in spite of its merits, with insufficient theoretical backing and under an excessive illusion of being 'new'. But this does not inhibit the feeling that it is dangerous; it is the source of a spontaneous offensive by ahistorical structuralism and by anti-historical sociology. This period admirably illustrates the following passage from *The German Ideology*: '...almost every ideology either is reduced to a false concept of history, or ends by reducing it to a total abstraction. Ideology itself is no more than one of the aspects of history.'
6   This repression (or interment beneath conservative theories) of all revolutionary human science is historically significant:

The thoughts of the dominant class are also, in every age, the dominant thoughts. In other words, the dominant material power of society is also its dominant spiritual power. The class that disposes of the means of material production disposes, by the same token, of those of intellectual production, so that generally speaking the thoughts of those who are deprived of the means of intellectual production are suppressed thoughts. And the dominant thoughts are themselves only the idealised expression of the dominant material relationships: they are those relationships seen in the form of ideas; they express all that makes a class the dominant class; they are in fact the idea of that domination.

Here arises a major new problem: must (or can) the historian think of a society of an earlier age in accordance with the criteria of today, which are, for their part, social and historical products? It is hence an anachronism, the cardinal sin, according to Lucien Febvre, who denounces it in speaking of Rabelais. But what is the use of defining a 'society of ranks' as a society in which the common man recognised a hierarchy of 'ranks'; or to say that a vassal was 'attached to his lord by the concept of loyalty'?

Let us content ourselves with the fact that such-and-such ideas dominated a certain era, without worrying about the conditions of production or of the producers of these ideas . . . we will then be able to say, for example, that at the time when the aristocracy ruled it was the reign of honour, loyalty etc., and that at the time when the bourgeoisie ruled it was the reign of liberty, equality etc.

In everyday life, any shopkeeper knows well enough how to distinguish between what a person claims to be and what he actually is; but our history has not yet reached this stage of common knowledge. It takes on trust how each age describes itself, and accepts the picture that every era paints.

We are told: is not the task of the historian accurately to re-discover the spirit of men in former times, to breathe life into their lives and collective thoughts? It is beyond doubt that this 'resurrection-history' can count its successes, can provide its intellectual pleasures. But it is not the scientific-history of societies; it is not destined to observe their evolution, or to take their mechanisms to pieces. A knowledge of this kind is not content with 'evocations' and 'reconstitutions'. It demands coherent analyses in which all the interdependent factors must figure. To say that history is 'made' by 'ideas' or by 'psychology' is as tautological and absurd as to classify an economic phenomenon as 'psychological'. All the resultant statistics express individual 'psychological' decisions. In the inflation process, however, the 'tendency to spend' does not mean that people will book into luxury hotels. Psychoanalysis itself, in spite of its materialist premises, is not a good basis for historical analysis. Occasionally it may cast light on forms redressed by men's reactions. But it cannot illuminate in any depth the social facts which justify them. Alas, 130 years after the appearance of *The German Ideology*, the same question remains: How much historical literature escapes, even today, the naïvetés that arise from the acceptance of sources.

7 I would like to add a further point concerning classes, where this book gives useful clues to the historian, the sociologist and the observer of our own societies. Marx's works, taken as a whole, have often been accused of lacking clarity as to the concept of class, whether through the incompleteness of the pages of *Capital* that should deal with it, through the extremely schematised form of the opposing elements attributed to capitalism (bourgeois-proletariat), or, on the contrary, by his use in the historical analysis of Germany, England and France of a complex and ill-defined vocabulary: proprietor, industrialist, petit bourgeois, peasant, smallholder etc.

I am tempted to propose (but tomes would be required for the unravelling) that the play between simplicity and complexity in the class system largely depends, not in Marx but in reality, on the stage reached by the mode of production that is being analysed. Simple divisions — feudal tripartition, capitalist bipartition — characterise the apogees, the social forms that approximate to the module, while the systems become complex, or give the illusion of doing so, during the periods of 'transition', which dovetail overdevelopment and underdevelopment, structurings and restructurings.

Besides, it is not difficult to distinguish, at the heart of the most cohesive classes, competing categories, groupings that are unequally linked to certain kinds of production; we find secondary divisions amidst the dominant classes — industrialist-agriculturist, importer-exporter, creditor-debtor — or indeed 'oppositions within the very body of the people'. There is nothing new in the classical difference between 'contradiction' and 'antinomy'.

Finally, when it comes to the expression of class struggles, a problem arises from the complicated play of intellectual agitation, the claims of the priestly classes, or their present day equivalent in the 'third power'.

Now, in *The German Ideology* there are to be found some singularly illuminating remarks on the shades of difference which emerge or fade between categories within one class, as the class struggles change in intensity. There are similar differences between the 'active' people in a dominant class and its 'intellectuals'. A revolutionary danger places a question mark over the power of a class, and the apparent complexity rapidly gives way to simplification.

[The division of labour] also manifests itself in the dominant class in the form of a division between material labour and intellectual labour, so that a proportion of the individuals within that class will be seen as the thinking part — ideologues, producers of ideas, who find a livelihood in the culture of the self-deceptions of the dominant class. While the rest passively accept and are receptive to these thoughts and illusions. These are the productive, practical members of this class, who have less time to meditate and dream for themselves. This division at the heart of the dominant class can reach the stage of oppositions, indeed hostilities, but these fall away as soon as conflict arises in which the entire class is jeopardised, when all appearance of distinction between dominant ideas and the ideas of the dominant class, and between the power of the ideas and of the class itself disappears.

This passage should be an inspiration to every historian who is faced with a conflict posed by the 'intellectuals' when social struggle emerges: to what class do these intellectuals belong? What class questions the ideology that they propose? The dominant class? How will it react? In our own age the words 'bourgeoisie', 'power', 'democracy', 'bureaucracy', 'ideology' are used so imprecisely, imprudently (or even deceptively). So these questions acquire an importance in distinguishing (or saving from confusion) the apparent conflicts and the true conflicts, the classes that came to power a long time ago, and those that are new to it, the traditional ideological machines, whether surviving or revitalised, and the revolutionary, pseudo-revolutionary or counter-revolutionary proposals. The task of politics here is the same as that of the historian, with this difference: that the historian, knowing the outcome of the conflict, is helped by this in his analysis. But politics will only become science when history does.

The German Ideology is far from being a 'history book'. It is certainly a book for historians, first of all for the principles we have drawn from the text. They are more explicit, less exposed to imprudent exegesis than certain later formulations, which have been reduced to syntheses whose brevity can be dangerously appealing; secondly, for some biassed developments which were subsequently to be better treated, but which already provide the ground plan, though more informatively in some parts than in others. We know enough of what Marx was reading at the time of *The German Ideology* to assess the progress he was making in his knowledge of the techniques, economics and social movements of the past. It remains to be said that if the all-too-general sociological views, such as 'division of labour', the town–country relationship and the succession of different types of property are still vague, given the absence of the central concept of the 'mode of production', several decisive episodes in the history of Europe have been grasped and felicitously characterised. Among these are the impotence of the medieval revolts, the emergence of manufacture, the role of vagrancy in early modern times, while in the higher reaches of trade there appeared a *bourgeoisie* that was *grande* in comparison with manufacturers and artisans, but *petite* in comparison with contemporary industrial enterprises. We find the dual nature of capitalism — national and protectionist, worldwide and committed to free trade, according to the exigencies of the moment, without forgetting his perceptive remarks on the American opportunity, a capitalism without a past, free before the free and open spaces. This grasp of proportions, of decisive facts, this absence of misinterpretation, even when the information is meagre, characterises the genius of Marx and Engels when confronted with historical material as soon as they discovered it, as soon as they discovered themselves.

Moreover, it is no less instructive to recognise them, from that time onwards, as critical historians, minutely comparing texts with Karl Grün's plagiarisms, or ridiculing Max Stirner's eight *geschichtliche Reflexionen*, whose deficiency is precisely that they are not 'historical'. They probe the consonance between ages and races (infancy, youth, maturity: Negroes, Mongols, Caucasians) or the similarity between Robespierre's dogmatism and papal dogmatism! It is true that one could say that this was equivalent to a critique; besides, its authors have gladly buried it. One may also say that this reaction in the name of history against absurd parallels across the expanse of time is not yet a need of our time. Does not the intellectual pseudo-scientific, pseudo-revolutionary over-production of Germany in 1840, have its equivalents in our own age? Who will perform the 'examination of the conscience' of our 'ideologues', of all our sins against history?

In 1847, however, a further step was to be taken by Marx and Engels. Not in *The Poverty of Philosophy*, in which the initial critique of the anti-historical Robinsonnades swiftly gives way to logical controversies, and in which various condensed formulations become the sport of facile criticism and tempt bad Marxists: 'The windmill will produce the society of the feudal lord, the steam-engine the society of the industrial capitalist'. All Marx's work contradicts this schematic approach, which is only explained by its context: and is a reply to Proudhon who identified the relationship between economic categories and reality. This does not prevent *The Poverty of Philosophy* from offering the historian some analyses–models, mechanism, strikes, considered at one and the same time as products and factors of history.

In the same period, in spite of all this, the *Communist Manifesto* erupts like an innovation, confronting the difficulty that Fustel was to emphasise, the lack of true syntheses, visionary flights that reveal the chief characteristics of a history. I have always suspected that Raymond Aron's aphorism: 'The historian's causal enquiry does less to draw the main lines of history than to restore to the past the uncertainty of the future' had its origin in a certain fear of history that the *Communist Manifesto* inspired in the bourgeoisie. If so striking a picture of the historical triumphs of the bourgeoisie should also announce its decline, this unfortunate prophesy must be exorcised. Positivist history set to work on it, forcing itself to reject Marx in the 'philosophy of history', and to reduce the insights of the *Communist Manifesto* to a number of unfulfilled 'prophesies'.

Unfulfilled? 'A spectre haunts Europe, the spectre of communism'. Let us substitute 'the world' for 'Europe', and we then arrive at present reality. But who still gives a thought to Rostow and his anti-manifesto fifteen years later? Not everyone can be a great historian.

I trust I may indulge in a personal recollection: in 1943, when I was in Germany in a prisoner-of-war camp for officers, I allowed myself the luxury (not too risky, thanks to our guards' level of culture!) of reading the *Communist Manifesto* to a large, restless and perplexed audience. One of my oldest friends, a renowned historian, and a leading professor of history said to me: 'What a work! You may think you know it by heart, but it never fails to astonish when you come back to it.' This review of world history from the decline of the Middle Ages — not a 'description' of the world, one hardly need say, but an enquiry into the elements and factors that have transformed it — is today confirmed and assimilated (but also diluted and rendered aseptic) by the common channels of information, so that its contents may seem banal, and its argument superficial, and you may fail to appreciate fully its profundity — (we have known that a long time) — and to reduce its revolutionary significance to the qualities of its form. But, in 1847, who could have written history in such a manner? As Althusser has pointed out in other respects, Marx was so 'new' in his own day that it takes time to appreciate him fully. The *Communist Manifesto* was only to reach its mark after 1870. We are to conclude that it emerged from the void: there had been Adam Smith; and the French historians of the Third Estate; and it was this conjuncture of enquiries which gave birth, around 1850, to German economic history; but Smith was to become a conventional reference for economists; and German economic history was to become trapped in the learned empiricism of 'our Roscher'. The *Communist Manifesto*, by contrast, remains the first shining success for synthesised history, for history-explication.

I shall not be considering it here as a revolutionary instrument. On the other hand I would like to say a word about the third part, which is often dismissed, as it provides an incomparable methodological lesson. Under the sole word 'socialism' he tries to find out what the various classes are about: 'feudal' socialism, the 'clerical' socialism of those classes recently dispossessed by the bourgeoisie, the 'petit bourgeois' socialism of the classes that it threatens, 'bourgeois' socialism, conservative socialism, seen as a counter-revolutionary dam, utopian socialisms that were once able to seduce some sections of the proletariat, but which quickly decline into impotence. Demystification of a word by class analysis, and in temporal conjunction: this is the work of the historian which was to be taken up again, and consciously copied by the young Stalin in 1904 around the word 'nationalism'; and this was to prove another masterpiece, not only of Marxist literature, but of history.

On account of this methodological aim of fragments that are far less frequently quoted than others, I have come to regret — but this regret will be seen as purely relative — a widespread tendency: that of not counting any of the works of Marx and Engels as 'historical works', except, of course, *The Peasants' War, Revolution and Counter-Revolution in Germany, The Class Struggle in France, The 18th Brumaire of Louis Bonaparte* and *The Civil War in France*. I say that this regret is purely relative in the sense that it is concerned with great works of history. But I fear that they are only recognised as such insofar as they resemble, more than Marx's other works, traditional 'history': men, parties, elections, riots, repressions, diplomacy. For some decades it has been the custom to fit everything into the socio-economic mould, whether economic crises, structures of society, the 'bourgeoisie' and the 'proletariat' or working-class struggles. So it comes about that one forgets, as with the

Communist Manifesto, that it is not Marx who wrote like us, but we who would like to write like Marx. To think like him is more difficult.

In the works we have cited, and which are called 'historical', it is always a matter (even in *The Peasants' War*), of revolutions that have miscarried. The first piece of advice that Marx and Engels give to historians and politicians (especially defeated politicians) on the subject of these setbacks is not to blame Mr X or Citizen Y — today we can add Comrade Z — for if 'the people' (the inverted commas are Engels') have been 'deceived' or 'betrayed', how and why did they let it happen? An explanation must still be found. To speak of collective 'mistakes' (by a 'party', 'peasants' or the 'petit bourgeois') is not an illuminating reply. It is the entire historical situation that must be rethought. Another danger lies immediately in wait for us: mechanism, the fatalism concerning 'conditions', which obliterates all responsibility and ends by considering every event legitimate.

Between 'It's the fault of...' and 'It couldn't have been otherwise...', how is one to distinguish the necessary conditions, the adequate conditions, the judgements and acts that have taken hold of them, respected them or made use of them, which have let history take its course? Global history is a much more complex matter than the mere presentation of objective data of military strategies, and it is a caricature to depict political decisions as an independently reached calculation, like a game in other words. Teams and individuals are themselves carriers of internal resolves; and in almost the whole course of history they have only acted intuitively, empirically. The historian, judging after the event, collates the results of decisions with the conditions which would have to have been taken into account. According to Raymond Aron the historian submits himself voluntarily to uncertainty. According to Marx the historian tries to assimilate it by reasoning and from the facts. Aron's definition is applicable to the classical historians from Thucydides onwards. The innovation of Marx and Engels was intended:

1 to dispel illusions concerning the freedom of individuals' decisions, not that he sees it as 'determined', but very broadly shaped by the property and position of the class that is responsible;
2 to measure the depth and determine the type of the information which politics has often lacked;
3 to distinguish between the appearance of the problems raised

(economic measures, types of power, moral arguments) and the reality, which is the class struggle.

This, then is the first undertaking: putting things in their rightful place, a synthesis (*Zusammensetzung*) of the social classes involved; no 'stratification', but reciprocal interests, aspirations and capabilities. The second undertaking is to locate their problems both in the world and in time. We say nowadays (i) analysis of structure; and (ii) analysis of conjuncture, but this vocabulary introduces nothing new to Marx. The picture achieves a balance of material and psychological notations. It opens with *The Class Struggle in France*, and ends with a lightning evocation of 'two world economic events': (i) the food crisis (today we would say the 'old type of crisis' — potato blight, bad harvests, high prices, provincial riots); (ii) 'the worldwide crisis in trade and industry', a capitalist crisis to whose nature and recurrence the *Communist Manifesto* had drawn attention.

As for this connective factor, at once precise and concise, one all too often forgets to associate it with the twenty closely-packed pages of the same *Cahiers*, written in the same year, which include a monumental documentation, of worldwide significance, not so much on 'the crisis' as on the cycle, since the return to prosperity was examined there, declared to be a temporary cessation of revolutionary conditions, with one sole outcome: that the crisis will return. When, as in *The Class Struggle*, Marx needs to analyse the connective factor in a political crisis, he does so judiciously, aware of the dulness of statistics and the obscurity of the sound of little known names. But his economic documentation always goes much further than the condensed material that he sees fit to retain. On the other hand, how often, in the 'politicology' of the day, can we guess the superficial character of the allusions to economics, while the economic reviews accumulate statistics and [diagrammatic] curves, as if either economics were something purely mechanical, or as if 'economic politics' alone counted, and not the social forces that give rise to them.

In this respect we should observe some peculiarities of *composition* in Marx and Engels' works that are called 'historical'. Those contemporary historians who admit (and sometimes believe they have discovered) the need to consider both the structure of a society, the temporal conjunctures and the events of the period, show a tendency to expound these three aspects of world history successively and separately. It is logical, therefore legitimate. This is hazardous to the extent that when one considers the events one risks misunderstanding what links them with the structures, the conjunctures. Marx and Engels avoid the danger of this rigid, pedagogical and conventional approach. For them, the strength of the links is what matters. The statement of the events may sometimes precede their explanation, at other times come after it. Sometimes the event will suggest an insistence upon the conjuncture, sometimes upon the structure. So Marx's history, as Schumpeter saw, neither separates nor 'fuses' the various aspects of economics — the social, the political and that of events. It combines them. Moreover, this *histoire raisonnée*, thanks to the spontaneous emergence of arguments, and the speed and irony of the narrative, is a living history.

It is also a militant history, and, whether directly or allusively, a history of reality. As far as these two points are concerned, it is in the opposite camp to positivist history, which claims 'objectivity', and demands a retrogressive movement. We shall not here go into the vast — and very often false — problem of 'historical objectivity'. Unless history is reduced to mere inquisitiveness about the past, wilfully deprived of significance, every account of events, every causal analysis, must, through its selectivity, clothe an ideology; it does little harm if it is openly declared; but it is dangerous if hidden. As for the vehement contemporaries, whom history no longer has any reason to abandon, when they constitute so many 'politicologies' and 'sociologies', I shall repeat what I have often written; dishonesty in contemporary history is to say one is objective when one knows oneself to be partisan; and the worst stupidity is to believe oneself to be objective when one is partisan (and who is not?). Marx and Engels (and later their great disciples) proclaim their political choice, and mean to serve it. But they believe that the best way to succeed is by bringing a sufficient intelligence to events, if not a 'science' of historical matter, whose principles they have given us, but not the entire working apparatus for different 'cases':

Thus, when we try to unravel, for *Tribune*'s readers, the causes that necessarily underlay the 1848 Revolution, and led, no less necessarily, to a progressive collapse in 1849 and 1850, we cannot be expected to provide an entire history of the events exactly as they occurred. Subsequent events and posterity's judgement will decide what is destined to enter world history. At present it is a chaotic mass of apparently fortuitous facts, lacking cohesion and kinship. The time for such a task has not yet arrived. We must keep within the limits of the possible, and be content when it falls to our lot to discover rational sequences. We must rely on incontrovertible facts, which explain the most important events and the decisive turns in each movement, affording us a view over the direction that the German people will take in the near future, or at least not too distant.

How unassuming! It is tempting to say: What a choice of words! — 'events', 'posterity's judgement', 'enter history'. We are a long way, however, from Raymond Aron, from his 'probable and relative judgements'. What Engels postulates is the *rationality of history*. A rationality that is penetrable. Without waiting — and penetrable by discriminating minds. Within certain limits, however: the limits of inevitably scant information, those of a relatively brief time for reflection, those of an insufficient opportunity to stand back, not for the sake of 'objectivity', but for the sake of ascertaining the consequences. I do not believe that Marx and Engels ever confused history and the political analysis of the present. They were widely read in the historians, just as they were widely read in the economists. They were harsh critics, capable of rejecting and condemning, but also of assimilating. They should be observed distinguishing, as with Guizot, the perceptive analyst from the blind pamphleteer. One looks in vain for any systematic condemnation, whether of the historian's metier as work required for information, or reflection on no matter what period of the past, provided it is intelligent. This needs to be pointed out to militant workers or young intellectuals who are tempted to dismiss scholarly history, not centred on the revolutionary and the immediate. In fact it is all history and first and foremost the history of the dominant classes that can and must permit us to assess the great political stakes.

If the 'historical works' of Marx and Engels are to be placed where they rightly belong, it is within the limits which they themselves assigned to them, in accordance with the cir-cumstances of their publication. In a preface to *The 18th Brumaire*, Ryazonov recalled that Weydemeyer's question which prompted the work reached Marx by way of a letter from Engels, dated 16 December 1851 requesting the article within the week! On 19 December Marx asked if he could have until 23 December. But he 'fell dangerously ill' so he was 'only' able to send the opening pages on 1 January 1852, and the rest 'only' on 13 February, says Ryazonov. Take note of the word 'only'. Remember that Marx was living in the depths of poverty: his family was in rags. It is astonishing that a masterpiece should have been written under such circumstances. Engels was expecting no more than a competent 'diplomatic' article — but one that could 'mark an epoque' if written by Marx, to whom he had sent his own impressions of the *coup d'état* on 3 December. Marx was pressed for time, and for his first despatch to Weydemeyer he merely paraphrased Engels' reactions, which were so immediate and familiar. The only difference was that he lent it all his literary genius. That is why the famous exordium — the historic tragedies have returned under the guise of farce; 'men make their own history', etc. — is so often recalled, so often imitated. Liebknecht evokes Tacitus, Juvenal and Dante.

Is this where Marx the historian is to be found? He himself says no; that he did not wish to exalt Bonaparte by insulting him, as Victor Hugo had risked doing, but to show how the class struggles (or perhaps we should call it the fear among the upper classes and the stupidity among the middle classes) could make heroes out of mediocrities, and even out of buffoons. Nor has the twentieth century given the lie to this: it is the century of Mussolini, Hitler and Franco. The history of a failed, confiscated revolution is not 'the history of a crime'. And we are urged, when confronted with Marx's 'historical works':

1   to avoid pastiche; one cannot imitate the inimitable; one does not write *The 19th Brumaire* about any event whatsoever;
2   to seek, behind the brilliance of the phrases, the seriousness of all the analyses that constitute the background; it is the sum of the works of Marx and Engels during five years of revolution that constitute a 'history' — the years 1847–52, which they lived through and upon which they deliberated;
3   not to base theoretical generalisations on the history of this one episode, situated concretely in time and space; its authors neither could nor would see it in this light; to say, as some have, that Marx recognised the existence of a 'peasant mode of production' merely because in 1852 he used the expression '*Produktionweise*' concerning the French peasantry is to forget that at that date he had not yet defined his theory of 'modes of production', that in comparing the mass of French peasantry to a 'sack of potatoes' he denied it even the ghost of a coherent structure, and that he described it as in a critical state — 4 million poverty-stricken people; this implies that they were scarcely a factor in the controversy into which he entered: had the Revolution's achievement created a contented peasantry, or a balanced France? Or, in slowing down the proletarianisation of the peasantry, did they jeopardise the rhythm of French

development? Both, without doubt. But there can be no adequate answer without close analysis. To put the question to Marx would be a poor way of rendering him homage.

Inversely, the general tendency is to demand less of those works of his that are considered 'political', rather than 'historical', that is to say the 1,000 articles inspired with 'the contemporary quality' of Marx and Engels, not to mention their enormous correspondence. Now, the historical content of these writings is considerable. Marx and Engels were brilliant journalists. If they were never reporters or interviewers, they nonetheless studied, in their reading and the notes they made, not only the standard old and modern works and the orthodox press of the most powerful countries but all kinds of documents — parliamentary debates, legislation, statistics, investigations. These they used, and further, they quoted from them profusely. They always, or almost always, read them in the original language. They wrote equally well in German, French and English. They also wanted to learn Russian; then Spanish. Their çopious references are irreproachable. Their account of Carlyle and Guizot is worthy of our best journals. In a word, technically they worked as historians.

Even so, is it enough, as has been done for all the countries and for a certain number of questions, to include the articles under 'complete works'? For the subjects range from Persia or Turkey to the Crimean War, Palmerston, religion and the arts. Would it not be better to draw a distinction between the unprepared fragments, or those written to order, and the carefully wrought series, the first often giving rise to the second? Apart from a few matters (Marx and his economics, Engels and his military affairs) our two authors never 'specialised'.

Marx himself contemplated writing a 'history', within a national framework, and extending through all periods: 'I shall confine myself to the case of Spain, which I know best, and which is perhaps the most distinctive.' Having to write for a newspaper on 'Revolutions in Spain', he felt the need to dwell longest on revolutionary Spain, which truly existed, and, because of that, to cover Spain in general. He did not write, as I have emphasised, a history of Spain. But he wanted to think about Spain historically. That is why he learned Spanish — by way of Calderón and Lope. From the time of *The German Ideology* he had loved quoting Cervantes, and sometimes Calderón. But this was in translation, and the allusions were literary, 'humanistic'. After 1856 they were to be historical: in *Capital* Don Quixote is cited as an instance of a man at odds with his era, an anachronism, rather than a human character. In the articles written during 1856 the War of Independence was reconstructed in terms of contrast: the guerillas — deeds without ideas; in the Cortes of Cadiz — ideas without deeds. He even passed judgement on the old Spain of Charles V without distorting the facts. When it came to the nineteenth century, Marx found in Marliani, the Italo-Spanish liberal and historian, a guide who sometimes had a quasi-Marxist turn of phrase that must have appealed to him. Alas, until about 1930 Spain was to know nothing of Marx's outline of her history. He was only to be known there as a remote theoretician, very poorly grasped by revolutionary militants. Engels and Lafargue tried in vain to remedy the situation.

Soon after this remarkable attempt at one particular national history, and ten years after the *tour de force* of the *Communist Manifesto*, Marx returned, in an 'Introduction' (unpublished) to his grand project: the idea of an economic treatise. But it had to be a sociological treatise, too, covering the capitalist world, and also, if the truth be known, a historical treatise — starting with war and ending with naturally occurring conditions ('subjective and objective; peoples, races etc.'), and encompassing the examination of types of historiography (including *Kulturgeschichte*), the dialectic between the forces and relations of production, the study of 'unequal developments' as between one country and another, and in levels of historical reality: law, culture, art. He ended with this important remark: 'World history has not always existed; in its world-history aspect, history is a result'.

This project marks the distance between the work that Marx would have wished to write and *Capital* as we know it. To limit one's reading of *Capital* to vol. I, if not to Chapter 1, to look down upon the historical developments as no more than simple 'illustrations' of the theory, is to impoverish an idea to the point of distorting it. But it is true that it is less irritating, if one looks for Marx the historian in *Capital*, to return every time to the chapters on the work day, on primitive accumulation and on the capitalist merchant. This, at any rate, is palpable, avowed history, not classical, it is true, but not too out-of-the-way, citing instances that are concrete in time and space. It is more difficult, but much more meaningful, to look for history at the point where it spontaneously disappears, where twenty years of fact-finding and reflection are condensed into twenty abstract pages:

I have tried elsewhere to point this out with regard to currency — briefly, it is true, but at sufficient length for me not to insist on it here. It would involve repeating the ideas found in *Capital*: wages, productive work, reserve army etc... behind which is hidden an enormous accumulation of information and analysis, which are historical in the strictest sense of the word.

With Marx this was existing knowledge, but he continually suggests developments of it; with him, every formula is also a *programme*: 'We shall confine ourselves to citing the list of factors relative to workers' average productivity, the development of science and the extent of its technological application, social combinations in production, its average scale and effectiveness, and purely natural conditions...'. What food for the historian at every stage!

We may add that this historical background is present from the very first pages of *Capital*, when Marx deals with 'value' and 'goods'. Barbon, Locke, Le Trosne, Butler, Petty, an anonymous writer of 1740, Verri etc. are not quoted in vain: English, French and Italian thought is imbibed directly from its source. And when Aristotle appears, this is no conventional reference. Every thought, explicitly or no, is placed within its time and elucidates its time. This Marx combines, step by step, not only as with Schumpeter, economic theory and historical analysis, but also, closely woven, the theory of history and the history of theory.

I always thought that one could condense *Capital*'s theory without too much difficulty into about 120 pages — the size of Hicks' book. But this would be to mutilate Marx. Hicks has now published, in 200 pages this time, a 'theory of economic history', and while he does not fail to compliment Marx's endeavour, he does propose using, he says, what the historians for over 100 years have had to add (or at least should have added) to the historical knowledge at Marx's disposal. But it would appear that Hicks has not personally spent countless hours in the British Museum to overtake Marx's direct investigation. *The Cambridge Modern History* seems to be enough for him. For him, as one soon realises, the old 'naïve anthropology' of the economists, more or less completed by the modern game of 'decisions', governs diplomacy as well as economics, without going through the hard, complex matter of classes and their struggles. Most decidedly, the economists' history, as so often with the historians' economics, scarcely seems destined to reach beyond Marx.

If, in conclusion, I have to define *Capital* in relation to the theme 'Marx and history', I would say, as for *The German Ideology*, that it is without doubt a 'history book', and, most assuredly, a 'historian's book'.

And, after all, if it is true that Marx has left us the task of defining the 'concept of history' (and even if our attempt at this task is poor enough) we can console ourselves by re-reading the early writings, in which he so vehemently stigmatised the absurd cult of the 'concept' among bad Hegelians.

4 MARX'S CRITIQUE OF POLITICAL ECONOMY
Maurice Dobb

Part I

It is commonly supposed that Marx's interest in economic questions (as distinct from philosophy and the understanding of history) dates from the attention he paid to the condition of the Mosel peasantry during the period of his editorship of the *Rheinische Zeitung* in the early 1840s. Serious study of the work of political economists, in particular Smith, Ricardo, James Mill, McCulloch and Say, certainly dates from his sojourn in Paris after his move there from Germany in 1843: a study that was later to be continued more intensively after the start of his London exile following the revolutionary events of 1848. Subsequently to 1850 Marx and Engels sponsored the view in the League of Communists of that era 'that revolution has become impossible in the immediately foreseeable future . . . and that the task of the League of Communists must be reset accordingly to give first priority to the work of education, study and development of revolutionary theory' — a notion that 'fell like cold water on the flames of exile fantasy' at the time.[1] The early 1850s were to witness both Marx's years of poverty in cramped Soho lodgings (characterised by frequent visits to the pawnshop and dependence on the financial generosity of Engels) and his use of the British Museum Reading Room for the deep and extensive studies which eventuated nearly two decades later in *Capital*.

Product of these years of study were the voluminous manuscript notes, covering some seven notebooks, called the *Grundrisse der Kritik der Politischen Oekonomie (Rohentwurf)*, which was not to see publication until as late as 1953.[2] By contrast the short work entitled *The Critique of Political Economy* was published in 1859, eight years before the first volume of *Capital*. This introductory work of 1859 has been called a 'curtain raiser' to the *magnum opus*. The focus of attention in the *Critique* can be said to be methodological and, like the first volume of the later opus, it starts with commodities and proceeds from there to the consideration of money and exchange. The *Grundrisse* is similarly concerned with methodological questions and in the main with the sphere of circulation and exchange. Value, for example, is dealt with explicitly only in a fragmentary paragraph

79

which breaks off in the middle of a sentence. Being composed, not
for publication, but primarily to develop and clarify his own ideas,
it consists of two outsize chapters called 'The Chapter on Money'
(which is the shorter of the two) and 'The Chapter on Capital'.
What Marx is apparently doing at this time in his 'rough draft' is to
deal with problems as these had already been posed by previous
economists about monetary exchange and exchange-value; thus
starting from the standpoint of his predecessors, whom he was
seeking to criticise and from whom he was trying to break free,
while grasping what was of positive value in their way of posing
problems. (This serves to explain the length and sometimes the
obscurity of what he here writes — even what has been described
as 'idealist defects'.)[3] In answer to the question as to why he was
so concerned here with Circulation or Exchange, rather than with
Production (as readers of his mature work might expect him to
do), one could say that it was because he sensed that in this lay the
source of the illusions characteristic of bourgeois political
economy — illusions which consciously or unconsciously
fulfilled a social role of masking both the existence and the source
of surplus value as the crucial feature of bourgeois economy, or
the capitalist mode of production. The illusion thus generated at
the level of 'appearance' he sought to unravel and dispel even
though he was still unclear as to the full nature of the essential
reality that lay behind it. In the process of circulation everything
had the semblance of an exchange of *equivalents*; buyers and
sellers freely contracting to barter what they had available to
exchange for what they sought to acquire. In such exchange the
competition of numerous individuals sufficed to ensure (at least
'on the average' or in 'the long run') that no exchanger could
utilise duress or bargaining power to tilt the balance to his own
advantage. If, accordingly, profit or surplus were to be made out
of such trade, this, it seemed, could only be due to the absence of
competition or to some limit on free trading. Thus the so-called
'Ricardian Socialists' such as Hodgskin and William Thompson
attributed profit on capital to 'unequal exchanges' or superior
bargaining power of those possessing capital. Yet, as Marx
observed, 'surplus value [is] not explicable by exchange'. He
goes on to say that exchange through the mediation of money as
'general equivalent' is the highest and most developed form of
free exchange:

It is in the character of the money relation . . . that all inherent contradictions of
bourgeois society appear extinguished in money relations as conceived in a

simple form; and bourgeois democracy even more than the bourgeois economists takes refuge in this aspect . . . in order to construct apologetics for existing economic relations.[4]

It follows that:

insofar as the commodity or labour is conceived of only as exchange value, and the relation in which the various commodities are brought into connection with one another is conceived as the exchange of these exchange values with one another, as their equation, then the individuals, the subjects between whom this process goes on, are simply and only conceived of as exchangers. As far as the formal character is concerned, there is absolutely no distinction between them, and this is the economic character, the aspect in which they stand towards one another in the exchange-relation . . . Each of the subjects is an exchanger; i.e., each has the same social relation towards the other that the other has towards him. As subjects of exchange, their relation is therefore that of *equality*. It is impossible to find any trace of distinction, not to speak of contradiction, between them; not even a difference. Furthermore, the commodities which they exchange are, as exchange values, equivalent, or at least count as such.[5]

Some pages later we find it said:

In present bourgeois society as a whole, this positing of prices and their circulation etc. appears as a surface process, beneath which, however, in the depths, entirely different processes go on, in which this apparent individual equality and liberty disappear . . . . What is overlooked, finally, is that already the simple forms of exchange value and of money latently contain the opposition between labour and capital etc.[6]

The *Critique* while opening with the same theme and emphasis as the *Grundrisse* (the opening paragraph indeed anticipating that of the first volume of *Capital*), commences to talk in terms of a reduction of exchange-value to *value* in the sense of labour-time expended in production (*social* labour in the sense that individual labours are assumed to be equal, or to be standardised).[7] This leads him to emphasise that 'although it is . . . correct to say that exchange-value is a relation between persons, it is however necessary to add that it is a relation hidden by a material veil'; adding that 'the conventions of our everyday life make it appear commonplace and ordinary that social relations of production should assume the shape of things' whereas 'exchange-values are really the relations of people to the productive activities of one another.[8] With this we meet a preliminary statement of what was later to be termed 'the fetishism of commodities', whereby a crucial element in his special approach to exchange and money is explained.

Following this, in the second of his two chapters, he proceeds to deal, somewhat verbosely, with 'Money or Simple Circulation' (opening it with a quotation from Gladstone to the effect that 'even love has not turned more men into fools than has meditation upon the nature of money'). Here he examines *inter alia* the views of English economists including Steuart, Smith, Ricardo and James Mill and what was to be called the Quantity Theory of Money, which he identifies with David Hume. What he seems to find lacking in such an approach is a sufficient recognition of money (gold) as itself a commodity, and hence of its exchange-value relatively to other commodities as determined by its cost of production or value.

When we come, eight years later, to his main work, we still find commodities and their circulation taken as starting-point (the first of the eight parts into which it is divided being entitled 'Commodities and Money'). But the focus of the work is on Capital ('The Transformation of Money into Capital') as money laid out in the purchase specifically of labour-power with an eye to the creation and acquisition of surplus-value. This was made possible under capitalism by the existence of a propertyless proletariat, separated from ownership of any means of production, such as land, and hence left with the hiring out of their working ability or labour-power for a wage as their sole means of livelihood; the concluding part 8 of vol. 1[9] being devoted to the historical process of so-called 'Primitive Accumulation' whereby a proletariat was brought into being.

From what has been said up to now (about the *Grundrisse* and the *Critique*) it might seem as though Marx's approach via concentration on money and exchange and his quasi-obsessive treatment of the latter was an excessively abstract even mystifying one. (He would probably have said that the degree of abstraction was what characterised the isolation of exchange *per se* in the treatment to-date by bourgeois political economy.) What strikes one, however, about *Capital* is his essentially *historical* approach and emphasis, to the extent that what he seeks to probe and analyse is the peculiarity in the functioning of capitalism as a socio-economic system owing to the historical conditions that characterise it as a mode of production. This latter concept was designed to include so-called 'social relations of production'; and the key feature of the bourgeois or capitalist mode that he was concerned to single out was the social polarisation whereby, on the one hand, ownership was concentrated in the hands of a minority (the bourgeoisie) and *ipso facto* the majority (or at least a substantial section) of the population had become deprived of it.

This socio-economic fact lying at the base of the system afforded the vital clue to explaining the crucial transaction on which the possibility of profit on capital rested — a transaction which a theory that devoted attention to exchange *per se* in isolation inevitably treated on a par with all other commodities as an exchange of 'equivalents'. Only if the peculiarity of this transaction was appreciated in its socio-historical setting could its true nature, and its role in the functioning of the economic structure as a whole, be fully and realistically appreciated. That they had failed to do this, at any rate at all completely, was his point of criticism of the classical economists — and this despite his undoubted admiration for their 'unprejudiced' and 'scientific' approach, and despite Ricardo's belief in Distribution as 'the principal problem in Political Economy' and his concentration of attention on the profit–wage relation.

In *Capital* Marx places this crucial exchange-relationship within the framework of the labour theory of value: a theory that had been used by the classical economists, at any rate by Ricardo.[10] As a result the rate of exploitation or of surplus-value was expressed as a ratio between two quantities of labour: namely, the surplus labour expended above the labour needed to produce subsistence for the labour-force (or embodied in wage-goods) as a ratio to the latter quantity of labour. In other words, from a money relationship it was translated into a relationship between two quantities of labour in production (for example, a relationship between surplus labour-time expended by a worker, or group of workers, in any day or week or year, to the 'necessary labour-time' in simply replacing his own used-up working energy or labour-power). It thus became a magnitude dependent upon, and determined by, conditions and relations of production, and *not* on circumstances attendant upon commodity circulation or exchange.

In the past this has been criticised as basing the whole theoretical structure on a false premise — on a primitive and outmoded theory of value which had subsequently been shown to be inadequate if not fallacious. If things did *not* in fact exchange in proportion to the labour embodied in them, but at prices governed by some other principle, then declared the Austrian economist Böhm-Bawerk writing at the end of the century, Marx's whole edifice crumbles, and the theory of so-called 'exploitation' is left hanging in the air. He concluded that Marx's theory 'has no abiding future'.

As a result of modern discussion attendant on revived interest in the classical economists and their distinctive approach, present-day economists are now aware[11] of the special significance of expressing macro-relations of the system in a homogeneous quantity such as labour: namely, that it affords a measure of those relations that is independent of changes in distribution of the product and their attendant effects on prices. It is a familiar fact that Ricardo initially[12] expressed his wage–profit relation in commodity-terms, namely in corn, when enunciating his theory of profit. As a first approximation this had its *raison d'être*, but it hardly fitted a many-commodity world, and was clearly inadequate in meeting Malthus's objections to the theory.[13] In his maturer *Principles of Political Economy and Taxation* he accordingly substituted for it measurement in terms of labour (on the assumption that prices were proportional to labour embodied — or at least approximately so). Marx can be said to have followed in this tradition in enunciating his theory of surplus value — his own signal innovation, and in a sense his *Aufhebung* to the classical economists.

Some have gone further, however, and have maintained that the theory of surplus value is in some way *derived* from the labour theory of value, and hence is in some sense logically dependent upon it. The precise nature of this dependence has not always been made clear — more often than not one could say that the connection has been unclear and is left open to various interpretations.[14] Both disciples *and* critics of Marx are here involved. The first question to be asked, therefore, is whether there is a *logical* dependence of one on the other that is being claimed — or only, perhaps, a rhetorical one?

The first and perhaps most obvious interpretation derives from the principle of *Naturrecht*. In the so-called 'natural order' of things, uncontaminated by the peculiar features of 'advanced' society, things exchange according to the labour required (on the social average) to produce them.[15] Such a 'natural order' affords a standard of what ideally *ought* to prevail. Without such a standard provided by the Labour Theory of Value, exploitation can be given no meaning. The meaning, be it noted, is a moral or ethical one.

This, however, is at best a very dubious interpretation of Marx's intention. There is no reason to suppose that he was seeking (or indeed would have been satisfied with) a moral or ethical theory of exploitation, or that he had any inclination at all towards 'natural right' theories. It is doubtful whether Adam Smith took it in this way, even though he made use of 'natural right' terminology, which was fashionable in the century in which he wrote. It would be much more dubious (indeed, highly disputable) to father such an interpretation upon Marx, writing seventy years later. What is more, Marx laid great emphasis upon the fact that labour-*power* was sold, not below, but *at* its value;[16] this value being determined by the historical conditions that characterised specifically the capitalist mode of production. The so-called Ricardian socialists, it is true, held that wages were depressed below the 'true value' of labour by the prevailing system of 'unequal exchanges' or the monopoly-power of employers. But Marx considered this explanation as inadequate, and produced his own theory of surplus value in substitution for this type of theory.

Another interpretation, sometimes met with, is that the Labour Theory, at any rate in Marx's version of it, represents labour as the only productive factor, or creator of wealth. This view of the matter seems, least of all, capable of being fathered on Marx, in view of his explicit statement (in the *Critique*) that 'it would be wrong to say that labour which produces use-value is the *only* source of the wealth produced by it, that is of material wealth'.[17]

Yet again it has been maintained that the essence of Marx's contribution, and in this respect contrary to classical political economy, is his depiction of the labour process of production, and that his theory of value expresses this and without it what is crucial to his contribution would be lacking. It is not easy, however, to see how much meaning can be given to such a proposition. Marx certainly laid emphasis on labour in the productive process; but it is not clear that his depiction of it was qualitatively different from that of his predecessors; while his very emphasis on it was in connection with labour-*power* and its value in the context of the creation of surplus-value rather than with anything else. Here, again, it is possible that what such people have in mind is the expository convenience of stating the whole matter in terms of labour. But this is not, of course, to say that a theory of exploitation would be logically incomplete without resting it on the postulate (or the assumption) that commodities exchange in proportion to embodied labour.[18]

What remains true is that the definition of exploitation (or for that matter of surplus-value) must explicitly or implicitly attribute some special role or quality to labour in social production: for example, that it is the sole productive *activity* (such as would not exist in a completely automated world), or, to borrow Alfred Marshall's terminology, it is in any ultimate sense the only social 'real cost'. This is no doubt the meaning of the statement often met with (and bearing an ambiguous if not tautologous sense in many cases) to the effect that labour is alone creative of value. Then it is possible to speak of capitalists (or landowners) 'appropriating' part of the fruits of productive activity, in a sense analogous to the 'appropriation' by a feudal lord or a slave-owner of the surplus product of serf or slave labour. But while this may conceivably share an assumption with a Labour Theory of Value, it is quite possible for such a statement (that is, about appropriation or exploitation) to be made of a world where commodities do *not* exchange in proportion to embodied labour.

In fact, of course, Marx did *not* believe that in the actual capitalist world exchange of commodities was in proportion to labour: this was a first approximation only, adopted in vol. I to facilitate his theory of surplus value. In fact, things exchanged, not at their (labour) 'values', but at 'prices of production',[19] as vol. III makes abundantly clear; the latter diverging from the former to the extent that what he termed the 'organic composition of capital'[20] was different in different lines of production. What he *did* maintain was that these prices of production were derivable (in quantitative sense) from 'values', given the rate of surplus value expressed in value-terms (that is, in terms of labour). *How* they are thus derivable is the crux of the much-debated 'Transformation Problem', which Marx himself did not satisfactorily solve. The reason why he failed to solve it satisfactorily is that in his own arithmetical examples of the 'transformation' only the final outputs of each productive sector were transformed from 'values' into 'prices of production', and *not* the constituent inputs. Indication is not lacking that Marx himself was aware that something more was needed for a complete solution; but vol. III, where his analysis reaches the level of 'prices of production', remained unfinished and was left by him largely in the form of incomplete drafts or notes. Suffice to say that it has subsequently been shown that a logical solution is quite possible, with all products, whether appearing as inputs or outputs, appropriately transformed into 'prices of production';[21] and this both for the kind of two- or three-sector case used by Marx (*vide* the Bortkiewicz 'solution') *and* for an indefinite number of individual commodities or *n*-products case (*vide* the Seton 'solution'). In other words, actual exchange ratios (at the 'prices of production' of Marx's vol. III) are logically (and mathematically) derivable from labour 'values', and there is no contradiction lying at the heart of Marx's system, as his foremost critic, von Böhm-Bawerk, maintained.

At the same time it becomes clear from these 'solutions' that not all the macro-relations of the system can remain the same in the two cases; and there has been some discussion as to which of these as determined by labour quantities in terms of values would have been regarded by Marx as the more crucial for preserving in the 'price of production' situation as well as in value-terms — whether the rate of surplus value, total surplus value and total profit or the ratio of total profit to total capital, both 'constant' and 'variable' (that is, the rate of profit). Some have even maintained (for example, Arghiri Emmanuel) that if the chief magnitudes as determined in labour-terms fail to survive the transformation-process (that is, fail to reappear in price-of-production terms) something of qualitative importance is lost by admitting the need for such a transformation. To the present writer, however, it would seem that, more important than whether any of these value-relations are preserved unchanged after all the relevant conditions for exchange under capitalism[22] have been introduced is the fact that the main relations in *price*-terms, however they appear, are capable of being *derived* from the value-magnitudes, and hence can be treated without any logical contradiction as *determined* by the latter. If they *can* be, then the analytical structure of *Capital* apparently stands.

Part II

An important aspect of Marx's treatment of capital accumulation is his emphasis upon a growing concentration and centralisation of capital as an inevitable tendency of this process. Some students of Marx have treated this as having more interest and importance than his theory of value. This concentrating tendency was associated with technical change and improvement, promoted by the capitalists' desire, under the pressure of competition, for higher productivity of labour. More advanced technique tended to enhance the importance of so-called constant capital relatively to variable capital and to give firms with larger aggregates of capital a competitive advantage. The buying-up by large capitalist firms of smaller competitors and the merging of several economic units into one promoted the economic strength and viability of the former and led to progressively higher degrees of centralisation of control and of economic decision-taking. After speaking of 'that change in technical composition of capital by which the variable constituent becomes always smaller and smaller as compared with the constant', he goes on to refer to accumulation as presenting itself 'as increasing concentration of the means of production and of the command over labour' and of 'an increase in the minimum amount of individual capital necessary to carry on a business under its normal conditions'.[23] As for centralisation of control of capital, this is greatly assisted by the growth of the credit system: 'not only is this itself a new and mighty weapon in the battle of competition', but it 'draws disposable money, scattered in large or smaller masses over the surface of society, into the hands of individual or associated capitalists'; thus 'it is the specific machine for the centralisation of capitals'.[24]

While orthodox economists such as John Stuart Mill were seeing competition as a progressively beneficial force (provided at least that population-increase was constrained), Marx emphasised its contradictory character: the dialectical contradiction, indeed, of competition producing ultimately a transformation into its opposite. Although he said relatively little about monopoly, and was concerned essentially with analysing the competitive stage of capitalism, Marx could thus be regarded as having offered a forecast, unique in its day, of the eventual transition to a final stage of monopoly capitalism.

Other closely associated tendencies, however, followed on the progress of capital accumulation, which we have seen that he regarded as being far from the smooth process of quantitatively widening investment that most other economists envisaged. First of these was the initial effect of technical change in displacing labour (as Ricardo in his chapter on Machinery added to the third edition of his *Principles* had admitted that it might do); with the resulting effect of augmenting the industrial reserve army. The industrial reserve army was in his view the principal mechanism in a competitive (and unorganised) labour market for regulating the level of wages, keeping this down, despite the progress of accumulation, to the conventionally accepted 'subsistence level' of the time:[25] 'The general movement of wages is exclusively regulated by the expansion and contraction of the industrial reserve army, and these again correspond to the periodic changes of the industrial cycle.'[26] In what was the nearest he came to providing a 'cycle' mechanism of employment, wages and profits, he pictured employment as expanding during years of investment-boom, with a consequential rising tendency of wages at the expense of profits. This expansive phase, however, could only be short-lived; the effect of the profit-squeeze in slackening the pace of accumulation and investment performed the function of recreating the industrial reserve army until something like the old level of real wages was restored, so that accumulation could quicken its pace once again:

As soon as . . . the surplus that nourishes capital is no longer supplied in normal quantity, a reaction sets in: a smaller part of the revenue is capitalised, accumulation lags, and the movement of rise in wages receives a check. The rise in wages, therefore, is confined within limits that not only leave intact the foundations of the capitalist system, but also secures its reproduction on a progressive scale.[27]

The other tendency, which has occasioned some considerable debate among Marxists was the so-called 'law of the tendency of the rate of profit to fall'. Discussion has centred on whether he regarded this as a periodic short-term tendency (as in the case referred to in the last paragraph) or as a long-period tendency of the system; and if the latter whether as an absolute 'law' operating over real time, or only in the absence of 'counter-tendencies' which might in actuality with varying degrees of probability supervene. The alleged tendency depended upon the influence of technical innovation upon the ratio between the two main constituents of capital, constant capital and variable capital (which he called the organic composition of capital): namely, to *raise* this ratio, at any rate in physical terms. A given rate of surplus value would then yield a lower *rate* of profit upon the total capital,[28] constant as well as variable, now employed. Marx was careful to point out that there were 'counter-tendencies', including a tendency for the rate of surplus value to rise as the result of a cheapening of goods consumed by wage-earners (with a lower money-wage consequently needed to yield a given level of *real* wages) and a 'cheapening of the elements of constant capital' (that is, the cost of machines and other material inputs) which if considerable enough could mean that constant capital in *value terms* showed a falling tendency not a rising one. Marx gave the impression of supposing that this would moderate or weaken the tendency, but would not suffice to reverse it, and that in the long run the main tendency to a falling profit-rate would still operate if at a moderated pace. But if they can moderate, these counter-tendencies can also when strong enough reverse the effect of rising (physical) organic composition. What has to be remembered in all this is that it was commonly assumed by economists of that time that the rate of profit had an actual tendency to fall. For this they offered different explanations: Adam Smith the competition of capitals entering industry in enhanced numbers; Ricardo diminishing returns on land and

hence rising cost of food as population increased over time.
Marx, in affording his own explanation and emphasising it as
opposed to theirs may well have implicitly shared their belief in an
actual tendency, and regarded himself as doing no more than
attribute it to a different cause.

Controversy and criticism have also been prompted by Marx's
so-called 'immiseration' thesis concerning an alleged tendency to
progressive impoverishment of the working class. Discussion has
centred upon whether this is to be interpreted as implying
absolute or merely relative impoverishment, or decline in the
working-class standard of living. Marx's references to this follow
discussion of capital accumulation and the reserve army from
which we have just quoted, and are entirely within this setting. In
other words, he was essentially concerned here with the
fluctuating mass of unemployed or casually employed workers on
the fringes of the industrial system. It has to be remembered that
in the period of the Industrial Revolution the reserve army was
being continually swollen by the redundant population of the
countryside (as is the case in underdeveloped countries today);
and Marx may well have envisaged his 'impoverishment'
tendency as operating during a whole initial industralising phase
of capitalism, but not necessarily beyond this. It has further to be
borne in mind that, as his terminology suggests, he may not have
been thinking in terms of wages alone, even if the size of the
reserve army was for him the principal regulator of the level of
wages, but of 'the general lot' of the working class — something
which included presumably social degradation and insecurity
within its scope as well as purely economic factors. Certainly it is
clear that he was referring to a purely competitive labour market
without collective bargaining, since in the last paragraph of the
section in question (section 3 of chapter XXV) he speaks of
workers' organisation in trade unions as something that can make
a positive difference to the situation — 'every combination of
employed and unemployed disturbs the 'harmonious' action of
this law' of supply and demand.[29]

Part III
Apart from controversies over the theory of value and the
transformation problem, the falling rate of profit and 'immiseration', to which we have already alluded, discussion since the
turn of the century about Marx's view of capitalism has largely
centred around two questions: the place to be occupied (if at all) in
his theory by the so-called 'realisation problem' and modern

imperialism and its association with concentration of capital and monopoly. The former of these questions has naturally been the preserve very largely of economists; whereas the latter has been the subject of commentary and debate more widely. In Marx's *Capital* there are one or two references to the problem of 'realising surplus value' (a problem arising from insufficiency of demand for what has been or could have been produced), but no more than this, and these references are inconclusive. They include the much-quoted passage in vol. III to the effect that:

the last cause of all real crises always remains the poverty and restricted consumption of the masses as compared to the tendency of capitalist production to develop the productive forces in such a way, that only the absolute power of consumption of the entire society would be their limit.[30]

— a passage which has an evident under-consumptionist ring.

In the early part of the nineteenth century the question of insufficiency of demand to take up the supply of goods produced, owing to the poverty of the mass of wage-earning consumers, had been referred to by a number of economic writers. Chief among these had been Sismondi who had attributed economic depression and periodic crises to this; and also Malthus who argued against excessive 'saving' or 'parsimony' and the lack of demand coming from wage-earners as justification for what he termed the 'unproductive consumption' of rent and profits. To this Ricardo had replied that what was saved out of profits became when invested demand for workers to be employed by the newly created capital, so that the process of saving-*plus*-investment represented a mere transfer of demand from one lot of consumers (the savers) to another (the newly employed workers): 'The wants of consumers . . . are transferred with the power to consume to another set of consumers' and 'the power to consume is not annihilated but is transferred to the labourer'.[31] The more general orthodox answer to the 'underconsumptionists', however, was to come from J.-B. Say and to become known as 'Say's Law'. This was to the effect that exchange was basically exchange of goods against goods, and that the production and supply of more of any one commodity automatically created additional demand for others to be exchanged against it. Thus while there could be over-production of particular goods whose production had been increased temporarily in excess of others, there could not be *general* over-production of all commodities.

Marx was far from being a friend of Say's Law. Indeed he ridiculed it as failing to notice that money customarily mediated between the two halves of any commodity-transaction (C–M–C), and there was no automatic reason for the first half always to be completed by the second. There could well be a tendency to hold the proceeds of the former as *money*, especially where expectations of profit were involved, without these money-receipts being spent on procuring another commodity. Yet he nowhere developed in detail the question of what circumstances might cause such additional purchase of goods or of labour-power. Moreover, in vol. II of *Capital* his famous expanded-reproduction *schema* or tables *seem* (at least) to emphasise proportionality between sectors, including the sector of pro-duction that produces capital goods or means of production,[32] as an assurance of smooth progress in expanding accumulation and production.[33] This led the Russian writer Tugan-Baranowski, for example, to conclude that there need be no hitch or crisis if only *proportionality* in production was observed.

Rosa Luxemburg at the beginning of the century was to become the leading opponent of this optimistic 'proportionality' view; criticising Marx, as she did in her *Accumulation of Capital* of 1913, for devoting too little attention to the problem of 'realising surplus-value' (by sale of 'the product'), as distinct from the conditions favouring its creation in the course of production. She accepted the fact that if what remained unconsumed by capitalists out of surplus-value were to be promptly reinvested in a fresh round of capital accumulation and 'expanded reproduction', no problem of realisation, or of deficiency of demand, would arise. But she stoutly denied that it was at all realistic to suppose that such a process could continue indefinitely (or even, indeed, for very long) solely under the impetus of capital accumulation for its own sake. Without the impetus of expanding demand and assured prospects of profit, the impetus to investment must surely falter, as indeed experience indicated that it did periodically. Capitalism and capital accumulation, accordingly, could only be kept going by the stimulus of some 'external market', in the shape of additional demand associated with development in some pre-viously under-industrialised and non-capitalistically developed area. New profit-expectations from investment in the latter would then sustain alike the process of accumulation and the pro-duction of capital goods in the older and more developed (but now lagging) capitalist sphere: 'International trade is a prime necessity for the historical existence of capitalism — an international trade which under actual conditions is essentially exchange between capitalist and non-capitalist modes of production.'[34] Upon this kind of expansion in the market developed capitalism relied for its continuance. But it was a procedure of expansion that could not continue indefinitely, and its effect as a 'boost' to expanded reproduction must eventually peter out. It will be noticed that Luxemburgian emphasis on external 'third markets' serves to link Marx's theory of capital accumulation with the facts of modern imperialism to constitute a theoretical explanation of the latter. She also anticipated more recent theories to the effect that militarism and State armament-expenditures could play the role of an expanding demand to sustain the investment-process:

Non-capitalist organisations provide a fertile soil for capitalism; more strictly: capital feeds on the ruins of such organisations, and although this non-capitalist *milieu* is indispensable for accumulation, the latter proceeds at the cost of this medium nevertheless, by eating it up.[35] Historically the accumulation of capital is a kind of metabolism between capitalist economy and those pre-capitalist methods of production without which it cannot go on and which in this light it corrodes and assimilates... . For capital, the standstill of accumulation means that the development of the productive forces is arrested, and the collapse of capitalism follows inevitably as an objective historical necessity.[36]

She concludes with the declaration that capitalism is:

the first mode of economy which is unable to exist by itself, which needs other economic systems as a medium and soil. Although it strives to become universal, and, indeed, on account of this its tendency, it must break down — because it is immanently incapable of becoming a universal form of production.[37]

It may be noted that in Russia, *per contra*, the general emphasis among Bolshevik writers was rather the opposite. Lenin previously in his *Development of Capitalism in Russia*, in the course of his polemic with the Narodniks,[38] had declared that the very development of an internal market by capitalist indus-trialisation was what essentially provided the expanding market needed to afford an impetus to the growth of capitalism itself. Later Bukharin, as a leading Bolshevik economist, wrote in criticism of Rosa Luxemburg's thesis.

Lenin, for example, in the first chapter of his book (a chapter entitled 'The Theoretical Mistakes of the Narodnik Economists') leaned towards the position of Tugan-Baranovski (with some reservations) on the matter of proportions between productive sectors, and still more that of Bulgakov whom Luxemburg was to criticise. In his view an essential feature of the development of capitalist production was that 'capitalist production and con-sequently the home market, grow not so much on account of

articles of consumption as on account of means of production';
increase in the latter outstripping the former:

The department of social production which produces means of production has,
consequently, to grow faster than the one which produces articles of
consumption. Thus the growth of the home market for capitalism is to a certain
extent 'independent' of the growth of personal consumption, taking place in
greater measure on account of productive consumption.

He admits, however, that there is a contradiction between this
expansion of production at a faster rate than that of consumption
— 'it is real production for production's sake'; but it is not a
contradiction such as can prevent such development from
happening — 'it is a contradiction, not of doctrine, but of actual
life; it is the sort of contradiction that corresponds to the very
nature of capitalism and to the other contradictions of this
system'. He goes on to deny that Marx 'attributed crises to
under-consumption'.[39]

Among modern economists, known in academic circles in West
Europe and America, the theory closest in nature to Rosa
Luxemburg (and one admittedly influenced by her) is that of
Michal Kalecki.[40] His theory which was first propounded in the
early and middle 1930s (that is, pre-Keynes) was chiefly
remarkable for two features of it. Firstly, it made the ratio of
profit to wages (the 'mark-up' on wage-cost) dependent on the
degree of monopoly, thus affording a monopoly-explanation of
the origin and basis of profit. Secondly, it made employment and
total output,[41] and, hence total profit, dependent on 'realisation'
factors, namely on total demand, and in particular on capitalist
consumption *plus* profit *invested*. In the third place he treated
total investment by capitalist — something which on both sides of
the 'realisation' debate had tended to be left hanging in the air —
as being dependent on the expected rate of profit on new
investment (that is, on total realised profit in relation to total
productive capacity). Thus both an increase and a decrease in
investment were self-reinforcing up to a point. An investment-
boom once started by expanding demand and hence realised
profit would encourage cumulatively further increases of
investment, until eventually the new productive capacity brought
into being by recent investment reacted adversely with sufficient
force upon the *rate* of profit earned (that is, total realised profit
divided by total productive capacity). Similarly, after the
downturn, the decline in investment would be self-reinforcing;
each decline of investment causing a shrinkage in total demand

and total realised profit (until the decline in productive capacity and employment had reacted sufficiently upon the *rate* of profit). Thus a logically rounded theory of economic crises and of the economic cycle in what could be called near-Luxemburgian terms. It is to be noted that while previous writers from Sismondi to J.A. Hobson of more recent times had focussed upon consumption and on *under-consumption*, Kalecki's theory faced squarely upon capital *investment*, and the reasons for its periodic and/or chronic inadequacy under conditions of capitalism (governed as this mode of production was by the profit-motive).

Since Rosa Luxemburg, as we have seen, discussion of the realisation problem has been closely linked with the problem of imperialism.[42] But the two names most commonly associated with Marxist interpretation of modern imperialism are those of Hilferding and Lenin. The former associated the phenomenon particularly with concentration of capital and monopoly, in particular with the growing dominance in later capitalism of the big banks over industry (specially exemplified at the time in Germany) and hence of the growing dominance of financial capital (whence the title of his work, *Das Finanzkapital*). Lenin's *Imperialism, The Highest Stage of Capitalism* (which he described in his Preface as a 'pamphlet') was written during the spring of 1916[43] and begins by acknowledging J.A. Hobson's *Imperialism*, which he described as giving 'an excellent and comprehensive description of the principal economic and political characteristics of imperialism'. Towards Hilferding Lenin was notably less generous, describing him as an 'ex-Marxist and now comrade-in-arms of Kautsky' (whom Lenin sharply attacked), and as taking 'a step backward compared with the frankly pacifist and reformist Englishman, Hobson, on this question'. But he acknowledges (with minor reservations) that Hilferding's *Finanzkapital* 'gives a very valuable theoretical analysis . . . of "the latest phase of capitalist development" '.

Lenin's work on imperialism is less an analysis in the theoretical sense than a descriptive account of the main features of capitalism in its new twentieth-century stage. Chief of these novel features is the supplanting of competition by monopoly:

the transformation of competition into monopoly is one of the most important — if not the most important — phenomena of modern capitalist economy ... . The enormous growth of industry and the remarkably rapid process of concentration of production in ever larger enterprises represent one of the most characteristic features of capitalism.[44]

This he dates from the period 'after the crisis of 1873', with a significant growth of cartels, even if these are 'still the exception' — by contrast with which the decade of the 1860s was 'the apex of development of free competition'.[45] He goes on to speak of that 'domination, and violence that is associated with it, such are the relationships that are most typical of the "latest phase of capitalist development" ', and to emphasise (following Hilferding) the new role of banks (that is, industrial investment banks of the German type) and of 'finance capital and financial oligarchy'. To this he adds the export of capital to less developed 'colonies' overseas in which can be said to have lain the essence of imperialism. All this he sums up with the statement:

> Imperialism is capitalism in that stage of development in which the dominance of monopoly and finance capital has established itself; in which the export of capital has acquired pronounced importance, in which the division of the world among the international trusts has begun; in which the division of all territories of the globe among the great capitalist powers has been completed.

He then proceeds to attack Kautsky's notion 'that imperialism must not be regarded as a "phase" or stage of economy, but as a policy... "preferred by finance capital" ' and that it 'cannot be "identified" with "contemporary capitalism" '.[46]

It is to be noted that, unlike Rosa Luxemburg or even Hobson, this theory does not connect colonial expansion, in a causal sense, with overproduction in the imperialist country (or countries) and with the mechanism of 'realisation' problems — nor for that matter with Marx's alleged 'falling profit-rate' tendency over time.[47] It is connected directly with the desire of big monopoly concerns to extend their domination and hence to strengthen their monopoly power over markets, whether for consumers' goods or means of production and particularly for the latter. The two types of emphasis need not, of course, be incompatible. They could be reconciled. But the difference of emphasis is nonetheless of some significance; and it is a difference that has continued to dominate modern controversy since World War II, with the large amount of attention paid to the role of state expenditure on armaments in warding off depression,[48] with its Luxemburgist emphasis and even a novel definition of 'surplus' appropriate thereto. It would accordingly not be incorrect to speak of the continuance of two trends in Marxist theory of such matters today: the one giving prominence in its anlysis of crises and imperialism and economic policy to the 'realisation' problem and to deficiency of demand, the other concentrating, rather, on sectoral 'proportions'.

It need hardly be said that the crux of Marx's various forecasts about the dynamics of capitalism was the progressive intensification of class struggle, which the system would have increasing difficulty in containing within its own structure. The industrial proletariat would grow in strength and cohesion, as well as in extent, with the growth of trade union organisation and of the acuteness of partial struggles over the division of the product between profits and wages. Out of economic struggles political class consciousness would grow, until finally the proletariat would rise up and take over the means of production themselves and transform the system. The Russian Revolution of 1917 with its pronounced class features[49] was widely accepted as a striking historical verification of this forecast. There have been many, however — notably the leading German Social Democrats of the time — who have claimed that this event was a contradiction rather than a vindication of Marx's forecasts, because the revolutionary breakthrough came in a relatively undeveloped capitalist economy, and one with a predominantly peasant population, while more capitalistically advanced countries of the West remained relatively stable and firm in face of calls to world revolution. Lenin and the Bolsheviks had an answer to this critique: namely, that in a crisis occasioned by World War I it was to be expected that cracks and breakdown would first come in the relatively weak structure of a no-more-than-partial industrial structure, even if the *existence* of an industrial proletariat and the degree of industralisation needed to produce it was a necessary condition of such a revolutionary outburst. The Soviet revolution came where and when it did because Russia happened to be 'the weakest link' in the network of world capitalism. Another way of putting the issue (a far from minor one in contemporary conditions) would be to say that the question depends on the relative weight to be assigned in assessing historical situations to so-called 'objective', largely mechanistic, factors in the situation and to 'subjective' factors, *non*-economic in the narrow sense and ideological-cum-political.

Part IV
What, then can be said by way of summary of Marx's critique viewed as a whole and in the perspective of a century? One thing to be noted so far as his theoretical system is concerned is the growing interest displayed recently, especially in the decades of the 1960s and 1970s, in academic circles, not only in England

which was to become his homeland and Continental Europe, but also in America. At least this has been true of the student population and the younger academic staff. This revival of interest is in large part due to a lively discussion and critique of 'bourgeois' doctrine consequent upon a work of Piero Sraffa published in 1960 devised (as the sub-title of the work has it) as a 'contribution to a critique of political economy'. Opinion among economists would certainly be divided, and divided sharply, as to which side in this academic debate have in a formal sense won the day. But most Marxists, at any rate, would certainly say that it has played the role of stimulating recognition of the importance of Marx's own peculiar approach, whether or not it has served to vindicate this.[50]

It may be asked why the theory of value should have played so large a part in Marx's system. Firstly, it can be said that, in common with Smith and Ricardo before him, he treated this as a clue to the 'automatic' working (and hence the 'objective laws') of a commodity, or market, system. More than a clue, it was, indeed, an abstract representation of such laws or tendencies. Secondly, and as we have earlier said, it afforded, when expressed in terms of labour a formal framework for his theory of surplus-value, because commodity-relations in terms of labour (as distinct from price-relations with some other commodity or commodities) were unaffected by changes in the exploitation-ratio itself. There could, perhaps, also be cited as a third reason the fact that to give 'exploitation' a clear meaning requires the postulate (or something very like it) that labour is the only *active* factor (or 'social cost'?) in production.[51] Accordingly to cast the theory of surplus-value in this form (if only as a first approximation) plays an important expositional role in conveying such a postulate which might otherwise remain concealed. This may be quite important where qualitative depiction is involved.

As regards social diagnosis and forecast Marx's doctrine in its time represented a unique contribution, and it is scarcely surprising that, after a period of initial neglect, it should have attracted the attention that it has. Classical political economy had certainly represented the system of individual enterprise and free competition as an ideal state if not the endterm of economic progress. The role of landlords formed the only anomaly blurring the simple lines of what Bastiat was to call the 'economic harmonies'; but while Quesnay had treated rent of land as a *produit net* or surplus, it was seen by him in no derogatory light but rather as constituent of the natural order; and only Ricardo had stressed the 'antagonism' between rent and profit, with the latter as the beneficial source of capital accumulation. A theory which depicted all property-income as 'exploitation' in some sense, and hence the source of social antagonism, was unprecedented, with the so-called 'Ricardian Socialists' as almost the sole exception hitherto — and they had attributed this, not to the inherent mechanism of a free competitive order but to the *imperfections* latent therein, such as Hodgkin's 'unequal exchanges'. Many economists today maintain that to bring in issues of this kind is to introduce 'sociological' considerations falling outside the proper sphere and competence of economic theory. True, it does imply a different frontier to the subject from what has grown (and increasingly grown) to be the traditional limits of orthodox price-theory. But then it may well be said in opposition to this view that the frontiers of the latter, conceived as mathematical analysis of market-equilibria, are too narrow: narrower than those envisaged by the classical economist economists, and too narrow to probe beneath the surface of what Marx himself would have called market 'appearance' as distinct from 'essence' and hence to pronounce upon what is of prime significance. At any rate, it is this emphasis on surplus-value and its social implications that gives to Marx's theory of capitalist production and exchange both its uniqueness and its special appeal.

As for the dynamic forecasts derived therefrom (or at least attached thereto), these as we have seen were also both varied and unprecedented, and discussion of them largely explains the lively interest in, and controversial debate around, his doctrines a century and more after the appearance of *Capital*.

Notes

1 Foreword by Martin Nicolaus to English edition of the *Grundrisse* (trans. M. Nicolaus, London, 1973), p. 8.
2 Among these was the short manuscript known as 'Introduction to a Critique', which was published by Karl Kautsky (in the magazine *Neue Zeit*) in 1903.
3 Foreword by Martin Nicholaus, *op. cit.* p. 17.
4 *Ibid.* p. 240.
5 *Ibid.* p. 241.
6 *Ibid.* pp. 247–8.
7 '... the labour-time of an individual, but of an individual in no way different from the next individual and from all other individuals insofar as they perform equal labour' *A Contribution to the Critique of Political Economy*, trans. S.W. Ryazanskaya, ed. by Maurice Dobb (London and Moscow, 1971) p. 32.

8 *Ibid*. pp. 34–5.
9 That is, what was published as a first volume (cf. the Moore-Aveling edition of 1886), and is commonly known as such, although it was originally conceived as two books or volumes and is described as such in the list of contents.
10 Smith had treated of it, but considered that it applied only to production and exchange in the 'original state' of society prior to the accumulation of capital and the private appropriation of land (that is, to pre-capitalist conditions).
11 Primarily as a result of the work of Piero Sraffa (esp. his *Production of Commodities by Means of Commodities*, Cambridge, 1960); also Professor P. Garegnani who has specially emphasised this corollary (*Il Capitale nelle teorie della Distribuzione*, Milano, 1960).
12 In his *Essay on Profits* of 1815, two years before the *Principles*.
13 See M. Dobb, *Theories of Value and Distribution since Adam Smith*, Cambridge 1973, chapter 3.
14 Dr Paul Sweezy, for example, has spoken of Marx's 'counter tradition' to that of the classical economists as being 'the production of commodities by means of human labour, (*Monthly Review*, February 1976, p. 55). If this latter be intended as a reference to the theory of value, it seems questionable whether this can be regarded as running 'counter' to the treatment of value by the classical economists. If it is meant to imply that human labour is the *sole* productive force, then (as we shall see) it is doubtful, to say the least, whether Marx intended anything of the kind.
15 In Marx's terminology this can be spoken of as 'petty commodity production' — by small owner-producers.
16 Accordingly, labour-power like other commodities subscribed to the laws of competition as propounded by classical political economy, and was not an exception to them.
17 K. Marx, *A Contribution to the Critique of Political Economy*, ed. with Introduction by Maurice Dobb (London, 1971), p. 36.
18 More plausibility can perhaps be given to the contention we are here discussing if we bear in mind that it is *not* sufficient for an economic theory to be logically coherent (which is what economists' discussion is apt to be about): while this is a necessary condition to be fulfilled, it is by no means a *sufficient* condition. Its concepts must be related to actual entities or processes in the real world — moreover to those that are the important ones in any determinative or causal sense, for it to have interpretative significance. Without this it must remain a 'pure' theory, without any specifically economic reference.
19 Equal to wages and material input costs *plus* an average rate of profit on the capital employed.
20 Or alternatively the 'turnover of variable capital'.
21 Including wages as the price of labour-power dependent on the price of wage-goods.
22 In particular the profit-motivated movement of capital between industries, establishing the tendency to an equal profit-rate as between industries.
23 K. Marx, *Capital*, vol. I (trans. Moore and Aveling), pp. 639–40.
24 *Ibid*. p. 641.
25 Marx followed Ricardo in treating this level, not as purely physical, but as containing a 'social element', subject to change with time and place. Moreover, he did not deny the ability of trade unions to affect the wage-level

— as he put it, 'to defeat the laws of supply and demand'.

26 *Ibid*. p. 651.

27 *Ibid*. p. 634.

28 With more constant capital used in conjunction with a given quantity of variable, it stands to reason that, with the rate of surplus value the same, when the surplus value created is spread over a larger quantity of constant capital, the rate of profit yielded will be lower the higher the ratio of constant to variable. Expressing it symbolically: with C and V as the two constituents of capital and S for surplus value, for any given rate of S/V,

$$\frac{S}{C+V} \quad \text{will be lower the higher is} \quad C/V$$

29 *Ibid*. p. 658.

30 K. Marx, *Capital*, vol. III (trans. Untermann), p. 568.

31 D. Ricardo, *Works and Correspondence of David Ricardo*, ed. P. Sraffa, vol. II, pp. 309, 311.

32 On the implicit assumption of prompt reinvestment of surplus-value over and above capitalist luxury-consumption.

33 It is to be noted, however, that towards the end of vol. II, after dealing with the proportions needing to be preserved between sectors or departments, Marx does cite a case where capitalists in consumer goods industries have difficulty in realising (by sale) their surplus-value in the form of money and hence investing this in new means of production. He gives the somewhat curious answer that they realise their products *against gold* from the gold producers; see M. Dobb, *On Economic Theory and Socialism* (London, 1955), p. 269.

34 R. Luxemburg, *Accumulation of Capital*, (trans. A. Schwartschild) p. 359.

35 She is thinking here particularly of small-scale peasant economy. Chapters 27 and 29 are headed respectively 'The Struggle Against Natural Economy' and 'The Struggle against Peasant Economy'.

36 *Ibid*. pp. 416–7.

37 *Ibid*. p. 467.

38 V.I. Lenin, *Development of Capitalism in Russia* (Moscow, 1956). The work first appeared in Russian in 1899, with a second edition in 1908, on which this English edition is based.

39 *Ibid*. pp. 31–2, 34, 36.

40 Who died in Warsaw in 1970. For facts about him cf. George Feiwel, *The Intellectual Capital of Michal Kalecki* (Tennessee, 1975).

41 There was always in Kalecki's system spare productive capacity, since (like Keynes) he denied any tendency to full employment and full capacity working, except quite exceptionally when total demand was at a high level.

42 J.A. Hobson, writing in 1902, indeed, had explained export of capital with colonial expansion and imperialism in terms of under-consumption.

43 Published in Russia after his return to Russia in April 1917.

44 V.I. Lenin, *Collected Works*, vol. XIX, pp. 92–3.

45 *Ibid*. p. 97.

46 *Ibid*. pp. 103, 160–1.

47 Cf. on this J.M. Gillman, *The Falling Rate of Profit* (London, 1957) who denies that the profit-rate in the USA has fallen after 1919, after which he claims that if anything it has risen.

48 Witness the discussion around the work of Bavan and Sweezy, *Monopoly Capital* (New York, 1966).

49 One need mention only the central role played by workers' Soviets and the fairly sharp social delineation of the personnel of the two sides of the civil war.

50 Opinion is sometimes also divided as to whether the discussion has served to vindicate specifically Marx's system rather than the approach of the classical economists as a whole.

51 Note that it is *not* the only necessary factor in producing wealth or use-values, in which, of course, nature and machines ('stored-up labour') played important roles.

5 MARX 'PHILOSOPHER'

István Mészáros

Marx's striking pronouncement on philosophy: 'The philosophers have only interpreted the world, in various ways; the point is to *change* it'[1] — is often understood in a onesided way: as a radical rejection of philosophy and a call for its supersession by 'scientific socialism'. What is not appreciated in such interpretations is that Marx's idea of such an *Aufhebung* is not envisaged simply as a theoretical shift from philosophy to science but as a complex practical programme whose realisation necessarily implies the dialectical unity of 'the weapon of criticism and the criticism of weapons'[2], which means that philosophy remains an integral part of the struggle for emancipation. As Marx put it: '*you cannot supersede philosophy without realising it*',[3] which cannot be accomplished *in* science itself, but only in practical reality or social praxis, — which includes, of course, the contribution of science. Furthermore, the original proposition cannot be divorced from Marx's assertion of the necessary interconnection between this 'realisation of philosophy' and the proletariat. For:

Just as philosophy finds its *material* weapons in the proletariat, so the proletariat finds its *intellectual* weapons in philosophy... . Philosophy cannot realise itself without the transcendence [*Aufhebung*] of the proletariat, and the proletariat cannot transcend itself without the realisation [*Verwirklichung*] of philosophy.[4]

The two sides of this dialectical interrelationship thus, according to Marx, stand or fall together.

But are such assertions to be taken seriously, or should they be considered no more than colourful examples of youthful exuberance and rhetorics? Can we assign any meaning — and if so, what exactly — to the idea of 'realising philosophy' without which 'the proletariat cannot transcend itself'? And since we cannot help seeing that the proletariat did not succeed so far in the historical task of transcending itself, should we turn our back to the embarrassing problem by pretending that Marx's programme has been accomplished in 'theoretical practice', through the supersession of philosophy by the *idea* of 'scientific socialism', 'the science of history', etc.? What role, if any, is left to

103

philosophy in the constitution of a socialist consciousness and in the realisation of the practical tasks facing us once Marx's critical remarks on past philosophy and on the relationship between philosophy and social life are consistently applied to the assessment of post-Marxian trends of development? These and similar questions are essential for our understanding of Marx's significance for philosophy as well as of philosophy's significance for the kind of social praxis which Marx himself had advocated.

Part I: The Realisation of Philosophy

Following his father's wishes, like Lukács seventy years later, Marx dedicated himself at first to the study of law. Soon, however, he felt the 'urge to wrestle with philosophy', realising that in view of the profound link between philosophy and his chosen field of study 'there could be no headway without philosophy'. He wrote half-apologetically to his father from Berlin in 1837: 'I became even more firmly bound to the modern world philosophy from which I had thought to escape'.[5] Philosophy for him was not a substitute to getting laboriously acquainted with the details of the technical literature: his reading of tedious juridical texts was just as phenomenal as his note-taking in his later years. He wasn't looking for some speculative *a priori* alternative to the minutiae of legal knowledge but for a guiding thread — an adequate theoretical foundation — to tie them together. He realised that the only way to gain a proper understanding of any object of study was grasping it in the network of its dynamic interconnections, and he proudly stressed the principle according to which '*the object itself must be studied in its development*'.[6] The refusal to uncritically assume the existent as simply given, and the demand for relating the particular points to their manifold dialectical interconnections in the overall process, understandably, led Marx to rigorously question the limits of his subject of study. Thus the transition from studying the empirical aspects of law ('administrative science',[7] as he called it) to Jurisprudence and from the latter to philosophy in general was natural for him and coincided with the deepening of his understanding of the problems at stake.

To be sure, this kind of progression is not a peculiarity valid for Marx alone. True, the depth and extent to which Marx was able to draw the philosophical conclusions from a critical examination of the empirical material (legal case studies as well as discussions of civil procedure, criminal law and the law of property, among other things) revealed a fast-maturing immense talent with a

Gargantuan appetite for knowledge matched by an unequalled power of generalisation and an ability to perceive the most far-reaching implications of any point at issue. An extraordinary single-mindedness of purpose coupled with a conscious effort to integrate life and work, the part and the whole, was clearly in evidence from the first moment of his recorded reflections, as we can see in his famous letter to his father to whom he wrote: 'allow me to review my affairs in the way I regard life in general, as the expression of an intellectual activity which develops in all directions, in science, art and private matters.'[8] No wonder, therefore, that witnessing Marx's Promethean determination to fuse life and work — that is, his way of addressing himself to the problems of philosophy with such an intensity that he didn't just study them but at the same time also lived them — made Moses Hess (by six years Marx's elder) write of him to a friend with boundless admiration and enthusiasm:

prepare yourself to make the acquaintance of the greatest, perhaps the *only* now living *true philosopher*, who soon, wherever he may appear (in print or on the lecture platform), will draw the eyes of Germany upon himself. Dr Marx — that is the name of my idol — is still a very young man (perhaps 24 years old at the most) who will deliver the last blow to the religion and politics of the Middle Ages. He combines the sharpest wit with the deepest philosophical earnestness. Think of Rousseau, Voltaire, Holbach, Lessing, Heine and Hegel united in one person; I say *united*, not thrown together — and there you have Dr Marx.[9]

All this is very true: the depth of insight of a Marx cannot be set up as a norm for all. Nevertheless, the general direction of the undertaking must be the same in that the inner logic of any particular field of study points beyond its own partiality and demands to be inserted into increasingly broader contexts until the point is reached where the full range of dialectical interconnections with the whole is adequately established. And philosophy is ultimately nothing but the comprehensive framework of such connections without which the analysis of particular areas is bound to remain fragmentary and hopelessly one-sided.

Nor could it be sensibly argued that Marx's subsequent critique of speculative idealism and contemplative materialism alike radically changed his attitude as to the importance of philosophy itself. To talk about Marx's 'youthful philosophical phase' as opposed to his later submergence in 'science' and in 'political economy' is a crude misrepresentation based on an appalling ignorance or distortion of quite elementary facts.[10] The target of his criticism with respect to philosophy was from the very beginning its remoteness from and opposition to the real world, and the impotence that necessarily followed from such an idealistic separation. This is why he wrote already in 1837: 'From the idealism which, by the way, I had compared and nourished with the idealism of Kant and Fichte, *I arrived at the point of seeking the idea in reality itself.*'[11] He was conscious of the fact that the problematical development of philosophy as an alienated universality was the manifestation of an objective contradiction and he was trying to find a solution to this contradiction. Thus when he reached the conclusion — in a critical rejection of the impotence of mere philosophical *interpretations* — that the problem did not arise from within philosophy itself but from the relationship between the latter and the real world, and that consequently the solution was in the *changing* of this world, he did not advocate a capitulation to fragmentariness and partiality, nor turning of one's back to the philosophical search for universality. On the contrary, he insisted that the measure of emancipation must be the degree to which social praxis regains its universal dimension: a task he also called 'the realisation of philosophy'.

Of course, Marx denied the legitimacy of an independent, self-oriented philosophy,[12] just as he scorned the idea of a separate existence of politics, law, religion, art, etc., in that all these areas ('ideological reflexes') had to be understood in relation to the objective development of the forces and relations of production as an integral part of the totality of social praxis. Equally, he rejected the idea that philosophy could have a privileged domain of its own and a separate medium of existence[13] which could be opposed to real life. And he stressed the role of the *division of labour*[14] in the formation of the illusions which philosophy had about itself. But he hastened to add that such developments whereby philosophy etc. come into contradiction with the existing relations 'can only occur because existing social relations have come into contradictions with existing forces of production'.[15] Thus the problem was identified as a profound contradiction of the social division of labour itself which made philosophy usurp — together with some other ideological forms — the dimension of universality. This did not mean in the slightest that the demand for universality itself was to be dismissed: only its speculative and imaginary realisation. This is why Marx insisted on the reintegration of philosophy with real life in terms of the *necessity of philosophy* as the necessity of its realisation in the service of emancipation. Thus philosophy, with these qualifications, continued to inform and orient Marx's work in a most significant sense to the very end of his life.

The idea of universality appeared in philosophy before Marx as an abstract principle. Another term of the same problematic, *totality*, was likewise articulated as a speculative philosophical and methodological concept. Marx revealed the true significance of these categories by putting into relief their real ground of existence and by treating them as the most general *Daseinsformen* ('forms of existence')[16] which were reflected in philosophy 'as in a *camera obscura*, in an inverted form' so as to be able to deduce actuality from the 'idea'. Marx described the real bases of universality and its historical corollary, 'world history', in the following terms:

1 'the universal development of productive forces';
2 'the actual empirical existence of men in their *world-historical*, instead of local being';
3 'universal competition' and the development of universal interdependence (*'universal* intercourse between men . . . makes each nation dependent on the revolutions of others');
4 the development of the 'universal class', the proletariat which 'can only exist *world-historically*, just as communism, its activity, can only have a "world-historical" existence', in other words, a 'world-historical existence of individuals, i.e. existence of individuals which is *directly* linked up with world history.'[17]

Consequently, the problem of universality, though at first perceived in a fictitious form in philosophy, was not simply a speculative philosophical perversion, but a real issue with a vital bearing on the life of every single individual now *directly* linked to world history in its actual unfolding. This is why it was not 'youthful rhetorics' to talk about the 'realisation of philosophy' as the work of actual historical development through the agency of real social individuals and their collective manifestations.

Marx raised the problem of universality and its realisation also under its other vital aspect: as *appropriation*. Again in place of mere conceptual transformations and solutions he presented us with the objective dialectic of real existence. And again in opposition to a speculative philosophical projection of the grandiose unfolding of the idea, the picture drawn was that of the harsh reality and potential liberation of actual historical development. For:

things have now come to such a pass, that the individuals must appropriate the existing totality of productive forces, not only to achieve self-activity, but, also, merely to safeguard their very existence. This appropriation is first determined by the object to be appropriated, the productive forces, which have been developed to a totality and which only exist within a universal intercourse. From this aspect alone, therefore, this appropriation must have a universal character corresponding to the productive forces and the intercourse. The appropriation of these forces is itself nothing more than the development of the individual capacities corresponding to the material instruments of production. The *appropriation of a totality of instruments of production* is, for this very reason, the *development of a totality of capacities in the individuals* themselves. This appropriation is further determined by the persons appropriating. Only the proletarians of the present day, who are completely shut off from all self-activity, are in a position to achieve a *complete* and no longer *restricted* self-activity, which consists in the *appropriation of a totality of productive forces* and in the thus *postulated* development of a *totality of capacities*. All earlier revolutionary appropriations were restricted; individuals, whose self-activity was restricted by a crude instrument of production and a limited intercourse, appropriated this crude instrument of production, and hence merely achieved a new state of limitation. Their instrument of production became *their property*, but they themselves remained *subordinate to the division of labour* and to their *instrument of production*. In all appropriations up to now, a mass of individuals remained subservient to a single instrument of production; in the appropriation by the proletarians, a mass of instruments of production *must* be made subject to *each individual*, and property to *all*, Modern *universal* intercourse can be controlled by *individuals*, therefore, only when controlled by *all*.[18]

Thus the philosophical concepts of universality and totality were shown by Marx to be closely linked to and dependent upon the possibility of a full appropriation which they anticipated in an abstract form in opposition to and in a speculative supersession of the deficiencies (partiality and conflict-ridden character) of empirical existence. Marx rejected this abstract negation and clearly identified the objective conditions, forces and tendencies of the social development which itself defined appropriation as the production of a totality of capacities in the individuals in conjunction with the development of a totality of productive forces and instruments of production in the framework of a universal intercourse. And in the same spirit later, in the *Grundrisse*, he projected the *'free development of individualities'*[19] and in *Capital* he anticipated for men 'conditions most favourable to, and *worthy of, their human nature...*; that development of human energy which is an *end in itself*, the *true realm of freedom'*.[20] The universality of such appropriation was characterised by Marx not only in terms of the highest level of the totality of productive forces and the corresponding all-round development of capacities in the individuals within a universal intercourse, but also in the radically new modality of property ownership: namely the exclusion of individuals as separate individuals from the ownership of the means of production in order to make possible their effective control by the totality of associated producers.

Guardedly, Marx used the expressions: '*postulated* development of a totality of capacities' and '*must* be made subject to *each* individual and property to *all*' (referring to the means of production). In this way he not only emphasised the necessary interdependence of the all-round development of the individuals and their conscious control of property and production, but also put into relief that so long as such developments are not actually accomplished in real life, philosophy is bound to continue to live a separate existence instead of being integrated in everyday life and thus 'realised'. For the separateness of philosophy is only the manifestation of an inner contradiction of a social praxis which as yet failed to realise its potential of developing the totality of capacities in the individuals appropriating the totality of productive forces under their combined control. This is the negative aspect of the problem. The positive is that philosophy, under such circumstances, is not merely the necessary manifestation of this failure — which itself cannot be swept under the carpet by pseudo-scientific verbal devices like 'theoretical practice', nor by haughtily dismissing Marx's theory of fetishism as Hegelianism and the outgrowth of 'German cultural Romanticism' — but at the same time also a vital reminder of a positive potentiality for transcending that failure. If partiality continues to prevail under our present-day circumstances, making the demand for universality appear extremely remote from reality, that is not philosophy's fault. The question is whether we resign ourselves to the triumph of partiality, elevating it to a permanent condition of existence, as Marx's critics tend to do, or negate it whichever way we can, including the form in which the philosophical 'weapon of criticism' can and must contribute to the success of a practical negation. There can be no doubt as to where Marx stands on this issue, with his advocacy of the 'development of free individualities' and of the 'true realm of freedom . . . worthy of human nature'. By contrast, the speculative verbal supersession of philosophy by 'Theory', 'Theoretical Practice', by the so-called 'rigorous scientific concepts of experimental reasoning', and the like, can only lead to a conservative rejection of the unity of theory and practice and to the sceptical dismissal of Marx's values as unrealisable dreams.

Part II: Marx's 'Positive Science'
Marx's philosophical development towards a radical watershed
in the entire history of philosophy was staggeringly fast. It goes
without saying that he did not simply break himself off the great
heritage of the past. On the contrary, he continued to make
generously positive references to the classics of philosophy —
from Aristotle to Spinoza and from Vico to Hegel — throughout
his almost half-a-century-long literary activity. But the ideas of
past philosophers, however fully acknowledged, were closely
integrated by him, as 'superseded-preserved' elements, into a
monumental conception of exemplary originality. He worked out
the basic outlines of this conception as a very young man, in his
early twenties, and he went on articulating and developing the
new world view in all its dimensions through his major works of
synthesis.

Engels wrote of Marx in 1886: 'Marx stood higher, saw further,
and took a wider and quicker view than all the rest of us.'[21]
Whatever we may think of Engels' own significance in the
elaboration of Marxism, there can be no doubt about the
fundamental validity of his statement. What Moses Hess
perceived and enthusiastically described in the letter quoted
above, and what Engels summed up in four equally enthusiastic
words ('Marx was a genius')[22] was clearly in evidence from the
outset. Marx's rightly famous letter to his father — written at the
age of barely nineteen — revealed an incommensurable passion
for synthesis coupled with an ability to treat not only the material
under his scrutiny but also his own efforts with remorseless
criticism, moving forward from one comprehensive framework of
assessment to the next in a relentless fashion, refusing to rest on
the laurels of his own achievements, though soberly acknowledging the relative merit of the enterprise. Talking of his
own first attempt at sketching a philosophy of law he wrote: 'The
whole thing is replete with tripartite divisions, it is written with
tedious prolixity, and the Roman concepts are misused in the
most barbaric fashion in order to force them into my system. On
the other hand, in this way I did gain a general view of the
material'.[23] The next step revealed that he was simply unable to
proceed in less than comprehensive fashion: 'I drafted a new
system of metaphysical principles, but at the conclusion of it I
was once more compelled to recognise that it was wrong, like all
my previous efforts.'[24] Intense dissatisfaction with this line of
approach made him look for a solution in a very different
direction:

I arrived at the point of seeking the idea in reality itself. If previously the gods had dwelt above the earth, now they became its centre. I had read fragments of Hegel's philosophy, the grotesque craggy melody of which did not appeal to me. Once more I wanted to dive into the sea, but with the definite intention of establishing that the nature of the mind is just as necessary, concrete and firmly based as the nature of the body. My aim was no longer to practise tricks of swordsmanship, but to bring genuine pearls into the light of day.[25]

But before this phase could be considered closed, the rather one-sided rejection of Hegel, based on no more than a fragmentary knowledge of his work, gave way to a much more balanced — though by no means uncritical — reassessment at the end of which again a yearning for a positive totalisation came to the fore:

While I was ill I got to know Hegel from beginning to end, together with most of his disciples . . . . In controversy here, many conflicting views were expressed, and I became ever more firmly bound to the modern world philosophy from which I had thought to escape, but all rich chords were silenced and I was seized with a veritable fury of irony, as could easily happen after so much had been negated.[26]

To be sure, these remarks, together with others contained in the same letter, did not amount to a coherent world view as yet. They were significant, nevertheless, as indications of an intense search for a new framework of totalisation: one capable of a dynamic comprehension of a growing and deepening range of knowledge. The moment the principle of 'seeking the idea in reality itself' appeared on Marx's horizon, a tension had been created which could not be resolved within the confines of philosophy as such. From this insight two further steps followed with compelling necessity, even if they were fully spelled out a few years later. First, that the insoluble character of past philosophical problematics was inherent in the philosophers' attempt to find the solutions in philosophy itself (that is, within the self-imposed limitations of the most abstract form of theory). And second, that the constitution of an adequate form of theory must be conceived as an integral part of the unity of theory and practice.

This latter principle in its turn made all theoretical solutions strictly transient, incomplete, and 'other-directed' (as opposed to the 'self-referential' coherence of past philosophy): in one word it made them *subordinate* — though, of course, *dialectically* subordinate — to the overall dynamism of self-developing social praxis. It had to envisage the historical supersession of all philosophical conceptualisations, including that of the new conception itself inasmuch as it was tied to a particular configuration of social forces and their antagonisms: an aspect which induced precisely those interpreters of Marx who could not understand the dialectic of theory and practice to attribute to the new world view nothing more than purely heuristic value, and, of course, even that of a very limited kind. We shall see in a moment the way in which Marx reached his radical conclusions, but first we have to glance at a few salient features of his new synthesis, worked out in a conscious opposition to the philosophical systems of his predecessors.

Engels, in his essay on Feuerbach, summed up his position on the problematical nature of past philosophical systems as follows:

With all philosophers it is precisely the 'system' which is perishable; and for the simple reason that it springs from an imperishable desire of the human mind — the desire to overcome all contradictions. But if all contradictions are once for all disposed of, we shall have arrived at so-called absolute truth — world history will be at an end. And yet it has to continue, although there is nothing left for it to do — hence, a new, insoluble contradiction. As soon as we have once realised — and in the long run no one has helped us to realise it more than Hegel himself — that the task of philosophy thus stated means nothing but the task that a *single philosopher* should accomplish that which can only be accomplished by the *entire human race* in its progressive development — as soon as we realise that, there is an end to all philosophy *in the hitherto accepted sense of the word.* One leaves alone 'absolute truth', which is unattainable along this path or by any single individual; instead, one pursues attainable *relative truths* along the path of the *positive sciences*, and the summation of *their results* by means of *dialectical thinking*.[27]

The important point in Engels' analysis is that the new world view, conscious of the fundamental contradiction in the way in which past systems treated the relationship between absolute and relative truth, had to be an *open system* replacing the *lonely philosopher* by the *collective subject* of successive generations that continue to advance knowledge in the progressive development of mankind. Indeed, Marx's completely unparalleled influence in the whole of human history cannot be separated from the fact that he had radically redefined philosophy as the collective enterprise to which many generations contribute their share in accordance with the requirements and potentialities of their situation. (In this sense in which we are talking about a radical reorientation of the whole framework of knowledge as a great collective enterprise, there can be only Marxism and not

'Marxisms'. The latter are socio-political specificities sharing the same basic orientation, and it is inherent in the spirit of the new world view that it must find its articulation through constant redefinitions and innovations, as the conditions of its further development significantly change through history and through the advancement of knowledge.) Thus it is not in the least surprising that the burden of producing a radically redefined general framework of orientation while undertaking the elaboration of socio-historically specific tasks made impossible for Marx to complete *any one* of his major works, from the *Economic and Philosophic Manuscripts of 1844* to the *Grundrisse* and to *Capital*, — not to mention countless other projects which he hoped to undertake but could not carry out. Nor should this worry us unduly, since the unfinished character of Marx's lifework is inseparable from the world historical novelty of his undertaking and from the challenging openness of his system. It goes without saying, not even the greatest talent can escape the consequences of historical and personal limitations. But much of today's talk about the 'crisis of Marxism' reveals a crisis of one's own convictions rather than some well-identified lacunae in Marx's vision.

On the other hand, Engels' characterisation of 'the end of all philosophy' — which deeply affected many subsequent interpretations — is disturbing in two major respects. The first is that even if philosophy is rightly defined as a collective enterprise, it is nonetheless one that is realised through the partial accomplishments of particular individuals — like Marx himself — who try to resolve the contradictions they perceive, to the best of their abilities, circumscribed not only by personal talent but also by the vantage point attainable at any given time in the progressive development of mankind. Thus nothing could be more Hegelian than Engels' idea of assuming 'the entire human race' as the materialist equivalent to Hegel's 'absolute mind' in possession of 'absolute truth', — although it is presented as the polar opposite to Hegel. In reality philosophy is advanced in the form of partial totalisations which of necessity constitute, at any given point in time, including the post-Hegelian phase of development, some kind of a *system* without which the very idea of 'relative truths' would make no sense whatsoever. The alternative to the Hegelian concept of absolute truth is not 'the entire human race' as the notional possessor of some such 'absolute truth', but the totalising synthesis of attainable levels of knowledge progressively superseded in the collective enterprise of particular systems. Consequently, no matter how consciously open was the Marxian world view in its inception and general orientation, it had to be *systematically* articulated at different stages of Marx's development — from the *Paris Manuscripts* to *Capital* — if it was to qualify as an adequate totalisation of knowledge.

The second respect in which Engels' analysis is extremely problematical is closely connected with the first. For having expelled from philosophy its vital function as the given system of totalising knowledge (that is, as a system which not only *arranges* but also *constitutes* knowledge, anticipating and furthering developments as well as following and synthesising them) he was left with a positivistic reduction of philosophy to a mere '*summation* of the results of the *positive sciences*.' Furthermore, the ambiguity between this vision of the 'positive sciences' and the Hegelian notion of 'positive knowledge' — wrongly attributed to Marx by Colletti and others — followed as an afterthought to this analysis when Engels asserted that 'though unconsciously, Hegel showed us the way out of the labyrinth of systems to real positive knowledge of the world.'[28] Although it was no part of Engels' conscious intentions, the tendency inherent in the shift we have seen in his analysis is that the criterion of truth is retransferred within the confines of *theory as such* — an orientation from which Marx so emphatically freed himself — and, modelled upon the 'positive sciences', becomes the foundation of a fictitiously self-sustaining 'theoretical practice' more or less openly opposed to Marx's principle which announced the dialectical unity of theory and practice as the real watershed between his line of approach and that of his predecessors. And, ironically, since no solid supporting evidence can be found in the whole body of Marx's massive work[29] to maintain the claimed adherence to the model of 'the positive sciences', he can now be also accused of 'Hegelianism' (or of an ambiguous wavering between empiricist scientism and romantic Hegelianism) for failing to provide the positivistic evidence required by the neat reductionist scheme.

In point of fact, Marx's development followed a very different route. He explicitly rejected modelling philosophy on the natural sciences, since he considered them 'abstractly material'[30] and subject to the same contradictions in the totality of social praxis which both divorced theory from practice and produced an ever-increasing fragmentation of theoretical and practical activities, sharply opposing them among themselves, instead of sustaining their unified development in an integrated framework.

His references to 'positive science' were neither idealisations of natural science, nor concessions to Hegelianism — let alone an uneasy mixture of the two — but expressions of a programme firmly anchoring theory to 'real life' and to the 'representation of practical activity' which could appear in the natural sciences, constituted on the basis of the social division of labour, only in an abstractly material and one-sided form. In opposition to speculative philosophy he wrote:

We set out from *real, active men*, and on the basis of their real life-process we demonstrate the development of the ideological reflexes and echoes of this life-process. The phantoms formed in the human brain are also, necessarily, sublimates of their *material life-process*, which is *empirically verifiable* and bound to material premises... . This method of approach is not devoid of premises. It starts out from the real premises and does not abandon them for a moment. Its premises are men, not in any fantastic isolation and rigidity, but in their *actual, empirically perceptible process of development* under definite conditions. As soon as this *active life-process* is described, history ceases to be a collection of *dead facts* as it is with the *empiricists* (themselves still *abstract*), or an *imagined activity of imagined subjects*, as with the idealists.[31]

And he emphatically added a clear definition of his meaning of 'positive science': 'Where speculation ends — in real life — there *real, positive science* begins: the representation of the *practical activity*, of the *practical process of development of men*.'[32] The same view is amplified a few pages further on:

This conception of history depends on our ability to expound the *real process of production* . . . to explain all the different *theoretical products and forms of consciousness*, religion, philosophy, ethics, etc. etc., and trace their origins and growth *from that basis*; by which means, of course, the whole thing can be *depicted in its totality* (and therefore, too, the *reciprocal action* of these various sides on one another). It has not, like the idealistic view of history, in every period to look for a *category*, but remains constantly on the *real ground of history*; it does not explain practice from the idea but explains the *formation of ideas from material practice*; and accordingly it comes to the conclusion that all forms and products of consciousness cannot be dissolved by *mental criticism* ['theoretical practice'] . . . but only by the *practical overthrow* of the actual social relations which gave rise to this idealistic humbug; that *not criticism but revolution is the driving force of history*, also of religion, of philosophy and all other types of theory.[33]

As we can see, Marx's concern with '*real, positive* science' was meant as an unmistakably clear and radical reorientation of philosophy towards '*real, active* men'; towards their '*actual, empirically perceptible* process of development'; towards their 'material life-process' dialectically grasped as an '*active* life-process'; in sum: towards the representation 'of the *practical activity*, of the *practical* process of development of men'. This was very much in line with the youthful inspiration of 'seeking the idea in reality itself', though, of course, grasped at a much higher level, in that the later formulation indicated in the references to social praxis also the *solution*, whereas the early one amounted to no more than a — however genial — intuition of the *problem* itself. Even the imagery used on both occasions revealed a striking similarity. The youthful letter, after the sentence which spoke of seeing the idea in reality itself, went on like this: 'If previously the gods had dwelt above the earth, now they became its centre.' And the paragraph quoted above (see note 31) from *The German Ideology* opened with these words: 'In contrast to German philosophy which descends from heaven to earth, here we ascend from earth to heaven. That is to say . . . we set out from real, active men.'[34] And again we can witness that the higher level of conceptualisation resolves the almost enigmatic ambiguity of the original imagery which reflected not only the problem — and the programme — of demystifying religion on the ground of earthly reality but at the same time also the young student's inability of satisfactorily doing so, whereas *The German Philosophy* firmly located religious and other fantastic conceptions as necessarily arising out of the contradictions of determinate modes of social praxis, and thus requiring for their solution the *practical overthrow* of the actual social relations of production.

The other point we cannot stress enough is the shift from Marx's singular — 'positive science', in the sense we have seen — to the empiricist plural of 'positive sciences', with the suggestion that the new philosophy simply 'summarises' the results of such 'positive' (natural) sciences ('their results') 'by means of dialectical thinking'. This is by no means a minor slip. On the contrary, its implications are very serious and far-reaching. For this is the Marxian passage so significantly transformed by Engels: '*Self-oriented* philosophy loses its medium of existence with the *representation of reality*.[35] It is replaced at the outset by a synthesis of the most general results which can be abstracted from surveying the historical development of men.'[36] Clearly, then, the 'results' mentioned by Marx are not those of the 'positive sciences' which leave to philosophy nothing but the role of 'summarising their results by means of dialectical thinking'. (Which itself is rather baffling. For how can thinking be dialectical if its role is not the production of ideas and results but merely the 'summarising' of what is handed down to it? Nor is it possible to see how could the whole enterprise turn out to be dialectical if the partial results were themselves not constituted dialectically, so as to make necessary some sort of a superimposition of the dialectic on them, as it were, from the outside.) In Marx's view, on the contrary, the results in question are themselves produced by the theory which also synthesises them, and they are produced through surveying the actual historical development of men, putting into relief their most significant objective — practically constituted — characteristics. Furthermore, this surveying is obviously not a matter of simple observation, but a dialectical process of taking hold of the immensely rich *'active life-process'* (in sharp contrast to the 'collection of dead facts as it is with the *empiricists*, themselves *still abstract'*) within a well defined, *praxis-oriented theoretical framework*, elaborating the great variety of factors involved in the surveyed practical activity of historically developing men in accordance with determinate *'material premises'* and thus actively dialectically reconstituting the theoretical framework itself which again encompasses the next round of survey. This is what Marx means by 'positive science' which is of necessity *totalising* and therefore cannot possibly exist in the plural — not in Marx's sense of the term. He makes this amply clear when he insists that in his conception — which explains all theoretical manifestations in relation to their material ground in conjunction with the principle of the unity of theory and practice — 'the *whole thing* can be depicted *in its totality'*, whereas 'the positive sciences' inevitably leave the vital task of totalisation untouched since it lies beyond any one of them. And the other, equally important, point stressed by Marx is that the dialectical interchange of the complex material factors with all the different theoretical products and forms of consciousness — 'the *reciprocal action* of these various sides on one another' — can only be grasped in such a framework of totalisation. Whether one calls it a new form of philosophy or — in a deliberate polemical opposition to speculative philosophy — 'positive science' is of little importance. What does matter, however, is that we cannot have a dialectical conception of history without such a framework of totalisation which 'the positive sciences' cannot possibly displace or replace.

Ironically for those who pay scant attention to historical evidence, the only time Marx treated philosophy approvingly as a *theoretical practice* was when he was still trapped within the confines of an idealist outlook. In his doctoral dissertation, written between early 1839 and March 1841, he argued that:

the *practice* of philosophy is itself *theoretical*. It is the *critique* that measures the individual existence by the essence, the particular reality by the Idea. But this *immediate realisation* of philosophy is in its deepest essence afflicted with contradictions, and this its essence takes form in the appearance and imprints its seal upon it.[37]

But even this approval, as we can see, was not unqualified. For it was coupled with a hint about some contradictions inherent in philosophy's opposition to the world, even though the author of the doctoral dissertation could not offer a precise definition of their nature, let alone an adequate solution to them. Given the limitations of his outlook then, he could depict the tensions and oppositions in question only as a most uneasy *stalemate*:

When philosophy turns itself at will against the world of appearance, then the system is lowered to an abstract totality, that is, it has become one aspect of the world which opposes another one. Its relationship to the world is that of reflection. Inspired by the *urge to realise itself*, it enters into tension against the other. The inner self-contentment and completeness has been broken. What was inner light has become consuming flame turning outwards. The result is that as the world becomes philosophical, philosophy becomes worldly, that its realisation is also its loss, that what it struggles against on the *outside* is its own *inner deficiency*, that in the very struggle it falls precisely into those defects which it fights as defects in the opposite camp, and that it can only overcome these defects by falling into them. That which opposes and that which it fights is always *the same as itself*, only with factors inverted.[38]

The contradictions could not be firmly identified because they were grasped as emanating from philosophy itself and thus tending toward a 'diremption [splitting up] of individual self-consciousness in itself' as regards the predicament of particular philosophers, and to an 'external separation and duality of philosophy, as two opposed philosophical trends'[39] as regards philosophy as a whole. The idea that the problem might arise out of the 'inadequacy of the world which has to be made philosophical'[40] appeared for an instant, but in terms of the problematic confined to the opposition of two philosophical trends it had to be subsumed as a 'moment' of the overall scheme of an ultimately self-oriented theoretical practice.

All the same, the problem itself appeared on the horizon and its unresolved character represented a challenge for Marx. His development in the years that immediately followed the completion of his doctoral dissertation consisted in the realisation:

1   that the subjective aspect of the problem cannot be confined to the consideration of *individual* subjectivity alone, in terms of which the dissertation tackled it,[41] but must be complemented by a dialectical conception of the actual historical development that produces a *collective agency* in relation to which the *actual realisation* — which necessarily escapes 'individual self-consciousnesses' — may be envisaged; and
2   that this demand for the realisation of philosophy — arising out of the 'inadequacy of the world' concretely defined as an antagonism inherent in a determinate mode of social praxis — must be linked to the programme of radically reconstituting theory in the *unity of theory and practice* and in a supersession of the prevailing *social division of labour*.

Such steps as were necessary to reach these conclusions were taken by Marx in circumstances of pressing practical problems. As he recalled it later: 'In the year 1842–43, as editor of the *Rheinische Zeitung*, I first found myself in the embarrassing position of having to discuss what is known as material interests.'[42] And indeed in his 'Justification of the Correspondent from the Mosel' he articulated a strikingly important point. He wrote that:

In investigating a situation *concerning the state* one is all too easily tempted to overlook *the objective nature of the circumstances* and to explain everything by the *will* of the persons concerned. However, there are *circumstances* which determine the actions of private persons and individual authorities, and which are *as independent of them as the method of breathing*.[43]

How hollow philosophical abstractions must have sounded to the ears of a man who arrived at holding such convictions. No wonder, therefore, that he was eager to set a standard to theory in accordance with the objective requirements of the actual circumstances. In a letter written in August 1842 he insisted that '*True theory must be developed and clarified within the concrete circumstances and in relation to existing conditions*.'[44] And in the spirit of his own principle, he undertook a meticulous study of the objective conditions and forces that manifest themselves in the concrete circumstances, with a view of understanding the dynamic of their interrelations and the possibilities of a conscious intervention in their development. The results of this undertaking were incorporated in his *Critique of the Hegelian Philosophy of Right*, in his essays 'On the Jewish Question', in his system *in statu nascendi* known as the *Economic and Philosophic*

Manuscripts of 1844, and in his celebrated 'Theses on Feuerbach' linked to his vital share in *The German Philosophy*. These works not only made the final reckoning with speculative philosophy but simultaneously also elaborated the framework of a new type of totalisation of actual historical development, with all its manifold, dialectically interacting factors, including even the most esoteric forms and manifestations of consciousness. Having identified in the proletariat the collective agency and material force through which 'the realisation of philosophy' could be reformulated in a radically new form and at a qualitatively higher level, he continued to insist that 'the proletariat finds its *intellectual* weapons in philosophy.'[45] Thus, situating his type of philosophy in relation to a concrete socio-historical force, and defining its function as both integral and necessary to a successful struggle for emancipation, enabled Marx to formulate the demand for the '*practical* overthrow of the actual social relations' as the guiding principle and measuring rod of the meaningfulness of the new philosophy. A philosophy which arises at a particular juncture in history from a determinate social praxis. A philosophy which — in accordance with the unity of theory and practice — vitally contributes to the unfolding and full realisation of the potentialities inherent in this emancipatory praxis.

Part III: Marx's Relation to Hegel
Marx's relation to the Hegelian philosophy was quite unique. In one sense, Hegelianism represented for him the polar opposite of his own approach which advocated ascertainable 'material premises' in contrast to 'self-oriented' philosophical speculation: an approach articulated from a dynamic vision of 'the standpoint of labour',[46] as against Hegel's adoption of the uncritical and ultimately ahistorical partiality of 'the standpoint of political economy'.[47] In another sense, however, Marx never stopped stressing the gigantic character of Hegel's achievements, brought to realisation at an immensely important juncture of historical development, in the aftermath of the French Revolution, in response to the most complex and dynamic interplay of social forces — including the emergence of labour as a hegemonic movement — in world history.

Marx's critical appropriation of this philosophy was very far from being confined to a youthful phase. Quite the contrary. For once he settled his accounts not only with Hegel himself but also with his 'neo-Hegelian' followers — basically in his *Critique of the Hegelian Philosophy of Right*, the *Economic and Philosophic*

Manuscripts of 1844, and *The German Ideology* — the road was cleared for putting to a positive use those acquisitions of the Hegelian philosophy which Marx considered to be of a fundamental value. Indeed, references to Hegel in the *Grundrisse* and in *Capital* were numerous and on the whole highly positive — much more so than in the early works. For reasons which we shall see in a moment, important affinities came to the fore precisely at a time when Marx was struggling with the task of synthesising some of the most intricate aspects of his conception of capital and of the manifold contradictions inherent in its dialectical and historical[48] unfolding. As Lenin himself insisted: 'It is impossible completely to understand Marx's *Capital*, and especially its first chapter, without having thoroughly studied and understood the *whole* of Hegel's *Logic*. Consequently, half a century later none of the Marxists understood Marx!'[49] Another half a century later still, alas, Marx's relation to Hegel is no less subject to prejudices and aprioristic pre-conceptions than at the time Lenin jotted down this famous aphorism.

The blatant misreading of Hegel's significance for the development of philosophy and with it the total incomprehension with which Marx's relationship to this great thinker is treated is by no means accidental. It reveals the stubborn persistence of attempts at discarding dialectics in favour of tempting simplifications of one kind or another. As Marx observed in a letter in this regard: 'The gentlemen in Germany . . . think Hegel's *dialectic* is a "*dead horse*". Feuerbach has much to answer for in this respect.'[50] And he sarcastically commented in another letter:

Herr Lange wonders that Engels, I, etc., take the *dead dog Hegel* seriously when Büchner, Lange, Dr Dühring, Fechner, etc., are agreed that they — poor dear have buried him so long ago. Lange is naïve enough to say that I 'move with rare freedom' in empirical matter. He hasn't the least idea that this 'free movement in matter' is nothing but the paraphrase for the method of dealing with matter — that is, the *dialectical method*.[51]

Thus an adequate evaluation of Marx's relationship to Hegel is not a minor matter. In a way it sums up Marx's relation to philosophy in general and his conception of dialectics in particular.

As we have already seen, Marx's original wholesale rejection of the Hegelian philosophy — on account of its idealistic remoteness from social reality — soon gave way to a much more differentiated appreciation. To be sure, he emphatically condemned 'that philosophic dissolution and restoration of the empirical world'[52] which he identified in an embryonic form already in the *Phenomenology*. But at the same time he insisted with no less emphasis that it is an outstanding achievement that Hegel 'grasps the essence of *labour* and comprehends objective man — true, because real man — as the outcome of man's *own labour*.'[53] Just how great an achievement this was, may be appreciated by bearing in mind that now for the first time in history the possibility of elaborating a truly comprehensive historical conception had been created, in sharp contrast to the fragmentary insights of earlier thinkers. Why Hegel himself could not consistently live up to the standard of his own great achievement will be clear when we compare his conception of history with that of Marx. This comparison will also show why Marx had no need whatsoever for treating Hegel as a 'dead dog' and his dialectic as a 'dead horse' in order to go radically beyond him. He could generously acknowledge that '*Hegel's dialectic is the basic form of all dialectic*'[54] precisely because he could 'strip it of its mystical form' at the crucial points where the 'standpoint of political economy' turned the basic form of all dialectic into a forced construction, so that the 'mystical veil' should make the antagonistic social contradictions disappear from sight through their merely conceptual resolution.

The first major step Marx took in his critical appreciation of the Hegelian philosophy was concerned with politics: his primary preoccupation at the time. It was his political radicalism which separated him from his young Hegelian friends, and he was also critical of Feuerbach already in March 1843 for the latter's inadequate treatment of politics. The point Marx firmly made was that Feuerbach refers '*too much to nature and too little to politics*, although that is the only link through which present-day philosophy can become true.'[55] Thus he found Feuerbach wanting in this crucial respect right from the beginning and therefore he could put the author of *The Essence of Christianity* only to a very limited use. When he later emphasised that Feuerbach had much to answer for the production of an anti-dialectical climate in Germany, he explained the positive impact of Feuerbach's principal work by comparing it with Proudhon's best work, *What is Property?* (*Qu'est-ce que la propriété?*):

Proudhon's relation to S. Simon and Fourier is about the same as that of Feuerbach to Hegel. Compared with Hegel, Feuerbach is very poor. All the same he was epoch-making *after* Hegel, because he laid stress on certain points which were disagreeable to the Christian consciousness but important for the progress of criticism, and which Hegel had left in mystic semi-obscurity.[56]

As the 1843 critique shows, this assessment was no hindsight. Belabouring nature and heavily underscoring politics, clearly, could not really help Marx in accomplishing what he had set out to do: the elaboration of a dialectical conception of actual social development in place of Hegel's idealistic synthesis of ingenious conceptual transformations. He insisted that 'The entire mystery of the *Philosophy of Right* and of Hegelian philosophy in general' is contained in paragraphs 261 and 262 of this work[57] which justifies the political state by presenting the conditions 'as the conditioned, the determining as the determined, the producing as the product of its product.'[58] And he did not stop at simply stressing the *'pantheistic mysticism'*[59] involved in speculatively deriving the family and civil society from the idea of the state, thus overturning the actual relations in a way whereby 'The fact, which is the starting point, is not conceived to be such but rather to be the mystical result.'[60] Pointing to such reversals could not resolve by itself anything at all. On the contrary, it could only serve to give the semblance of a new-found rationality to extremely problematical, indeed contradictory, social structures by insisting that they are at the roots of the various ideological pictures. Such work of demystification — as, for instance, pointing out the connection between the earthly and the 'holy family' — must be complemented, if it is not to be turned into a new form of mystification, by an adequate analysis of the social contradictions which manifest in those problematical social structures themselves which in turn generate the mystifying images of false consciousness. The real object of criticism is always the *fundamental determinant* — in this case the specific mode of social metabolism which assigns the individuals to determinate (indeed, one could say 'predestined') functions within the boundaries of the unholy triad of the family, the civil society and the state — and not merely the however correct assertion of the *immediate determination* between the family and civil society on the one hand, and the political state on the other, which would leave all three just as massively standing as Feuerbach's critique of religion does not affect in the slightest the earthly family. The suggestion that one could have one side without the other naïvely and undialectically severs their necessary connections, giving the illusion of a solution in the form of a one-sided, false rationality: a great impoverishment with respect to Hegel — and this is why 'compared to Hegel, Feuerbach is very poor' — who undoubtedly puts into relief the dialectical interconnections, even if in a speculative form, as a set of 'logical-metaphysical determinations.'[61]

How can one avoid the 'dialectical circularity'[62] which characterises the Hegelian solution in that the development of dialectically interconnected moments is 'predestined by the nature of the concept'?[63] This is all the more important since all such 'dialectical circularity' leads a very uneasy existence on the very border of undialectical tautology.[64] Marx's answer consisted in breaking the circle while not only retaining the dialectical framework of explanation but simultaneously also revealing its real ground of determination. He showed that Hegel was forced into the kind of solution he gave because of the *unresolved antinomy*[65] between *external necessity and immanent end* in his conception of the actuality and ideality of the state. Since 'the standpoint of political economy' makes the solution of this antinomy impossible, though insisting on its solution (thus introducing another contradiction and determining the feasible lines of reasoning) 'empirical *actuality* is admitted *just as it is* and is also said to be *rational*; but not rational because of its own reason, but because the empirical fact in its empirical existence has a significance which is other than it itself... . The actual becomes phenomenon, but the Idea has no other content than this phenomenon.'[66] Thus it is the necessary retention of the underlying social contradiction which sunders the Idea from its content, degrading actuality to the status of mere phenomenality which of course calls for ideality as its counterpart and in its otherness its own ground of rationality. In this way an '*Idea–Subject* which is differentiated from the fact itself'[67] is speculatively generated, and in turn it produces the identical Subject–Object through which 'that philosophic dissolution and restoration of the empirical world (with all its actual contradictions) to which we referred earlier can be accomplished.

As we can see, Marx did not stop at the point of asserting the 'upside-down' character of the Hegelian conceptual framework, but pressed on to demonstrate its revealing ideological function, identifying the — for Hegel insoluble — contradiction as its fundamental ground of determination. Such an analysis pointed in the direction of the most radical *practical* conclusions. Just as he wrote one year earlier in his 'Comments on the Latest Prussian Censorship Instruction' that 'The real, *radical cure for censorship* would be its *abolition*',[68] he could see no solution to the problems of the state short of its radical negation and supersession, with all the necessary implications for the family and civil society. Indeed, it was in view of the insoluble contradictions of the 'civil society' (inseparably linked to the family) that the conclusion about the radical supersession of the state asserted itself as inescapable. Thesis X on Feuerbach — 'The standpoint of the old materialism is civil society; the standpoint of the new is human society, or social humanity' — put in a nutshell one of the most striking innovations of the Marxian philosophy. For the *whole*[69] of bourgeois philosophy treated as a self-evident axiom the constitution of human society as 'civil society', based on the irreconcilable antagonism of its individual members, which in turn predicated with an equally axiomatic validity the unquestionable necessity of the state as the benevolent manager of the pre-existing antagonisms, and consequently as the absolute *pre-condition* of social life as such. The outrageous logic of all such reasoning — which not only dualistically severed the rule-constituting political sphere from its material base, but simultaneously also established the absolute primacy of the political over social life of which it was in fact a historically specific manifestation and dimension — had to be called by its proper name, even if such logic of political legitimation assumed in Hegel an immensely complex and rather opaque form as compared to the relatively naïve transparency of the Hobbesian scheme. To envisage the reintegration of the political dimension with the material life-process of society, it was necessary to negate both the political state itself and that fictitious individualistic 'human nature' (the alleged producer of the irreconcilable antagonism) which reciprocally postulated one another in the self-sustaining ideological circle — a vicious circle if there ever has been one — of bourgeois rationality. 'Human society, or social humanity' as the standpoint of the new philosophy was the only basis on which an objectively unfolding process of social recuperation could be conceived, in opposition to the arbitrarily frozen historical dynamism as encapsulated in the various self-legitimating schemes of the state and civil society.

Another point that clearly emerges from the Marxian critique of Hegel's philosophy of right is that — contrary to Lukács's *History and Class Consciousness* and its followers — the 'identical Subject–Object' could not play a positive part in Marx's reasoning. On the contrary, it was precisely his critique of this problematic which helped Marx to reconstitute the dialectic on a radically different footing. Marx not only demonstrated the apologetic function of the identical Subject–Object in the Hegelian scheme of things — namely 'that philosophic dissolution and restoration of the empirical world' which we have seen above — but also put into relief that in order to make this ideological function possible, the objective dialectical factors had to be artificially dissolved by Hegel into the 'Idea–Subject and the fact itself' so as to be reunited again in the prefigured construct of legitimation. This is no place to enter into a discussion of the far reaching implications of this complex of problems in any detail. Let it suffice to indicate simply the diametrically opposed tendencies manifest in Marx's and in Hegel's approach. For insofar as the problematic of the identical Subject–Object can embody a movement, it is one tending towards a point of *rest*: the resolution of the originally postulated teleological end. In Marx, on the contrary, the movement is *open-ended* and its fundamental intent is subversive, not reconciliatory. And as far as the synthesis of the complex forces is concerned which makes intelligible the dynamism of social transformations, Marx's explanation — quite unlike Hegel — concentrates on:

1　The unity of the *individual and the collective subject* (of which the 'übergreifendes Moment' is the latter, even if it is given the most subtle conceptual and historical qualifications); and
2　the unity of *the ideal and the material*, mediated through the dialectic of *theory and praxis*.

Clearly, in both instances the feasible points of rest are of necessity strictly transient, amounting to a relative unity only, but never to identity,[70] while the superseding drive forward retains its ultimately overriding importance[71] — notwithstanding the partial stabilisation of determinate phases, and notwithstanding the institutional inertia which tends to petrify them — in the course of historical development.

Thus Marx's conception of the dialectic went beyond Hegel right from the moment of its inception in two fundamental respects, even if he continued to maintain that Hegel's dialectic is the basic form of all dialectic. First, the critique of the Hegelian transformation of the objective dialectic into a speculative conceptual edifice (through the dualistic opposition of the Idea–Subject to empirical existence degraded to mere phenomenality) established the interplay of objective forces as the true framework of dialectics and as the real ground of determination of even the most mediated subjective factors. And second, the demonstration of the ideological determinants of Hegel's speculative-conceptual dialectic — the 'philosophic dissolution and restoration of the empirical world' as an ahistorical construct which contradicted the profoundly historical potentialities of the Hegelian conception itself — emphatically put into relief the irrepressible dynamism of the actual historical developments, together with a precise indication of the necessary levers through which the revolutionary agency is enabled to intervene in accordance with its conscious aims in the positive unfolding of the objective dialectic. These accomplishments were *structurally incompatible* with Feuerbach's philosophy, and they were worked out by Marx in the years 1843–4 when, according to a crude schematism, he was supposed to be a 'Feuerbachian humanist'.

However, stressing the exemplary originality of Marx's approach should be no reason for minimising the immense philosophical significance of the Hegelian dialectic. Attempting a demonstration of the validity of the Marxian solutions merely in terms of their opposition to Hegel hopelessly distorts and underscores not only the historical importance of the Hegelian philosophy but also the real scope of Marx's own discourse, making it to be thoroughly dependent on the theoretical problematic of his great predecessor. Such an assessment, in other words, only manages to attack Hegel in the name of Marx while undermining Marx's own significance. In truth it was finding his own angle — a standpoint radically different from 'the standpoint of political economy' — which enabled Marx both to understand 'the entire mystery of Hegelian philosophy' and to appreciate its historical achievements notwithstanding its all too obvious mystifications. The radical negation of Hegel cannot be the measure of Marx's greatness, just as the lasting importance of the Hegelian achievements cannot be simply confined to their relative consonance with Marx.

While the unsparing critique of the Hegelian philosophy of right and of its unquestioning attitude towards the state was a necessary precondition for an adequate theoretical grasp of the historical dialectic, some of the more positive acquisitions of Hegel's conception became visible to Marx only after he had reached his own conclusions on the problems concerned. Thus to view such matters in terms of 'Hegelian influence' or an alleged liberation from it would be totally beside the point. To give a typical example, one of Marx's major discoveries concerned the role of *labour-power* as a commodity in the development of capitalism. Marx stressed in this respect the specificity of the capitalistic production relations in that the owner of labour-power could only sell his labour-power for a limited period, otherwise he would convert himself from the owner of a commodity into a commodity (a slave), thus undermining the necessary form of reproduction of the new mode of production. Obviously, Marx drew qualitatively different conclusions from this insight than Hegel could from the standpoint of political economy. However, the limitation of the Hegelian standpoint does not diminish in the least the importance of the fact itself that Hegel succeeded in identifying with great clarity the specificity mentioned above, and Marx did not hesitate for a moment to acknowledge this when he quoted in *Capital* the relevant passage from none other than the *Philosophy of Right*:

I may make over to another the use, *for a limited time*, of my particular *bodily and mental aptitudes and capabilities*; because, in consequence of this restriction, they are impressed with a character of alienation with regard to me as a whole. But by the alienation of all my labour-time and the whole of my work, I should be converting the substance itself, in other words, my general activity and reality, my person, into the property of another.[72]

Similarly, the instrument of production as the crucial mediatory factor in human development has a paramount importance in Marx's theory:

An instrument of labour is a thing, or a complex of things, which the labourer interposes between himself and the subject of his labour, and which serves as the conductor of his activity. He makes use of the mechanical, physical, and chemical properties of some substances in order to make other substances subservient to his aims.[73]

Clearly, the problem at stake involves a principle of the highest order, with the most far-reaching consequences for the understanding of the historical dialectic, and for the reasons which we have seen earlier it would be most unreasonable to expect the philosopher who assigns to empirical existence the status of mere phenomenality to articulate it along the same lines as Marx. What is significant, however, is that even if in a highly abstract form (indeed, with a touch of mysticism in the mode of its expression) the crucial dialectical principle of mediation is defined by Hegel at the highest level of philosophical generality as the interplay of factors which follow their own inherent logic of unfolding, as we can see in the footnote Marx added to his own formulation: 'Reason is just as cunning as she is powerful. Her cunning consists principally in her *mediating activity*, which, by causing objects to act and re-act on each other *in accordance with their own nature*, in this way, without any direct interference in the process, carries out reason's intentions.'[74]

We can notice a significant change in Marx's orientation with respect to Hegel's *Logic* in particular. In the *Critique of Hegel's Philosophy of Right* he treated with utmost sarcasm 'the holy register of the Santa Casa (the *Logic*)'[75] and he complained that 'Hegel's true interest is not the philosophy of right but logic. The philosophical task is not the embodiment of thought in determinate political realities, but the evaporation of these realities in abstract thought. The philosophical moment is not the logic of fact but the fact of logic.'[76] Which was all right as far as it went, but it did not go deep enough. For it remained oblivious to a vital dimension of the *Logic*, namely the systematic elaboration of the principles which constitute 'the basic form of all dialectic', even if shrouded in mystical veil.

The Hegelian logic was in fact the outcome of two fundamental determinations: one extremely problematical and the other far less so. (That is to say, the second was problematical only to the extent to which it was necessarily tied to the first and therefore was bound to suffer its consequences.) The author of the *Critique of Hegel's Philosophy of Right* was acutely aware of the first — namely the ideological transsubstantiation of determinate social-political realities into logical-metaphysical determinations so that they can evaporate in one sense only to be restored in another — but he had at the time very little concern for the other. Once, however, he identified the task as the systematic investigation of the nature of capital and of the manifold conditions of its socio-historical supersession — which inevitably put the earlier prevalent concern with politics in perspective, as 'the political-legal superstructure' the contradictions of which cannot be unravelled on their own but only in the context of a precise understanding of the material base and of its complex dialectical interactions with the totality of highly mediated social structures — the need for a dialectical totalisation of the whole complex became imperative. For now Marx had to investigate not only the given realities (and still less only the 'determinate political realities') but also various embryonic forces and tendencies, together with their most far-reaching ramifications and implications, in the framework of a rigorous dialectical assessment. Working out the full implications of complex problems, putting into relief the rich connections of their inner determinations, following consistently and systematically their developments to their logical conclusions 'in accordance with their own nature', anticipating their future developments on the basis of their objective determinations as opposed to simply postulating uselessly abstract possibilities — all this had to be done in *Capital*, and to do it was conceivable only in the form of a dialectical totalisation. Significantly enough, the constantly recurring category in the *Grundrisse* and in *Capital* is '*Sichsetzen*'[77] or 'self-positing', which in a way sums up the mode in which objective determinations appear and assert themselves in the course of actual socio-historical development. The inspiration in the use of this and similar categories[78] is, of course, Hegel. Not in the sense of some problematical 'influence' which would leave a foreign element in the body of Marxian thought, but categories considered as '*Daseinsformen*'[79] in the framework of a profoundly original theory are transferred from Hegel into Marx's universe of discourse and reactivated there with a qualitatively different meaning.

All the same, Marx was anxious to stress, more than anybody else, that it was Hegel who first produced a coherent system of dialectical categories — even if in a highly abstract and speculative form — which put him far above his predecessors and contemporaries. In a letter to Engels Marx stated that Comte is '*miserable* compared to Hegel. Although Comte, as a professional mathematician and physicist, was superior to him, i.e. superior in matters of *detail*, even here Hegel is *infinitely greater as a whole*.'[80] It was Hegel's unprecedented ability to make his totalising conception of dialectical categories bear on all matters of detail — whenever, that is, ideological determinations did not structurally prevent him from doing so — which made him infinitely superior to all positivist worshippers of reified 'fact' and lifeless 'science'.[81]

In a letter quoted above, Marx made a similar point about his own work. As we have seen, he stressed that 'Lange is naïve enough to say that I "move with rare freedom" in empirical matter. He hasn't the least idea that this "free movement in matter" is nothing but the paraphrase for the *method* of dealing with matter — that is, the *dialectical method*.'[82] The 'free movement in matter' when, as in Hegel's case, the matter in question has been transposed into the homogeneous medium of a speculative-conceptual universe, was relatively easy, as compared to the task Marx himself had to accomplish. For he could not merely explore the intricate logic of his concepts on their own, but constantly had to refer them back to empirical reality. Having masterfully succeeded in doing so, in the framework of a dialectical philosophical conception firmly anchored to actuality, is the true measure of Marx's intellectual greatness.

Notes

1 K. Marx, *Theses on Feuerbach* (Spring 1845). Italics indicate emphases added by myself.
2 K. Marx, *Introduction to the Critique of the Hegelian Philosophy of Right* (December 1843–January 1844).
3 *Ibid.*
4 *Ibid.*
5 The last three quotations are from Marx's letter to his father, Berlin, 10 November 1837.
6 *Ibid.*
7 *Ibid.*
8 *Ibid.*
9 Letter by Moses Hess to Berthold Auerbach, Berlin, 2 September 1841.
10 In this respect see chapter VIII. 'The Controversy about Marx' of I. Mészáros, *Marx's Theory of Alienation* (London, 1970).
11 From Marx's letter to his father quoted above.
12 'There is no history of politics, law, science, etc., of art, religion, etc.' (Marx's note on the manuscript of *The German Ideology*, London, 1965, p. 671);

Since the Young Hegelians consider conceptions, thoughts, ideas, in fact all the products of consciousness, to which they attribute an *independent existence*, as the real chains of men (just as the Old Hegelians declared them the true bonds of human society) it is evident that the Young Hegelians have to fight only against these illusions of the consciousness.; . . . Morality, religion, metaphysics, all the rest of ideology and their corresponding forms of consciousness, . . . no longer retain the *semblance of independence*. They have no history, no development; but men, developing their material production and their material intercourse, alter, along with this their real existence, their thinking and the products of their thinking. . . . If these theorists treat really historical subjects, as for instance the eighteenth century, they merely give a history of the ideas of the times, torn away from the facts and the practical development fundamental to them. (*Ibid.* pp. 30, 38, 53.)

13 'When reality is depicted, *philosophy as an independent branch of knowledge* loses its medium of existence.' (*Ibid.* p. 38).
14 Division of labour only becomes truly such from the moment when a division of material and mental labour appears. From this moment onwards consciousness *can* really flatter itself that it is something other than consciousness of existing practice, that it *really* represents something without representing something real; from now on consciousness is in a position to emancipate itself from the world and to proceed to the formation of 'pure' theory, theology, philosophy, ethics, etc. (*Ibid.* p. 43).
15 *Ibid.*

16 The expression is from Marx's Introduction to the *Grundrisse*, but the idea itself dates back to the early 1840s.

17 These quotations are from *The German Ideology*, *op. cit.* pp. 46–8. A marginal note by Marx to *The German Ideology* reads as follows: 'Universality corresponds to (1) the class versus the state, (2) the competition, world-wide intercourse, etc., (3) the great numerical strength of the ruling class, (4) the illusion of the *common* interests (in the beginning the illusion is true), (5) the delusion of the ideologists and the division of labour.' (*ibid*. pp. 62–3). As we can see, Marx is talking about very important objective factors, and one should not misinterpret the terms 'illusion' and 'delusion' in a subjectivistic-voluntaristic sense. For he himself explicitly states that 'common interest' is very real in the first place (it becomes an illusion in the course of the development of capitalistic contradictions) and by linking the 'delusion of the ideologists' to the division of labour he reasserts his view about the need for an objective practical supersession of such manifestations of consciousness.

18 *Ibid*. pp. 84–5.

19 K. Marx, *Grundrisse* (London, 1973), p. 706.

20 K. Marx, *Capital* (Moscow, 1957), vol. III., p. 800.

21 F. Engels, 'Ludwig Feuerbach and the End of Classical German Philosophy', in *Marx-Engels: Selected Works* (Moscow, 1951), vol. II., p. 349.

22 *Ibid*.

23 K. Marx, F. Engels, *Collected Works* (London, 1975), vol. I, p. 17.

24 *Ibid*.

25 *Ibid*. p. 18.

26 *Ibid*. p. 19.

27 F. Engels, 'Feuerbach and the End of Classical German Philosophy', *op. cit.* pp. 330–1.

28 *Ibid*. p. 331.

29 Marx was always anxious to stress the fundamental distinction between levels of analysis — corresponding to qualitatively different types of social phenomena — to which appropriately different methods of enquiry must apply. He wrote in 1859:

The changes in the economic foundation lead sooner or later to the transformation of the whole immense superstructure. In studying such transformations it is always *necessary to distinguish* between the *material transformation* of the economic conditions of production, which can be determined with the *precision of natural science*, and the legal, political, religious, artistic or philosophic — in short, *ideological forms* in which men become conscious of this conflict and *fight it out*. (*A Contribution to the Critique of Political Economy*, London, 1971, p. 21.)

Clearly, there is no sign whatsoever of a 'scientistic reductionism': on the contrary, the impossibility of such reductionism is rigorously asserted. Nor is there any wavering between 'empiricist scientism' and 'romantic Hegelianism'. Instead we find the establishment of a clear line of demarcation between different forms of social praxis, pointing to a need for methods of analysis appropriate to 'material transformations', the 'ideological forms', and to the complex interactions of the two. Indeed, Marx repeatedly scorned bourgeois political economy for its attempt at reducing complex human relations into categories subsumed under claimed natural laws:

> The *crude materialism* of the economists who regard as the *natural properties of things* what are *social relations* of production among people, and qualities which things obtain because they are subsumed under these relations, is at the same time *just as crude an idealism*, even *fetishism*, since it imputes social relations to things as inherent characteristics, and thus mystifies them. (*Grundrisse*, p. 687).

Even when he asserted the necessary implications of socio-economic developments in England for the Continent of Europe, he hastened to add that on the Continent the consequences 'will take a form more brutal or more humane, *according to the degree of development of the working-class itself.*' (*Capital*, vol. I, p. 9). It goes without saying, the latter cannot be determined 'with the precision of natural science', and since the development of a complex social totality always involves a multiplicity of qualitatively different factors, even the analysis of the material transformation of the economic conditions of production must be always qualified by the necessary implications of the manifold *dialectical interconnections*. Social processes, according to Marx, are inseparable from their *historical determinations*, and thus they cannot be forced into the Procrustean bed of immutable 'natural laws', conceived on the model of a schematic 'natural science'. In sharp contrast to scientism Marx identified the necessity manifest in social processes as *historical necessity* (*historische Notwendigkeit*) and he defined it as a *disappearing necessity* ('*eine verschwindende Notwendigkeit*', *Grundrisse*, pp. 831–2.), thanks to the active involvement of the human agency in all such processes which therefore must be opposed in principle to any form of reductionism.

30 Natural science has invaded and transformed human life all the more *practically* through the medium of industry; and has prepared human emancipation, however directly and much it had to consummate dehumanisation. *Industry* is the actual historical relation of nature, and therefore of natural science, to man. If, therefore, industry is conceived as the *exoteric* revelation of man's *essential power* we also gain an understanding of the *human* essence of nature or the *natural* essence of man. In consequence, natural science will lose its *abstractly material* — or rather, its *idealistic* — tendency, and will become the *basis of human science*, as it has already become the *basis of actual human life*, albeit in an estranged form. One basis for life and another basis for *science* is *a priori* a lie. (K. Marx, *Economic and Philosophic Manuscripts of 1844*, pp. 110–1).

31 *The German Ideology*, pp. 37–8.

32 *Ibid.* p. 38.

33 *Ibid.* p. 50.

34 *Ibid.* pp. 37–8.

35 In other words, through the reorientation of philosophy as 'real, positive science' concerned with 'the representation of the practical activity, of the practical process of development of men.' *The German Ideology*, p. 38.

36 *Ibid.* Translation is my own. Rendering '*Betrachtung*' is particularly difficult. In addition to 'surveying' it also means 'consideration', 'contemplation', 'meditation', 'reflection', 'observation', etc. When we talk

about a synthesis based on the comprehensive historical development of men, the empiricist immediacy of 'observation' is clearly out of place.

37 K. Marx, *Difference between the Democritean and Epicurean Philosophy of Nature, Marx-Engels, Collected Works*, vol. I, p. 85.
38 *Ibid.*
39 See *ibid.* p. 86.
40 *Ibid.*
41 Having defined the 'immediate realisation of philosophy' as the *objective* aspect of the problem, Marx turns to the *subjective* aspect:

> This is *the relationship of the philosophical system* which is realised *to its intellectual carriers*, to the *individual self-consciousnesses* in which its progress appears. This relationship results in what confronts the world in the realisation of philosophy itself, namely, in the fact that these individual self-consciousnesses always carry a *double-edged demand*, one edge turned against the world, the other against philosophy itself. . . . Their liberation of the world from un-philosophy is at the same time their own liberation from the philosophy that held them in fetters as a particular system. (*Ibid.*, pp. 85–6).

42 K. Marx, Preface to *A Contribution to the Critique of Political Economy*, January 1859.
43 *Collected Works*, vol. I, p. 337.
44 Marx to Dagobert Oppenheim, 25 August 1842, *Werke*, vol. 27, p. 409.
45 K. Marx, 'Introduction to the Critique of the Hegelian Philosophy of Right.'
46 The reason why this is of a capital importance is that the *same phenomena*, inasmuch as the competing classes are directly involved, appear quite different as viewed from the opposite standpoint, and thus yield *radically different* interpretations. As Marx noted in the *Grundrisse* (p. 832): 'this process of *objectification* appears in fact as a process of *alienation* from the standpoint of labour, and as *appropriation* from the standpoint of capital.' Marx's critical adoption of the standpoint of labour meant a conception of the proletariat not simply as a sociological force diametrically opposed to the standpoint of capital — and thus remaining in the latter's orbit — but as a *self-transcending* historical force which cannot help superseding alienation (that is, the historically given form of objectification) in the process of realising its own ends that happen to coincide with 'reappropriation'. For Marx's remarks on the proletariat as the 'universal class' in this sense, see his 'Introduction to the Critique of the Hegelian Philosophy of Right.'
47 'Hegel's standpoint is that of modern political economy. He grasps *labour* as the *essence* of man — as man's essence in the act of proving itself: he sees only the positive, not the negative side of labour.' *Economic and Philosophic Manuscripts of 1844* (London, 1959), p. 152.
48 See in this respect Marx's letter to Engels, 2 April, 1858.
49 V.I. Lenin, *Collected Works*, vol. 38, p. 180.
50 To Engels, 11 January 1868.
51 To Kugelmann, 27 June 1870.
52 *Economic and Philosophic Manuscripts of 1844*, p. 150.
53 *Ibid.* p. 151.
54 To Kugelmann, 6 March 1868.
55 K. Marx, F. Engels, *Werke*, vol. 27, p. 417.
56 To Schweitzer, 24 January 1865.

57 K. Marx, *Critique of Hegel's Philosophy of Right* (Cambridge, 1970), p. 9.

58 *Ibid.*

59 *Ibid.* p. 7.

60 *Ibid.* p. 9.

61 *Ibid.* p. 18.

62 To use Sartre's expression. See his *Critique of Dialectical Reason*, especially its Introduction.

63 *Critique of Hegel's Philosophy of Right*, p. 15.

64 In fact Marx often points to such tautologies. See for instance his *Critique of Hegel's Philosophy of Right*, p. 11, and also his Introduction to the *Grundrisse*.

65 *Critique of Hegel's Philosophy of Right* p. 16.

66 *Ibid.* p. 9.

67 *Ibid.*

68 K. Marx and F. Engels, *Collected Works*, vol. I, p. 131.

69 No doubt, what Marx meant to stress in his aphorism was that *even* the materialistic approaches — including Feuerbach's — remained anchored to the standpoint of civil society shared also by the classical political economists.

70 Not even at the moments of the 'apocalypse': a concept which plays such a vital role in Sartre's thought, from some early works to the *Critique of Dialectical Reason*.

71 In view of this, it is amazing to find accusations of 'Millennial utopianism' and of 'bringing history to a standstill' levelled against Marx.

72 K. Marx, *Capital*, vol. I, p. 168. (cf. also p. 293 of the *Grundrisse*.)

73 *Ibid.* vol. I, p. 179.

74 *Ibid.* (The quote is from Hegel's *Enzyklopädie*, Pt. I., *Die Logik*, Berlin, 1840, p. 382).

75 *Critique of Hegel's Philosophy of Right*, op cit. p. 15.

76 *Ibid.* p. 18.

77 For lack of space, let us see only two examples. The first concerns capital in relation to circulation and exchange value:

The first quality of capital is . . . that circulation is not the movement of its disappearance, but rather the movement of its real self-positing [*Sichsetzen*] as exchange value, its self-realisation as exchange value. It cannot be said that exchange value as such is realised in simple circulation. It is always realised only in the moment of its disappearance. (*Grundrisse*, pp. 259–60).

The second analyses the value-positing (*Wertsetzen*) function of capital:

Capital is now posited . . . as not merely sustaining itself formally, but as *realising itself as value*, as value relating to itself as value in every one of the moments of its metamorphosis, in which it appears at one time as money, at another time as commodity, then again as exchange value, then again as use value. The passage from one moment to the other appears as a particular process, but each of these processes is the transition to the other. Capital is thus posited as value-in-process, which is capital in every moment. It is thus posited as *circulating capital*; in every moment capital, and circulating from one form into the next. The point of return is at the same time the point of departure and vice versa — namely the *capitalist*. All capital is originally circulating capital, product of circulation, as well as producing circulation, *tracing in this way its own course. (Ibid.* p. 536).

78 They are far too numerous even to be mentioned, ranging from '*Fürsichsein*' and '*Sein für andres*' to '*Aufhebung*', 'negation of the negation', etc. Let us see, instead, an unexpected but important distinction between 'boundary' and 'barrier' which Marx adopted with reference to the Hegelian *Logic*:

Every boundary [*Grenze*] is and has to be a barrier [*Schranke*] for it [that is, capital]. Else it would cease to be capital — money as self-reproductive. If ever it perceived a certain boundary not as a barrier, but became comfortable within it as a boundary, it would itself have declined from exchange value to use value, from the general form of wealth to a specific, substantial mode of the same. . . . The quantitative boundary of the surplus value appears to [capital] as a mere natural barrier, as a necessity which it constantly tries to violate and beyond which it constantly seeks to go.

And the relevant passages in Hegel's *Logic* read as follows: 'Something's own boundary posited by it as a negative which is at the same time essential, is not merely boundary as such but barrier.' 'The sentient creature, in the limitation of hunger, thirst, etc., is the drive to go beyond its limiting barrier, and it does overcome it.' (*Grundrisse*, pp. 334–5.)

79 See Marx's Introduction to the *Grundrisse* in particular.
80 To Engels, 25 July 1866.
81 Cf. Marx's letters to Engels, 1 February 1858 and to Schweitzer, 24 January 1865.
82 To Kugelmann, 27 June 1870.

6 MARX AND THE QUEST FOR COMMUNIST LIBERTY
Nicola Badaloni

Part I: On the Depreciation of Capital

In a letter dated 14 August 1881, Marx discusses Proudhon's theory of capital with Engels. For Proudhon, says Marx, 'the pure affirmation of capital is interest': profit is no more than 'a particular form of wage'.[1] If interest is eliminated, we once again have a healthy bourgeois society. When Proudhon proposes reducing the rate of interest to *annuité*, his yardstick, quite patently, is that which normally prevails in bourgeois society. No one in actual fact has ever received (or is ever likely to receive) interest in the form conceived by Price. Marx writes:

Capital fails to pay its own interest: but not only that: it also fails to reproduce itself in such a manner as to maintain its value. And because of this simple law the value is originally determined by initial production costs, according to the labour time that was originally required for the object itself to be produced. Once produced, however, its price is determined by the costs necessary to reproduce it. And the costs of reproduction fall constantly and more rapidly the more an era is industrialised. Hence the law of the constant depreciation of the value of capital itself. This puts paid to the law of rent and interest which would otherwise lead to absurdity. This, moreover, explains the thesis [put forward by Engels] that no factory covers its own production costs, so that Proudhon is unable to rejuvenate society by introducing a law to which it already basically conforms without need of his advice.[2]

This letter follows a discussion between the two friends in the course of which Marx had devised a project to bring about the lowering of interest rates by founding 'a national bank with a monopoly of paper currency so that gold and silver are withdrawn from circulation'.[3] Engels had objected that such a plan would fail because it would constrain small tradesmen to resort to usurers. The increase in the money supply would only help the big businessman. Nonetheless, Marx's argument is not groundless. The classical thesis (even Ricardo's) was that the paper currency had to be proportionate to the shifts in gold, and hence increase when gold flowed in during a phase of expanding production and intensive export, and decrease in a time of depression, when it was the export of gold that was increasing. For Marx, however, the bank in this second case would have to act in the opposite

137

way, stimulating rather than restricting the mechanisms of exchange. In other words, the demand for greater liquidity would have to be satisfied. If it acted in any other way, the bank would be interfering 'unnecessarily', aggravating 'the crisis developing in the market'.[4] Marx arrived at this conclusion in the conviction that the intensification of movement in the currency, whether in the form of paper money or gold, did not act as a cause but as an effect 'of the greater quantity of capital set to work'.[5] The depression could be effectively combated by increasing the money supply, that is to say by devaluing the existing capital, the debts that had been contracted, the rate of interest and the stock, thus giving fresh impetus to profits at the expense of wealth accumulated and legitimised in the form of property.

Engels is in only partial agreement with this proposal. He believes that the depression in itself sets the currency free to some extent, acting spontaneously upon it. It is true that in the course of a depression the circulation of money perceptibly decreases 'only at the end' and that 'this process begins spontaneously at the outset of the depression, even if it is impossible to put one's finger on it in individual cases'.[6] Engels nonetheless fails to see the point of intervening in the spontaneous chain of the various movements of circulation, whereas Marx perceives that an action upon the interest rate which is not dictated by the immediate preoccupations of the bank could attenuate the effects of the commercial crisis because the depreciation of capital would have positive effects upon the rate of profit.

Marx, as is well known, had been concerned with this problem of depreciation in *The Poverty of Philosophy*. In this work, following Ricardo, he had written that the law of value as a measure of real labour was also 'the law of the continual *depreciation* of labour... . There will be depreciation not only of the commodities brought into the market, but also of the instruments of production and of whole plants'.[7] To counteract this uninterrupted process of depreciation, Marx had then proposed a 'new agreement', which was based upon the sum total of productive forces (immediate labour as an index of the productive possibilities of accumulated labour) and the sum total of needs. He wrote:

It is in the nature of large-scale industry that working hours should be equal for all. What is today the result of capital and the competition of workers among themselves will be tomorrow, if you sever the relation between labour and capital, an actual agreement based upon the relation between the sum of productive forces and the sum of existing needs.

But such an agreement is a condemnation of individual exchange, and we are back again at our first conclusion!

In principle, there is no exchange of products — but there is the exchange of the labour which co-operates in production. The mode of exchange of products depends upon the mode of exchange of the productive forces.[8]

The social relations 'produced by men' who are 'authors and . . . actors of their own history', develop this history by a triple movement: a 'growth' in productive forces, a 'destruction' in social relations, and a 'formation' in ideas.[9]

In present society founded on wage labour, the three models of rationality indicated here (accumulation of knowledge and technology, hence increased valorisation; the criticism, des-truction and restructuring of knowledge and technology, hence depreciation; the changes in social relationships, hence the formation of ideas), operate under the spur of competition. The basic condition is the development of the productive forces (the logic of accumulation and expansion). But this arises within the framework of capitalism only through competition, the continual destruction (depreciation) of these same productive forces (whether living or dead). This double movement takes on the historical form of the contrast between accumulated labour (which has become private property) and the creation of new profit. The positive condition for valorisation is indubitably the injection into the system of new labour-power. Nevertheless, this would not be enough to charge the system with the necessary mobility without the negative condition, namely the depreciation of both living and accumulated labour. In a time of crisis, capital does no hesitate to reorganise itself. The capitalist system of production can function because the sum total of productive forces, both present and past (the available social labour) is exposed to tensions and antagonisms (a reduction in the labour time necessary for the reproduction of labour-power and the depreciation of accumulated capital). Capital is 'Accumulated labour which serves as a means of new production'.[10]

The early 1850s were the watershed between Marx the critic of ideology and theorist of the driving forces in history and Marx the critic of political economy. The attention he pays to the problem of the depreciation of capital, both as internal contradiction and as the instrument of the system's vitality, indicates that he attributes great importance to the phenomenon of competition in connection with the need for depreciation and crises. In the letter we have examined there is something more besides, namely an indication of possible ways of intervening in the negative

movement where depreciation occurs. A process which arises
spontaneously within the capitalist system can be consciously
regulated, within certain limits, by an economic policy.
Bourgeois society institutionalises private property and tends to
turn it into the reason for the security and sometimes even the
livelihood of individual property-owners; and it is precisely for
this reason that capital, which is its very basis, must continually
modify its proportions of value. History, as the terrain on which
accumulation occurs, becomes the stage for this play which turns
the depreciation of wealth into an instrument for setting out to
produce and accumulate new wealth. The philosophy of capital is
the philosophy of the crisis of what has historically occurred, and,
within the limits which derive from the reproduction of the former
conditions, of the creation of new levels of equilibrium. The
positive condition of this continual imbalance is that it always
keeps the door open for renewed accumulation.

**Part II: Inflation, Wages and the Positive Condition for
Accumulation**

The outline of an explanation of the relationship between
variation in the monetary value of commodities and the
movement of wages is to be found in another of Marx's letters to
Engels, written on 22 April 1868. Marx says:

> I will only give you a short account now of a 'little thing' which occurred to me as
> I was just glancing at the part of my manuscript dealing with the rate of profit.
> Thanks to it one of the most difficult questions is simply solved. The question is,
> namely, how it happens that when the value of money, i.e., of gold, is falling, the
> rate of profit rises, while it falls when the value of money rises... .
>   If, when the value of money is falling, the price of labour does not rise to the
> same degree, then it falls, the rate of surplus value rises, and therefore, all other
> things remaining the same, the rate of profit also. The rise of the latter — so long
> as the ascendant oscillation in the value of money continues — is simply due to
> the fall in wages, and this fall is due to the fact that the change in wages only
> slowly accommodates itself to the change in the value of money.[11]

Here Marx discusses the question of price inflation in relation
to variations in the profit level. Prices change more quickly than
the cost of labour-power. This is a problem Marx had tackled in
vol. III of *Capital*, where he had maintained that an increase in
the monetary value of the profit level was incapable of producing
a real reduction in wages because the increase had to be
accompanied by 'an increase in wages, and also an increase in the
price of commodities forming the constant capital'.[12] In the letter
quoted above the question is further clarified, and a new

observation is introduced. He is concerned with the different rates of this proportional alignment, which result in an increase in the surplus value, and hence in the profit. For a certain length of time, the market price of wages fails to adjust to the changes in the nominal value of profits, which is thereby rendered not merely nominal but actual. Moreover, Marx discusses whether the phenomonen has exhausted all its effects when a levelling-off is achieved between the price of labour and the value of money. The theoreticians (including Ricardo) reply that at this point both the wage and the profit are expressed in a greater quantity of money, and hence that nothing is changed; to this the 'specialists who are concerned with the history of prices [that is, the practical men] reply with facts'.[13] In reality, if we assume that 'the elements, or some elements, of the *constant* part of the capital fall in value owing to the greater productivity of labour, whose products they are', and if 'their fall in value only corresponds to the fall in the value of money', 'their price remains unchanged'.[14]

The matter can also be expressed as follows: the time required to restore the balance between surplus value and wages is normally used by capital to increase the productivity of labour in a given branch of production. When the prices, including those of wages, come back into balance, the rate of surplus value and that of profit are found to be increasing in relation to a simultaneous and unobserved development in the productivity of labour. The restoration of balance seems to have come about through the increase in monetary wages to the old level. But in the meantime the old balance has again been upset, since there has been a hidden increase in the productivity of labour. This creates a drop in the value of the constant capital. The effect is an increase in the rate of profit. The combination of a system of exchange with the availability of a better technology also produces modifications in the prices of the constant part of capital. An extreme case would arise when technological development had induced a drop in the prices of the elements of constant capital (or at least some of them) which would perfectly balance the monetary increase. In this case the fall in the value of money and hence the rise in the prices of all the other goods would result in contrary changes in wages and surplus value, leaving the rate of profit unchanged. Besides, while the rate of surplus value at the end of the pendulum movement would achieve balance, the rise in the rate of profit would be greater if 'the value of the constant capital dropped faster than the value of money, and less if it dropped more slowly'.[15]

The productivity of labour, especially in industries proper, thus receives a stimulus 'from the falling value of money, the mere inflation of money prices, and the general international scramble for the increased mass of money'.[16] Extending the case from a single branch so as to embrace the entire system of production, one can observe how

the extent . . . to which in the one case the increase in the rate of profit with the fall in the value of money and in the other fall in the rate of profit with the increase in the value of money acts upon the *general rate of profit* will partly depend upon the *relative increase* in the particular branches of production in which the change takes place, partly upon the *duration* of the change, because the rise and fall of the rate of profit within the particular branches of industry need time to affect the others. If the fluctuation is only temporary, it remains local.[17]

In the case that Marx outlines, the model of exchange is combined with a direct reference to the theme of the development of productivity. His reasoning is based on the premise that the apparent movements whereby balance is restored conceal an actual variation in the rate of profit, which in practice tends generally to increase. To explain this variation, one must hypothesize the combined effect of the variation in relations of exchange on the price of labour, and its function as stimulant to the development of productivity. Behind the monetary movement, which tends towards balance, there is another tendency, hidden from view and acting differently. This is the tendency, virtually constant in capitalist production, to develop the productivity of labour. Its effect is to increase the rate of profit.

We have here, in a nutshell, two problems which were to remain at the centre of Marx's thought. Firstly, there is the system of relationships which allows the exchange between capital and the labour-power to be transformed into the fundamental condition for the maintenance and development of private property, the devision of labour and class domination. Secondly, there is this increase in the productivity of labour, which, given the foregoing premises, permanently operates in favour of the dominant classes. In Marx, the two questions become the single problem of the way (or ways) in which, by a change in social relationships, the increase in the productivity of labour may be diverted into a different channel. His entire theoretical construction is directed towards rendering visible within the complex interrelationships of exchange those which canalise the development of the productive forces towards class domination, while at the same time allowing one to perceive how the very highlighting of these channels in the analysis not only renders them visible as such, but also shows that no logical or natural necessity attaches to them, but a historical necessity that depends upon factual presuppositions taken into the system and assimilated by it. For this reason the analysis of the capitalist system was never separated in Marx from legal relationships and in particular those governing property, and he refused to adopt the reductive point of view of Ricardo where the existing relations of production became those which reflected in absolute, without mediations or diaphragms, the development of the productive forces. On the other hand, this analysis never lost sight of the problem that Ricardo had tackled: the development of the productive forces. It is not only a question of seeing how the old relations of exchange reappear under the new circumstances. That could lead to Proudhon's illusion that by reducing their autonomy, they could pave the way for a more civilised organisation of society. It is rather a question of creating conditions whereby new social relationships — freer ones — may make the increased productivity of labour available to all.

Part III: On Bourgeois Power and the Enrichment of the Individual

The depreciation of existing capital and labour-power derives from the relations of exchange; the increase in the productivity of labour derives from the interference of science and technology within exchange. Exchange appropriates human nature just as it appropriates man's intelligence and his capacity to make use of things. The reduction of human nature to mercantile relationships of exchange and the identification of the individual with private property are not concepts that Marx invented but assertions repeated and defended by almost all the philosophers of his age. It is Marx who critically maintains that 'natural human talents' are something different from the aptitudes of other species. They are not so much the cause as the effect of the division of labour.[18] At the centre of Marx's attention are the theories of the *idéologues*, especially Destutt de Tracy, according to whom (and to J.B. Say) society is a series of reciprocal exchanges, and production cannot occur without exchange. Ricardians like James Mill had attacked the monetary system, but this attack, says Marx, for 'all its ingenuity . . . cannot lead to a decisive victory'. Indeed,

the primitive economic superstitions of people and governments cling to tangible, palpable and visible bags of money and hold that the sole reality of wealth lies in the absolute value of the precious metals and in the possession of them. Of course, the enlightened, wordly-wise economist comes along and proves to them that money is a commodity like any other and its value, like that of any other commodity, depends on the relations between the costs of production and supply and demand (competition), between the costs and the quantity of competition of other commodities. However, such an economist will be confounded by the observation that the *real* value of things is their exchange value and that in the last analysis this resides in money, which resides in its turn in the precious metals and that consequently money is the *true* value of things and the most desirable thing of all. The economist's theories in fact amount to the same thing except that his powers of abstraction enable him to perceive the existence of money behind all the commodity forms and destroy his faith in the exclusive value of its official metal existence. The existence of money in metal is only the official, visible expression of the money-soul which has percolated all the productions and movements of civil society.

The opposition of the modern economists to the money system does not go beyond the fact that they view money in its abstract and general form. [19]

Further on, Marx observes:

Economics — like the process of reality itself — begins with the relations between men as relations between private property owners. If we proceed from the premise that man is a private property owner, i.e. an exclusive owner whose exclusive ownership permits him both to preserve his personality and to distinguish himself from other men, as well as relate to them, if we assume that private property is man's personal, *distinguishing* and hence essential existence — then it follows that the loss or sacrifice of that private property signifies the *alienation of the man* as much as of the *property* itself. [20]

Money 'possesses the *property* of being able to buy everything and appropriate all objects, [it is] the *object* most worth possessing';[21] money, as the existing and active concept of value, confounds and exchanges everything; it is the universal *confusion* and *exchange* of all things, an inverted world, the confusion and exchange of all natural and human qualitites.'[22]

In contrast to the alienation of money stands man as an objective being, as a being who needs objects to perpetuate his own natural existence, and needs social relationships to enrich himself. At the root of Marx's idea of man as an objective being lies a new vision of objectivity, intimately connected to the need for objects, and a new idea of exchange as a social relation between individual human beings. Marx writes that 'A being which is not itself an object for a third being has no being for its *object*, i.e. it has no objective relationships and its existence is not objective.'[23] In the present state of things:

the social relation I bear to you, the labour I perform to satisfy your need, is likewise merely an *appearance* and our mutual supplementing of each other is equally but an appearance, based on our mutual plundering of each other. The intention to *plunder*, to *deceive*, inevitably lurks in the background, for, since our exchange is self-interested on your side as on mine, and since every self-interested person seeks to outdo the other, we must necessarily strive to deceive each other. Of course, in order for the power which I confer upon my own possession at the expense of yours to become a real power, it must be *acknowledged* by you. But our mutual recognition of the mutual power of our possessions is a struggle and the victory in the struggle goes to the man who has the greater energy, strength, insight or agility. If my physical strength is great enough, I will plunder you directly. If the realm of physical force has been neutralised then we each attempt to delude the other and the shrewdest will get the better of the bargain.[24]

The contrast between the objective human being and the alienated reality of mercantile relations — and these too are objective, but reduced to a mere appearance — does not consist in a regression to a state prior to and outside exchange, but in a reappropriation of the alienated social objectivity. The point of departure is the new situation in which 'each of us really *does* act out the role in which the other casts him'. Another person's production 'signifies expressly: *the acquisition* of my object . . . Our mutual value, then , is the *value* of our mutual objects.'[25]

How is one to overcome this state of alienation, in which our power is expressed in the ability to make use of the power of others, in which, just as with money, so also the master-slave relationship is barely stripped of its most immediate aspects, and yet 'Our mutual servitude to the object really appears at the beginning of the development of the relation of dominance and slavery'?[26] Marx's reply is that this relationship of reciprocal utilisation is simply the naïve expression of our essential relationship, and that if we could conceive of producing like men, 'My labour would be the *free expression* and hence the enjoyment of life.' In reality

In the framework of private property it is the *alienation of life* since I work *in order to live*, in order to procure for myself the *means* of life. My labour is *not* life.

Moreover, in my labour the *specific character* of my individuality would be affirmed because it would be my *individual* life. Labour would be *authentic, active, property*. In the framework of private property my individuality has been alienated to the point where I loathe this activity, it is torture for me. It is in fact no more than the *appearance* of activity and for that reason it is only a *forced* labour imposed on me *not* through an inner necessity but through an *external* arbitary need.[27]

From the above passage, which presents in a drastic manner

the theme of needs as the basis of the problem of liberty, as the reappropriation of a social essence which in historical reality is still bound up in master-slave relationships, one can see how Marx reveals with his critique the property relations intrinsic to the whole world of exchange and that of wealth. The influence of Fourier can be markedly felt. The critical exercise is centred, as we said, on the *idéologues* and the 'doctrinaires'. For the latter, human faculties and property relations constitute a unity, and nature is subsumed and resolved within the property relation. The critique of exchange, in this very wide sense, which lies at the centre of the pages we have been examining is, simultaneously, the critique of the naturalisation of a specific social relationship, which would still seem to be imbued with the cloaked presence of the master-slave structure. In *The Holy Family* Proudhon is given recognition as the most acute critic of the 'ideological', 'doctrinaire' and 'positivist' reduction of the individual human being to his property-owning form. It was Proudhon who raised the objection against Comte that the finite dimensions of the earth will not admit of any right to property. Precisely because the availability of land is limited, Comte should have reached the conclusion that it cannot be subject to appropriation. The appropriation

of air and water causes no prejudice to anybody because, as they are unlimited, there is always enough left. The arbitrary appropriation of land, on the other hand, prejudices the enjoyment of others precisely because the land is *limited*. The use of the land must therefore be regulated in the interests of *all*.[28]

Nature is a prerequisite for the productive capacities that are created by man when matter is given as a prerequisite.[29] But Proudhon's critique is limited. He assails all economic relations except *labour time* and the *material of labour*. He uncritically turns labour time into 'the immediate existence of human activity as activity, the measure of wages and the determinant of the value of the product'. He thus makes *the human side* the decisive element in political economy (a judgement which Marx will ascribe to Ricardo in almost exactly the same words) but he reinstates man as far as his rights are concerned 'still in an economic and therefore contradictory way.'[30] Proudhon's critique of political economy 'recognises all the essential determinants of human activity, but only in an estranged, alienated form.' Hence it 'converts the importance of time for *human labour* into its importance for *wages*, for wage labour'.[31]

With due respect to the critics who have seen the link between the young Marx and the mature Marx as the passage from philosophical interests to scientific ones, or from a humanistic vision of man to a structural consideration of social relationships, it must be said that the peculiar character of Marx's first critique of bourgeois society consists in the general attack on the bloc constituted by property relations and their mobilisation in political economy, in order to subject both to the same criticism. Wealth in the form of real estate, money, the ownership exercised upon labour and the products of labour, and their exchange, are all property relations. The diversity of their phenomenology should not deceive us. The societal nature of exchange presupposes these relations in which a power lies hidden. During these years Marx did not pose the problem of the development of productive forces as an instrument of liberation. It was Ricardo and his followers who gave property relations a more modern definition, which involves labour time. Proudhon confined himself to stripping property relations and hence the master-servant figure of its most archaic characteristics. The search for a more radical solution, however, does not tend in the direction of recognising in the development of the productive forces at least a condition for the communist revolution: on the contrary, political economy (Ricardo) affords a more logical description of bourgeois wealth. In the *German Ideology*, to be sure, there is a very strong awareness that the world has been transformed by industry. The simplest sensuous certainty, says Marx, is the result of 'social development, industry and commercial intercourse.'[32] Man is sensuous activity. It is individual human beings living in their social interconnection who have subsumed their animality into history. Man's tribal 'consciousness receives its further development and extension through increased productivity, the increase of needs and, what is fundamental to both of these, the increase of population.'[33] Man's social potentialities are multiplied, but in the process they give way to 'a material power above us, growing out of our control, thwarting our expectations, bringing to naught our calculations'.[34]

Of the two great schools of law — one of which considers power to be the basis of all regularising of relations between men, while the other derives laws from the will — Marx sides decisively with the former. The power that expands over the masses and dominates them is considerably more organised than the State. If we take 'power as the basis of right, as Hobbes, etc., do, then right, law, etc., are merely the symptom, the expression of *other* relations upon which state power rests.'[35] In the State,

moreover, power emanates (as we have already seen) from the
propertied classes, and also from the 'theological strata'. In the
capitalist mode of production, intellectual labour must take on
peculiar forms. The various functions

mutually presuppose each other, . . . the contradictions in material production
make necessary a superstructure of ideological strata whose activity — whether
good or bad — is good, because it is necessary; . . . all functions are in the
service of the capitalist, and work out to his 'benefit'; . . . even the most sublime
spiritual productions should merely be granted recognition and *apologies* for
them made to the bourgeoisie, that they are presented as, and falsely proved to
be, direct producers of material wealth.[36]

Taking his cue from the lectures given by H. Storch to the Grand
Duke Nicholas, Marx observes that according to Storch 'the
physician produces health'.[37] But he objects:

It can just as well be said that illness produces physicians, stupidity produces
professors and writers, lack of taste poets and painters, immorality moralists,
superstition preachers and general insecurity produces the sovereign. This way
of saying in fact that all these activities, these services, produce a real or
imaginary use-value is repeated by later writers in order to prove that they are
productive workers in Smith's sense, that is to say, that they directly produce
not products *sui generis* but products of material labour and consequently
immediate wealth.[38]

The same way of presenting one's own work as productive, in
Smith's sense of the word, is found in Nassau Senior. In relation
to the bourgeois, he expresses the servility that consists in
presenting 'all functions as serving the production of wealth for
him'. In relation to the workers he puts forward the thesis 'that
the unproductive ones consume the great mass [of products],
since they contribute just as much as the labourers to the
production of wealth, even though in their own way'.[39] What
Marx wants to stress is a new intellectual climate in comparison
with Adam Smith's time. With reference to Pellegrino Rossi he
observes:

In dealing with the division of labour, Smith explains how these operations are
distributed among different persons; and that the product, the commodity, is the
result of their co-operative labour, not of the labour of any individual among
them. But the 'spiritual' labourers à la Rossi are anxious to justify the large share
which they draw out of material production.[40]

It is important to emphasise this difference of intellectual
climate to understand some of Marx's theoretical viewpoints too.
In the first place — and here he takes up the line of thought that

derives from Smith — there is his way of measuring what he calls 'false costs of production'. According to Smith:

State, church, etc., are only justified insofar as they are committees to superintend or administer the common interests of the productive bourgeoisie; and their costs — since by their nature these costs belong to the overhead costs of production [*faux frais de production*] — must be reduced to the unavoidable minimum. This view is of historical interest in sharp contrast partly to the standpoint of antiquity, when material productive labour bore the stigma of slavery and was regarded merely as a pedestal for the idle citizen [*citoyen oisif*], and partly to the standpoint of the absolute or aristocratic-constitutional monarchy which arose from the disintegration of the Middle Ages — as Montesquieu, still captive to these ideas, so naïvely expressed them in the following passage [*Esprit des Lois*, VII, Ch.4]: 'If the rich do not spend much, the poor will perish of hunger'.[41]

With Adam Smith the bourgeoisie has changed this relationship but as soon as it has become master of the field

and has partly itself taken over the State, partly made a compromise with its former possessors; and has likewise given recognition to the ideological professions as flesh of its flesh and everywhere transformed them into its functionaries, of like nature to itself; when it itself no longer confronts these as the representatives of productive labour, but when the real productive labourers rise against it and moreover tell it that it lives on other people's industry; when it is enlightened enough not to be entirely absorbed in production, but to want also to consume 'in an enlightened way'; when the spiritual labours themselves are more and more performed in its *service* and enter into the service of capitalist production — then things take a new turn, and the bourgeoisie tries to justify 'economically', from its own standpoint, what at an earlier stage it had criticised and fought against.[42]

What must be underlined is the importance that the relationship between productive and unproductive classes has when we consider the establishment of the various modes of production and the social relations which correspond to them. This, as we shall see, is one of the fundamental keys to an understanding of historical materialism. The mystery which a product of labour conceals derives precisely from the relations of production from which it emerges as a 'thing'. A coat is a coat. But have it made in a manner that corresponds to an exchange in which the figures of contractor and worker are separated and 'you have capitalist production and modern bourgeois society'; have it made in the manner that corresponds to production for direct consumption and 'you have a form of handicraft which is compatible even with Asiatic relations, or those of the Middle Ages'.[43] Secondly, it must be underlined that the urge of the intellectual classes to be recognised as having a productive function is in itself erroneous, but historically important. It marks the divide between the era of Adam Smith and that of the Garniers and Storches, the *idéologues* and the positivists.

The *German Ideology* is the basic text in which this problematic is expressed, although it is also a deviant text, because it is still directed against the speculative interpretation and transformation of the philosophy of the *idéologues*. An important passage refers to civil society as 'the true focus and theatre of all history'.[44] The power of civil society is expressed as 'an invisible hand', which has come to dominate both above and beyond individuals. The object of Marx's criticism, like Owen's and Fourier's, is the universal dependence imposed by the invisible hand of commerce. Salvation lies solely 'in the control and conscious mastery of these powers, which, born of the action of men upon one another, have till now overawed and ruled men as powers completely alien to them.'[45] In the *German Ideology* the productive forces are understood as the expression of human activity and they regulate its history. In capitalist society, as seen by Marx in this period, the relationship between human creativity and its products tends to disappear, because a utilitarian relationship is always interposed. In this regard, Destutt de Tracy is central to Marx's critical thinking: he identifies property and human personality in general.[46] Marx speaks of the need to recognise 'his frankness and shamelessness'. In reality a bourgeois 'believes himself to be an individual only insofar as he is a bourgeois': but the theoretical identification of bourgeois property with human individuality cannot be upheld.[47] Similarly Bentham, the English ideologue *par excellence*, always inserts interest 'between himself and his mode of action'.[48] From each human ability 'a product alien to it is demanded.'[49] Human creativity is subjected to utilitarian relationships, whose supreme material expression is money, 'which represents the value of all things, people and social relations.'[50]

Thus, the critique of human alienation is in the last analysis a critique of utilitarian relations of a mercantile kind. In this critique Ricardo already plays an important role because he allows Marx to interpret the entire complex of bourgeois social relations as an expression of a vast system of power that is well articulated in its structures, from those of property to the State and the ideological classes, yet whose substance consists in the form of wealth in general. Ricardo is therefore more advanced than Proudhon, because his idea of wealth is more abstract and can therefore contain within itself a greater number of particular forms. Nevertheless, this interpretation of the contribution made by Ricardo to economics as a science, though it remains a permanent acquisition for Marx, transforms Ricardo's theory into an internal moment of this general conceptual mobilisation of wealth, which, once it has been rendered abstract, can embrace all these new manifestations of power and domination which the transformed character of the master-slave relationship permits. Marx's research will never abandon this interpretative line: nor is it without significance that *Capital* will take commodities and value as the starting-point of its enquiry. Value is therefore the concretisation of the relations of domination and power that condition it.

Nonetheless, Marx's researches of the 1850s head him to a new conviction: that although Ricardo had fully accepted the social form of exchange, he had recognised that the primary and fundamental element was the increase in the productivity of labour, and that this tended to create a contradiction with the presumed form of the exchange. There is no trace of this in the young Marx. His critique of the system of exchange is the critique of the utilitarian relationships which are superimposed as alien relationships on the needs of that objective being: man. The new factor (the increase in the productivity of labour) interferes with the social relations, and shows them to be unsustainable in the long run. It gives autonomy to the value of free time, releases labour time from its function as the primary condition of wealth, and creates the material conditions for the formation of mass individualities.

Marx struggled to unify the two strands of his research, and *Capital* is the result of this effort. Nevertheless, it is precisely on this welding that criticism has always centred. Marx the 'prophet', 'humanist', 'philosopher' was always the one who subjected to criticism the bourgeois relations of production and exchange. Marx the scientist is the one who gleaned from Ricardo the theme of the increase increase in the productivity of labour. The welding, whereby 'freed time' became the material condition for the practical and theoretical critique of the system of exchange, has not been seen in all its fulness. Politically speaking, this has left room to the capitalist system and in general it has made it hard to recognise the link between socialism and liberty. Yet only through the juxtaposition of the two strands could Marx's research programme, which, as is well known, extended into politics, the theory of the State and that of the individual, be completed. In this sense, after developing the theme of the contradiction between relations of property and material productive forces, and dictating the rules for the birth, life and death of social formations, Marx concluded the Preface to *A Contribution to the Critique of Political Economy* with these words:

In broad outline, the Asiatic, ancient, feudal and modern bourgeois modes of production may be designated as epochs marking progress in the economic development of society. The bourgeois mode of production is the last antagonistic form of the social process of production . . . but the productive forces developing within bourgeois society create also the material conditions for a solution of this antagonism. The prehistory of human society accordingly closes with this social formation.[51]

This diagnosis of the process of social transformation will remain an accepted premise for Marx. He will repeat it in *Capital*, where he criticises the view that only relationships of distribution are historical, not those of production. This view — particularly in John Stuart Mill — is based:

on the confusion and identification of the process of social production with the simple labour-process, such as might even be performed by an abnormally isolated human being without any social assistance. To the extent that the labour-process is solely a process between man and Nature, its simple elements remain common to all social forms of development. But each specific historical form of this process further develops its material foundations and social forms. Whenever a certain stage of maturity has been reached, the specific historical form is discarded and makes way for a higher one. The moment of arrival of such a crisis is disclosed by the depth and breadth attained by the contradictions and antagonisms between the distribution relations, and thus the specific historical form of their corresponding production relations, on the one hand, and the productive forces, the production powers and the development of their agencies, on the other hand. A conflict then ensues between the material development of production and its social form.[52]

What this second theoretical picture of the transformation of historical forms adds to the preceding quotation is the reference to productive capacity, to the subjective side of the productive forces. Furthermore, the conflicts in the sphere of distribution are taken to be signs of a deeper crisis.

This latter aspect of the question should be brought to the attention of those who even today reduce the reason for conflict to the sphere of the distribution of wealth alone. In fact the mode of production is also involved and it is to this that Marx refers when he cites an anonymous work on *Competition and Cooperation*.[53] His opinion is that the development of productivity creates the material conditions for the historical transformation of a mode of production based on competition into one based on co-operation. It is no longer just alienation (the negative condition) that comes into the discussion: it is also re-appropriation — as the positive condition deriving from the possibility of directing the new levels of productivity towards a free association of producers. Economics reveals the material conditions of liberty and also indicates the path by which it is to be realised, if its presuppositions are subjected to criticism. Nevertheless, the idea that it also reveals the maximum alienation in the relations of property, and also constitutes the point of arrival of their modernisation, is constantly at loggerheads with the first possibility. In fact, such incompatibility pinpoints the site of the struggle between the classes, as well as the reasons for this struggle.

Part IV: The Development of Production and Monetary Circulation
According to Marx, money has three determinations. First, it is to be conceived as an ideal measurement, the allocation of a price to commodities. At this level the price is a presupposition of circulation, a possibility which is not necessarily put into effect. In order for the possibility to become a reality, the commodity must really circulate, be 'actualised'. As purely ideal measures, as relative prices attributed to commodities before they actually circulate, commodities may all be compared on the basis of the social work of which they are the materialisation. In the actual reality of the process of exchange, these commodities must be measured in money. At this second level the relationship is no longer 'ideal'. In the process of measuring one by the other, commodities and money can trip against accidental circumstances, such as a fluctuation in the value of the commodities, or of the money, or of the movements involving both of them. The economists (Ricardo, Say, James Mill, etc.) tend to equate the two. They turn the buyer-seller relationship into the expression of an identity, so that each is the reflection of the other. In such a manner, they deny the divide between the two concepts; the very life that informs crises is strangled by them at birth: they see harmony where there are the seeds of contradictions. Historically speaking, it is this divide that has made a separate corporal reality of the mercantile classes. Exchange is not in itself an exclusively capitalist fact; nor are the phenomena of a general rise and fall in prices. The phenomenon only becomes capitalist when money becomes the *representative form* of general wealth. At this point,

something must be added to the ideality of price as measurement, to the reality of exchange as the encounter and clash of prices on the market; and that something is the typically mercantile phenomenon of the *autonomising* of money as the equivalent of general wealth, as *treasure*.

On the appearance of this third determination, money can no longer be presented as a mechanism of exchange, an apparatus that enables wealth to circulate. It is the object of the desire for riches, the source of the property relationship. As regards this third aspect, Marx recoups the great theorists of mercantilism (W. Petty and P. Boisguillebert), although he recognises their fetishism. Modern political economy has criticised this fetishism, in fact refining it without becoming entirely free of it. Property relations, the object of the desire for riches, have not diminished in the least. The legal superstructures, the ideologies, tend to equate all human activities with the form taken by the property relation — even those that are quite foreign to it. Modern bourgeois society, because of the stimulus to own, adapts its forms to this impulse. This results in the potentially all-embracing mobility of possession. Bourgeois property is subjected to revolutions in value, that is, to the possible stranglehold of being forced to re-enter the movement of relations of exchange. On the other hand, the impulse towards the autonomising of wealth, that is, the tendency to stabilise the property relationship and to exercise relative power, is the stimulus on which exchange itself depends.

The simple model that is here set forth — it is however reproduced in the more complex one which involves capital, even if in a more elaborate form — was thus constructed by Marx with the *ideality* or *generality* of prices (values) as the starting-point, to pass on to the *accidentality-particularity* of exchange in which prices must be realised as exchange values, finally to reach the *substance* of exchange value which emerges from the process, becomes autonomised by it, and is its aim and stimulus. The starting-point is the initial *ideality* (wealth as the sum of prices), which is made concrete and takes on accidentality in real exchange, and emerges as money which has been valorised. The nature of the problem may be clarified by contrast with Ricardo. The latter recognises that in political economy one is dealing with exchange value, but he then restricts himself to speaking of the distribution of the product, 'as if the form of wealth based on *exchange value* were concerned only with *use value*, and as if exchange value were merely a ceremonial form . . .'[54] He reaches the conclusion that wealth only increases in its material form, as use value. Objectively speaking, however, when the surplus value and the capital increase, the one relatively and the other absolutely, the exchange value also increases as such, and the money as such. The realisation process, creates the exchange value which 'does not exist as equivalent for already present exchange values or for already present labour time.'[55]

In Ricardo's eyes 'the exchange value of products declines in the same proportion as there is an increase in the productive force of a given quantity of labour (of a given sum of capital and labour) and the redoubled production now has the same *value* that the half previously had'.[56] It is already established *a priori* that one can sell a certain quantity of the products of labour and one can sell twice the amount of the same commodity. But the increase in quantity is only a means to determine an excess of value. If it is true that value is relative, it is equally true that 'in order that the value of the profit may increase, there must be a third thing whose value declines . . . The excess does not consist in that exchange, although it is only realised in this. It consists in the fact that . . . the value of the wage declines to the same extent as the productive force of labour increases'.[57] Moreover, exchange is decisive for the realisation, that is, to pass from the ideality of prices to the reality of the market which determines their reciprocal friction. Exchange, that is to say, 'finds its limits in the means and needs of others for all specific goods that can be produced in a country and even in a particular market within the worldwide one.'[58] This means that production must tally with a counterproduction, an active demand. Ricardo does away with the problem by maintaining that capital can always be shifted into some other kind of commodity; and yet, Marx observes, it is 'precisely in the ''some'' that the problem lies'.[59] Besides, while Ricardo always speaks of a capital which, if it is taken away from one productive branch, is injected into another, capital often 'consists to a large extent of the fixed investment', and this is destroyed when labour's link with it is broken.[60]

To sum up, Marx discusses Ricardo because he has erased the third aspect of money, and decisively shifted the second towards the first. On the one hand, the desire for money has become the normal motivation in a system where profit is the sole index of productivity; on the other, the relative determining factors of value, which are expressed in the movement of capital, are drawn back into the field of an 'ideality' which attenuates their contradictions. The systematic increase in the productivity of labour is effortlessly reconciled with the market. In reducing money and capital to tools of circulation (in many respects ideal) the autonomising of money as the source of historically determined relationships of property and power is forgotten. Marx reads Ricardo's theory of increased productivity through the lens of J.D. Steuart's modern mercantilism,[61] not as a mechanism of the organic social process, which is nothing other than exchange, but as the breeding-ground of the dominant classes' lust for power. In this respect, 'mercantilism' refuses to lend itself to Ricardo's 'reductionism'.

Part V: On Production and Circulation in General
We have already referred to a passage in *Capital* where Marx alludes to the fact that insofar as 'the labour-process is solely a process between man and Nature, its simple elements remain common to all social forms of development.' Immediately afterwards Marx adds that 'each specific historical form of this process further develops its material foundations and social forms'.[62] He repeats almost exactly the same argument in his letter to Kugelmann of 11 July, 1868 (but, as we shall see, it will also be repeated elsewhere):

even if there were no chapter on value in my book, the analysis of the real relationships which I give would contain the proof and demonstration of the real value relation. The nonsense about the necessity of proving the concept of value arises from complete ignorance both of the subject dealt with and of the method of science. Every child knows that a country which ceased to work, I will not say for a year, but for a few weeks, would die. Every child knows too that the mass of products corresponding to the different needs require different and quantitatively determined masses of the total labour of society.[63]

This statement has been singled out as indicating a residual naturalism in Marx. The category of production in general has been understood as an abstraction that designates the material control of every form of production, which therefore remains constant and unchanged through mutations. There can be no doubt that one finds in Marx the reasonable idea that all societies are producers of use values, of goods that allow the original interchange between the human race and nature. The forms of this appropriation change, the content remains. Bourgeois capitalist society is a form of social organisation which turns the valorisation of wealth into the means to increase the availability of the means of exchange. In this lies its specific quality, the barriers that social relationships raise against the mode of production, the crisis by which it is continually threatened.

It should be emphasised that the 'general' does not have only this meaning in Marx. He uses to his own ends the grammar offered by Hegel's logic, particularly the logic of the concept with its three dimensions of *general* or *universal*, *particular* and *individual*. When he sets up his own analysis as a research into *capital in general*, he presupposes that all the historical potentialities contained in the concept 'capital' are or can be developed. Particularity and individuality are not only parts of the general concept; they are also instances that contradict it, or, as is the case with the 'individual', they 'deprive' it of the abstractness of universality. Thus it is in the sphere of the *particular* that competition and crises are to be found; in the sphere of the *individual* may be seen the way out of the capitalist system by the formation of the 'social individual'. The specific object of Marx's research is indeed capital in general, the kind of capital that is hypothetically capable of developing all its own capabilities. Only in this way did Marx think he could measure the capacity for resistance in the mode of production, the development of its own internal logic in the face of the barriers and contradictions which defined its concept. Nonetheless, capital in general or capital in accordance with its concept is not the definition of the meaning of a noun. If it makes any sense to speak of capital — and if it is not simple production found in all eras — it can only be defined within history; and in the facts one must recognise the elements from whose articulation capital itself has taken off. Capital presupposes specific social realities; these, taken in isolation, are not capital, but this is what they become from the moment when they enter into relationship with one another and give to society a certain movement. The pre-suppositions of capital are thus 'posed' within it; they constitute its basis and are developed to the extent that is permitted by that basis.

These presuppositions are of social origin — they are not the simple technical conditions of production which have become socially available. Instead, they imply the existence of classes and the exploitation of one by another. In Marx's language this can be expressed by indicating that capital is not an absolute form of production, but a *historical* form of production; that is, it is such that the elements of its genesis become the 'natural' conditions by which the development of the productive forces is held in check. Nevertheless, it exhibits a tendency towards an absolute form of production, and this tendency is expressed by capital in its own peculiar forms, connected to the desire for wealth of which we have already spoken. Capital is thus a particular reality which exhibits a universal tendency. In the comparison between Ricardo and Sismondi, it is the former who has better understood capital's 'universal tendency'; while the latter has better understood its 'particular restrictedness' as an underlying factual reality.[64] For Ricardo the capacity to overcome obstacles is 'in the nature of capital'. Sismondi uncovers the contradictions and would like to limit them with obstacles external to production, of an ethical, juridical nature. Ricardo stresses the element of 'universality', raising simple production, which as such exists also in capitalist production, to *production in general*, whereas its tendency towards the 'absolute' is peculiar to capital. Therefore, rather than admit that capital is subject to crises, Ricardo must leave out 'all its specific qualities . . . and their specific character as forms', and conceive capitalist production 'as simple production for immediate use value'.[65] R. McCulloch, James Mill and J.B. Say, as we have already pointed out, immediately identify supply and demand. The moment when the exchange value becomes autonomous is eliminated, and production and consumption are identified, as if one were faced with an absolute form of production and not a historically determined one.

To avoid confusion it is worth remembering that by absolute production Marx means a type of organisation in which the universal development of the productive forces has as its sole presupposition the 'advance beyond the point of departure'.[66] In other words the absolute form of production means that which is based solely on the state of technology, on the development of the productive capacities, and on the capacity of individuals to foresee social needs. Capitalist production is not an absolute production of this type, even if it betrays a tendency to be so, that is, as Marx puts it, to develop *production in general*. The latter is an abstraction which allows us to determine the type of the absolute form of development of the productive forces. Thus, referring to Ricardo, Marx writes: 'Ricardo, rightly for his time, regards the capitalist mode of production as the most advantageous for production in general'.[67] Elsewhere he indicates a limit *'not inherent to production generally, but to production founded on capital.'*[68] In an even more binding way, this meaning of the term *production in general* emerges when it is connected with the operation of abstraction from the various forms of production, through their common basis. It is as if Marx had said: If we take away the particular determinants of the various modes of production, the abstraction which results is what Hegel calls the basis, that is, a tendency, a potentiality that takes on significance in relation to the particular determinants that have 'gone deep'. In other words, if I consider the common substance that is realised in the various modes of production, stripping it of its particular determinants and not identifying it with any of them, I do not remain with a simple abstraction, but I bring a tendency to light, a movement of reality. Marx too attempts the logical operation of exposing the basis. When this is seen against the background of the various modes of production, it has something that is determined, the determinant nature of production in general or absolute production. If we read the passage that follows, it might seem totally incomprehensible but for the pointers given above:

if wages are reduced to their general basis, namely, to that portion of the product of the producer's own labour which passes over into the individual consumption of the labourer; if we relieve this portion of its capitalist limitations and extend it to that volume of consumption which is permitted, on the one hand, by the existing productivity of society (that is, the social productivity of his own individual labour as actually social), and which, on the other hand, the full development of the individuality requires; if, furthermore, we reduce the surplus-labour and surplus-product to that measure which is required under prevailing conditions of production of society, on the one side to create an insurance and reserve fund, and on the other to constantly expand reproduction to the extent dictated by social needs; finally, if we include in No. 1 the necessary labour, and in No. 2 the surplus-labour, the quantity of labour which must be performed by the able-bodied on behalf of the immature or incapacitated members of society, i.e., if we strip both wages and surplus-value, both necessary and surplus labour, of their specifically capitalist character, then certainly there remain not these forms, but merely their foundations, which are common to all social modes of production.[69]

At the conclusion of the passage, the reader would scarcely expect the reference to the *common foundation*, but rather a line of argument that led towards what Marx called absolute production, (that is, that which starts from the state of technology and the development of human personalities). It will be remembered how, in the *Critique of the Gotha Programme*, Marx maintains that from the overall social product one must deduct whatever is necessary to reintegrate the consumed means of production, a supplementary percentage for the expansion of production, a reserve fund to cover insurance against casualties, damage due to natural causes, etc.; not to mention the expenses of general administration which are not part of production, of the expenses earmarked to fulfil social needs — schools, health institutions, etc.; a fund for the incapacitated; and lastly the individual distribution of what remains of the total social product. The argument runs in the reverse order (from total social product to distribution in the second case, and from the stripping away of the forms of capitalist distribution to obtain the social fund in the first) but the substance of the argument is the same. Yet in the second instance Marx is referring to communist society, and in the first to the stripping away of the foundations of capitalist society. The mystery can only be resolved by admitting that the stripping away of foundations reveals the foundations as the root of that absolute tendency which in capitalist society is opposed by the historico-factual bases of the mode of production, (that is, in essence by the division and exploitation of classes). Through the foundations one arrives at production in general, and from its combination with rich individuality one reaches the correct subject-object relationship, and hence the possibility of a communist society. I do not feel that this combination of rich individuality and productive forces, this problematic of the stripping away of the forms, should be treated as an example of naturalism. The argument turns, rather, on two conditions: productivity on the one hand, and rich personality on the other. As long as the material conditions of production permitted the labour of the majority to serve to create the rich individuality of the few, no operation aimed at stripping away the foundations was possible. But when the development of labour productivity makes it possible to combine the two elements of productivity and personality in such a way that it is materially possible to secure free time for the masses, so that they can have a rich individuality of their own, then this operation takes on the significance of a profound restructuring of the whole of human history, of a revolutionary re-foundation; and at its centre lies the development of wealth and the liberty of the masses. Having turned *production in general* into the absolute form of production, it becomes possible to consider capital as a form that has only a tendency towards the absolute, but which through its own presuppositions is prevented from effecting it.

The desire to attain production in general or absolute production without stripping the forms and returning them to their foundation involves exalting capitalist production as an absolute form of production. It means treating a propensity as a reality. Only rarely and to a partial extent does Ricardo attain a grasp of the historicity of the capitalist mode of production. Usually he speaks of capitalist production as absolute, quashing the bases, forgetting the origin of the categories. Typical of his scientific method is his 'reduction' and elimination of those aspects that conflict with or contradict his generalisations. For example, it is typical of the way he considers capitalist production that the problem of 'realisation' is treated as being already resolved. In the eyes of the capitalist producer, the difficulties of realisation are considered non-existent. Rciardo takes this concept to the extreme conclusion, that crises do not exist as possibilities, and that the phenomena which certain economists label with this name are simply frictions produced by the shift of capital from one branch to another.

If one then adopts the point of view of productive, interest-bearing capital (a point of view that antedates Ricardo which Marx nonetheless considers indispensable to the depiction of capitalist society) the same productive process takes on the appearance of a stumbling block, a harsh necessity which nonetheless is merely the reflection of the only thing that matters for these capitalists, namely the increase in the exchange value. In this case, the development of productivity becomes a mere means to increase the production of exchange value. Marx's idea is that the figure of the capitalist as producer of interest 'arises necessarily, because the juridical aspect of property is separated from its economic aspect and one part of the profit under the name of interest accrues either to capital which is completely separated from the production process, or to the *owner of this capital*.'[70] As we have already pointed out, Proudhon believed he had rendered absolute production visible by expelling these forms from the arena. For Marx, as we know, they are quite uneliminable. To erase them is merely to pretend not to see them. This does not alter the fact that he too, in the complex movement of commodities and capital, tends to isolate methodologically the area of production from that of circulation. Yet this is a way of visualising a complex articulation which in the last resort must be at least approximately represented in a non-reductive manner. Theoretically speaking, this type of methodology has as its double butt the reductionism of Ricardo and Hegel's game of reflections, understood as the immediate identification of production with consumption, of accumulation with income. In other words, Marx generously concedes that the real movement can appear in such a way as to justify the reduction of reality to a game of reflections, from which Ricardo escapes only by making a norm of the exceptional aspects of reality. Nonetheless, the universal to which bourgeois production tends is wealth in its general form, money:

Capital posits the *production of wealth* itself and hence the universal development of the productive forces, the constant overthrow of its prevailing presuppositions, as the presupposition of its reproduction. Value excludes no use value; i.e. includes no particular kind of consumption etc., of intercourse etc. as absolute condition; and likewise every degree of the development of the social forces of production, of intercourse, of knowledge etc. appears to it only as a barrier which it strives to overpower. Its own presupposition — value — is posited as product, not as a loftier presupposition hovering over production. The barrier to *capital* is that this entire development proceeds in a contradictory way, and that the working-out of the productive forces, of general wealth etc., knowledge etc., appears in such a way that the working individual *alienates* himself [*sich entäussert*]; relates to the conditions brought out of him by his labour as those not of his *own* but of an *alien* wealth and of his own poverty. But this antithetical form is itself fleeting, and produces the real conditions of its own suspension. The result is: the tendentially and potentially general development of the forces of production — of wealth as such — as a basis; likewise, the universality of intercourse hence the world market as a basis.[71]

The possibility that the development of the productive forces may be transfused into that of enriched personality lies in the fact that the wealth produced, now as before, is rendered autonomous; it becomes restricted and alienated through property relationships. Capital is not a social function, but a relationship of power and enjoyment. This relationship is concealed under the appearance of exclusive social functionality, but leaves open a margin for a subjective appropriation.

In capital the tendency towards absolute production is expressed in the endeavour to assimilate 'all points which are presuppositions of circulation'.[72] The circulation time emerges as itself 'a barrier to . . . realisation of value'.[73] The tendency to reduce circulation time to zero is the inevitable consequence of all this. If 'circulation caused no delay, if its velocity were absolute and its duration = 0(that is, if it were accomplished in no time), then this would only be the same as if *capital* had been able to begin its production process anew directly it was finished'.[74] It is equally obvious that the reduction of circulation time to zero is, if we take Marx's model, the maximum to which production time can attain, where one gives this term the meaning of the production of value. Nevertheless, it is mediated by a process of real production, because if one reduced the entire production to the realisation of value, the real time of production, from the point of view of value, would have to tend towards zero. But staying with Ricardo's point of view on the primacy of commodity-producing capital, 'No velocity of circulation could increase the reproduction of capital, or rather the repetition of its realisation process, beyond that point' of zero duration. 'Circulation time in itself is not a *productive force* of capital, but a barrier to its productive force, arising from its nature as exchange value.'[75] According to Ricardo's viewpoint, the difficulties in realising value from a specific capital are automatically resolved in the multiplicity of the investment alternatives offered to capital in general. For Marx this is only an ideal tendency of capital, which conflicts with the reality of circulation, and yet, as a tendency, it forms part of that reality, because it inspires modes of behaviour, suggests expectations and obscures aspects of reality which are in contradiction with such modes of behaviour.

If one remains on the 'general' level, the continuity of production presupposes 'that circulation time has been suspended.'[76] Quite evidently there is a divergence between the ideality and the reality. Mercantile capital has a function of the utmost importance.[77] And yet this, even as bank capital, operates in favour of the development of this appearance of ideality. Credit as a 'measure' of surplus value subordinates to itself money as a medium of circulation. Marx shows how Ricardo tends to take as read 'the general standard of profit' on the basis of a relation 'between total profit and total wages, and this is not altered through competition.'[78] In the explanatory model proposed by Ricardo we find the condition of 'competition without restriction'. This amounts to saying 'that the laws of capital are completely realised only within *unlimited competition* and *industrial production*. Capital develops adequately on the latter productive basis and in the former relation of production; that is to say its immanent laws enter completely into reality.' But if this is how things stand, Marx says, 'it would have to be shown how this *unlimited competition* and *industrial production* are conditions of the realisation of capital, conditions which it must itself little by little produce'. Here, however, the hypothesis assumes the ideal aspect 'externally and arbitrarily . . . not as developments of capital itself, but as imaginary presuppositions of capital'. This, besides, is the only way in which Ricardo has 'a faint notion of the *historic* nature of the laws of bourgeois economy.'[79] In other words, according to Marx, Ricardo takes for granted the relations of capital to itself in its pure form of self-realisation of value, which, by means of interest, effects the passage from the economic form of wealth to that of poverty. In Ricardo's eyes, such a form, apparently pure, is not a tendency that conflicts with the harsh reality of commodity capital (and which has, besides, like landed revenue, an origin in master-slave relationships which go beyond the capitalist form of production). He sees it as a reality. Ricardo failed to understand the formation of capital, its history: he 'speaks only of the division of an available, *ready* amount, not of the original positing of this difference'.[80]

In substance, then, Marx sees in the circulation process and its agents a formation that with its genesis conditions the present, even if it has been so modified as to correspond to the concept of capital. The correspondence is neither logical nor naturalistic, but logico-historical, that is to say it is constituted of historical elements that were originally autonomous, and hence have become a functional part of the capitalist mode of production. This does not alter the fact that if one lays bare the historical forms, it is possible to recognise in them what Marx has defined as their common foundation.

But the stripping away of the forms, the rediscovery of the common foundation, is in reality the origin of what in Ricardo appears as the development of the productivity of labour, as production in general and the tendency towards the absolute. This tendency manifests itself in capitalist society in a specific historical context, which works both in the sense of ideally reducing it, and in the sense of 'contradicting it' in practice. Even the capital that ideally appears as a subject which develops itself (which generates its own value) actually remains blocked in each of its fixed forms. For instance, until it enters the market, it is the simple product of labour; as long as it remains motionless in the market, it is commodity; until it can be exchanged with the conditions of production (labour-power and objectified labour) it is money. Capital's intrinsic tendency towards the absolute includes not only production in general but also circulation in general, capital's irresistible tendency to refrain from standing still in any of its forms. At the same time, just as capital is not production in general but only a tendency in that direction, so also it is not circulation in general, but only a tendency in that direction. To borrow the expression of the *Critique of the Gotha Programme*, in capitalist society (and even in the first phase of a communist one) 'the enslaving subordination of the individual to the division of labour' has not vanished; labour is a means of life, and not 'life's prime want'; the productive forces have not increased with the all-round development of the individuals, 'and all the springs of co-operative wealth' do not 'flow . . . abundantly'.[81] Circulation in general is precisely this flow of all the sources of social wealth in their abundance. Ideally speaking, even in a communist society this would correspond to an absence of external impediments, to an exclusion of crises. Yet crises are something from which capital cannot free itself in reality, but only ideally; because, as we know, the circulation cost is presupposed as equal to zero. In the ideal type of capitalist production, the realisation is preliminarily and entirely taken as already realised.

The reduction to zero of the time of distribution does not arise in the reality but only the 'ideality' of a capital that has already presupposed that the entire product is realised. Ricardo claims that it arises, even if with some friction, in reality. For Marx it is a question of two ideal experiments (production in general and circulation in general) which refer in reality to an innate tendency within capitalist society. It is as if Marx had told us: this is how it would be if the concept of capital included its reality. This reality, however, is profoundly different, because it took shape on the basis of the servile assumptions of ground rent, the exploitation of labour, the division of labour, property relations, and the desire for wealth and power. The presupposition of the whole argument is the ideal experiment (for Ricardo the reality) whereby capital in its aggressive vitality considers its *ideality* as already *realised*, its 'tendencies' as 'facts'. The scientific value of the experiment lies in the fact that it is considered as such by the scientist.

It is precisely by accepting Ricardo's ideal presuppositions that Marx makes use of them to show how the 'poetry' of capital, generating value by 'self-reflection', hides the prose of the appropriation of unpaid work. But apart from this, there is also in Marx a far broader rejection of the reduction of reality to its idealisation. It is scientifically useful to presuppose circulation in general (the absence of crises) as being realised. But it is equally useful to remain aware of the reality of crises, as of the pre-capitalist barbarity which emerges from ᵗhe master-slave relations hidden under the form of property-ownership. Of course, it is not easy to understand this combination of historico-factual elements, real tendencies and experimental idealisations. Gramsci, on this subject, pointed to tendential laws, attributing them to Ricardo. In fact, they have to do with the way Marx interpreted Ricardo, making the natural laws of the system the manifestation of its ideal tendencies. Nowadays one tends to skim casually over this problematic, one takes it as given that relations of servitude and exploitation cannot be proved, that relations of property and power have disappeared off the face of the earth, that money is simply the means of exchange and crises a thing of the past. Marx's critique of Ricardo is glossed over and the difference between a type of production which tends to become absolute and absolute production loses all meaning. Above all, one loses sight of what was central in Marx, even if it was undeveloped, namely that the tendency expressed in the concept of production in general and circulation in general meant, in the last instance, that the development of the productivity of labour would interfere with the relations of exchange and of property. If money was the autonomising of relations of exchange into property relations, free time was the autonomising of the development of labour productivity as a material condition for the rise of a new civil order. The terms of this alternative need to be clarified further, even more so now that while on the one hand what is obvious has become unprovable (namely that property relations generate power and exploitation in a way which is specific to them), on the other hand the idea seems to be taking hold that the will to power is something ahistorical, inherent in human nature and at work in all human relationships. According to this view, the only way out of reflectionism and perspectivism is through the will to power. In the present context, it is interesting to note that for Marx one breaks out of this pre-scientific state by reasserting that '*omnis determinatio est negatio*', and that in our specific case the free time of the masses can become the negation of those conditions of servitude that have also penetrated the capitalist mode of production.

Part VI: Free Time and the Formation of the Social Individual
There is a long, important footnote in the *Grundrisse* in which Marx observes that

the creation of surplus labour on the one side corresponds to the creation of minus-labour, relative idleness (or *not-productive labour* at best), on the other. This goes without saying as regards capital itself; but holds then also for the classes with which it shares; hence of the paupers, flunkeys, lickspittles etc. living from the surplus product, in short, the whole train of retainers; the part of the servant [*dienenden*] class which lives not from capital but from revenue. Essential difference between this *servant* class and the *working* class. In relation to the whole of society, the creation of *disposable time* is then also creation of time for the production of science, art etc. The course of social development is by no means that because one individual has satisfied his need he then proceeds to create a superfluity for himself; but rather because one individual or class of individuals is forced to work more than required for the satisfaction of its need — because *surplus labour* is on one side, therefore not-labour and surplus wealth are posited on the other. In reality the development of wealth exists only in these opposites [*Gegensätze*]: in potentiality, its development is the possibility of the suspension of these opposites. Or because an individual can satisfy *his own* need only by simultaneously satisfying the need of and providing a surplus above that for *another* individual. This brutal under slavery. Only under the conditions of wage labour does it lead to *industry, industrial labour*. Malthus is therefore quite consistent when, along with surplus labour and surplus capital, he raises the demand for surplus idlers, consuming without producing, or the necessity of waste, luxury, lavish spending etc.[82]

The passage is interesting in one respect because it alters the image of Marx the prophet: here it is explicitly stated that the progress of free time towards the formation of a rich mass individuality is only a possibility. Even theoretically the forecast is taken into the realm of the theoretical establishment of the possibility. It is the circumstances that are not harmonised, and not harmonisable (the economic contradictions as antitheses to the economic harmonies of Bastiat and Carey) which open the door to possibilities.[83] It is also interesting from the point of view of the depiction of reality, because, while the capitalist system remains, those who are dominant have every interest in developing that servile class which exchanges its work for income. Capital is seen by the bourgeoisie as their own private property, and, as such, allows them to express socially a function of mastery. Nonetheless this function serves a social function. At times the capitalist himself has sought self-justification in presenting himself as a dependent labourer in the service of that social function. In actual fact it is a property relationship. Hence Marx insists on the fact that the capitalist, as an individual, has the possibility of choosing the moment when his profit is presented socially as income, and, only appearing to be such, can be reconverted into capital. Nonetheless, this choice, though real on an individual plane, remains theoretical on the plane of the class, which must not only produce and consume, but provide and reproduce its capital. Hence the increase in real power which accrues to the capitalist at the moment when, remaining such, it can nonetheless also multiply the servile figures who exchange their work for his income. Thus there is an element of truth in Malthus, and Marx does not hesitate to say so, notwithstanding the justified aversion that he shows towards his thesis. Even when seen from this angle, the question shows how the conveyance of free time towards a shortening of labour time, and hence towards the conquest of conditions of mass cultural development, can only be a 'possibility', (that is, the result of a whole set of struggles co-ordinated in time and space in accordance with a historical pattern).

But returning to the other possibility: by keeping the condition of the workers unchanged, or scarcely changed, free time leads to the luxury of the dominant class and the development of servile functions, and this is something that Marx found in other writers besides Malthus. In one way or another the question engages the interest of the whole range of political economists, including Ricardo. To him, as we know, Marx raises the objection of not having been able to develop a theory of money that corresponded to the capitalist system. In this way Marx means to rebuke Ricardo for not having detected, within the relations of exchange, the process whereby money is rendered autonomous and relations of property are formed. The class conflict is grasped at one of its essential knots — the conflict between wages and what Ricardo calls profit — but it is restricted to this. The antithesis takes the form of the search for the maximum net production in relation to gross production, and this search is justified and sublimated as a natural necessity. The sociological consequence of all this is that 'in this contradictory form those classes in society whose time is only partly, or not at all, absorbed in material production although they enjoy its fruits, should be as numerous as possible in comparison with those classes whose time is totally absorbed in material production and whose consumption is, as a consequence, a mere item in production costs, a mere condition for their existence as beasts of burden. There is always the wish that the smallest possible portion of society should be doomed to the slavery of labour. This is the utmost that can be accomplished from the capitalist standpoint.'[84]

This exposition of the sociology implicit in Ricardo's economic thought can be referred back to the passage on Malthus above. The conclusion in both cases is that an increase in the unproductive and middle classes follows inevitably from the development of capitalist society in its evolved form. In another significant passage from Marx's permanent dialogue with Ricardo, Marx points to two tendencies which continually interweave in the attempt to interpret the antagonistic relationship between capital and wage labour: one tends towards the liberation of labour-power, the other towards absorbing it to an ever greater extent. One tendency, Marx writes:

throws the labourers on to the streets and makes a part of the population redundant, the other absorbs them again and extends wage-slavery absolutely, so that the lot of the worker is always fluctuating but he never escapes from it. The worker, therefore, justifiably regards the development of the productive power of his own labour as hostile to himself; the capitalist, on the other hand, always treats him as an element to be eliminated from production. These are the contradictions with which Ricardo struggles in this chapter. What he forgets to emphasise is the constantly growing number of the middle classes, those who stand between the workman on the one hand and the capitalist and landlord on the other. The middle classes maintain themselves to an ever increasing extent directly out of revenue, they are a burden weighing heavily on the working base and increase the social security and power of the upper ten thousand.[85]

A few pages previously in the same work, Marx had referred to Ricardo's theory of machinery, stating that 'while one section of the workers starves, another section may be better fed and clothed, as may also the unproductive workers and the middle strata between worker and capitalist'.[86]

This discussion with Malthus and Ricardo (which is also directed against J.B. Say) is important on the philosophical plane as well. The capitalist's tendency to create intermediary non-productive classes who are in a position to live on the productive work of others had already been observed by Bentham. The relationship between Bentham and Ricardo can be summed up as follows: for Ricardo a society's wealth does not lie in the extension of productive labour at the expense of non-productive labour, as with Smith, but in the intensity of the former: the number of those who are condemned to labour must be relatively small, and the productivity of labour must be as high as possible. When this second condition is achieved, a society is rich. The intuition that leads to this conclusion is philosophically expressed in Bentham's thought through the formula of the greatest happiness of the greatest number. I believe we can see an affinity between the residual balance of unhappiness implicit in Bentham's utilitarianism and the condemnation of productive work of the smallest possible number, which Marx sees in Ricardo's 'cynicism'. There are those who can enjoy increased social wealth, and there are those who are condemned to produce in the worst conditions. Utilitarianism echoes this solution in the limits it sets on the achievement of happiness, which is confined to a proportion of men only.

Nonetheless, the relationship between philosophy and political economy does not end with this affinity. Bentham sees the bourgeois as the type of the normal man, whereas John Stuart Mill does not wholly accept this limitation, but goes beyond it and develops progressive tendencies within the limits of the capitalist system. Marx writes:

To avoid misunderstanding, let me say that, while it is quite right to rebuke men like John Stuart Mill for the contradiction between their traditional economic dogmas and their modern tendencies, it would be very unjust to lump them together with the herd of vulgar economic apologists.[87]

Mill's progressive tendencies can be identified in three points:

1   He does not accept that the quota of social wealth, which must serve as the labour fund or wage, is enclosed by natural chains and impenetrable barriers. As historical experience has proved, there is a margin for the increase of wages, without altering the capitalist relationship of production.
2   He rejects the idea that the happiness of the greatest number, in the given historical conditions, is inseparable from the unhappiness of those who are condemned to productive labour. Hence his advocacy of the associative forms of the organisation of labour, and his rejection of man's relationship of legal and moral dominance over women. The way he explains the psychological acceptance of the existing relationship of dominance is connected with a logic of association, which is hardened by habit and behaviour. These, however, can be changed, yielding to new forms of association of ideas that are less restrictive in their tendency. For Mill, a socialist organisation based on the association of producers is a possibility; it is arrived at through a speculative comparison where the decisive element is the increase of liberty it can bring about.[88]
3   The process of intellectual development, in the sense of transmitting and perfecting skills, is found in all productive labour.

Marx stood by this correction of Mill, yet he criticised him severely on other points, first and foremost for his apologia for profit as the effect of the capitalist's abstaining from consumption. This was the theory of Nassau W. Senior, who had solemnly averred his willingness to supplant the words labour and capital by labour and abstinence.

John Stuart Mill, on the contrary, both copies Ricardo's theory of profit, and annexes to it Senior's 'remuneration of abstinence'. He is as much at home with absurd and flat contradictions as he is at sea with the Hegelian 'contradiction', which is the source of all dialectics.

And he adds:

It has never occurred to the vulgar economist to make the simple reflection that every human action may be conceived as an 'abstinence' from its opposite. Eating is abstinence from fasting, walking is abstinence from standing still, working is abstinence from idling, idling is abstinence from working, etc. These gentlemen would do well to ponder occasionally over Spinoza's '*Determinatio est négatio*'.[89]

Secondly, he criticises him for his 'naturalisation' of the productive process which he severs from history. While distribution is seen as historically modifiable, the productive process is almost natural. The combination of the productive process with natural conditions is so close that it tends to debase the sphere of production to mere technology. On the whole, Mill set in motion a mechanism of social needs to which he was unable to unite a theory where the capitalist limits of the labour fund were superseded. On the question of communism, with Robert Owen specially in mind, Mill observes that 'if a conjecture may be hazarded, the decision will probably depend mainly on one consideration, *viz.* which of the two systems is consistent with the greatest amount of human liberty and spontaneity'.[90] This marks the most fruitful point in Mill's thought; nonetheless he refuses to consider how much liberty would be concretely and historically realisable if one created Owen's condition of 'self-management' by labour and a deliberate process of redirecting free time away from the intrinsic wealth of the dominant class, and those who depend directly on their income, towards the free time of the masses.

Bentham thus anticipates a tendency that Ricardo will make his own when he sets impassable boundaries on the 'unhappiness' of the direct producers and defines 'happiness' as the relationship of implicit or explicit slavery that the majority establish with the income of the dominant class. Ricardo never fails to maintain a relationship with the truths of science, and, confronted with the choice between these and class interests, opts for the former.[91] Bentham, going beyond this 'cynicism', remains wholly bound up in bourgeois relations. The ferociously polemical page that Marx devotes to him is well known:

Classical political economy has always liked to conceive social capital as a fixed magnitude of a fixed degree of efficiency. But this prejudice was first established as a dogma by the archphilistine, Jeremy Bentham, that soberly pedantic and heavyfooted oracle of the 'common sense' of the nineteenth-century bourgeoisie. Bentham is among philosophers what Martin Tupper is among poets. Both could only have been manufactured in England. This dogma in fact renders the commonest phenomena of the production process, for instance its sudden expansions and contractions, and even accumulation itself, absolutely incomprehensible. It was used by Bentham himself, as well as by Malthus, James Mill, MacCulloch, etc., for apologetic purposes, and in particular so as to represent one part of capital, namely variable capital, or that part convertible into labour-power, as being of fixed size. Variable capital in its material existence, i.e. the mass of the means of subsistence it represents for the worker, or the so-called labour fund, was turned by this fable into a separate part of social wealth, confined by natural chains and unable to cross the boundary to the other parts.

Of course, to set in motion the means of production one needs a 'definite mass of living labour'. But 'the number of workers required to put this mass of labour-power in a fluid state is not given, for it changes with the degree of exploitation of the individual labour-power. Nor is the price of this labour-power given, but only its minimum limit, which is moreover very elastic.' At the basis of this dogma lie the following facts: 'on the one hand the worker has no right to interfere in the division of social wealth into means of enjoyment for the non-worker, it is only in favourable and exceptional cases that he can enlarge "labour" at the expense of the "revenue" of the rich.'[92]

As we have already said, John Stuart Mill's thesis is quite different. Socialism remains open as a possibility. The barriers are not erected in any drastic way. The intermediary classes can also favour social changes, provided they do not restrict their own freedom. Part in accordance with this line (but not Bentham's) certain things have developed in advanced capitalist societies which pose the problem of administering the redistribution of social wealth in accordance with Ricardo's principles, (that is, maintaining profit as an independent relation).[93] Marx's critique, nonetheless, still succeeds in being comprehensible: he writes:

The law of capitalist accumulation, mystified by the economists into a supposed law of nature, in fact expresses the situation that the very nature of accumulation excludes every diminution in the degree of exploitation of labour, and every rise in the price of labour, which could seriously imperil the continual reproduction, on an ever larger scale, of the capital-relation. It cannot be otherwise in a mode of production in which the worker exists to satisfy the need of the existing values for valorisation, as opposed to the inverse situation, in which objective wealth is there to satisfy the worker's own need for development. Just as man is governed, in religion, by the products of his own brain, so, in capitalist production, he is governed by the products of his own hand.[94]

Marx's fundamental thesis is essentially as follows: capitalism develops the productive forces, and releases labour time. The mechanism of capitalist society ploughs back this freed time into the productive process, widens the field of production of luxury goods, servants, overseers, priests, civil servants and managers.[95] It follows from this that capitalist society (although not moving between the Pillars of Hercules hypothesised by Bentham) impedes the increase of the producers' free time, restricting itself to a cut in the time that is required to produce goods, (that is, contributing in practice to a diminution of the sum for wages). The lower class can intervene in this field by way of struggles: in fact the history of the working-class movement in the course of the nineteenth century, besides being a struggle for wages, was a struggle for shorter hours. Marx writes of this in a letter to Bolte, dated 23 November 1871:

every movement in which the working class come out *as a class* against the ruling classes and attempts to force them by pressure from without is a political movement. For instance, the attempt in a particular factory or even a particular industry to force a shorter working day out of the capitalists by strikes etc. is a purely economic movement. On the other hand the movement to force an eight-hour day, etc., *law*, is a *political* movement. And in this way, out of the separate economic movements of the workers there grows up everywhere a *political* movement, that is to say a movement of the *class*, with the object of achieving its interests in a general form, in a form possessing a general social force of compulsion. If these movements presuppose a certain degree of previous organisation, they are themselves equally a means of the development of this organisation.[96]

Potentially, however, the question presents other aspects. The reduction in the working day is closely connected with the increase in productivity. The two questions are closely linked, because, while small circulation persists (the exchange between capital and labour-power), the increase in productivity could make up for or actually increase the mass of value the ruling class appropriates. The real problem is thus political, as Marx explains in the letter to Bolte. But the political outlet must derive from a development of what he calls the worker's 'enormous aware-ness', that is to say labour's capacity to recognise its 'products as its own', and at the same time its separation from them as an 'improper — forcibly imposed' separation.[97] In the existing social reality, the machine that governs labour confronts it 'as the power which rules it', as a power which 'is the form of capital'.[98] The accumulation 'of knowledge and of skill, of the general productive forces of the social brain, is thus absorbed into capital, as opposed to labour',[99] it becomes the 'technological application of science.'[100] Machines do not come to the aid of the worker (as Ricardo had recognised in his famous self-criticism of chapter 31 of the *Principles*). But if the enormous awareness is formed, then it is 'the development of the social individual which appears as the great foundation-stone of production and of wealth. The *theft of alien labour time, on which the present wealth is based*, appears a miserable foundation in face of this new one, created by large-scale industry itself.'[101] In place of production based on the value of exchange, there arises the 'free development of individualities'.[102]

The theory of the social individual is thus the exact equivalent in the field of subjectivity of the discovery of the 'foundation' of the capitalist form of production in the field of objectivity. Marx emphasises that the necessary labour time will be measured in terms of the needs of the social individual, inasmuch as 'real wealth is the developed productive power of all individuals'.[103] The individuals under the new conditions 'reproduce themselves as individuals, but as social individuals.'[104] Yet the presence of the three Hegelian dimensions of the concept (universal, particular and individual) is still in evidence. The means of escape from capitalism is the productivity of labour, which is combined with rich individuality. The material preconditions are now located within the individual.

United in this combination are two critical strands of Marx's research. The first is the one that is directed against Ricardo and Ricardianism. The arrival point of this critique can be symbolised in the passage in which Marx observes, concerning an anonymous follower of Ricardo, that:

Labour-time, even if exchange-value is eliminated, always remains the creative substance of wealth and the measure of the *cost* of its production. But free time, *disposable time*, is wealth itself, partly for the enjoyment of the product, partly for free activity, which — unlike labour — is not dominated by the pressure of an extraneous purpose which must be fulfilled, and the fulfilment of which is regarded as a natural necessity or a social duty according to one's inclination.[105]

On the other hand, the formation of the social individual does not involve any particular training in the sense whereby man is taught to overcome his own natural limits.

From this point of view one observes both the affinity to, and distance from, the problematic of utopian communism. John Stuart Mill's concessions to Nassau Senior arose precisely when 'On this side of the Channel began to spread Owenism; on the other side, Saint-Simonism and Fourierism.'[106] The theoretical limit of this great current of thought consisted in the fact that it reproduced, inverting the terms, the philosophy of the *idéologues*. Just as the latter had, so to speak, found bourgeois man in nature and had made property-owning man into natural man, so the currents of utopian socialism found in the liberation of natural man the roots of a healthy sociality. For Marx the naturalness to be reconquered as the life that is lived, to be led back, as it were, to the human capacity for fulfilment and enjoyment, was that which has been accumulated by human labour and become the property of the ruling classes. Hence he does not confine himself to criticising Mill for having impoverished Owen's great project, but he criticises him above all for not having theorised the historicity of the bourgeois mode of production. Thus Marx's anthropology is not the theory of a natural enrichment of the faculties, even if the development of sensibility is accompanied by the refinement of the senses which has become the exclusive possession of the dominant classes. Marx's anthropology is at one and the same time the theory of a historical appropriation of culture and science and of a consequent overall development of the capacities of the social individual.

In a late passage, which therefore cannot be accused of reflecting a youthful discipleship of Feuerbach, Marx writes concerning the profound movement that leads to the formation of the human individual:

Like any other animal, [men] begin by *eating*, *drinking*, etc., that is to say, not with 'standing' in a relationship, but with *behaving actively*, with mastering certain objects of the external world through action, thus satisfying their needs. (In other words, they begin with production.) With the repetition of this process the quality which these objects have to 'satisfy their needs' is impressed on their brains . . . At a certain level of evolution, when their needs and their activities, geared to satisfying them, have multiplied and developed, men will give a name to the entire category of these objects which experience has taught them to distinguish from the rest of the external world . . . . But this linguistic denomination only expresses, in the form of a description, what the repeated confirmation has transformed into experience, that certain external objects serve to satisfy the needs of men who already live in a certain social context. (This is a necessary presupposition because of language). . . . These objects are useful to them, and they confer on the object this character of utility as a character possessed by the object, though it is hard to imagine a sheep considering its 'utility' as consisting in its being a foodstuff for men.[107]

There are a number of problems in this passage. In the first place, Marx presupposes an active behaviour of men with respect to things, in full correspondence with his early writings; in the second place the process of naming (already social because it presupposes language) serves to represent a usefulness which fixes and selects active forms of behaviour; in the third place, this process, insofar as it involves language, itself indicates the peril of reification, namely the tendency to transfer to the ownership of objects those characteristics which experience has established as utilitarian relationships. One must deduce from this that critical reflection involves language from the outset. This is an important warning to establish the lay character of all knowledge, and of Marxism itself and its theoretical refinement. One must presuppose, moreover, that science works upon linguistic codifications. It too is a form of man's active behaviour. In a passage that has become famous through recent epistemological discussions, Marx writes: 'What distinguishes the worst architect from the best of bees is that the architect builds the cell in his mind before he constructs it in wax.'[108] But, to render his thought more complete, this passage should be put alongside the other in which Marx maintains that, 'Science, unlike other architects, builds not only castles in the air, but may construct separate habitable storeys of the building before laying the foundation stone.'[109]

This conclusion is a representation of what Marxism itself is or should be (besides being a characterisation of the state of science in the nineteenth century, as far as Darwinism, chemistry, mathematics and physics itself are concerned). It is certainly interesting that Marx was aware of it. Basically it is to this very awareness that he commits the destiny of his critique of Ricardo's science. It concerns itself with the fact that the increase in productivity becomes a reality that is immediately graspable at the level of common awareness, and that the division into classes with the increase in the free time of the masters and the development of the mass of unproductive people become equally recognisable. To link the two categories of phenomena there are the social contradictions, the crises. Marx does not believe that the 'refinement' of consciousness can assume a mass character independently of the insight into common sense of these two presuppositions. Hence his immense scientific work and the hope that it may in one form or other cause the fundamental elements of his argument to emerge in common consciousness.

There is a passage in what, in Marx's project, should have been the fourth volume of *Capital*, in which he indicates with great precision the results of the historical development that he expected. The passage, which comes from his discussion with T. Hodgskin, goes like this, expressed in nervous note form:

Accumulation of large amounts of capital by the destruction of the smaller capitals. Attraction. Decapitalisation of the intermediate links between capital and labour. This is only the last degree and the final form of the process which transforms the conditions of labour into capital, then reproduces capital and the separate capitals on a larger scale and finally separates from their owners the various capitals which have come into existence at many points of society, and centralises them in the hands of big capitalists. It is in this extreme form of the contradiction and conflict that production — even though in alienated form — is transformed into social production. There is social labour, and in the real labour process the instruments of production are used in common. As *functionaries* of the process which at the same time accelerates this *social* production and thereby also the development of the productive forces, the capitalists become superfluous in the measure that they, on behalf of society, enjoy the usufruct and that they become overbearing as *owners* of this social wealth and *commanders* of social labour. Their position is similar to that of the feudal lords whose exactions in the measure that their *services* became superfluous with the rise of bourgeois society, became mere outdated and inappropriate privileges and who therefore rushed headlong to destruction.[110]

One may observe that this passage gives the lie to the oversimplified accounts of the 'collapse'. Marx speaks here of the concentration of capital, but this theory is in no way tantamount (as eminent scholars of social classes have recently maintained it is) to a reduction of the intermediary classes. These, as we know, tend to increase in number, but with a different social function. Marx maintains that this change corresponds to a diminished intensity of social function and an increase in power, the function of command. The function of the producer shifts towards that of the property-owner. Marx was wholly consistent in maintaining that behind the bourgeois producer, whom Destutt de Tracy identified with the human individual, stood the property-owner. The historical tendency he observes is characterised precisely by a diminution of the productive function and an increase in property ownership. This marks the terms of a historical transition. The productive functions are transferred to social individuals, while the proprietary ones remain concentrated in the old classes whose historical function decreases.

Moreover, even if one holds fast to the human form of the bourgeois individual as producer and proprietor, this is something profoundly different from that of the 'social individual'. Marx, with reference to Bentham, has given a ferocious description of the former, but already the comparison exhibits some characteristics of the latter:

The principle of utility was no discovery made by Bentham. He simply reproduced in his dull way what Helvétius and other Frenchmen had said with wit and ingenuity in the eighteenth century. To know what is useful for a dog, one must investigate the nature of dogs. This nature is not itself deducible from the principle of utility. Applying this to man, he that would judge all human acts, movements, relations, etc. according to the principle of utility would first have to deal with human nature in general, and then with human nature as historically modified in each epoch. Bentham does not trouble himself with this. With the dryest naïveté he assumes that the modern petit bourgeois, especially the English petit bourgeois, is the normal man.[111]

Let us compare these characteristics with those of the new producer, the social individual. He holds fast to the principle of productive labour, but the supreme value, wealth *per se*, is free time; he has no need to disguise *universal labour* ('all scientific labour, all discovery and all invention'; it depends partly on co-operation among the living, partly on the utilisation of the labour of the dead)[112] under the form of productive labour. He can judge his own past, detaching it from himself. Marx writes of Fourier that he

characterises the eras of civilisation by means of monogamy and private landed property. The modern family contains in nucleus not only *servitus* (slavery), but also *serfdom*, because from the start it exists in relation to services for the cultivator of the fields. It contains within itself, in miniature, all the antagonisms which, on a broader scale, develop in society and its history.[113]

History, science, the repossession of life as enjoyment of free time, as the socialisation of the development of productivity and as the realisation of this liberation through the removal of all the servile forms: these are the characteristics of the social individual in contrast with bourgeois utilitarianism. Already in *The German Ideology* Marx had said:

the productive force, the state of society and consciousness can and must come into contradiction with one another, because the *division of labour* implies the possibility, nay the fact, that intellectual and material activity, that enjoyment and labour, production and consumption, devolve on different individuals, and that the only possibility of their not coming into contradiction lies in negating in its turn the division of labour.[114]

From the above-quoted passage it emerges how Marx attributes a step-by-step character to the solving of the contradiction. What remains unchanged is a direction of movement, a mark which men stamp upon history, where one is aware of the contradiction, and it becomes the spur to action. Today, Bentham's old cynicism (an expression of a class that justifies itself as productive) has obviously taken other forms and it is the ideologies of the masters, the property-owners and the non-producers, which depict the 'coolie' condition of the masses as a necessity.

Part VII: On the Method of 'Provisional' Abstractions
It is impossible to grasp the socialism-liberty relationship without

pointing the political struggle in the direction indicated by Marx. The development of productivity is part of the struggle of the masses for 'liberation'. This is achieved through a historical process of class struggle, diffusion of culture, limitation of the social division of labour, and a reduction in the power and property of the ruling class. The condition necessary for the development of this process is that the various analytical 'blocs', which allow us to consider capitalist society as a 'whole', remain visible and co-existent (that is, what is provisionally isolated as an object of analysis should not be irreversibly 'removed'). In other words, Marx proceeds in accordance with the method of reductions or provisional abstractions. It is not simply a matter of analysing phenomena in their pure state, but of letting them pass provisionally in review so that the whole receives light now from this side and now from that, and to a corresponding extent its other zones are thrown to a greater or lesser extent into the shade.

If, for instance, the labouring process is considered as the process of valorisation, as dead labour which is transformed into self-realising value, then it is necessary to make a provisional abstraction from the process of large circulation. This comes about not by removing it, but on the contrary by 'idealising' it as fully functioning, as if no problem of 'realisation' existed for capital. In this case, 'small circulation' is the only one that is absorbed within the production process as a variable (that is, as the variable of exploitation). From the whole process of large circulation it is possible to make an abstraction, because the prices are fixed ideally, and, as we said, are presupposed as realised. Moreover, if one wants to proceed in isolating the analytical bloc of 'exploitation', it is impossible to stop at this point. The study of value produced from scratch requires not only the ideality of prices and their realisation, but also the abstraction from the fluctuations of value of that part of capital which Marx defines as constant. That is to say, even to constant capital one must apply 'a mathematical rule, employed whenever we operate with constant and variable magnitudes, related to each other only by the symbols of addition and subtraction.'[115] If in this sense the constant capital is reduced to zero, the value in general appears as simple objectivised labour, and the surplus value equally as coagulation of labour time.

In the first case examined, the reduction of circulation to zero allows the whole formation of value to be led back ideally to the productive process. Only under these conditions (that is, within the orbit of this ideality), do prices and values coincide. In the second case, the reduction of constant capital to zero enables the value produced from scratch to be recognised only by allowing the variable part of anticipated capital to play an exclusive role. According to Hegel's logic (analogous in this respect to Ricardo's reductionism) it would be easy to interpret the provisional reduction to zero as an operation of reduction to unity. For instance, following this logic, absolute surplus value and relative surplus value could be identified, or supply and demand, by changing places, could be considered the same thing. At first glance, nothing could be simpler. Absolute surplus value is *relative* because it requires a development of productivity that allows the necessary labour-time to be limited to *a part of the working day*. But if one looks at the *movement* of surplus value, this appearance of identity disappears. When the capitalist mode of production has developed, there arises an alternative as to the manner of raising the *rate of surplus value*: it can be raised '*by prolonging the working day*' or else, 'if the length of the working day is given . . . by a change in the relative magnitudes of the components' of the working day itself (necessary labour and surplus value). At this point, within the provisional abstraction of surplus value, the part of constant capital which Marx calls fixed reappears as 'a change in either the productivity or the intensity of the labour'.[116] Constant capital is thus reintroduced, even if only for that part which can serve to lower the cost of the labour-power.

In appearance only do Ricardo and his followers pursue the same path. For example, John Stuart Mill idealises prices. For him, 'exchange, buying and selling (that is, the general condition of capitalist production), are a mere incident, and there would always be profits, even without the purchase and sale of labour-power!'[117] In other words, the method of provisional abstractions is replaced by a reduction that leads to identity. The entire relationship is halted at its moment of ideality. Shifting the question to surplus value, we find that Ricardo and Mill do not understand 'that the rate of profit may depend on circumstances which in no way affect the rate of surplus-value. I shall show in volume 3', Marx continues 'that the same rate of surplus-value may be expressed in *the most diverse rates of profit*, and that *different rates of surplus-value* may, under certain circumstances, be expressed in *the same rate of profit*'.[118] Marx means that by identifying rate of profit with rate of surplus value, Ricardo precludes the possibility of conditionally (so to speak) isolating the phenomenon of surplus value. Although he has grasped the centrality of the problem, he does not confine himself to circumscribing it within the space that serves to isolate it temporarily from the whole, but reduces the whole to that one problem. Thus, having reduced surplus value to profit, he cannot imagine circumstances by dint of which the variation in the rate of profit does not depend on its antagonism to wage costs. Surplus value is precisely the category which, given the 'combined labourer', can show the connection between the development of productivity and small circulation, without falling into that reductionism which excludes other factors from having an impact on the rate of profit.

The question, as we know, is important for Marx, because he always considers the capitalist mode of production as a way of giving autonomy to wealth, as a system of ownership which exercises its power on living labour and dead labour. He therefore does not find himself up against the dramatic problems of those who, having refused to look at this aspect of the problem and having determined to consider economics not as the science of given human relationships that are known by means of idealisation, but as the science of functional idealisations, are no longer in a position to see modes of exploitation, class domination and property relationships. In the second volume of *Capital* Marx considers the process of circulation as a potential flow that knows no interruptions. This does not correspond in any conceivable way to the real movement of things. Instead, as a provisional abstraction, it reveals both the 'ideality' of the circulatory movement (its tendency towards a reduction to zero time) and the forces that actually operate in this direction. Hence the particular manner of calculating the times of circulation on which we have dwelt. We recalled above that in contrast to Ricardo, Marx's theory of money gives new meaning to the theoretical research which had originated with bourgeois society. Initially conducted with a coherence between ends and means, the research had subsequently relegated this coherence to second place to the advantage of other interests. And yet in actual fact volume II of *Capital* is to a great extent a polemic against mercantilism, against 'profit upon alienation'. Surplus value, Marx writes, has its source 'neither in the money-form of wages nor in the form of wages paid in kind, nor in the capital laid out in the purchase of labour power. It arises out of the exchange of value for value-creating power, out of the conversion of a constant into a variable magnitude.'[119] And again: a capital's 'time of circulation . . . limits, generally speaking, its time of production and hence its process of generating suplus-value.'[120] The importance of these statements can be readily understood: they have no bearing on the possibility of calculating circulation costs, but they confer a particular meaning on them. The negative sign with which circulation costs are calculated serves to indicate their historicity and the tendency to limit them in a communist community. In other words, planned, socialised production will be far more able to approach the ideal model of a production realised without contradictions.

Nevertheless, if Marx's argument points in this direction, there is a place in the second volume of *Capital* to which we have already alluded, which clearly displays the problem of the relationship with the origin of bourgeois society and its investment of power. Marx takes up the cudgels against 'profit upon alienation', but is unshakeable in his affirmation that the 'capitalist class remains . . . the sole point of departure of the circulation of money.'[121] Here, in a 'provisional abstraction', there reappears the historical complexity of the mode of capitalist production. For Marx, the risk to face is the one whereby production and income can be presented as concepts that reflect each other (that is, as substantially identical). The central point is that:

the purchase and sale of labour-power . . . rests on a distribution of the *elements* of production which preceded and presupposed the distribution of the social *products*, namely on the separation of labour-power as a commodity of the labourer from the means of production as the property of non-labourers.[122]

In other words, if it is true that specific parts of value function as income, it is equally true that others function as capital. Returning to this same problem at the end of *Capital*, vol. III Marx attacks 'the absurd dogma . . . that in the final analysis the value of commodities resolves itself completely into income, into wages, profit and rent.'[123] Logically speaking, the difficulty comes from 'the definite designations of revenue and capital interchanging, and altering their position, so that they seem to be merely relative determinations from the point of view of the individual capitalist and to disappear when the total process of production is viewed as a whole.'[124] Notwithstanding the many good reasons that can militate in favour of this logic of a 'perspective' type of reflection, they founder on the fact that capital must reproduce itself in mercantile value and constitutes an element of it. To the logic of relations that reflect one another, or to that of reductionism, Marx opposes the logic of provisional abstractions, which disappear, leaving definite traces, and whose functional shift is representative of possible historical modifications. The element of truth in the reflective relation is, as we know, that profit appears to the individual capitalist as convertible into income, and 'can just as well be consumed productively as individually, equally well as capital or revenue'.[125] The form of the reflective relations thus conceals the possibility of decision-making and choice at the level of the individual capitalist, and thereby constitutes the source and the form of his power as possessor of social wealth. In reality, such an alternative of power remains, within the system, on the individual level. On the general plane (that is, on that of the overall social relations), the capitalist system's *laws of nature* operate (that is to say, in Marx's terminology, its historical laws). The capitalist process could not even last a week if the decisions not to invest became general. The fact is that they remain individual, and, as such, give to the historical laws the appearance of being natural ones.

Production in general, then, is based on the assumption that goods are sold at their value. The shift towards 'reality' that Marx proposes to make in *Capital*, vol. III is substantially a loosening of the bonds that come from 'idealisation', that is to say to the precedence that value-prices take over real circulation. Exchange is progressively severed from this ideality, even if its real mechanisms are presented in such a way as not to depart radically from the presupposed ideality. Nevertheless, 'realisation' becomes an open problem, and, in conjunction with it, competition. Commercial capital is not only posed ideally as 'false expenditure' in relation to an ideal condition in which prices are already realised, but it also interferes in reality with the rate of profit. Even landed revenue is no longer made into an abstraction. Its capitalist origin is explained in terms of the specific characteristics of such a branch of production as agriculture, whose organic composition revealed in Marx's day a distinct prevalence of living over objectified labour. Nonetheless, even in this process of drawing near to reality, the procedure by provisional abstraction remains central. Precisely in relation to the theme of the logic of 'reflection' Marx observes:

Although the rate of profit thus differs numerically from the rate of surplus-value, while surplus-value and profit are actually the same thing and numerically equivalent, profit is nevertheless a converted form of surplus-value, a form in which its origin and the secret of its existence are obscured and extinguished. In effect, profit is the form in which surplus-value presents itself to the view, and must initially be stripped by analysis to disclose the latter.[126]

Elsewhere Marx wrote that profit was the most highly developed form of surplus value.[127] In any case the path that Marx traced in the first volume of *Capital* is one to which he continued to point. Surplus value and profit are not a mere play of reflection. Simply because the visibility of small circulation has not been obliterated, Marx can see in the development of the productivity of labour not only an increase in use values which, if idealised, become realisable in every circumstance, but also either a clue to the shattering of the wretched basis of the theft of a man's labouring time and to posing the question of free time for the masses, or a basis for rendering exchange value autonomous, for the formation and solidification of property-owning relations or relations of power connected to them.

The famous question of 'transformation' must also be seen against this background. The mode of determining market values, Marx wrote, 'which we have here outlined *abstractly*, is promoted in the real market by competition among the buyers, provided that the demand is large enough to absorb the mass of commodities at values so fixed.'[128] The reality which is approached is thus kept deliberately close to its concept (that is, to its idealised provisional abstraction). On the other hand this real condition with which Marx is most concerned (the increase in the productivity of labour) is reduced to zero, and will reappear only in the sphere of the law of the tendential fall in the rate of profit. The assumed ideal conditions are thus that commodities are sold at their value. It should be noted, moreover, that Marx here means by surplus value not the original condition of the appropriation of labour power, from which arise capital and all the property relations, but, as even a disciple of Ricardo must realise, the peculiarity of the relation of exploitation of those branches that are statically productive under various technological conditions. Given the competition among capitals, given the diverse organic composition of the productive branches, given the wage and its size, which is taken as an index of a specific quantity of labour-power and surplus value which are set in motion by it, given the rate of surplus value and the productivity of labour, given that the commodities are all sold at their value (that is, that the total of price-values is realised), given all these ideal conditions, one may deduce the transformation of surplus values into average profit. The conclusion could not be drawn without bringing into play the elements of provisional idealisation, which presuppose that commodities are sold at their value, and which put a stop to all other conditions of variability.

One should not speak of a naturalistic residue, but, if anything, of a permanent use of a method of 'idealisations' or provisional abstractions. Immediately afterwards, in fact, the variation in the productivity of labour reemerges as a permanent tendency. In the effort to approximate to reality, this leads to the assertion of the tendential law of the fall in the rate of profit, and hence to the objective emergence of limits and barriers to the capitalist system which present themselves as its contradictions. It has been said of the tendential laws that they are scientifically irrelevant.[129] But in Marx's method the concern is still to render visible the traces which, in an examination which was not centred upon provisional abstractions, would remain completely unnoticed. It is these traces that allow Marx to construct the alternative between a society in which the autonomisation of exchange value leads to a permanent increase in the imbalance between living labour and the ownership of dead labour, and a society in which the traces, observed in a context which had apparently erased them, serve to convey the development of individual capacities towards mass liberation. Such are the signs, the points of reference, that Marx has left us for the building of a communist liberty.

I do not mean by this to defend to the death the validity of Marx's scientific method. He is sometimes approximate in his methods; the suggestions are at times inspired but tortuous, the idealisations not always consonant with the results. What I have wanted to point out in these pages is something quite different. From the first pages in which attention was drawn to the depreciation of capital and the thesis that capital never entirely covers its debts, through to the examination of the way in which exchange value is rendered autonomous along with the relations of property and mastery that derive from them, up to the encounter and clash with Ricardo concerning the increase in the productivity of labour and the alternative between the ruling class's enjoyment and the free time of the masses, Marx offers us his coherent research which aims to separate economics from its traditional link with the property-owning classes and at the same time to retain its character as a science. The result is the hypothesis of a new type of producer (the social individual) who puts 'the conditions of the free development and free movement of individuals under their control'. Marx does not arrive at this hypothesis either on philosophical grounds or on politico-economic ones, but by conveying economics towards a hypothesis of transformation, and going on to see with disenchanted eyes a present in which the residues of violence and barbarism which are to be overthrown still operate within a system of chains that are compatible with them, and hence whose very rationality must also be radically transformed.

Notes

1 K. Marx and F. Engels, *Marx-Engels Werke* Dietz Verlag, (Berlin, 1962–8), vol. 27 pp. 312-5.
2 *Ibid.*
3 *Ibid.*
4 *Ibid.*
5 *Ibid.*
6 *Ibid.*
7 K. Marx, *The Poverty of Philosophy*, in *Collected Works* (Lawrence & Wishart, London, 1975), vol. 6, p. 135.
8 *Ibid.* p. 143.
9 *Ibid.* p. 166.
10 K. Marx, *Wage Labour and Capital*, in *Selected Works*, (Progress, Moscow, 1969), vol. 1, p. 159.
11 K. Marx and F. Engels, *Selected Correspondence* (Lawrence & Wishart, London, 1936), p. 238.
12 K. Marx, *Capital. A Critique of Political Economy* (Lawrence & Wishart, London 1977), vol. III, p. 180.
13 K. Marx and F. Engels, *Selected Correspondence* (Lawrence & Wishart, London, 1943), p. 239.
14 *Ibid.* p. 239.
15 *Ibid.* p. 240.
16 *Ibid.* p. 240.
17 *Marx-Engels Werke*, vol. 32, p. 67 (this passage is deleted in the English translation of the letter of 14 August 1851 in *Selected Correspondence*).
18 K. Marx, *Economico-Philosophical Manuscripts*, in *Early Writings* (Penguin, Harmondsworth, 1976), p. 373.
19 *Ibid.* p. 261-2.
20 *Ibid.* p. 266.
21 K. Marx, *Early Writings*, p. 375.
22 *Ibid.* p. 379.
23 *Ibid.* p. 390.
24 *Ibid.* p. 75-6.
25 *Ibid.* p. 277.
26 *Ibid.* p. 277.
27 *Ibid.* p. 278.
28 F. Engels and K. Marx, *The Holy Family, or Critique of Critical Criticism. Against Bruno Bauer and Company. Collected Works*, vol. 4, p. 45.
29 *Ibid.* p. 46.
30 *Ibid.* p. 49.
31 *Ibid.* p. 50.
32 K. Marx and F. Engels, *The German Ideology. Critique of Modern German Philosophy according to its representatives Feuerbach, B. Bauer and Stirner, Collected Works*, vol. 5, p. 39.

33 *Ibid*. p. 44.
34 *Ibid*. p. 47.
35 *Ibid*. p. 329.
36 K. Marx, *Theories of Surplus-Value* (Lawrence & Wishart, London, 1969), part 1, p. 287.
37 *Ibid*. p. 287.
38 *Ibid*. p. 287.
39 *Ibid*. p. 290.
40 *Ibid*. p. 295.
41 *Ibid*. p. 301.
42 *Ibid*. p. 301.
43 *Ibid*. p. 296.
44 K. Marx and F. Engels, *The German Ideology, Collected Works*, vol. 5, p. 50.
45 *Ibid*. pp. 51-2.
46 *Ibid*. p. 228.
47 *Ibid*. p. 229.
48 *Ibid*. p. 213.
49 *Ibid*. p. 410.
50 *Ibid*. p. 410.
51 K. Marx, *Early Writings*, p. 426.
52 K. Marx, *Capital*, vol. III, pp. 883-4.
53 The work referred to here is entitled *A Prize Essay on the Comparative Merits of Competition and Cooperation* (London, 1834). Appearing anonymously, it treated with the utmost realism that condition whereby, if machines cut the cost of those goods that are necessary to life, they 'cheapen labour too'. (p. 27) Elsewhere it showed how the contribution by parishes had been utilised to maintain competition between mechanical looms and manual ones: 'Competition between the manual loom and the mechanical loom was maintained with the poor tax.' Workers are reduced 'from respectable and to a certain extent independent artisans to wretched, fawning creatures who live off the degrading bread of charity'. (*ibid*. p. 29).
54 K. Marx, *Grundrisse* (Penguin, Harmondsworth, 1974), p. 331.
55 *Ibid*. p. 348.
56 K. Marx, *Grundrisse* (Backhaus, Turin, 1976), p. 979.
57 *Ibid*. p. 1011.
58 *Ibid*. p. 1014.
59 *Ibid*. p. 1015.
60 *Ibid*. p. 1005.
61 'Steuart is . . . the *rational* expression of the Monetary and Mercantile systems' (Marx, *Theories of Surplus-Value*, part I, p. 43). In fact Steuart is utterly immersed in the illusion of 'profit upon alienation', but one must not forget that this illusion is a necessity for the capitalist system, which presents the gratuitous appropriation of labour-power as exchange.
62 K. Marx, *Capital*, vol. III, p. 883.
63 K. Marx and F. Engels, *Selected Correspondence*, p. 246.
64 K. Marx, *Grundrisse*, p. 410.
65 *Ibid*. p. 411.
66 *Ibid*. p. 540.
67 K. Marx, *Theories of Surplus-Value*, part II, p. 117.
68 K. Marx, *Grundrisse*, p. 415.
69 K. Marx, *Capital*, vol. III, p. 876 (translation amended).

70 K. Marx, *Theories of Surplus-Value*, part III, p. 462.
71 K. Marx, *Grundrisse*, pp. 541-2.
72 *Ibid.* p. 542.
73 *Ibid.* p. 543.
74 *Ibid.* p. 545.
75 *Ibid.* p. 545.
76 *Ibid.* p. 548.
77 In a letter to Engels of 30 April, 1868, Marx, on the basis of given production costs, tries to calculate how commercial capital influences the mean rate of profit. If the society's productive capital is given, and if the total of merchants' capital is also given, Marx's hypothesis is that the trader derives the mean rate of profit from his capital. The introduction of commercial capital lowers the mean rate of profit calculated for productive capital alone. In this way the 'commodities — taken as a whole, and on a social scale — are sold *at their value*'. The commercial capitalist realises the total of social wealth, while his own capital, added to productive capital, serves him only as circulating monetary capital. 'Whatever more the merchant swallows up he gets either simply by trickery, or by speculation on the oscillations of commodity prices, or, in the case of the actual retailers, as wages for labour — wretched unproductive labour though it is — all these appearing under the form of profit.' (*Selected Correspondence*, pp. 244-5).
78 K. Marx, *Grundrisse*, p. 557.
79 *Ibid.* pp. 559-60.
80 *Ibid.* pp. 595-6.
81 *Ibid.* pp. 595-6.
82 K. Marx, *Critique of the Gotha Programme* (Progress, Moscow, 1978), pp. 17-18.
83 K. Marx, *Grundrisse*, p. 401-2.
84 See on this question G.W.F. Hegel, *Science of Logic* (London, 1969), vol. II.
85 K. Marx, *Theories of Surplus-Value*, part 3, p. 257. Notwithstanding the condemnation this inflicts on productive workers, it never reaches the brutal picture that is conjured up by Nietzsche's assessment:

I do not see what can be done about the European worker. He finds himself too well placed not to make more immediate demands: ultimately he has the majority on his side. Hope has vanished that a species of man can be created that is both modest and moderate, a slavery in the least rigorous sense of the word, a class. something that has unalterability. A worker has been created who is militarily proficient: he has been given the right to vote, the right of association; everything has been done to destroy the instincts on which can be based a swarm of servile coolies, so that the worker already feels and makes felt his existence — now — as a state of penury (in moral terms, as an *injustice*). But what do you expect? . . . If you aim at something, you want the means as well; if you want slaves (and they *are* needed!) you should not educate them in such a way as to turn them into gentlemen.' (F. Nietzsche, *Posthumous Fragments*.)

Elsewhere, in relation to the way in which Nietzsche sees to the solution of free time: 'One recognises the superiority of Greek man and the man of the

Renaissance, but one would wish to have them without their causes and conditions' (*ibid.*). This note, like the exposition of Ricardo's implicit sociology, aids the understanding of Marx's theory of production in general as the possibility of free time for the masses. I do not conceal the fact that they intend to avoid concealing (behind a Wittgensteinian silence) the fact that neo-Ricardians and neo-Nietzscheans aspire to cultural hegemony over the working-class movement.

86 K. Marx, *Theories of Surplus-Value*, part 2, p. 573.

87 *Ibid.* p. 561.

88 K. Marx, *Capital* (Penguin, Harmondsworth, 1976), vol. I, p. 760, footnote. Nietzsche, on the other hand, is:

> against justice . . . against *John Stuart Mill*. I abhor his triviality when he says: There is no need for two weights and two measures; that which you would not, do not unto others. He would gladly base all human relationships on *reciprocity* in such a way that every action is presented as the repayment of an action that has been done to us. This premise is plebeian in the basest sense of the word. It presupposes an equivalency of action for me and for you. The *ultra-personal* value of an action is simply obliterated. Reciprocity is a gross piece of vulgarity . . . In a profound sense one never pays back because one is unique and makes only *unique things*. This fundamental conviction contains within itself the cause of the *aristocratic isolation from the multitude*, since the multitude believes in equality and *therefore* also in the possibility of compensation and reciprocity. (F. Nietzsche, *Posthumous Fragments*).

89 It is yet to be ascertained whether the communistic scheme would be consistent with that multiform development of human nature, those manifold unlikenesses, that diversity of tastes and talents, and variety of intellectual points of view, which not only form a great part of the interest of human life, but by bringing intellects into a stimulating collision, and by presenting to each innumerable notions that he would not have conceived of himself, are the mainspring of mental and moral progression. (J.S. Mill, *Principles of Political Economy*, Penguin, Harmondsworth, 1970, p. 361.)

90 K Marx, *Capital*, vol. I, p. 744, footnote.

91 J.S. Mill, *Principles of Political Economy*, p. 360.

92 Ricardo's ruthlessness was thus not only *scientifically honest*, but a *scientific necessity* from his own point of view. But, because of this, it is also quite immaterial to him whether the advance of the productive forces slays landed property or workers . . . Ricardo's conception is, on the whole, in the interests of the *industrial bourgeoisie*, only *because* and *insofar as* their interests coincide with that of production and the productive development of human labour. Where the bourgeoisie comes into conflict with this, he is just as ruthless towards it as he is at other times towards the proletariat and the aristocracy. (K. Marx, *Theories of Surplus-Value*, part II, p. 118.) This is the essence of Marx's theory of the lack of impartiality in science.

93 K. Marx, *Capital*, vol. I, pp. 758-60.

94 The choice of the wage as the independent variable in the preliminary stages was due to its being regarded as consisting of specified necessaries determined by physiological or social conditions which are independent of prices and the rate of profits. But as soon as the possibility of variations in

the division of the product is admitted, this consideration loses much of its force. And when the wage to be regarded as 'given' in terms of a more or less abstract standard, and does not acquire a definite meaning until the prices of commodities are determined, the position is reversed. The rate of profits, as a ratio, has a significance which is independent of any prices and can well be 'given' before the prices are fixed. It is accordingly susceptible of being determined from outside the system of production, in particular by the level of the money rates of interest (P. Sraffa, *Production of Commodities by Means of Commodities: Prelude to a Critique of Economic Theory*, Cambridge, 1975, p. 33.) Nor must one forget that while for Bentham the wage was fixed by natural limits, corresponding to the laws of nature, the externality of the level of profit and its dependence on that of interest, depend, if we adhere to Marx's interpretation, on the property relations which are autonomised with respect to the productive system. If it is supposed that the working classes govern the relation between wages and the rate of profit and determine prices, property relations are excluded from control by the productive system; indeed they exercise a fundamental influence on it. On this point, Marx's argument about not separating the critique of political economy, the critique of power and the critique of property relations is difficult to sidestep, unless one also makes power into an independent variable.

95 K. Marx, *Capital*, vol. I, pp. 771-2. There is an element of wit in the juxtaposition of such social figures. That of the manager enjoys a good press in late-capitalist circles.

96 But Marx maintains:

If man attributes an independent existence, clothed in a *religious form*, to his relationship to his own nature, to external nature and to other men so that he is dominated by these notions, then he requires *priests* and *their* labour. With the disappearance of the religious form of consciousness and of these relationships, the labour of the priests will likewise cease to enter into the social process of production. The labour of priests will end with the existence of the *priests* themselves and, in the same way, the labour which the capitalist performs *qua* capitalist, or causes to be performed by someone else, will end together with the existence of the capitalists. (K. Marx, *Theories of Surplus-Value*, part III, p. 496.)

97 K. Marx and F. Engels, *Selected Correspondence*, pp. 318-9.

98 K. Marx, *Grundrisse*, p. 463.

99 *Ibid*. p. 693.

100 *Ibid*. p. 694.

101 *Ibid*. p. 699.

102 *Ibid*. p. 705.

103 *Ibid*. p. 706.

104 *Ibid*. p. 708.

105 *Ibid*. p. 832.

106 K. Mark, *Theories of Surplus-Value*, part III, p. 257.

107 K. Marx, *Capital*, vol. I, pp. 743-4.

108 The so-called *Notes on Wagner* from which this passage is taken may be read in English translation in *Theoretical Practice* (1972) no. 5.

109 K. Marx, *Capital*, vol. I, p. 284.

110 K. Marx, *Contribution to the Critique of Political Economy* (Lawrence &

Wishart, London, 1971), p. 57.
111 K. Marx, *Theories of Surplus-Value*, part III, p. 315.
112 K. Marx, *Capital*, vol. I, pp. 758-9, footnote.
113 K. Marx, *Capital*, vol. III, p. 104.
114 *The Ethnological Notebooks of Karl Marx*, (Studies of Morgan, Phear, Maine, Lubbock) transcribed and edited, with an introduction by Lawrence Krader (Assen, 1972), p. 120.
115 K. Marx and F. Engels, *The German Ideology*, in *Collected Works*, vol. 5, p. 45.
116 K. Marx, *Capital*, vol. I, p. 322.
117 K. Marx, *Capital*, vol. I, p. 646.
118 *Ibid*. p. 652.
119 *Ibid*. p. 660.
120 K. Marx, *Capital*, vol. II (Lawrence & Wishart, London, 1961), p. 220.
121 *Ibid*. p. 125.
122 *Ibid*. p. 334.
123 *Ibid*. p. 385.
124 K. Marx, *Capital*, vol. III, p. 841.
125 *Ibid*. p. 844.
126 *Ibid*. p. 848.
127 *Ibid*. p. 48.
128 Ricardo's disciples, just as Ricardo himself, fail to make a distinction between *surplus-value* and *profit* . . . It does not occur to them that, even if one considers not capitals in different spheres of production but *each* capital separately, insofar as it does not consist exclusively of variable capital, (i.e. of capital laid out in wages only), rate of profit and rate of surplus-value are different things, that therefore profit must be a more developed, specifically modified form of surplus-value. They perceive the difference only insofar as it concerns equal profits — average rate of profit — for capitals in different spheres of production and differently composed of fixed and circulating ingredients. (K. Marx, *Theories of Surplus-Value*, part III, p. 85.)
129 K. Marx, *Capital*, vol. III, p. 185.

7 THEORY OF EVOLUTION, REVOLUTION AND THE STATE: THE CRITICAL RELATION OF MARX TO HIS CONTEMPORARIES DARWIN, CARLYLE, MORGAN, MAINE AND KOVALEVSKY

Lawrence Krader

Part I: Natural and Human History

The Relation of Man to Nature

The relation to nature of the human kind is at once the natural history of humanity, whereby the material continuity between man and nature is posited, and the material interchange between the two sides is effected. Therefore there is but one universal history, the history of man and nature; this history is one, being the history of human labour in relation to nature, or the history of production, industry and science. Human history is the history of society as the act of its development, even in the alienated form of industry, hence it comprises the true anthropological nature of history; it is a real and actual part of natural history, as the becoming human of nature. Natural history thus comes to comprise human history within itself, just as human history comes to comprise natural history. In actuality the universal history is divided, nature and mankind being alienated from one another, potentially the two histories are one.[1] The alienation of labour in society is the secondary alienation in history, which follows from the primary alienation of man from nature by his labour, the first alienation being the historical condition of the second; the second does not follow out of any logical necessity from the first. The second alienation is the condition of labour in civil and bourgeois society. Were that second alienation to flow of necessity from the first, which is the real and actual position of man in the cosmos, then it would follow that the bourgeois condition of alienation is of the nature of things.[2]

History is the universal solvent. There is nothing that is not subject to change; all is history by virtue of its coming into being and passing away. The notion of immutable laws was on the contrary soothing to the ears of the kings of the Medes and Persians, and accounts of the eternal laws of being are alike pleasing to the speculative philosophers and to the church, just as the doctrine of unchanging laws of the market and of profit are a myth of the classical economists,[3] presupposing an unchanging human nature, which is the fantasy of the speculative anthropologists. History was thereby hypostasised, being made into the metaphysical subject, a Person apart; it is therefore a fetish, the self-actor, endowed with a will and consciousness of its own, instead of what it really is, inseparable from its bearers, the real, human individuals.[4] Human history is from its beginning and continuously thereafter the history of the activity whereby we produce our existence; this continuity is the process of social reproduction itself, and is as such that part of the history of labour which is the relation of labour to nature. The history of our labour and work[5] is the history we make. There is thus but one science, the science of history,[6] which is divided as the universal history of nature and the particular history of the human kind.

History and Ideology
The interpretation of history is the expression of an ideology which has a practical effect on the brains of human beings, whereby the consciousness comes into historical play. The first ideologues were those such as Cabanis and Destutt de Tracy who held that scientific ideas would have a historical action, which would be realised by their engagement in the politics of Napoleonic France; but as is well known, Napoleon would have none of them, whereat their frustration was activated by Saint-Simon.[7] The German ideologists, L. Feuerbach, Bruno Bauer, Moses Hess and Max Stirner, developed their ideas from the breeding grounds of pure speculation, with the end of practical engagement in the German political arena. This was not history but metaphysics.[8] It is at the same time an interested speculation, a speculation with a particular political expression in view; that this speculation was proposed as the basis for history by the German ideologists does not make it into a science, for it poses only the cerebral activity of man as the basis of history, history *en philosophe*, abstract history. History is of itself concrete history, the opposite of abstract, speculative history. The human individual on the contrary is both abstract and concrete. On the one side, the human individual is the same as the generic being of man, with generic consciousness. On the other, the society is not a mere abstraction, as opposed to the individual. The natural history of mankind is its biological history, the record of homo sapiens. (Thus, the history of the species is one; any other doctrine would be racism. The history of mankind as social history is many; the totality of the history of the human kind is the opposition between the many histories and the one.) Neither society nor history has any force, save through the activity of the individuals in their combination, the consciousness exists only in

and through the brain of the living individuals; and the generic life is not separate from these individuals, the two are one.[9] Thereby the doctrine of fatalism, which arises out of the abstraction of the total course of history from its concrete moment, the human individuals, and posits the historical movement as being subject to a goal of its own, is overcome. By the process of abstraction, the individual activities are subordinated to a supervening force, and history is itself made into a god.

The Basis and Superstructure of Society

Production by labour consists of a double relation, natural and social, social in the sense that the work together of several individuals is implied in all labour. Hence a given mode of production or industrial stage determines the condition of society, and not the converse. The history of humanity is a discontinuous series of stages of development, divided according to the different modes in which production is organised and carried through.[10] The history of humanity is therefore an evolution in the strict sense of the word, being a development of one stage out of another by forces inherent in one stage and connected in an unbroken line with the next, the transformation from the one to the other being effected likewise by inherent forces common to both stages of the development. These inherent forces in the history of the modes of production, in the transformation from one industrial stage to the next, are the productive powers, which are in no way a development external to the historical course of production itself, the relation of labour to nature being the direct application of the work whereby the natural materials are transformed within the process of production.

The notion of developmental stages in evolutionary sequence from lower to higher, in linear progression, is implicit in the articles written by Marx on India, according to which, England stood at a higher stage of development than India. Moreover, because England stood high industrially, it therefore stood high in its civilisation, or stage of social development. India was inferior because its productive powers were less developed than the productive powers of English capitalism, a stage to which India had not yet attained, because it was inferior as a trading nation to the English, and because it was held back in its development as a colony by the conquering power. India had been able to win quietly over its previous conquerors, the Arabs, Turks, etc., who had not stood higher than the Indians in productive powers, and therefore did not stand higher in their civilisation.[11]

The history of nature is only concrete, the history of humanity is both abstract and concrete, being constituted of the relations of labour to nature and the relations in society, the construction of civilisation upon the basis of the natural relation of labour and the social relation thereof. The history of mankind is developmental both in the sense that man by his labour has developed out of the animal stage of natural history and in the sense that man by his labour has developed from one stage or mode of production to another. The concept of development is an abstraction made by those who stand outside the historical course, by abstracting themselves from it, and comparing the productive powers of one stage of development with another. The development of human history is therefore both extrinsic and intrinsic, the abstraction being the extrinsic history which is brought to bear upon the intrinsic, concrete history. The stages of development are at once classificatory devices, hence externalities, and containers of the substance, or the productive powers, which are the inner dynamism of human history.

The modes of production are classified accordingly as the Asiatic, the classical-antique, the feudal and the modern bourgeois, which stand to each other as the progressive epochs of the economic formation of society. They are successive stages, the one chronologically following upon the other, as *dramatis personae*, in the order of their historical appearance, and they are progressive in the sense that the productive power of the successive stage is higher than that of the preceding one.[12] A mode of production is the economic formation of a society, constituting a stage in the historical course of its development, and thereby periodic wholes. The mode of production is not the society as a totality, but its economic basis, the basis being bound together with the superstructure of the society. A mode of production, moreover, is not multiple within a given society, save in periods of transition or chaos through war and conquest, revolution; a society is likewise a whole, save when it is torn apart by the same processes of revolutionary transformation.

Part II: Evolution of Nature and Society
Marx and Darwin

The concept of evolution as the development in common of a related group of organisms by common factors within the individual members of the group, and common relations to the environment, was powerfully developed by Darwin's researches, the publication of which Marx noticed in letters to Engels and Lassalle.[13] Darwin's work, wrote Marx, provides a natural-scientific basis for the class struggles in history, dealing a death-blow to teleology in the natural sciences;[14] the connection of Darwin's doctrine was made to the Malthusian 'struggle for existence' [this phrase was used in a metaphorical sense by Darwin: LK], the war of each against all, of Thomas Hobbes, and to Hegel's theory of civil society as the spiritual animal kingdom by Marx.[15] From Darwin's doctrine, Marx drew support for the premise in his thinking which he had already established, whereby the unity of natural and human history is posited as intrinsic, in opposition to the doctrine of the grand design for nature and man which is imposed by a deity. Teleology is a doctrine of godly, extrinsic guidance, opposed to which are the processes of natural maintenance and natural selection, which are the internal and concrete dynamisms of the origin of species.[16]

The relation between natural and human history was brought into focus by Marx in his critique of the notion advanced by Thomas Hodgskin regarding the storage of labour skills. What is at issue is the accumulation and transmission of skills, their maintenance and reshaping, by living labour. This is then related by Marx to the accumulation of past, crystallised labour, or the product of living labour. The passage from the storage (*Aufhäufung*) of the inherited traits, according to Darwin, to the accumulation by man is made, according to Marx, by an already modified human nature, and already modified non-human nature transformed into an organ of man's activities. The accumulation is the result of a two-fold process, on the one side historical, over periods of time greater than the span of an individual's life, on the other the transmission of a skill on the part of the individual worker.[17]

Darwin, according to Marx, had brought out the history of natural technology, the process of natural selection being the process of adaption of the plant and animal organs as instruments of production. The difference between the two processes of production lies in the modification of nature by man. Yet the parallel between the two processes was drawn by both Darwin and Marx relative to specialisation, and to the relation between form and function: thus, in natural organs and human instruments of production, the greater the specialisation of function, the less freedom in the form of the instrument is possible; a knife to cut all sorts of things can be, on the whole, of any shape, while on the contrary, a knife to be used to cut in only one way on one thing must have a particular shape.[18] Both men sought to prove at this point that the laws of natural and of human history are the same.

Concrete and Abstract History

The movement of history depicted by Marx is the process of an internal development of the productive forces, the relations of production and exchange, and the forms of property related to them, the conflict between the productive forces and the forms of property. The movement of history proceeds through stages or discontinuities, in which the inner development is contradicted by the external, juridical forms. The historical movement of dissolution of the archaic gentes, clans, sibs, lineages, village communities was at the same time contradicted by the process of formation of the ancient states which were founded upon tribes, whereby the principles of the archaic collective life were carried forward.[19] Given that these processes of continuation and dissolution of the archaic collective and communal forms of the social life are world-wide in scope, then it follows that they are the subject of another kind of history than that of a particular people, whether Roman, Germanic, or Inca, etc.[20] These world-wide movements are concrete historical processes, whereby the history of civil society is worked out, but they are not particular courses of history; they are processes which are carried forward on different continents, under different historical and cultural circumstances, hence they are general processes, but they are not universal, for they are not the processes in which all the peoples participate of necessity, such as the processes of labour and production. History, general and concrete, is opposed to the abstract universal history, such as had been set down in the eighteenth century by the philosophers Kant and Condorcet, and is opposed to the concrete and particular histories which had been written by Niebuhr and Mommsen.

The process of human evolution is at once the same and not the same as the general human history; they are the same insofar as both are concrete, but at this point they then diverge, as may be shown in connection with the history of particular institutions.[21] The application by Marx of the philological and historical researches of Niebuhr, Grimm, Maurer, Haxthausen, Kovalevsky, etc. on the history of the peasant commune among the Romanic, Germanic, Slavic and Indic peoples is an aspect of the history of particular institutions and at once a part of the evolution of humanity.[22]

Evolution and Revolution: The History We Do Not Make and the History We Make

The history we make is opposed to the history we do not make.[23] The separation between the two histories is not absolute, for the history we do not make is a major determinant factor in the history we make; the history we do not make is determined in a minuscule but developing way by the history we make. The history we do not make is natural history, the history of the evolution of the cosmos, the Earth, the human species; the history we do not make is subject to laws we do not make, but only discover, whereas the history we make is subject both to these laws of nature and to human acts and relations, and the laws willed and conscious, unwilled and unconscious, natural and legislated, laws manipulative, predictive and prescriptive. The great act of the history we make is the act of radical transformation of society; the course of human history is the interaction of the several historical moments, conscious and unconscious, voluntary and involuntary.[24] The radical transformation of society is the history of the development of the universal human consciousness, the social consciousness in general, and the class consciousness in particular, divided as the social classes are divided and opposed to one another.

The system of the history we do not make was worked out by Marx at first relative to the discoveries made by Darwin, and then related to conceptions introduced by Vico. It was in this connection that Marx called for the history of technology which would compose for humanity the material basis of each particular social organisation, the history of the productive organs of man, parallel to the history of natural technology. The two histories are the same and at once not the same, being continuous and discontinuous with one another, the human history disclosing a four-fold process:

1   The active relation of man to nature.
2   The process of direct production of human life.
3   The social relations of human life.
4   The mental or spiritual representations which spring from these relations.[25] (The order in which these moments appear in the theory is important.)

This would then constitute the critical history of technology, and the critical relation between nature and culture.

The active relation to nature has its history; without

co-operation in the labour process there is no production, without production there is no life. The beginnings of culture, such as are found among the hunting peoples, provides evidence of such co-operation; the agriculture of the communities in India likewise. These are evidences of co-operation on the communal, or small scale. Large-scale co-operation in simple form was undertaken by the agencies of the Asiatic, ancient Egyptian and Etruscan sovereignties. Sporadic large-scale and complex co-operation was applied in European antiquity and in the Middle Ages. The capitalist form of co-operation is undertaken on a large scale, is systematic as opposed to sporadic, and is complex as opposed to simple, whereby it is opposed to the pre-capitalist economic formations.[26] The development of co-operation in the capitalist mode of production is on the one hand the negation of that which was undertaken at the beginnings of human culture, on the other continuation, by the actualisation of the potentiality and the realisation of the possibility that was inherent therein.

The sequence from the primitive to the pre-capitalist to the capitalist modes of production is an ordered sequence abstractly considered, and it is carried through concretely by multilinear developments, false starts and detours. The progression is not uniform, but proceeds by quiet metamorphoses, which are succeeded by rapid overturns. A classless society is constituted out of opposed historical moments: a mass of contradictory forms of within the social unity has a contradictory character which will not be exploded by gradual change. Yet if we do not find hidden in the society as it is the material conditions of production and exchange for the constitution of the classless society, then all attempts at exploding the present society would be vain.[27]

The history we do not make is our natural history or the evolutionary process. It is history without the historical subject, history that is solely concrete. The history we make is history abstract and concrete, history with both subject and object. The history we make is the history of society and its formation, the history of the theatre of war between the social classes, as the necessary condition for that conflict, just as it is the necessary condition for class consciousness. The history of class consciousness follows the same historical course and is subject to the same criteria of development as was noted above in the case of the social history of co-operation. In the ancient states and empires of Asia, Africa, Europe and the New World, the class consciousness achieved at first a sporadic expression on the part of the immediate producers in society; in modern capitalist society, on the contrary, class consciousness has been systematically developed, both qualitatively in terms of strength of commitment, and quantitatively, in terms of the numbers of those in the working class involved. It has attained a peak of its historical expression in the history of modern bourgeois society, during the time of revolution, and it diminishes as the revolutionary activity, whereby it is brought forth, and which in turn it serves to heighten and express, lessens in its social force, with reference to the oppositions between the social classes. The class consciousness is expressed in a positive manner during the height of revolutionary activity, and on the contrary, is reified when the latter is reduced, not in a unitary mode, but accordingly as the social classes are divided. The history we make is nothing other than the processes of the relation of labour with nature, the interaction within society, and the mental and spiritual representations which arise from these relations and interactions. As such it is different from the history we do not make, which lacks the abstract and theoretical representations thereof, save as they have been introduced by the human kind. In practice, the course of the history we make is separate from the history we do not only in the fantasies of the speculative philosophers and the religious world of the mystics.[28]

The notion advanced by the evolutionary socialist, Eduard Bernstein, that socialism will be achieved through the quiet metamorphosis of bourgeois society rests on the simplification of the process of history on the one side, and the confusion of evolution as the history we do not make with the history we make on the other. The propaganda of the act, or terrorism, achieves nothing but its self-destruction unless it is directly related to the processes of the material base of society, the radical transformation of society and its material base, and therewith of their mental and spiritual representations.

The Individual and Society

The individual was made into the prime mover of history, and a cult of the individual was thereupon manufactured by Thomas Carlyle.[29] Not unrelated to this act of devotion was the fable whose central figure was Robinson Crusoe, the self-made man, alone on his tropical isle.[30] The problem of the individual in history is a two-fold one, on the one hand, that of the reality of the individual in society, and hence in history; on the other the question of the primary motive force in history. That the individual is real, and not a mere abstraction, was the subject of

Marx's early polemic against Feuerbach and Feuerbach's interpretation of Hegel.[31]

The state, wrote Marx, is the form in which the individuals of a ruling class bring out their common interests, and in which the whole of civil society of a given epoch is concentrated. The illusion is then promulgated that the act of legislation rests on the free will of the individual; it is in fact torn forth from its real basis in society. The abstract individual has no history, the concrete individual is not only in history, but is the sole basis for the productive forces, for the private labours, for the consciousness, and hence for social reality, materially and historically. The capacities of the individuals are not developed by the individuals themselves, however; they are developed only by the individuals in their combination, in their interaction with another, and by their appropriation in concert of the instruments of production, their combined applications of these instruments.[32] The individual is the ensemble of social relations.[33] Society, however, is not of the same material reality as the individuals who make it up: society is the expression of the sum of the relations between the individuals who make it up; it is not made up of the individuals themselves, nor is it directly the nexus of the relations between the individuals.[34] The relation between the individual and society is therefore asymmetrical.

The history of society is divided into periods or stages. That history, we have seen, is not an independent construction, but is constituted by the relations to one another of individuals over the course of time. The stages themselves are not historically real, or accessible to the senses, they only appear to be so. The activities of the individuals in their combination with one another and in relation to the world of nature make up the given stage of their achievements. The society is not real in the same sense that our physical bodies are real, or the planets and stars are real; hence the social fact is not real in the same sense that the facts studied by the physiologists and physicists are real.[35] Questions of social ontology have a bearing both on the being of the human individual and on the ideology of the ruling class both in the ancient and the modern bourgeois epochs of the history of civil society. The priest at the shrine of Diana Nemorensis, elected king for a year, prowled about his glade with naked sword in hand; this struggle of each against all had begun in ancient Rome. The rugged individualist was celebrated by the Republican Party in the campaigns conducted from 1932 to 1944 against Franklin Delano Roosevelt. Society is but a congeries of individuals, according to

Hobbes. The alternative to this viewpoint had been put forward by Aristotle, who considered the individual outside society to be either a beast or a deity, in any case, inhuman.[36] The cult of the individual, the doctrine of social contract — according to which each enters society of his own free will — whereby society is formed to begin with, is the reduction of social ontology to individual ontology, and of social problems to problems of the individual and the individual conscience. On the contrary: the freedom of the individual is the freedom of the ruling class-individual, and this freedom lacks the substance of freedom. The agencies of the state must bring under control not only the working class, guarding against the general strike, and against the industrial army of the reserve, but also against the aberrations of the individual capitalist, who seeks his profit at the expense of the interest of the whole of the social class of which he is a member, and against the declassed terrorism of the alienated youth emerging out of the alienating ruling class.

The question of the individual is not raised directly in the doctrine of socialism, it is raised by the enemies of socialism. The status of the individual is not the central problem of socialism, on the contrary, the end and fundamental problem of socialism is the constitution of the social whole by social labour. The individuality is then stripped of its class character. The false individuality of the ideologists of the mode of production of modern bourgeois society was founded, during the nineteenth and twentieth centuries, not on the philosophical doctrines of classical antiquity, of Aristotle and Epictetus, but on the atomistic individualism of Descartes, Hobbes and Leibnitz during the seventeenth century. The current ideological expression, however, is but a subterfuge, whereby the agencies of the state, the ruling class, and the private sphere attached to either are divested of responsibility for the care of the sick, the hungry, the aged; relief from the burden of taxation of the rich is the point behind the philosophy of the individual.[37]

The historical category in the doctrine of Marxism is the relation of man by his labour to nature and the relations of human kind in society, the society being in turn the expression of human relations in their combination, in a given period. The period is the form of the combination; it is not independent of the relations between the human beings. The individual as the bearer and nodal point of the social relations is determined therein by the actual and the antecedent relations in the same historical course; the consciousness of these relations is borne by the individual, existing nowhere else than in his nervous organs. The conscious human being, however, is not the prime mover but the derivative of the present and past relations in their combination to the other human beings and to the natural surroundings; the relations are divided in their social expression according to the relations in production, which are the determinants in their turn of the formation and the opposition between the social classes in modern bourgeois society. The measure of history is not the individual but the social whole and the relations of the social classes in their division therein. Thus the socialist canon, 'From each according to his abilities, to each according to his wants',[38] is to be read in a different way: we are not concerned with the capacities and wants of the individual, but with the totality of the capacities of social labour, and the totality of the wants of the social whole.

Part III: History and Ethnology
Marx and Morgan

The evolutionary thesis was embraced by Marx not because it took up natural history in the light of human history, but on the contrary, because it is possible by the application of this thesis to subsume human history under natural history, whereby the materialist doctrine is strengthened, and to posit natural history as a moment of human history.[39] The conception of human evolution as a part of universal evolution, hence as a part of our internal human history — yet that history which is outside our control as the history we do not make — was undertaken by E.B. Tylor, John Lubbock, L.H. Morgan, J.B. Phear, and, in a marginal way, by H.S. Maine; M.M. Kovalevsky was associated with both the Darwinian and the Mainean movements.[40] Nature had been considered by Hegel to be practically both in a direct and external relation to mankind,[41] whereas in the evolutionary school, nature was in a direct but not external relation; the practical as well as the theoretical relations are not different from one another in this matter. Marx in taking up the evolutionary school of ethnology turned his back on the Hegelian doctrine of nature on the one hand, and on the position of the non-evolutionary ethnologists on the other.[42]

The evolutionary doctrine of Morgan posits a progression of mankind as an organic development each out of the preceding one, over three stages, from savagery to barbarism to civilisation. The highest stage is reached by the dissolution of the gentes at the last formation of the stage of barbarism. The evolutionary process is world-wide, but assumes different forms in the different parts of the world, hence the progression is plurilinear; yet each stage is a whole, and is one, even though it is attained by varying means. Moreover, it is not the individual human being that is real, nor yet the historical people; it is the stage of culture that is real. The impulsion to change from one stage to the next is given by discoveries and inventions, the motor of history, according to Morgan being the technics, whereby the foundation of society upon the relations between persons is changed, being replaced by a foundation upon territory and property. The past, argued Morgan, is not dead, its record can be traced among present-day peoples; thus, the family had its origin in the promiscuous horde, and the practice of marriage in groups is still to be observed among peoples today, whereas it had been long superseded among others.[43]

Property was traced by Morgan from the primitive stage to the modern civil stage; Morgan closed his work with a peroration denouncing property for the unmanageable power which it has come to exert on the human mind. Marx drew from the study of Morgan's work the affirmation that the time-scale of human history is very great, and that the distortions worked by property are but a momentary aberration (and indeed a short one, commented Marx)[44] in the present stage of society. The notes taken by Marx, together with Marx's comments, have had their effect on the history of socialism. Morgan's criticism of property are perhaps sharper than that which is found in the comfortable writings of the others of the evolutionary school whom Marx studied, but he is not to be taken as a critic of the social system of capitalism; Marx referred to Morgan's opinions in order to support his own, not because they shared the same standpoints but because Morgan adhered to the opposite camp, and is to be reckoned as one therefore who strengthened the socialist cause against his will.[45]

The attack on the individualist interpretation of history which Marx unceasingly conducted found support in the researches of Morgan who held that Theseus was not an individual but a period or a series of events.[46] Morgan brought out as a general rule the objective factors in history, the technological, as we have seen, and the institutional; in this sense he was a materialist, if a naïve one, and for this reason he was celebrated by Engels. Among the institutions listed by Morgan, the gens is the predominant one in barbaric society. Marx applied this formulation to the theory of formation of castes in history, which are to be accounted for by the petrification of the gens principle. The gentes are ranked in barbaric society, just as the castes in civil society, higher and lower; equality and fraternity are practiced within the caste and the gens alike, which are expressed by the bond of kinship. Equality and fraternity are contradicted by the principle of aristocracy,[47] which is based on the formation of social classes. The formation of the social classes does not arise, according to Marx, from the differentiation of ranks between the gentes, however, but from the conflict of interests between the chiefs of the gentes on the one side, and the common people of the gentes on the other. The chiefs are rich, and this is connected with private property in houses, lands, herds and thereby with the monogamous family; the common people are poor.[48] Private property, however, is neither the cause of the differentiation between rich and poor, nor of the formation of the monogamous family; it is the expression in law of historical moments whose force lie elsewhere.

Morgan's conception of the stage prior to the formation of civil society and the state makes the dissolution of the gens, or the principle of kinship, into the motive force of history. This principle, which was taken over by Marx implicitly, and by Engels explicitly, from Morgan, is a contradiction of the formulation by Marx of the transition to civil society. Marx had written that the tribes of the ancient states were founded in two ways, either by kinship groups or by local groups. To this he added that the Roman gentes were corporations.[49] Instead of kinship alone, Marx had a general theory of the collectivity in its various forms, clans, tribes, gentes, or groups founded on kinship; localities, village communities, or groups grounded on neighbourhood, proximity; and associations, corporations, hereditary and voluntary societies. This is a broader and more scientifically apt formulation than that which the book by Engels has made current. The formation of civil society and the state is grounded on the dissolution of the archaic collectivities (the gentes, clans, village communities, associations), and the equality and fraternity connected thereunto.

Marx and Maine

Civil society is made up of the public and the private spheres, and cannot be reduced either in its origin or in its development to the private sphere, of which the modern civil and bourgeois family is a part, alone. To the kinship bond which the family exemplifies, the relations of the public sphere of civil society, of social labour, social production, exchange, trade, and the superstructure, the law, politics, the state, are added; by the relations between the social classes, civil society is formed and separated into the public and the private spheres. Maine, in treating of the traditional chiefs of the Irish septs, or clans, and of the heads of the joint families, village communities, of India, had considered them to be mere agglomerations of private families; further, he had in mind the English private family in considering the clan and community in Ireland and India.[50] Marx brought out his opposition to the confusion between the public and private spheres no less strongly in his comments to the book by Phear, who, in his account of the Indo-Aryan social and land system began with the assumption that the dynamism in the history of society and of land tenure came from within the private family.[51]

Maine's theory of social progress based on evolution presupposed the determination of history by legal and moral factors; Marx criticised him for making the moral the primary instead of the derivative in the determinant factors of history, which are, said Marx, economic before everything else. Maine made the state into a real historical substance, instead of what it really is, a mere appearance; he was criticised for failing to see the state as an excrescence of society, for failing, that is, to have related them to particular and concrete social conditions which determine the historical appearance of the state, and which will cause the state to disappear when those conditions themselves disappear. This contention by Marx is the opposite of an organic theory of society and the state. There is no thought, for example, that the state will wither away as a fruit; the society is subject to conditions, relations between people, and the state is the resultant of these historically concrete relations and conditions. The theses that the state is a formation of particular social conditions, that economic factors underlie the formation of the state, and that the state is a transitory phenomenon of history, are commonplace because Marxism has made them so today. The separation of the social classes and the public from the private sphere is based upon the factors at work in the archaic communities. The individuals who eventually form the ruling class in society are torn forth from these communities, and therewith the individuality is elaborated. These individuals then develop interests which are opposed to the interests of the immediate producers in the communities, who form the working class. The interests are class interests, and the individualities express a class-individuality; their interests have economic conditions at their base, and upon these bases the state is constructed.[52] The communities have been formed into the exploited social class of the immediate producers, while at the same time they have retained their communal character pro forma. The social conflict at the beginning of the history of civil society, therefore, is in its substance between the social classes, but in its form it is at first the conflict between class persons, the ruling class-individuals on the one side, the community as a person on the other. The persons are legal persons, whether individuals or groups, their interests, however, are neither communal nor individual, but social class interests, and the persons social class-persons. The individual interest of the ruling class is an ideological figment, as we have seen. The human individual is on the other hand opposed in his private, interior life to the externally formed social class interest, which is internalised by the class individual, in the history of civil society. The ruling class interest has the disposition of the surplus value at its base, the whole of social labour has the valorisation of the total production in society as its interest. In its present and actual situation the working class presupposes the capitalist class, just as the latter presupposes the working class; potentially the whole of social labour bears within itself the social totality.[53]

Part IV: Modes of Production and the Theory of Stages
The Theory of the Mode of Production
A mode of production is the economic formation of society; it is not the society itself. During the history of society, four economic formations have been identified: the Asiatic, the classical-antique, feudal, and modern bourgeois; to each of these economic formations there is a corresponding epoch of society. The four economic formations in their historical span comprise the history of the social and political economy; the corresponding epochs of society, the Oriental, the slave society of antiquity, the serf society of medieval Europe, and the modern bourgeois society, in their combination span over the history of civil society. This combined history of economy and society is identical with the history of the social classes, the opposition between them, the separation of the public from the private sphere, and the formation of the state. The four formations of the economy and society are listed in the order of their historical appearance; at the same time they are progressive stages of development in their relations to one another, the productive powers of the later ones being generally higher than the foregoing.

Labour in the stage of human history prior to these formations of civil society was organised in the clans, gentes, village communities, tribes, being collective and communal both in form and substance; in this stage of social development the form and the substance of labour are not separate from one another, nor are the public and the private spheres of the society. In the earliest phase of the history of the Asiatic mode of production, labour is still organised formally in the village communities, hence it is communal in form, whereas it is social in substance, since these village communities are brought together in the bonds of mutual dependence through exchange of commodities, just as they are brought together by the forced supply of surplus labour and the surplus product to the agencies of the overarching community, the state. Labour in this second condition, by the relations of exchange and of the alienation of the surplus, is the producer of exchange value on the one side, surplus value on the other; by virtue of these relations of value, the communal labour in the Oriental villages is transformed into social labour in substance. The Asiatic mode of production appears to have been primitive, but it merely retained certain primitive forms.

The course of history is at once a continuous and a discontinuous succession, in which factors making for stability and change oppose one another. In a given historical course the attainment of a stage implies the establishment of a number of factors of stability, whereby an economic and social system is maintained over a period of time. All the modes of production enumerated have been and are made up of the conflicting forces. Thus the earliest of these in time, which is the Asiatic mode of production, appears on the surface to have been a stagnating economic formation, whereas within it the forces making for its dissolution were at work. The development of the specialisation of functions in production, and the division of labour in society, of the mutual dependence of the village communities on one another, thus the separation and opposition between the units of production and consumption in society; the development and expansion of commodity exchange; and the separation of private rent from public tax, which had at first been indistinguishable from one another, in this sense, qualitative changes in the *form* of surplus value, were all historical developments at work within the Asiatic mode of production and the Oriental society. These internal factors did not lead to the dissolution and transformation of the Asiatic mode of production, but it was not for want of their dynamism; rather it was the intervention of an external force

which led to the finish of the Oriental society as such, the force of
the colonialisation by early capitalism, which interrupted the
process of its dissolution.[54]

It has sometimes been asserted that the development of private
property, not only in land but generally also in the Asiatic mode of
production, was weak; this assertion is then applied to explain
that rent and tax, or the private and public expression
respectively of the surplus value, tended to coincide therein. This
is the inversion of the theory of property in the Asiatic mode of
production and Oriental society: in the early phase of the history
of this economic and social formation, the ownership of the land
was communal, whereas the tiller of the soil had but possession of
the arable as the condition and means of production, as opposed
to proprietorship thereof. The land was conceived to be
communally owned in this stage; the state, through its concrete
agencies, had no other way, there existed no alternative juridical
expression, to assert ownership of the land save as the
community magnified. The community, formally speaking, had
no way to give juridical expression to the difference between the
public and private spheres, at this time; therefore, rent and tax
were not differentiated at the beginning of the history of the
Oriental society, whereas in the later phase they were. Again, in
the early period of the history of the Oriental society, production
in the countryside and in the towns were not differentiated from
one another, presenting an indifferent unity. In the later history of
the Asiatic mode of production and the Oriental society,
however, the urban and rural production were opposed to one
another while giving the appearance of an absence of differentiation between them.[55] The urban centres of ancient China,
India, the Mediterranean world, Mexico were political and
ceremonial centres whose economic functions and specialisations differed little from non-agricultural functions and
specialisations of the countryside in the early period of the history
of civil society; in the later historical development of these
civilisations urban trade and manufacture came to be differentiated both quantitatively and qualitatively from the rural.

Marx and Kovalevsky

Of the four modes of production listed, two are limited and two
are world-wide in their historical scope. The two that are limited
are the classical-antique and the feudal modes of production, or
the economic formations founded on the exploitation of slaves
and serfs respectively, arising as they do out of the conditions of

social labour in ancient and medieval Europe; to be sure, not all of
social labour was bound in the one form or the other of servility in
those epochs, but they were so predominantly, or considered
themselves to be so bound. If these categories are exported to
other parts of the world, it is only by the elaboration of a
Eurocentric viewpoint toward history, whereby European
scholars follow in their minds the paths traced for them by the
European gunboats. Marx was faced by ethnocentrism when
studying the works of Maine, Phear and Kovalevsky.[56] Because
Kovalevsky had found evidence of benefices, farming out of
offices, and commendation, in the history of India, he concluded
that here feudalism is found. Marx's argument against this
conception is as follows:

1   Benfices and farming out of offices are also found in ancient
Rome; there is nothing specifically feudal about these practices.
2   Serfdom, an essential moment of Western European feudalism, is not found in India.
3   Kovalevsky himself admitted that patrimonial jurisdiction,
such as was practiced in feudal Europe, was absent in the Mogul
Empire of India.[57]

The appellation 'Asiatic mode of production' is in one sense a
misnomer, for it is, together with the social formation corresponding to it, the stage of the earliest formation of civil society
and the state. The transition to civil society, the formation and
opposition between the social classes did not occur once and for
all time, the opposition between the public and private spheres,
and between communal versus social labour, took place in the
history of many peoples, in different parts of the world,
independently of one another. Out of these several moments, a
unitary economic and social formation emerged, which is called
the Asiatic or Oriental merely because it was first detected in that
part of the world, but it could just as well be termed the
Afro-Asiatic, or the Inca, or the ancient Mexican, for the
conditions of its formation are repeated in the various parts of the
Americas, Eurasia and Africa. The later history of the Asiatic
mode of production is not one but many, although it is usually
treated as a unitary history; thus the history of the Oriental
society is to be treated in two phases, an early one, in which the
social labour is communal in form, in which rent and tax tend to
coincide, and the opposition between town and countryside is not
at all developed; and a later one, in which the lands of the Oriental

society, China, India, Persia, Indonesia, Inca Peru, Aztec Mexico, Asante and Oyo in Africa, all follow separate historical courses.

The Asiatic, classical and feudal modes of production are grouped together as pre-capitalist, for they have a distinct and important common feature in opposition to the capitalist, namely, that labour is unfree in all the pre-capitalist modes of production, whereas it is free pro forma in the capitalist. Social labour in the Asiatic mode of production was subject to a two-fold bondage: village labour there was unfree by virtue of the communal bonds of habit and feeling,[58] while at the same time it was bound by the forcible extraction of surplus value through the agencies of the state, whereby the Oriental communities sustained the class that ruled over them. In the economic formation of classical antiquity, the chief form of social labour was that of slavery, or the related form, clientage, likewise the precarious tenure of the land held by a private landowner, in practice but another form of clientage. Labour in this condition was not bound to the means of production, which was the land above all, nor was it bound by custom as it was in the Asiatic mode of production, but in the form of slavery could be bought and sold separately from the land. The slave stood in a relation of personal bondage to the master; at the same time there was a small amount of free, wage labour (in Greece *mistharnes*, in Rome *mercenarius*); labour in the Athenian polis during Aristotle's time exceeded free labour by a ratio of 2:1 or 3:1.[59] Production on the Roman *latifundia*, which as Pliny said led to the destruction of ancient Italy, was the task chiefly of slave labour. Labour in medieval Europe was unfree, being bound to the soil, in the form of adscription or pre-dial bondage; hence it was freed from the bondage to the person of the master, but was impersonally bound to the means of production, and could not be sold separately from the latter. Town labour was then freed from this form of constraint, but was otherwise bound by rules of apprenticeship and indentures in close corporations, guilds and companies. This form of unfreedom was denounced by Adam Smith in the eighteenth century, that is, long after the capitalist mode of production had replaced the feudal.[60]

The capitalist mode of production is, as Marx set it forth, a world-wide historical phenomenon, and as such is unlike the classical antique and the feudal. It is unlike the Asiatic mode of production as well, being the movement developed in certain parts of Europe, northern Italy, England and the Low Countries, Catalonia and adjacent places, whence it was imposed by conquest over the rest of the world. Here the chief form of labour is wage labour, which has the right of free disposition of its labour power. Wage labour, however, is not the invention of the capitalist mode of production, but is found to have been developed in a modest degree in the pre-capitalist economic formations; it is found in the later phase of the Asiatic mode of production, and in classical antiquity: Aristotle wrote about this form of labour, which he held to be unnatural, slavery the natural form. In the capitalist mode of production, the freedom of social labour to dispose of its power for a wage is distributed over virtually the entire working class. Nevertheless, labour in this condition, while free pro forma has not yet gained the substance of its freedom, which is the most radical of the wants thereof.

The Peasant Community in History

In the centre of Morgan's historico-evolutionary conceptions lay the gens, in the centre of Kovalevsky's lay the village community. Neither theoretical representation is incorrect, neither is correct, both are part of a greater theory of the history of the stage of primitive society and of its dissolution in the transition to civil society, which, as we have seen, Marx adumbrated in a brief insight in 1857–8. That he later appears to have abandoned the theory at once more general and more profound, according to which the collective institutions of the primitive society, both those based on neighbourhood and those based on kinship were dissolved in the formation of civil society, in favour of an exclusively kinship-based theory, which he derived from Morgan's work, and was so interpreted by Engels, has had a narrowing effect on the development of the study of history and theory of society by Marxists and socialists, both in the Second and Third Internationals.[61] Moreover, at the time that he composed the *Grundrisse*, he grasped what was later forgotten both by himself and by his co-workers and followers, that the gens itself has its history, becoming in the time of the Roman republic a corporation, or guild.

The village community too has its history, which is a complex one, for the community encountered at the beginnings of written history among the peoples of China, India, Persia, Egypt, or among the Slavic and ancient Germanic peoples, is not the same as the community encountered by van Enschut among the Dutch, Olufsen among the Danes, Karadzić and Csaplowics among the South Slavs, in the early nineteenth century, nor yet that which was encountered by Wilks, Raffles, Campbell, Maine and Phear in South Asia, at the same time. The community in the early period of the history of civil society, whether in ancient Rome or in the even more ancient Oriental societies, was in its form continuous with the prehistoric communities, yet in its substance it was hanged. Thus when Marx referred to the communal village in India in the nineteenth century as appearing in ruined form, as the caricature of what it had formerly been,[62] the same applied as well to the gens at the beginning of Roman historical society, and of the historical society of India, the Incas, etc. While Marx was critically aware of the transformation which the archaic community underwent in the period of civilisation, this critical awareness on the part of those whom he studied, Maurer on the Germanic past, Mommsen on the Roman, Maine and Kovalevsky, was not at all developed.[63]

When Haxthausen drew attention to the existence of the Russian peasant commune in the nineteenth century, he awakened the conviction among many socialists that the peasants had already mastered the principle which would guide the future of humanity beyond the social revolution.[64] The study of the prehistory and history of the peasant community was undertaken by these socialists with the intent to show that the soil was originally owned and worked in common, hence that man is by nature a communal animal. The enemies of socialism at that time seized upon the socialist thesis and sought to show that property was not in its origin communally but individually owned, hence that man is not a communal but an individual animal by his nature.[65] The anthropologists, historians and sociologists whom Marx studied had as their starting point the thesis of the continuity of the peasant communal practices from the highest antiquity down to the contemporary times.[66] The entire controversy is perhaps of interest for those who wish to study the past for itself; it should be evident, on the contrary, that our comprehension of the nature of human nature will not emerge out of the study of the peasant communes, still less will it determine the nature of society under socialism. The study of the peasant commune during the nineteenth century was undertaken as a kind of simplification of complex issues by Maine, Kovalevsky, among others. Thus B. Cicerin held the view that the prehistoric and ancient peasant community had disappeared with the formation of the Kievan state, in medieval Russian history, and that the modern community of the Russian peasantry was a creation of events and policies posterior to that formation: administrative acts of the government, the intervention of the landlords in the interest of their own rent collections, and so forth.[67] Finally, ink has been spilled over the question, whether the communes and collectives in contemporary, post-revolutionary China and the Soviet Union are determined by and continuations of the peasant communes of the Asiatic mode of production and the Oriental society, which is a simplification even more drastic than the foregoing, gliding over already proposed distinctions and differentiations, and seemingly unconscious of them. The peasant community at the same time is an abstraction, if we think to find out what it might have been at the dawn of civilisation; moreover, the historically concrete course of the peasant communities of China, India, Persia, Russia, Germany, differ from one another.

Peasant communities are little republics, capable of sustaining and governing themselves, combining the various branches of production within themselves, with little dependence on the outside world.[68] The unit of consumption is the same as the unit of production, in this case, for these communities produce all or virtually all that they consume. Exchange and commodities are not introduced by the relations inside the communities; on the contrary, exchange relations, and in particular commodity exchange, begin between the producing communities, whereby exchange value is historically introduced,[69] hence commodities come into being. Commodities are not brought into being by virtue of their having been produced; useful things, having first been exchanged as commodities are thereupon transformed, and the production of these things, which are now expressed as use values, is transformed in this way into commodity production. The quantitative and qualitative increase in the exchange relations between the villages, and between villages and towns, transforms the communal relations into social relations; and the process is given expression as the creation of exchange value. By means of the development of the exchange relations, the communal village autonomy and autarky is overcome, and the society as the expression of the relations between the human beings who make it up, is historically created, in our modern sense. By the relations of exchange, abstract value is separated from concrete or use value, the abstraction of the individual, of society and of value is created; the formality of the individual, of society, and of value is created; the public side as the formal side of the individual and of society is separated from the private side, and each is opposed to the other. The process of alienation of the surplus value proceeds *pari passu* with the creation of exchange value, yet each process is independent of the other and is the condition of the other; the creation of exchange value determines the creation of surplus value, and conversely, the creation of surplus value determines the creation of exchange value in the history of civil society. These processes are developed on the basis of the dissolution not of the form but of the substance of the archaic communes, gentes, clans, villages and tribes, and their transformation into modern corporate groups.

Part V: The Motor of History: From Bondage to Freedom of Labour
The relations of labour to nature and the relations thereof in society together constitute the form and substance of human life. These relations of substance and form have their history. The relation to nature is the material interchange between man and nature, whereby human life is produced and reproduced by the processes of alienating the materials and forces of nature, and appropriating them to human use, whereby our human wants, creature wants, are met. The relation of labour in society is the combination and division of labour, by means of which the production of the means of subsistence is organised and carried through. The production, distribution and exchange of these products is the material interchange in society. The history of society is determined by the two elements of labour, the organisation and the relations thereof in society. We will take up these elements in reverse order, in reference to the primary motive force of history.

Labour in the primitive condition of human life is collectively organised. Thus each one, in labouring for another, labours for himself, there being no unearned surplus in primitive society. In civil and bourgeois society the collective primitive labour is transformed into social labour by the developments of special- isations of function in production, by the division of labour and the combinations thereof, by exchange of products as com- modities, hence by the increasing mutual dependence of the producers on one another. At the same time that the social relations of labour are developed they are destroyed by the production and alienation of a social surplus, which is the antisocial relation of labour in civil and bourgeois society, whereby one man labours both for himself and for another, but his labour is not reciprocated. By the creation and destruction of the bond of social labour, the fundamental relation in society is created and destroyed.[70]

Historically, the transformation of communal into social labour by the processes of creation of exchange value and the alienation of surplus value has brought about the submission of social labour to a condition of bondage. This bondage is imposed by coercion or the threat of coercion, for the process of exploitation by extraction of surplus value from the hands of its immediate producers does not proceed logically but against the interest of the latter. The opposite of this is the contention of naïve materialism, in the strict sense. In all the modes of production preceding the capitalist in the history of civil society, social labour was in one form or another unfree, being bound by the obligation to provide surplus labour and surplus product to the ruling class, which is socially defined as the exploiting class, because it reciprocates the labour living and dead which is provided to it, not by returning value of the same order or kind to its producers, but by ruling, by imposing its force for the purpose of alienating the surplus, in return for that which it has taken away. In order to meet these enforced impositions of obligation, labour is bound to the villages in the Asiatic mode of production; to the person of the master or patron in the classical, and to the soil in the feudal modes of production; to the guildmasters in the early period of capitalism; by indentures and long-term contracts of servitude; by unsurious conditions of indebtedness; and by the superstructure raised upon these conditions, the false consciousness of a social bond to the king, lord, master, patron, capitalist, church, god, or country. Labour in the latest period of the industrial capitalist mode of production is free only to the extent that it can change its masters, moving from the condition of exploitation by one capitalist to the next, and from one country to the next.

A stage of history is not a phenomenon of primary social reality; it is a derivative construction, determined by the social relations of the primary order. Thus the change from one historical stage to the next is determined by the change in the relations of labour, from the primitive to the civil social condition through the transformation of labour from the communal to the social condition, and within the civil condition from the unfree to the pro forma free condition in the period of industrial capitalism. The most radical want (*Bedürfnis, besogno*) of social labour is the substance of its freedom, but the realisation of that radical human want requires the radical transformation of society.

The combinations, specialisations, divisions, accumulations of skills, and their transmission together constitute the social organisation of labour. The mode of organisation of society, whether communal or civil, determines the mode of organisation of labour, whereby production is socially organised; thus the communal organisation of society determines the communal organisation of labour and of production, the bourgeois organisation of society determines the bourgeois organisation of production, and conversely, the communal organisation of production determines the communal society, the bourgeois organisation of production determines the bourgeois organisation of society, etc. Bourgeois society itself constitutes the organisation of production in the bourgeois period of history, civil society generally constitutes the organisation of production in the history of the society divided into social classes.[71] The motive force of history is thus two-fold, being constituted of the relations of labour, as we have said, and the organisation of society as a whole.

Notes

1 K. Marx, *Oekonomisch-Philosophische Manuskripte* (1844), in *Werke*, vol. 1, p. 544.
2 *Ibid.* p. 510. G. Markus, *Marxism and Anthropology: The Concept of Human Essence* in the Philosophy of Marx, Van Gorcum (Assen, 1978) shows that Ludwig Feuerbach had adopted a position in which the anthropological determination is an ontological determination. Anthropological alienation is therefore ontological alienation; a bourgeois condition of alienation which is considered indifferently from anthropological alienation is therefore the same as ontological alienation.
3 K. Marx, *Misère de la philosophie* (1847), chapter 2, Metaphysics of political economy, 1, seventh remark, in *Werke*, vol. 4, p. 139. See also *Werke*, vol. 23, p. 96 note; and K. Marx, 'Kritische Randglossen zu A. Wagner, *Lehrbuch*', *Werke*, vol. 19, p. 359.
4 K. Marx, '*Die Heilige Familie*' (1845), chapter VI. First Campaign (against Bruno Bauer) in *Werke*, vol. 2, p. 83.
5 F. Engels, *Notes to English Edition of Capital by Marx* (New York, 1936), pp. 54 and 207. Engels here distinguished work as the creation of use-value, or the finished product, labour as the continuous process of production, the creation of value. He put this distinction in another way in his 'Dialectics of Nature', in *Werke*, vol. 20, p. 383: here work is applied in the physical sense, as opposed to labour, which is used in the economic sense. This is a particularity of the English language, which is not generally found.
6 K. Marx, *Die Deutsche Ideologie*, in *Werke*, p. 18. Here German philosophy is treated as a special branch of the ideology in general. The two thoughts have a somewhat different connection as treated by D. Rjazanov, *Marx–Engels Archiv* (1926), vol. 1, p. 237, where they appear to be in direct juxtaposition; they are separated, to judge by the new *Probeband* (Marx/Engels Gesamtausgabe, 1972), pp. 37 and 425. The attribution of the passage to Marx is my own.

7 F. Picavet, *Les idéologues* (Paris, 1891). On Cabanis and Destutt de Tracy *passim*; Saint-Simon, pp. 453f.
8 K. Marx, *Werke*, vol. 3, *loc cit*:

The history of nature, the socalled natural science, is not our concern. We will have to do with the history of mankind since almost the entire ideology is reduced either to a twisted interpretation of the latter history, or to a total abstraction of it. The ideology is itself but one side of this history.
9 K. Marx, *Oekonomisch-Philosophische Manuskripte, op. cit.* pp. 537f; *Die Deutsche Ideologie, op. cit.* pp. 25, 66ff., 71.
10 K. Marx, *ibid.* pp. 29f. Marx wrote, 'Die Produktion des Lebens, sowohl des eignen in der Arbeit wie des fremden in der Zeugung... .' Here the connection between the economic and social act of labour is separated from the biological act of procreation of the life of another human being. The combination of the biological and the economic activities is firmly rejected, having no place in Marxist theory and practice, and having unacceptable consequences in the further development of the theory: Friedrich Engels, in *Ursprung der Familie, des Privateigentums und des Staats* (1884), evidently taking the program advanced in the unpublished work, *Die Deutsche Ideologie*, promulgated the non-distinction between the biological act of reproduction and the social-economic act of reproduction, with particular reference to the primitive condition of human life. Marx had written previously (*ibid.* p. 18), that 'The history of nature is not our concern'. Here he contradicts himself.
11 K. Marx, 'The Future Results of the British Rule in India', *New York Daily Tribune*, 8 August 1853. See also K. Marx, 'The British Rule in India', *ibid.* 6 June 1853; and K. Marx, 'The East India Company — its History and Results', *ibid.* 11 July 1853. Cf. L. Krader, *The Asiatic Mode of Production* (Assen, 1975), pp. 80f., 159f. Cf. K. Marx, *Capital*, vol. III, in *Werke*, vol. 25, p. 804.
12 K. Marx, 'Zur Kritik der politischen Oekonomie: Vorwort', in *Werke,* vol. 13, p. 9; see also K. Marx, *Grundrisse der Kritik der politschen Oekonomie* (Berlin, 1953), p. 25.
13 C. Darwin, *The Origin of Species* (London, 1859).
14 K. Marx, letter to Ferdinand Lassalle, 16 January 1861. See K. Marx, letter to Engels, 19 December 1860.
15 K. Marx, letter to Engels, 18 June 1862.
16 K. Marx, letter to Laura and Paul Lafargue, 15 February 1869; K. Marx, letter to L. Kugelmann, 27 June 1870. Marx sent a copy of *Capital* to Darwin, who acknowledged receipt of it in a letter of 1 October 1873. A report has been circulated according to which Marx offered to dedicate some (unnamed work) of his to Darwin which Darwin declined on personal grounds. P.T. Carroll of Philadelphia has found that Darwin, in a letter of 13 October 1880, declined the offer of E. Aveling, Marx's son-in-law, to dedicate his book of essays to him, Darwin. It is this letter, or rumours of its existence, which probably initiated the report which is otherwise without foundation that Marx had offered to dedicate a work to Darwin.
17 K. Marx, 'Theorien über den Mehrwert III, in *Werke*, vol. 26.3, p. 289. Cf. K. Marx, *Capital*, vol. I, on inheritance in castes and guilds, in *Werke*, vol. 23, p. 360; see also L. Krader, *Dialectic of Civil Society* (Assen, 1977), pp. 260ff. The subject matter in the passages mentioned, both in the 'Theorien

über den Mehrwert' and in *Capital* both refer to the accumulation of labour skills and their social transmission; both refer to the relation between man and the laws of nature; the passage in the 'Theorien über den Mehrwert' is at once more accurate and subtler than that in *Capital*; it is the former that is applied and developed here.

18 C. Darwin, *op. cit.*; K. Marx, *Capital*, vol. I, *op. cit.* p. 361 note.
19 K. Marx, *Grundrisse, op. cit.* p. 378.
20 K. Marx, *Capital*, vol. I, *op. cit.* pp. 92, 102; *Grundrisse, op. cit.* pp. 391, 395; *Die Deutsche Ideologie, op. cit.* chapter I.
21 The calculation of labour time is a case in point. The amount of labour time expended in the production of socially useful things is the substance of the theory of value. But the reckoning and calculation of the amount of labour time so expended is the specific characteristic of commodity exchange and production; it is not found in primitive society, but is developed in conditions where exchange of commodities predominates, that is, in civil society: Cf. K. Marx, *Capital*, vol. II, in *Werke*, vol. 24, pp. 236f. This chapter in the history of economic institutions is cited by Marx from E.B. Tylor, *Researches into the Early History of Mankind* (1865). The passage is cited by Marx with some irony in order to hit W.N. Senior, the author of a theory of abstinence in consumption for the purpose of capital accumulation, and likewise the author of a theory of the last, unearned labour hour, on the head. Tylor, perhaps the chief cultural evolutionist of his time, then virtually disappears from Marx's view.
22 For bibliographic references, see K. Marx, *Chronik seines Lebens in Einzeldaten* (Moscow, 1934). Further additions are in L. Krader (ed.) *The Ethnological Notebooks of Karl Marx* (Assen, 1974), pp. 379f., Note 125. The opposition between the two aspects of history is evident in the passages relative to land practices in ancient Mexico and Peru, in conjunction with the same in relation to Eurasia in antiquity. To this we may add the coeval practices in the ancient Near East and in Africa south of the Sahara. These matters were under debate in the nineteenth and early twentieth centuries. The issue was whether in primitive society land was held in common or in severalty (see Part IV, of this paper, particularly the section entitled 'The Peasant Community in History'.
23 G. Vico, *Principi di Scienza Nuova* (1744); K. Marx, *Capital*, vol. I, in *Werke*, vol. 23, p. 393n. Marx recommended Vico's philosophy of right to F. Lassalle (letter of 28 April 1862). The doctrine according to which all is subject to history, nature and man alike, is owed to Francis Bacon in modern times, and this conjunction of the history of all matter is later developed by Buffon, Kant, Laplace and Adelung. The historical doctrine of Vico is contradicted by his own doctrine, of *corsi* and *ricorsi*, which leads everything to history, but it does not lead to change; it on the contrary leads to the Nietzschean concept of the eternal return.
24 The role of the consciousness in history was explored by Marx and Engels in the *Communist Manifesto*, and in many other places. The positivists of that time, Auguste Comte were concerned with the workings of unconscious laws, whereas the juridical-legal positivists were dealing with positive, man-made (that is, conscious) laws, as opposed to divine or natural laws. This view of the law, which is owed to F. Bacon and William Blackstone, for example, would appear to stand opposed to the treatment of the history of positivism by L. Kolakowski, *The Alienation of Reason* (New York, 1968).

The consciousness cannot be considered a determinant factor in human history; it is excluded by Marx even as a defining factor:

One may distinguish mankind from the beasts by consciousness, religion, or whatever else you will. Men themselves begin to distinguish themselves from the beasts as soon as they begin to *produce* their means of subsistence'. (K. Marx, '*Die Deutsche Ideologie*', in *Werke*, vol. 3, p. 21.)

The consciousness is itself from the beginning a social product and remains so as long as men exist in any way. (*Ibid.* p. 31.)

25 K. Marx, *Capital*, vol. I, in *Werke*, vol. 23. pp. 392f. note.

26 *Ibid.* pp. 353f.

27 K. Marx, *Grundrisse, op. cit.* p. 77. Here the theory of the social whole within which the class divisions take place is implicitly developed. The concept of the totality in reference to the class-divided society was made explicit by A. Gramsci, *Il Materialismo Storico* (Torino, 1948); K. Korsche, *Marxismus und Philosophie* (Berlin, 1923); and by G. Lukács, *Geschichte und Klassenbewusstsein* (Berlin, 1923). The first thesis of Marx posits the process of revolution, the second the process of evolution, each being a necessary condition for the other.

28 Further on the history we make and do not make, see K. Marx, *Die Deutsche Ideologie*, in *Werke*, vol. 3, p. 28; K. Marx, 'The Eighteenth Brumaire of Louis Napoleon', in *Die Revolution* (New York, 1852), in *Werke*, vol. 8, p. 115.

29 T. Carlyle, 'On Heroes, Hero-Worship, and the Heroic in History', in *Latter-Day Pamphlets* (1850) (reviewed by K. Marx in *Werke*, vol. 7, pp. 255 sq.). See T. Carlyle, *Essays*, vol. I (Dent/Everyman), and in reference to this, *Werke*, vol. 23, p. 270n. Here the irony with which Marx polemicised against Carlyle's cult of the individual is brought out.

30 K. Marx, *Zur Kritik der politischen Oekonomie,* in *Werke*, vol. 13, p. 46 criticised David Ricardo for postulating the existence of the primitive hunter isolated from all society, much as Robinson Crusoe. Cf. also *Werke*, vol. 23, pp. 90f. Daniel Defoe did not intend to have Robinson Crusoe represent the archtype of the self-made man; on the contrary, he described in detail the effort with which Robinson removed all that he could from his wrecked ship, equipping himself with everything his civilisation had to offer, to prepare himself for the dangers of his new home. He was not alone, but the heir of his past. The account by Defoe lists both the skills that Robinson could and could not master, the manufacture of ink fell outside his capacities.

31 K. Marx, *Oekonomisch-Philosophische Manuskripte, op. cit.* pp. 557, 539, 544.

32 K. Marx, *Die Deutsche Ideologie, op. cit.* pp. 62ff., 67ff. Marx had been accused by T.G. Masaryk, *Die philosophischen und sociologischen Grundlagen des Marxismus* (1899), pp. 147 sq., and 184f., of the sin of illusionism, that is, of having separated the individual consciousness from the individual and depositing it in the social class, hence of making the consciousness an illusion. This is the opposite of the significance of the passages here, and immediately preceding, cited. The argument of Masaryk should have borne on the motor of history, whether driven by the individual or by the social class.

33 The sixth thesis of Marx on Feuerbach reads, 'The human being is not an abstraction dwelling within the individual. In reality, the human being is the

ensemble of social relations'. (*Werke*, vol. 3, pp. 6, 434). The argument is against the abstraction, man as man, which Feuerbach had culled from Hegel. On the contrary, the phrase, man as man, occurs in Hegel's lectures on freedom only in connection with specific and concrete historical circumstances, the ancient Germanic, and the subsequent extension thereof. The consequence is that the consciousness that all men are in themselves, man as man, free. See G.W.F. Hegel, *Vorlesungen über die Philosophie der Weltgeschichte (1822/1828)* (Hamburg, 1955), vol. 1, pp. 62f.

34 K. Marx, *Grundrisse, op. cit.* p. 176.
35 The conception put forward by E. Durkheim, *Les règles de la méthode sociologique* (1895), which affirmed that the social facts are no different from the facts of physics and of physiology, are a remarkable simplification of the problem of social reality. Durkheim, to be sure, had to guard against the interested nonsense of the doctrine of the church at that time, and against the individualistic sociology and individualistic psychology of Gustave Tarde. Nevertheless, Durkheim's programmatic assertions, which have been repeated, and with the same end, to guard against the parallel dangers of reduction of the social sciences to an individualising social science by the father of British structuralism, A.R. Radcliffe-Brown, in *The Natural Science of Society* (Chicago, 1957). The issue of individualism had been revived briefly by our latter-day Thomist, Mortimer J. Adler.
36 The priest of the wood is the tale with which James George Frazer begins his work, *The Golden Bough*. Aristotle returned to his attack on individualism in his works on the *Politics*, the *Ethics*, and the *Morality*, with the teaching, man is by nature an animal of the *polis*. Epictetus, according to Arrian, began his polemic, *Against Epicurus*, with the words, 'Epicurus knows as well as we do that we are by nature social beings'. The wise men of antiquity had separated the question of social and individual being from the question of the ideology of the ruling class.
37 The defence of the individuality is undertaken by the ideologists of the ruling class in modern bourgeois society on the grounds that unless the individual is free we will be in danger of losing the Leonardo da Vincis or Shakespeares of the future. This self-serving doctrine cannot be applied to assurance of artistic merit of the future, for we know only of its negation: the conditions under which Homer, Monteverdi and Bach made their creations will not be those of future creativity. On the irrelevancy of past canons to the present and the future, see K. Marx, *Grundrisse*, Einleitung, *op. cit.* pp. 30f.
38 K. Marx, *Kritik des Gothaer Programms, op. cit.* p. 21. (G.V. Plekhanov, *The Role of the Individual in History*, which originally appeared in 1898, provides a well-known statement from the tradition of Marxism, on this question, which is put in the title of his work.)
39 Darwin developed his model of natural history in accordance with the social doctrine of Thomas Malthus: C. Darwin, *op. cit.* Chapter 3. See also his *Descent of Man* (1871), Part I, Chapter 2.
40 L. Krader (ed.), *The Ethnological Notebooks of Karl Marx* (Assen, 1974). The works excerpted by Marx are: L.H. Morgan, *Ancient Society* (New York, 1877); J.B. Phear, *The Aryan Village in India and Ceylon* (London, 1880); H.S. Maine, *Lectures on the Early History of Institutions* (London, 1875); and J. Lubbock, *The Origin of Civilisation* (London, 1870).
41 G.W.F. Hegel, *Enzyklopädie der philosophischen Wissenschaften*, 1830, § 245.
42 K. Marx on Adolph Bastian, in letter to Engels, 12 December 1860.

43 Engels wrote his book, *Ursprung der Familie*, in connection with Morgan's *Ancient Society*. In doing so he felt he was fulfilling a legacy of Marx. Engels, in keeping with Morgan's position on the origin of the family, wrote a notice published in *Die Neue Zeit*, 1892, vol. 11, Part 1, pp. 373–5, entitled 'A Newly Discovered Case of Group-Marriage'. The note was published on the basis of the researches among the Gilyaks by L. Sternberg.

44 K. Marx, *Ethnological Notebooks, op. cit.* p. 139.

45 K. Marx, Draft of letter to Vera Zasulic, in *Werke*, vol. 19, p. 386: An American author who is in no way suspect of revolutionary tendencies, and is supported by the government in Washington... (thus Marx refers to Morgan.) On the other hand, a complex error has been made in regard to Morgan, who cited Gaius and Theodor Mommsen regarding slavery in the ancient Roman family. Marx then referred to Fourier who characterised the modern epoch of civilisation by monogamy and private property in land. The modern family, so reads Marx's note, contains in germ not only slavery but also serfdom; it contains in miniature all the antagonisms within itself which later develop broadly in the society and its state. (This brief note is in need of further development: by the modern family is meant the modern family in its ancient Roman form, which included the famul, or slave, within itself. The later history of the family is opposed to the history of society and its state, as we shall see. On Fourier, cf. K. Marx, *Ethnological Notebooks, op. cit.* p. 120.) F. Engels, *Ursprung, op. cit.*, at the end, expressed his intention to place this idea of Fourier's beside Morgan's and his, Engels's, own. But this did not make Morgan into a critic of the modern family, such as Marx and Engels were in the *Communist Manifesto*, or Fourier was. Nevertheless, Eduard Bernstein, in the Foreword to the Italian translation of Engels, *Origine della Famiglia*, considered Morgan to be a utopian socialist. Morgan had been a lawyer for the railroad interests in New York State. He had nothing to do with the utopian socialists of that time.

46 K. Marx, *Ethnological Notebooks, op. cit.* p. 209.

47 *Ibid.* p. 183.

48 *Ibid.* p. 210.

49 K. Marx, *Grundrisse, op. cit.* pp. 381f. Morgan has been criticised for bringing out only the consanguineal and ignoring the community factor other than the consanguineal, in his well-known ethnographic works on the Iroquois, by W.N. Fenton and others. Cf. K. Marx, *Ethnological Notebooks, op. cit.* pp. 357 and 376. He is no less to be criticised for omitting the factor of the community, the local or the proximal group, in his theory of evolution; this concerns the use made as well by others of his theories.

50 K. Marx, *Ethnological Notebooks, op. cit.* p. 310.

51 *Ibid.* p. 281: 'The asinus lets everything be grounded on private families.' The family in civil society is the private family, falling within the private sphere of civil society. Thus the joint family of India, the house-community or zadruga of the Yugoslavs during the traditional historical period, the extended family of the Mongols, are all private families in one form or another, for the society in which they are found is civil society, in one form or another, wherein, throughout its history the public and private spheres are separated from one another. The prehistory of the Slavic great or extended family, the house community of the South Slavs, the joint family in India, and the like formations in China, Africa, and the New World, before the foundation of civil society, with its basis in the differences between the social

classes, is therefore neither public nor private, for civil society itself is founded on the difference between the public and private spheres. The collective and communal institutions themselves are divided into public and private segments by the organisation of civil society. The family of civil society is not the family of the primitive condition of social life. Nor is the gens, clan, or village community the same in civil society as any of these had been in the primitive, collective and communal condition. The gens in the time of the Roman Republic became a kind of publicly and officially recognised corporation.

52 K. Marx, *Ethnological Notebooks, op. cit.* p. 329. This is perhaps the most extensive and precise statement by Marx on the process of formation and connections of the state in society. It is adumbrated in the draft of Marx's correspondence with Vera Zasulic, where Maine is, moreover, denounced for having hypocritically defended the British empire in its work of destruction of the ancient Indic communes, while Maine proclaimed at the same time that these had been wrecked by the force of spontaneous laws of economics. (*Werke*, vol. 19, p. 386f.)

53 K. Marx, *Grundrisse*, p. 362: The capitalist produces the workers, the worker produces the capitalist, etc.

54 On the question of stagnation, see L. Krader, *Asiatic Mode of Production, op. cit.* pp. 153, 160, 185.

55 K. Marx, *Grundrisse, op. cit.* pp. 377–82: community as person, p. 377; community as state, p. 379. Asian history as indifferent unity of town and countryside, p. 382. On the sources for these ideas, cf. L. Krader, *Asiatic Mode of Production, op. cit.* Part I, Chapter I.

56 K. Marx excerpted the work of M.M. Kovalevsky, *Obščinnoe Zemlevladenie* (Moscow, 1879). Marx's notes and comments on this book are published in L. Krader, *Asiatic Mode of Production, op. cit.* Part II.

57 L. Krader, *op. cit.* p. 383. Kovalevsky then sought to establish the category of feudalism in Algeria before the French colonisation, which Marx found untenable (*ibid.* p. 403). Phear likewise sought to interpret the history of India as feudal, at which point Marx exclaimed, 'This ass Phear calls the constitution of the village *feudal.*' (*Ethnological Notebooks, op. cit.* p. 256.) In fact Phear criticised his contemporary, J.J.D. La Touche, who had in his report on Ajmere and Mhairwarra falsified the facts by terminology borrowed from feudal Europe. (*Ethnological Notebooks, op. cit.* p. 283.)

58 *Ibid.* p. 255. Phear thus perceived one of the forms of unfreedom of social labour in the Asiatic mode of production.

59 These figures are taken from V. Ehrenberg, *The Greek State* (London, 1974), p. 31. They give a very approximate estimate of the condition of social labour in the middle of the fourth century B.C.

60 A. Smith, *Inquiry into the Wealth of Nations* (1776), vol. I.

61 Yet his interest in the history and theory of the ancient commune continued into the period 1879–81, when he took up his ethnological-evolutionary studies. Thus the commune lay in the centre of his attention in the drafts (unposted) of his correspondence with Vera Zasulic (see above). Moreover, although he scolded Maine for not having taken up the tribe and gens in his work, instead of speaking prerogative (*Ethnological Notebooks*, p. 309); yet Marx concentrated his attention on the Indian village community, not only in the connection with *Capital* (among others, the study of the Indian village community by Wilks, Raffles, Campbell) but also later (Kovalevsky, Phear,

Maine). Bibliographic references in: K. Marx *Ethnological Notebooks*, Asiatic Mode of Production, *op. cit.* and *Dialectic of Civil Society, op. cit.* p. 124.

62 K. Marx, *Zur Kritik der Politischen Oekonomie, op. cit.* p. 21 (ruinenweise); *Grundrisse*, Einleitung, *op. cit.* p. 26.

63 K. Marx on Theodor Mommsen: cf. *Ethnological Notebooks, op. cit.* pp. 218, 221f., and notes, pp. 408f. Marx had a high opinion of G.L. v. Maurer's scholarship in regard to the ancient and medieval history of the Germans, and measured the work of Maine (cf. *Ethnological Notebooks, op. cit.* pp. 295, 299, etc.) and Kovalevsky (cf. L. Krader, *Asiatic Mode of Production*, p. 383 etc.) according to the standards of Maurer. Yet Marx had already begun to differentiate critically that which Maurer, whom Marx had cited in *Capital* vol. I, had not. (Marx in a letter to Engels of 25 March 1868 considered that the peasants about Trier, on the Hunsrück, had maintained the old Germanic system down to the time of the Napoleonic invasions, and he remembered his father talking about it from a lawyer's point of view.)

64 Marx read August v. Haxthausen, *Die ländliche Verfassung Russlands* (Leipzig, 1862), in May, 1875. The study of the Russian peasant commune, mir, was first published by Haxthausen, in *Studien über die inneren Zustände, das Volksleben, und insbesondere die ländlichen Einrichtungen Russlands*, 3 vols. (Hannover, 1847–52). Marx referred to Haxthausen in his drafted but unposted letter to the journal, *Otečestvennyje Zapiski*, written in 1877 (November?). See *Werke* vol. 19, p. 107; also pp. 407f. and 582 (note 242). See also the drafts of his correspondence with Vera Zasulic, February–March 1881 (*ibid*. pp. 384–406). These considerations underlie the references made to the Russian commune, obščina, by Marx and Engels, *Communist Manifesto*. Engels added the following footnote to the English edition of the *Communist Manifesto* in 1888:

...Haxthausen discovered communal ownership of land in Russia, Maurer proved it to be the social foundation from which all Teutonic races started in history, and by and by villages were found to be, or have been the primitive form of society everywhere from India to Ireland. The inner organisation of this primitive communistic society was laid bare, in its typical form, by Morgan's crowning discovery of the true nature of the *gens* and its relation to the *tribe*. With the dissolution of these primeval communities society begins to be differentiated into separate and finally antagonistic classes.

Marx and Engels were one person in their revolutionary praxis, in 1848, in the organisation and activities of the International Working-Men's Association ('First International'), etc. In their theoretical developments, the further these were removed from the praxis, they were to a decreasing degree one. See L. Krader, *Ethnologie und Anthropologie bei Marx* (Ullstein, 1976), pp. 11f.

65 N.D. Fustel de Coulanges, G. v. Below and Max Weber were among those who attributed the ownership of land in severalty to the ancient Romans and Germans, both before and after the establishment of the state and historical society among them. (Fustel at the same time attributed to the nomadic Tartars the practice of common ownership of the land.) Weber and Below thought to strike a blow at the socialist doctrine thereby. On this controversy, cf. L. Krader, *Dialectic of Civil Society, op. cit.* Chapter 2, Agrarian Communism.

66 In the nineteenth century, the opinion varied regarding the communal beginnings of history. The first editor of *Russkaja Pravda*, J.P.G. Ewers, held that the Russian state emerged out of tribal antecedents; this view followed by the later Russian historians, S.M. Solov'iev and K. Kavelin. The Slavophile K.S. Aksakov, took up the thesis of the peasant community in opposition to Solov'iev and Kavelin. M.M. Kovalevsky and F.S. Leontovic̆ were of the opinion that the family community, Yugoslav zadruga, preceded the village community in the evolution of social institutions. In the generation immediately preceding the Russian Revolution, V.O. Kljucevsky held that the kinship group based on common descent in the paternal line (in Russian, rod) was the fundamental social unit prior to the formation of the state; S.F. Platonov, his contemporary, shared this view. Among the Soviet historians, B.D. Grekov traced the prehistory of the Slavs from the *rod* to the obs̆c̆ina, thence to the state. (Further on this, also bibliographic references in: L. Krader, *Dialectic of Civil Society, op. cit.* pp. 137 sq.)

67 B. Cicerin. *Oblastnye uc̆rez̆denija Rossii*, vol. XVII v (Moscow, 1856). *Idem. Obzor istoric̆eskogo razvitija sel'skoj obs̆c̆iny v Rossii* (Russkij Vestnik, 1856).

68 The term 'little republic' appears to have been the invention of William Blackstone: writers on Indian villages communities probably without consciously knowing the source took to applying it as a commonplace at the end of the eighteenth century, and the beginning of the nineteenth. Marx then took it over, in his writings on India. On the sources for the use of the term by Marx see L. Krader, *Asiatic Mode of Production*, pp. 63ff., 83f.

69 K. Marx, *Capital*, vol. III, in *Werke*, vol. 25, pp. 186f. See also *Werke*, vol. 23, p. 102. To be sure, exchange is practiced in primitive conditions as well, but it is of a different sort from that found in civilised conditions. On the other hand, ritual exchange is practiced under both conditions. Marcel Mauss, *Essai sur le Don: Forme et raison de l'échange dans les sociétés archaiques* (1923–24) dealt with ritual exchange; he did not take up the question of commodity exchange. While both ritual exchange and commodity exchange have been developed historically by the routinisation and rationalisation of either and of both, the practices differ in the two forms of exchange. By the routinisation and rationalisation of commodity exchange, trade, commerce and the market, what Whately and Ruskin called catallactic. The rationalisation and routinisation of ritual exchange leads to the further development of the ritual itself.

70 On the definition of social labour as the relation whereby each works for another, see K. Marx, *Capital*, vol. I, in *Werke*, vol. 23, p. 86: 'Finally, as soon as men in any way labour for another, their labour takes a social form as well.' Labour as here formulated has its history, and its socialisation has its history as well. In a work which is now in press, *Dialectic of Civil Society*, vol. II, we show that the formulation itself has its history, being traced back to Aristotle, Ethics, Book V. Cf. K. Marx, 'Auszüge aus Mill' *Eléments d'économie politique'*, in *Werke*, Ergänzungsband I, p. 462:

Our *reciprocal* value is for us the *value* of our reciprocal objects . . . . Given that we had as men produced: Each of us would have *affirmed doubly*, himself and the other. . . . I have directly in my life expression shaped your life expression, thus in my individual activity I have *confirmed* and *realised* directly my true being, my *human*, my *communal being*.

71 K.Marx, *Grundrisse*. Einleitung, *op. cit.* p. 25: 'Civil society is the most highly developed and most complex organisation of production in history'.

8 MARX, ENGELS AND POLITICS

Eric J. Hobsbawm

The present chapter deals with Marx's and Engels' views about the state and its institutions, about the political aspect of the transition from capitalism to socialism — the class struggle, revolution, and the organisation, strategy and tactics of the socialist movement, and indeed with their thought on politics and political theory in the general sense. Analytically these were in one way secondary problems: 'Legal relations as well as forms of State could not be understood from themselves . . . but are rooted in the material conditions of life', in that 'civil society' whose anatomy was political economy.[1] What determined the overthrow of bourgeois society were the internal contradictions of capitalist development, and more particularly the fact that capitalism generated the proletariat which would be its gravedigger. Moreover, while state power was crucial to class rule, the authority of capitalists over workers as such 'is vested in its bearers only as a personification of the requirements of labour standing above the labourer. It is not (vested in them in their capacity) as political or theocratic rulers, in the way that it used to be in former modes of production.'[2] Hence politics and the state did not need to be integrated into the basic analysis, but could be brought in at a later stage.[3]

In another sense, however, politics was primary, not only because Marx and Engels were active revolutionaries, but also because for the proletariat, as for earlier classes, the conquest of political power was the precondition of the transcendence of an earlier form of society, because in class society 'social evolutions' must be 'political revolutions'.[4] Hence an enormous amount of Marx's writings deals with politics. Yet these writings differ in character from his main theoretical work. Though he never completed his comprehensive economic analysis of capitalist development, its torso exists. Marx also devoted systematic attention to the critique of social philosophy, to what may be called the philosophic analysis of the nature of bourgeois society and communism in the 1840s. There is no analogous corpus of work on politics. His writings in this field after he became a communist are almost entirely in the form of

227

journalism, inquests on the immediate political past, contributions to discussion within the movement, private letters and
reading notes. There are signs that in later life he took an interest
in the problem of the historic origins of the state, in connection
with his increasing preoccupation with primitive communal and
pre-class social organisation, but he found no time to present the
results of his studies in connected form.[5] Engels attempted a more
systematic treatment of the state in *Anti-Dühring* and various
writings after Marx's death, notably the *Origin of the Family,
Private Property and the State*.

The precise nature of Marx's and to a lesser extent Engels'
views is therefore often unclear, especially about matters which
did not particularly preoccupy them; which indeed they may have
wishes to discourage, because 'what blinds people most is above
all the illusion of an autonomous history of state constitutions,
legal systems and ideological conceptions in all specific fields'
(1894).[6] Engels himself admitted, late in life, that though he and
Marx had been right to emphasise, first and foremost, 'the
derivation of political, juridical and other ideological conceptions
from the basic economic facts', they had somewhat neglected the
formal side of the process for the content. This applies not only to
the analysis of political, legal and other institutions as ideology,
but also — as he pointed out in the well-known letters glossing the
materialist conception of history — to the relative autonomy of
superstructural elements. There are thus considerable gaps in the
known ideas of Marx and Engels on such topics, and hence
considerable uncertainty about what they were or might have
been. Subsequent Marxists who attempted to fill these gaps (for
example, on law) when the need for a fuller Marxist theory arose,
thus found little in the classic texts to guide them. There is no
reason to believe that Marx and Engels — particularly Marx, with
his enormous range of erudition and intellectual interests —
would have had any difficulty in developing their thought on these
topics. On the other hand the absence of suitable texts from them
was in some ways to bias and distort subsequent Marxist
theoretical developments.

There is, of course, no difficulty in understanding why Marx
and Engels did not bother to fill gaps in their theory which now
seem obvious. The historical epoch in which and about which
they wrote, differed from all subsequent ones, including (except
for an overlap in the last years of Engels' life) the one in which
Marxist parties developed into mass organisations or otherwise
into significant political forces. Marx's and Engels' own situation

as active communists was only occasionally comparable to that of
their disciples who led or were politically active in these later
movements. For though Marx, perhaps more than Engels, played
an important role in practical politics, especially during the 1848
revolution as editor of the *Neue Rheinische Zeitung* and in the
First International, neither ever led or belonged to political
parties of the kind which became characteristic of the movement
after Marx's death. At most, they advised those who led them
from afar; and party leaders (for example, Bebel), in spite of their
enormous admiration and respect, did not always accept their
advice. The only political experience of Marx and Engels which
might be compared with that of some later Marxist organisations,
was their leadership of the Communist League (1847–52), which,
for this reason, provides a point of departure for the later Leninist
development of Marxism. The historically specific situations of
Marx's and Engels' lifetime, and the specific character of their
political interventions in them, must never be forgotten.

Nevertheless, though most of their writing was *ad hoc*, some of
it was based on a coherent analysis, which was gradually shaped,
modified and elaborated in the light of successive historical
experiences, though never fully formulated. This is notably the
case with the two problems of State and Revolution which Lenin
correctly linked in his attempt to produce such a systematic
formulation.

Marx's own thinking about the state began with the attempt to
settle accounts with the Hegelian theory on the subject in the
Critique of Hegel's Philosophy of Law (1843). At this stage Marx
was a democrat, but not yet a communist, and his approach thus
has some analogies with Rousseau's, though students who have
tried to establish direct links between the two thinkers have been
defeated by the undoubted fact that 'Marx never gave any
indication of being remotely aware' of his alleged debt to
Rousseau.'[7] The crux of his critique is the demonstration that the
state is simply an aspect of civil society which (to use the phrase
of the *German Ideology*) comprehends, but goes beyond state
and nationality, though in its external relations it presents itself as
nationality, while 'internally it must structure itself as state'.[8] It
may be noted — the thought continues to be present in Marx's
later theory of the state, though hardly ever dominant — that in
civil society, 'which develops as such only with [the development
of] the bourgeoisie' (*ibid.*), the state has among its functions the
regulation of the conflict between the private interests of the
bourgeois individuals and the public interest of the system.[9]

The *Critique* anticipated some aspects of Marx's more familiar later ideas: the identification of the state with a specific form of production-relations ('private property'), the state as a historic creation and its eventual dissolution (*Auflösung*) together with that of 'civil society' when democracy ends the separation of state and people, the conflict between private and public interest. However, it is chiefly notable as a critique of orthodox political theory, and consequently forms the first and last occasion on which Marx's analysis operates systematically in terms of constitutional forms, problems of representation etc.[10] We note his conclusion that constitutional forms were secondary to social content, and his critique of government by representatives (that is, by introducing democracy as a *formal* part of the state rather than recognising it as its essence).[11] Marx envisaged a system of democracy in which participation and representation would no longer be distinct; a point later stressed in connection with the Paris Commune.

In his communist phase the problem of the state became indissolubly linked with the problem of revolution; political theory with politics which, as Marx reminded Proudhon, were inseparable from the class struggle.[12] Marx therefore stressed four main points: the essence of the state was political power, which was 'the official expression of the opposition of classes within bourgeois society' (*ibid.*), it would consequently cease to exist in communist society; in the present system it represented not a general interest of society but the interest of the ruling class(es); but with the victory of the proletariat it would not disappear immediately but, during the expected transition period, take the temporary form of 'the proletariat organised as a ruling class'.

These ideas, though consistently maintained for the remainder of Marx's and Engels' lives, were considerably elaborated, particularly in two respects. First, the concept of the state as class power was refined, especially in the light of post-1848 regimes which (like that of Napoleon III) could not simply be described as the rule of the bourgeoisie. This will be further discussed below, though we note that Marx incidentally elaborated the theme of the state's relative independence — even against 'its own' class, as in the not wholly ironic formula (1850) that the state 'is nothing more than the reciprocal insurance of the bourgeoisie against both its own members and the exploited class, an insurance which must become increasingly expensive and apparently increasingly independent as against bourgeois society, because the subjection of the exploited class becomes increasingly difficult.'[13]

Second, mainly after 1870 Marx, but more especially Engels, outlined a more general model of the historical genesis and development of the state as a consequence of the development of class society, most fully formulated in the *Origin of the Family* (1884), which incidentally forms the starting-point of Lenin's later discussion. Unfortunately Marx's own development of these themes, which appear in connection with a revived and intense interest in primitive communal, (that is, pre-state society and consequently in the communist society of the future),[14] can only be reconstructed from reading-notes and other fragmentary material. The speculative discussion of this phase of Marx's political thought only began in the 1970s,[15] and it therefore did not affect the subsequent history of Marxism before that date. Engels argues that with the growth of irreconcilable and unmanageable class antagonisms in society, 'a power apparently standing above society became necessary for the purpose of moderating this conflict and keeping it within the bounds of "order" ' (that is, to prevent the class conflict from consuming both the classes and society 'in sterile struggle'). Though plainly 'as a rule' the state represents the interests of the most powerful and dominant class which by its control acquired new means of holding down the oppressed, it should be noted that Marxian state theory, then as earlier, was considerably more complex than the simple equation: state = coercive power = class rule. It accepts the state as at least a negative mechanism to prevent social disintegration during class society and, as we have seen, a positive mechanism for regulating the conflict between private and public interests of the bourgeois. It also accepts the element of concealment of power or rule by mystification or ostensible consent, which is implicit in the state's appearance of standing above society. There are evident reasons why in the political practice of Marx and the proletarian movement, these elements were not stressed.

Since Marx and Engels believed both in the eventual abolition/dissolution of the state and in the necessity of a transitional (proletarian) power, as well as in the necessity of social planning and authority after the revolution, the future of political authority raised problems which have troubled their successors, both in theory and in practice. These could not be solved by the semantic device of denying that political authority in the new society was a 'state', since state, politics and political power were by definition confined to the realm of class society, though Engels came close to saying this by arguing that it would begin to 'wither away' in an unspecified manner ('of itself') with 'the first act in which the state will appear as the real representative of the whole of society', namely the conversion of the means of production into social property. Two main ways of giving such formal statements substantial content are sketched.

First, with the end of bourgeois society the scope of political authority as a force imposed from above will disappear both with the end of class exploitation and of alienation, which, out of the contradiction between individual and communal interest, gives 'communal interest in the form of the *state* a separate shape'.[16] Second, in the absence of the need to rule men, the apparatus of management which would survive the state would be confined to 'the administration of things'. The distinction between the government of men and the administration of things was probably taken over from earlier socialist thought. It had been made familiar, especially by Saint-Simon. It becomes more than a semantic device only on certain very optimistic assumptions, (for example, the belief that the 'administration of things' would be technically rather simpler and less specialised than it has so far turned out to be, and thus within the scope of non-specialist citizens: Lenin's ideal of every cook as competent to govern the state). There seems no doubt that Marx shared this optimistic outlook.[17] Nevertheless, during the transitional period the rule of men, or in Engels' more precise phrase 'the intervention of state power in social relations'[18] would disappear only gradually.

Marx and Engels' preoccupation with the disappearance of the state is interesting not for what prognoses can actually be read into it, but chiefly as powerful evidence of their hopes for and conception of the future communist society; all the more powerful because their forecasts on this matter contrast with their habitual reluctance to speculate about an unpredictable future. The legacy they left to their successors on this problem remained puzzling and uncertain.

One further complication of their theory of the state must be briefly mentioned. Insofar as it was not merely an apparatus of rule, but one based on *territory*,[19] the state also had a function in bourgeois economic development as the 'nation', the unit of this development; at least in the form of a number of large territorial units of this kind (see below). The future of these units is not discussed by Marx or Engels, but their insistence on the maintenance of national unity in some centralised form after the revolution, though raising problems noted by Bernstein and confronted by Lenin,[20] is not in doubt. Marx always disclaimed federalism.

Marx's ideas on revolution, equally naturally, began with the analysis of the major revolutionary experience of his era, that of France from 1789 on.[21] France was to remain for the rest of his life the 'classical' exemplification of class struggle in its revolutionary form and the major laboratory of historical experiences in which revolutionary strategy and tactics were formed. However, from the moment he made contact with Engels, the French experience was supplemented with the experience of the mass proletarian movement, for which Britain was then and remained for several decades the only significant example.

The crucial episode of the French Revolution from both points of view was the Jacobin period. It stood in an ambiguous relation to the bourgeois state[22] since the nature of that state was to provide a free field for the anarchic operations of bourgeois/civil society, while in their different ways both the Terror and Napoleon sought to force them into a state-directed framework of community/nation, the one by subordinating them to 'permanent revolution' — used in this connection by Marx (*loc. cit.* p. 130) — the other to permanent conquest and war. The real bourgeois society first emerged after Thermidor, and eventually the bourgeoisie discovered its effective form, 'the *official* expression of its *exclusive* power, and the *political* recognition of its *specific* interests' in 'the constitutional parliamentary state' (*Repräsentativstaat*) in the revolution of 1830 (*ibid.* p. 132).

Yet as 1848 approached, another aspect of Jacobinism was emphasised. It alone achieved the total destruction of the relics of feudalism, which might otherwise have proceeded over decades. Paradoxically this was due to the intervention in the revolution of a 'proletariat' as yet too immature to be able to achieve its own objectives.[23] The argument remains relevant, even though we would not today regard the Sansculotte movement as 'proletarian'; for it raises the crucial problem of the role of the popular classes in a bourgeois revolution, and of the relations between bourgeois and proletarian revolution. These were to be the major themes of the *Communist Manifesto*, the writings of 1848 and the post-1848 discussions. They were to remain a major theme of Marx's and Engels' political thinking and of twentieth-century Marxism. Moreover, insofar as the coming of bourgeois revolution provided a possibility, following the Jacobin precedent, of leading to regimes which went *beyond* bourgeois rule, Jacobinism also suggested some political characteristics of such regimes (for example, centralism and the role of the legislative).

The experience of Jacobinism therefore threw light on the

problem of the transitional revolutionary state, including the
'dictatorship of the proletariat', a much-debated concept in
subsequent Marxist discussion. The term first entered Marxian
analysis — whether it was derived from Blanqui is unimportant —
in the aftermath of the defeat of 1848–9 (that is, in the setting of a
possible new edition of something like the 1848 revolutions).
Subsequent reference to it occurs chiefly in the aftermath of the
Paris Commune and in connection with the perspectives of the
German Social Democratic Party in the 1890s. Though it never
ceased to be a crucial element in Marx's analysis[24] the political
context in which it was discussed thus changed profoundly.
Hence some of the ambiguities of subsequent debate.

Marx himself never seems to have used the term 'dictatorship'
to describe a specific institutional form of government, but
always only to describe the *content* rather than the form of group
or class rule. Thus for him the 'dictatorship' of the bourgeoisie
could exist with or without universal suffrage.[25] However, it is
probable that in a revolutionary situation, when the main object of
the new proletarian regime must be to gain time by immediately
taking 'the necessary measures to intimidate the mass of the
bourgeoisie sufficiently',[26] such rule would tend to be more
overtly dictatorial. The only regime actually described by Engels,
if not literally by Marx as a dictatorship of the proletariat was the
Paris Commune, and the political characteristics of it which he
emphasised were the opposite of dictatorial (in the literal sense).
Engels cited both the 'democratic republic' as its specific political
form, 'as the French Revolution already demonstrated'[27] and the
Paris Commune. However, since neither Marx nor Engels set out
to construct a universally applicable model of the *form* of the
dictatorship of the proletariat, or to predict all types of situations
in which it might be in force, we can conclude no more from their
observations than that it ought to combine the democratic
transformation of the political life of the masses with measures to
prevent counter-revolution by the defeated ruling class. We have
no textual authority for speculations about what their attitude
would have been to the post-revolutionary regimes of the
twentieth century, except that they would almost certainly have
given the greatest initial priority to the maintenance of
revolutionary proletarian power against the dangers of overthrow. An army of the proletariat was the precondition of its
dictatorship.[28]

As is well known, the experience of the Paris Commune
suggested important amplifications to Marx's and Engels'

thought on the state and the proletarian dictatorship. The old state machinery could not be simply taken over, but had to be eliminated; Marx here seems to have thought primarily of Napoleon III's centralised bureaucracy, as well as army and police. The working class 'had to secure itself against its own representatives and officials' in order to avoid 'the transformation of the state and state organs from servants of society into its masters', as had happened in all previous states.[29] Though this change has been interpreted in subsequent Marxist discussion chiefly as the need to safeguard the revolution against the dangers of the surviving *old* state machinery, the danger envisaged applies to *any* state machinery which is allowed to establish autonomous authority, including that of the revolution itself. The resulting system, discussed by Marx in connection with the Paris Commune, has been the subject of intensive debate ever since. Little about it is unambiguously clear except that it is to consist of 'responsible [elected] servants of society' and not of a 'corporation standing above society'.[30]

Whatever its precise form, the rule of the proletariat over the defeated bourgeoisie has to be maintained during a period of transition of uncertain and doubtless variable length, while capitalist society is gradually transformed into communist society. It seems clear that Marx expected government, or rather its social costs, to 'wither away' during this period.[31] Though he distinguished between 'the first phase of communist society, as it has emerged after long labour-pains from capitalist society' and 'a higher phase', when the principle 'from each according to ability, to each according to need' can be applied, because the old motivations and limitations on human capacity and productivity will have been left behind,[32] no sharp chronological separation between the two phases seems envisaged. Since Marx and Engels rigidly refused to paint pictures of the future communist society, any attempt to piece their fragmentary or general observations on this subject together to form one, must be avoided as misleading. Marx's own comments on those points suggested to him by one unsatisfactory document (the Gotha programme) are obviously not comprehensive. They are mainly confined to restating general principles.

Throughout, the post-revolutionary prospect is presented as a lengthy, complex, by no means necessarily linear and essentially at present unpredictable process of development:

The general demands of the French bourgeoisie before 1789 were more or less established, as — *mutatis mutandis* — are the immediate demands of the proletariat today. They were more or less standard for all the countries of capitalist production. However, no pre-revolutionary Frenchman of the 18th century had the slightest idea, *a priori*, of the way in which these demands of the French bourgeoisie were actually to be carried out.[33]

Even after the revolution, as he observed in connection with the Commune, 'the replacement of the economic conditions of the slavery of labour by those of free and associated labour can only be the progressive work of time', that 'the present "spontaneous operation of the natural laws of capital and landed property" can only be replaced by "the spontaneous operation of the laws of social economy of free and associated labour" in the course of a lengthy process of development of new conditions,'[34] as had happened in the past with the slave and feudal economies. The revolution could only initiate this process.

This caution about predicting the future was largely due to the fact that the chief maker and leader of the revolution, the proletariat, was itself a class in process of development. The broad outlines of Marx's and Engels' views on this development, evidently based in the main on Engels' British experience of the 1840s, are presented in the *Communist Manifesto*: a progress from individual rebellion through localised and sectional economic struggles, first informal, then increasingly organised through labour unions, to 'one national struggle between classes', which must also be a political struggle for power. 'The organisation of the workers as a class' must be 'consequently into a political party'. This analysis was substantially maintained for the remainder of Marx's life, though slightly modified in the light of capitalist stability and expansion after 1848, as well as of the actual experience of organised labour movements. As the prospect of economic crises precipitating immediate workers' revolt receded, Marx and Engels became somewhat more optimistic about the possibility of successes for the workers' struggle within the framework of capitalism, by means of trade union action or the achievement of favourable legislation,[35] though the argument that the workers' wage depended to some extent on a customary or acquired living-standard as well as on market forces, is already sketched by Engels in 1845.[36] It follows that the pre-revolutionary development of the working class would be more prolonged than Marx and Engels had hoped or expected before 1848.

In discussing these problems it is difficult but essential to avoid reading a century of subsequent Marxist controversies back into the text of the classic writings. In Marx's lifetime the essential task, as he and Engels saw it, was to generalise the labour movement into a class movement, to bring into the open the aim implicit in its existence, which was to replace capitalism by communism, and most immediately, to turn it into a political movement, a working class party separate from all parties of the possessing classes and aiming at the conquest of political power. Hence it was vital for the workers neither to abstain from political action, nor to allow any separation of their 'economic movement from their political activity'.[37] On the other hand the nature of that party was secondary, so long as it was a class party.[38] It must not be confused with later concepts of 'party', and no coherent doctrine about these is to be found in their writings. The word itself was initially used in the very general sense current in the mid-nineteenth century, which included both the supporters of a particular set of political views or cause and the organised members of a formal group. Though Marx and Engels in the 1850s frequently used the word to describe the *Communist League*, the former *Neue Rheinische Zeitung* group or the relics of both, he carefully explained that the League, like earlier revolutionary organisations, 'was merely an episode in the history of the party, which forms spontaneously and everywhere in the soil of society' (that is, 'the party in the wider historical sense').[39] In this sense Engels could speak of the workers' party as a political party 'being already in existence in most countries' (1871).[40] Evidently from the 1870s Marx and Engels favoured, where possible, the constitution in some form of an *organised* political party, so long as this was not a sect; and in the parties formed by their followers or under their influence (on the model initially introduced by Lassalle), problems of internal organisation, party structure and discipline etc., naturally called forth suitable expressions of opinion from London. Where no such parties existed, Engels continued to use the term 'party' for the sum-total of the political (that is, electoral) bodies expressing the independence of the working class, irrespective of their organisation, 'never mind how, so long as it is a separate workers' party'.[41] They showed little except incidental interest in the problems of party structure, organisation or sociology which were to preoccupy later theorists.

Conversely, he wrote that:

sectarian 'etiquettes' must be avoided... . The general aims and tendencies of the working class arise from the general conditions in which it finds itself. Therefore these aims and tendencies are found in the whole class, although the movement is reflected in their heads in the most varied forms, more or less imaginary, more or less related to these conditions. Those who best understand the hidden meaning of the class struggle which is unfolding before our eyes — the communists — are the last to commit the error of approving or furthering sectarianism.[42]

The party must aim to be the organised class, and Marx and Engels never deviated from the declaration of the *Manifesto*, that the communists did not form a separate party opposed to other working class parties, or set up any sectarian principles of their own by which to shape and mould the proletarian movement.

All Marx's political controversies in his later years were in defence of the triple concept of: (a) a *political* class movement of the proletariat; (b) a revolution seen not simply as a once-for-all transfer of power to be followed by some sectarian Utopia, but as a crucial moment initiating a complex and not readily predictable period of transition; and (c) the consequently necessary maintenance of a system of political authority, a 'revolutionary and transitory form of the state'.[43] Hence the particular bitterness of his opposition to the anarchists, who rejected all of them.

It is thus vain to seek in Marx for the anticipation of such later controversies as those between 'reformists' and 'revolutionaries', or to read his writings in the light of subsequent debates between right and left in the Marxist movements. That they have been so read is part of the history of Marxism, but belongs to a later phase of its history. The issue for Marx was not whether labour parties were reformist or revolutionary, or even what these terms implied. He recognised no conflict in principle between the everyday struggle of the workers for the improvement of their conditions under capitalism and the formation of a political consciousness which envisaged the replacement of capitalist by socialist society, or the political actions which led to this end. The issue for him was how to overcome the various kinds of immaturity which held up the development of proletarian class parties (for example, by keeping them under the influence of various kinds of democratic radicalism — and therefore of bourgeoisie or petit-bourgeoisie — or by trying to identify it with various kinds of Utopias or patent formulas for achieving socialism, but above all by diverting it from the necessary unity of economic and political struggle). It is an anachronism to identify Marx with either a 'right' or 'left', 'moderate' or 'radical' wing in the international or any other labour movement. Hence the irrelevance as well as the absurdity of arguments about whether Marx at any point ceased to be a revolutionary and became a gradualist.

What form the actual transfer of power, and indeed the subsequent transformation of society, would take, would depend on the degree of development of the proletariat and its movement, which reflected both the stage reached in capitalist development and its own process of learning and maturing by praxis. It would naturally depend on the socio-economic and political situation at the time. Since Marx patently did not propose to wait until the proletariat had become a large numerical majority and class polarisation had reached an advanced stage, he certainly conceived of the class struggle as continuing after the revolution, though 'in the most rational and humane manner'.[44] Before and for an undefined period after the revolution the proletariat must thus be expected to act politically as the core and leader of a class coalition, its advantage being that, thanks to its historic position, it could be 'acknowledged as the only class capable of social initiative' (*ibid.*), even though still a minority. It is not too much to say that Marx saw the only potential 'dictatorship of the proletariat' he actually analysed, the Paris Commune, as destined ideally to proceed by something like a popular front of 'all classes of society which do not live by others' labour' under the leadership and hegemony of the workers.[45] However, these were matters of concrete assessment. They merely confirm that Marx and Engels did not rely on the spontaneous operation of historical forces, but on political action within the limits of what history made possible. At all stages of their lives they consistently analysed situations with action in their minds. The assessment of these changing situations must therefore be considered.

We may distinguish three phases of the development of their analysis: from the mid-1840s to the mid-1850s, the following twenty-five years, when a lasting victory of the working class did not seem on the immediate agenda, and Engels' last years, when the rise of proletarian mass parties appeared to open new perspectives of transition in the advanced capitalist countries. Elsewhere a modification of the earlier analyses remained valid. We shall consider the international aspects of their strategy separately below.

The '1848' perspective rested on the assumption, which proved correct, that a crisis of the old regimes would lead to widespread social revolution, and on the assumption, which proved incorrect, that the development of the capitalist economy had proceeded far enough to make possible the eventual triumph of the proletariat as the outcome of such a revolution. The actual working class, however defined, was at this time clearly a small minority of the population, except in Britain where — against Engels' prediction — no revolution took place. Moreover, it was both immature and barely organised. The prospects of proletarian revolution therefore rested on two possibilities. Either (as Marx, in some ways anticipating Lenin) foresaw, the German bourgeoisie would prove unable or unwilling to make its own revolution, and an embryonic proletariat, led by communist intellectuals, would take over its leadership,[46] or (as in France) the radicalisation of bourgeois revolution initiated by the Jacobins, could be continued.

The first possibility clearly proved quite unrealistic. The second still seemed possible even after the defeat of 1848–9. The proletariat had taken part in the revolution as a subaltern, but important member of a class alliance ranging leftwards from sections of the liberal bourgeoisie. In such a revolution possibilities of radicalisation arose at various moments, as moderates decided that the revolution had gone far enough, while radicals wished to press further with demands 'which were, or seemed, at least in part, to be in the interest of the great mass of the people'.[47] In the French Revolution this radicalisation had only served to reinforce the victory of the moderate bourgeoisie. However, the potential polarisation of class antagonisms during the capitalist era, as in the France of 1848–9, between a now united and reactionary bourgeois ruling class and a front of all other classes, grouped round the proletariat, might for the first time make it possible that a defeat of the bourgeoisie could make 'the proletariat, made wise by defeat, into the decisive factor' (*ibid.* p. 514). This historical reference back to the French Revolution lost much of its point with the triumph of Louis Napoleon.[48] Of course much — in the event too much — depended on the specific dynamic of the revolution's political development, since the continental working classes, including the Parisian, had behind them a very inadequate development of the capitalist economy.

The major task of the proletariat was therefore the radical-isation of the next revolution from which, once the liberal bourgeoisie had gone over to the 'party of order', the more radical 'democratic party' was likely to emerge as victor. This was the 'maintenance of the revolution in permanence' which forms the chief slogan of the Communist League in 1850[49] and which was to be the basis of a shortlived alliance between Marxians and Blanquists. Among the democrats the 'republican petit-bourgeoisie' was the most radical, and as such the most dependent on proletarian support. It was the stratum which must primarily both put under pressure and be combated by the proletariat. Yet the proletariat remained a small minority and therefore required allies, even as it sought to replace the petit-bourgeois democrats as the leader of the revolutionary alliance. We may note in passing that during 1848–9 Marx and Engels, like most of the left, underestimated the revolutionary or even the radical potential of the countryside, in which they took little interest. Only after the defeat, perhaps under the impetus of Engels (whose *Peasant War*, 1850, already showed an acute interest in the subject), did Marx come to envisage, at least for Germany, 'some second edition of the peasant war' to back proletarian revolution (1856). The revolutionary development thus envisaged was complex and perhaps lengthy. Nor is it possible to tell at which stage of it the 'dictatorship of the proletariat' might arise. However, the basic model was evidently a more or less rapid transition from an initial liberal phase through a radical-democratic one to one led by the proletariat.

Until the world capitalist crisis of 1857 failed to lead to revolution in any country, Marx and Engels continued to hope for, and indeed expect, a new and revised edition of 1848. Thereafter, for some two decades, they had no hope of any imminent and successful proletarian revolution, though Engels maintained his perennial youthful optimism better than Marx. Certainly they did not expect much of the Paris Commune, and were careful to avoid optimistic statements about it during its brief lifetime. On the other hand the rapid world-wide development of the capitalist economy, and especially of industrialisation in western Europe and the USA, now generated massive proletariats in various countries. It was on the growing strength, class consciousness and organisation of these labour movements that they now pinned their hopes. It must not be assumed that this made a fundamental difference to their political perspectives. As we have seen, the actual revolution, in the sense of the (presumably violent) transfer of power, could take place at various stages of the lengthy process of working class development, and would in turn initiate a lengthy process of post-revolutionary transition. The postponement of the actual transfer of power to some later stage of working class and capitalist development would no doubt affect the nature of the subsequent transition period, but though it might disappoint revolutionaries eager for action, it could hardly change the essential character of the predicted process. Nevertheless, the point about this period of Marx's and Engels' political strategy is that, though willing to plan for any eventuality, they did not consider a successful transfer of power to the proletariat imminent or probable.

The advance of mass socialist parties, particularly after 1890, for the first time created the possibility, in some economically developed countries, of a direct transition to socialism under proletarian governments which had come to power directly. This development occurred after Marx's death, and we therefore do not know how he would have confronted it, though there are some signs that he might have done so in a more flexible and less 'orthodox' manner than Engels did.[50] However, since Marx died before the temptation to identify himself with a flourishing mass Marxist party of the German proletariat was so great, this is a matter for speculation. There is some evidence that it was Bebel who persuaded Engels that a direct transition to power now became possible, bypassing 'the intermediate radical-bourgeois stage'[51] which had been previously regarded as necessary in countries which had failed to make a bourgeois revolution. At all events, it seemed that henceforth the working class would no longer be a minority, with luck at the head of a broad revolutionary alliance, but a vast stratum growing towards a majority, organised as a mass *party* and rallying allies from other strata *round that party*. Herein lay the difference between the new situation and that (still unique) of Britain, in which the proletariat formed the majority in a decisively capitalist economy and had achieved 'a certain degree of maturity and universality', but — for reasons into which Marx hardly bothered to enquire — had failed to develop a corresponding political class movement.[52] To this perspective of a 'revolution of the majority' achievable through mass socialist parties, Engels devoted his last writings, though these must be read to some extent as reactions to a specific (German) situation in this period.

Three peculiarities characterised the new historical situation with which Engels now attempted to come to terms. There was virtually no precedent for mass socialist working class parties of the new sort and none for what increasingly became common, single national 'social-democratic' parties virtually without competition on the left, as in Germany. The conditions which allowed them to develop, and became increasingly common after 1890, were legality, constitutional politics and the extension of the right to vote. Conversely, the prospects of revolution, as traditionally conceived, were now substantially changed. (The international changes will be considered below.) The debates and controversies of socialists in the era of the Second International reflect the problems arising out of these changes. Engels was only partly involved in their early stages, and they certainly became acute only after his death. Indeed it may be argued that he never fully worked out the possible implications of the new situation. Nevertheless, his opinions were obviously relevant to them, helped to shape them, and were to be the subject of much textual debate, because of the very impossibility of identifying them with any one of the diverging trends.

What was to give rise to particular controversy, was his insistence on the new possibilities implicit in universal suffrage, and his abandonment of the old insurrectionary perspectives; both clearly formulated in one of his last writings, the *aggiornamento* of Marx's *Class Struggles in France* (1895). It was the combination of both which was controversial: the statement that the German bourgeoisie and government 'are much more afraid of the legal than of the illegal action of the workers' party, of electoral success than of rebellion' (*ibid.*) Yet in fact, in spite of some ambiguity in Engels' last writings, he certainly cannot be read as approving or implying the legalistic and electoralistic illusions of later German and other social democrats.

He abandoned the old insurrectionary hopes, not only for technical reasons, but also because the clearer emergence of class antagonisms which made possible the mass parties, also made more difficult the old insurrections with which all strata of the population sympathised. Reaction would thus now be able to gather support from much larger sectors of the middle strata: ' "The people" will therefore always appear divided and thus a powerful lever disappears, which was so effective in 1848.' (*loc. cit.* p. 521). Yet he refused — even for Germany — to abandon thoughts on armed confrontation and with his usual and excessive optimism predicted a German revolution for 1898–1904.[53] Indeed, his immediate argument in 1895 tried to show little more than that, in the then situation, parties like the SPD had most to gain by utilising their legal possibilities. Violent and armed confrontation was thus likely to be initiated not by insurrectionaries but from the right against the socialists. This continued a line of argument already sketched out by Marx in the 1870s[54] in connection with countries in which there was no constitutional obstacle to the election of a socialist national government. The suggestion here was that the revolutionary struggle would then (as in the French Revolution and the American Civil War) take the form of a fight between a 'legitimate' government and counter-revolutionary 'rebels'. There is no reason to suppose that Engels ever disagreed with Marx's then view that 'no great movement has been born without the shedding of blood'.[55] Engels clearly saw himself not as abandoning revolution, but simply as adapting the revolutionary strategy and tactics to a changed situation, as he and Marx had done all their lives. It was the discovery that the growth of mass social-democratic parties did not lead to some form of confrontation but to some form of integration of the movement into the existing system, which threw doubt on his analysis. If he is to be criticised, it is for underestimating this possibility.

On the other hand he was keenly aware of the dangers of opportunism — 'the sacrifice of the future of the movement for the sake of its present'[56] — and did his best to safeguard the parties against these temptations by recalling, and indeed largely systematising, the main doctrines and experiences of what was now coming to be called 'Marxism', by stressing the need for 'socialist science',[57] by insisting on the essentially proletarian base of socialist advance,[58] and especially by establishing the limits beyond which political alliances, compromises and programmatic concessions for the sake of winning electoral support, became impermissible.[59] Yet in fact — and against Engels' intention this contributed, especially in the German party, to the widening of the gap between theory and doctrine on the one hand, actual political practice on the other. It was the tragedy of Engels' last years, as we can now see, that his lucid, realistic and often immensely perspicacious comments on the concrete situation of the movements served not to influence its practice, but to reinforce a general doctrine increasingly separate from it. His prediction proved only too accurate: 'What can the consequence of all this be, except that the party will suddenly, at the moment of decision, not know what to do, that there is unclarity and uncertainty about the most decisive points, because these points have never been discussed?'[60]

Whatever the prospects of the working-class movement, the political conditions for the conquest of power were complicated by the unexpected transformation of bourgeois politics after the defeat of 1848. In the countries which had undergone revolution the 'ideal' political regime of the bourgeoisie, the constitutional parliamentary state, was either not achieved or (as in France) abandoned for a new Bonapartism. In short, the bourgeois revolution had failed in 1848 or led to unpredicted regimes whose nature probably preoccupied Marx more than any other problem concerning the bourgeois state: to states plainly serving the bourgeoisie's interest, but not directly representing it as a class.[61] This raised the wider question, which is far from having exhausted its interest, of the relations between a ruling class and the centralised state apparatus, originally developed by the absolutist monarchies, strengthened by bourgeois revolution in order to achieve 'the bourgeois unity of the nation' which was the condition of capitalist development, but constantly tending to establish its autonomy *vis-à-vis* all classes, including the bourgeoisie[62] (This is the starting-point of the argument for the argument that the victorious proletariat cannot merely take over the state machinery, but must break it.) This vision of the convergence of class and state, economy and 'power elite', clearly anticipates much of twentieth-century development. So does Marx's attempt to provide French Bonapartism with a specific social basis, in this instance the post-revolutionary petit-bourgeois peasantry, in other words a class:

incapable of asserting their class interests in their own name... . They cannot represent themselves, but must be represented. Their representative must at the same time appear as their master, as an authority above them, as an unrestricted government power protecting them from other classes and sending rain and sunshine from above (*ibid*. pp. 198–9).

Here various forms of later demagogic populism, fascism etc., are anticipated.

Why such forms of rule should prevail, was not clearly analysed by Marx and Engels. Marx's argument that bourgeois-democratic government had exhausted its possibilities and that a Bonapartist system, the ultimate bulwark against the proletariat, would therefore also be the last form of rule before proletarian revolution,[63] evidently proved mistaken. In a more general form a 'class-balance' theory of such Bonapartist or absolutist regimes was eventually formulated by Engels (mainly in *Origin of the Family*), based on various formulations of Marx derived from the French experience. These ranged from the sophisticated analysis in the 18th Brumaire of how the fears and internal divisions of the 'party of order' in 1849–51 had 'destroyed all conditions of its own regime, the parliamentary regime, in the course of its struggle against the other classes of society' (*loc. cit.* pp. 176–85), to simplified statements that it rested 'on the fatigue and impotence of the two antagonistic classes of society'.[64] On the other hand Engels, as so often theoretically more modest but also more empirical, pursued the suggestion that Bonapartism was accept-able to the bourgeoisie because it did not want to be bothered with, or 'has not the stuff for' governing directly.[65] A propos of Bismarck, joking about Bonapartism as 'the religion of the bourgeoisie', he argued that this class could (as in Britain) let an aristocratic oligarchy conduct the actual government in its interest, or in the absence of such an oligarchy, adopt 'Bonapartist semi-dictatorship' as the 'normal' form of gov-ernment. This fruitful hint was not elaborated till later, in connection with the peculiarities of bourgeois-aristocratic co-existence in Britain,[66] but rather as an incidental observation. At the same time Marx and Engels after 1870 maintained, or reverted to, the emphasis on the constitutional-parliamentary character of the typical bourgeois regime.

But what was to happen to the old perspective of a bourgeois revolution, to be radicalised and transcended by 'permanent revolution', in the states where 1848 had simply been defeated and the old regimes re-established? In one sense the very fact that the revolution had taken place proved that the problems it raised *must* be solved: 'the *real* [that is, historical] as distinct from the illusory tasks of a revolution are always solved as a result of it.'[67] In this instance they were solved 'by its testamentary executors, Bonaparte, Cavour and Bismarck'. But though Marx and Engels recognised this fact, and even welcomed it — with mixed feelings — in the case of Bismarck's 'historically progressive' achieve-ment of German unity, they did not fully work out its implications. Thus the support of a 'historically progressive' step taken by a reactionary force might conflict with the support of political allies on the left who happened to be opposed to it. In fact this happened over the Franco-German war, which Liebknecht and Bebel opposed on anti-Bismarckian grounds (supported by most of the ex-1848 left) while Marx and Engels inclined privately to support it up to a point.[68] There is a danger in supporting 'historically progressive achievements' irrespective of who carries them out, except of course *ex post facto*. (Marx's dislike and contempt for Napoleon III saved him from similar dilemmas over Italian unification.)

However, more seriously, there was the question of how to assess the undoubted concessions made from above to the bourgeoisie (for example, by Bismarck), sometimes even described as 'revolutions from above'.[69] Though regarding them as historically inevitable Engels — Marx wrote little on this topic — was slow to abandon the view that they were impermanent. Either Bismarck would be forced towards a more bourgeois solution, or the German bourgeoisie 'would once more be compelled to do its political duty, to oppose the present system, so that at long last there will be some progress again.'[70] Historically he was right, for in the course of the next seventy-five years the Bismarckian compromise and Junker power were swept away, though in ways unpredicted by him. However, in the short run — and in their general theory of the state — Marx and Engels did not quite come to terms with the fact that the compromise solutions of 1849–81 were, for most of the European bourgeois classes, substantially the equivalent of another 1848 and not a poor substitute for it. They showed little signs of wanting or needing more power or a more completely and unequivocally bourgeois state — as Engels himself hinted.

Under these circumstances the fight for 'bourgeois democracy' continued, but without its former content of bourgeois revolution. Though this fight, increasingly conducted under working-class leadership, won rights which enormously facilitated the mobilisation and organisation of mass working-class parties, there was no real evidence for the late Engels' view that the democratic republic 'the logical [*konsequente*] form of bourgeois rule', would also be the form in which the conflict between bourgeoisie and proletariat would be polarised and finally fought out.[71] The character of the class struggle and of bourgeois–proletarian relations within the democratic republic, or its equivalent, remained cloudy. In short, it must be admitted that the question of the political structure and function of the bourgeois state in a developed and stable capitalism did not receive systematic consideration in the writings of Marx and Engels, in the light of the historical experience of the developed countries after 1849. This does not diminish the brilliance, and in many cases the profundity, of their insights and observations.

However, to consider Marx's and Engels' political analysis without its international dimension, is to play *Othello* as though it did not take place in Venice. The revolution was for them essentially an international phenomenon, and not simply an aggregate of national transformations. Their strategy was essentially international. Not for nothing does Marx's *Inaugural*

Address to the First International conclude with a call to the working classes to penetrate the secrets of international politics and to take an active part in them.

An international policy and strategy was essential not only because an international state system existed, which affected the chances of survival of any revolution, but more generally, because the development of world capitalism necessarily proceeded through the formation of separate socio-political units, as is implied in Marx's almost interchangeable use of the terms 'society' amd 'nation'.[72] The world created by capitalism, though increasingly unified, was 'a universal interdependence of nations' (*Communist Manifesto*). The fortunes of revolution, moreover, depended on the system of international relations, because history, geography, uneven strength and uneven development placed its development in each country at the mercy of what happened elsewhere, or gave it international resonance.

Marx's and Engels' belief in capitalist development through a number of separate ('national') units, is not to be confused with a belief in what was then called 'the principle of nationality' and today 'nationalism'. Though initially they found themselves attached to a deeply nationalist republican-democratic left, since this was the only effective left, nationally or internationally, before and during 1848, they rejected nationalism and the self-determination of nations as an end in itself, as they rejected the democratic republic as an end in itself.[73] Many of their followers were to be less careful to draw the line between proletarian socialists and petit-bourgeois (nationalist) democrats. That Engels never lost some of the German nationalism of his youth and the associated national prejudices, especially against the Slavs, is common knowledge.[74] (Marx was rather less affected by such feelings.) Yet his belief in the progressive character of German unity, or support for German victory in wars, was not based on German nationalism, though it certainly gave him pleasure as a German. For much of their lives both Marx and Engels regarded France rather than their own country as decisive for the revolution. Their attitude to Russia, long the chief target for their attack and contempt, changed as soon as a Russian revolution became possible.

Thus they may be criticised for underestimating the political force of nationalism in their century, and for failing to provide an adequate analysis of this phenomenon, but not for political or theoretical inconsistency. They were not in favour of nations as such, and still less in favour of self-determination for any or all nationalities as such. As Engels observed with his habitual realism: 'There is no country in Europe in which different nationalities are not placed under the same government... . And in all probability it will always be so.[75] As analysts they recognised that capitalist society developed through the sub-ordination of local and regional interests to large units — probably, they hoped from the *Manifesto* on, eventually into a genuine world society. They recognised, and in the perspective of history approved, the formation of a number of 'nations' through which this historic process and progress operated, and for this reason rejected federalist proposals 'to replace that unity of great peoples which, if originally brought about by force, has nevertheless today become a powerful factor of social pro-duction'.[76] Initially they recognised and approved the conquest of backward areas in Asia and Latin America by advanced bourgeois nations for similar reasons. They correspondingly accepted that many smaller nations had no such justification for independent existence, and some might actually cease to exist as nationalities; though here they were clearly blind to some contrary processes visible at the time, as among the Czechs. Personal feelings, as Engels explained to Bernstein,[77] were secondary, though when they coincided with political judgement (as with Engels on the Czechs) they left undue room for the expression of national prejudice and — as was to appear later — for what Lenin was to call 'great nation chauvinism'.

On the other hand as revolutionary politicians Marx and Engels favoured those nations and nationalities, great or small, whose movements objectively assisted the revolution and opposed those which found themselves, objectively, on the side of reaction. In principle they took the same attitude to the policies of states. The chief legacy they thus left to their successors was the firm principle that nations and movements of national liberation were not to be regarded as ends in themselves, but only in relation to the process, interests and strategies of world revolution. In most other respects they left a heritage of problems, not to mention a number of deprecatory judgements which had to be explained away by socialists trying to build movements among peoples dismissed by the founding fathers as unhistorical, backward or doomed. Except for the basic principle, later Marxists were left to construct a theory of 'the national question' with little aid from the classics. It must be pointed out that this was due not only to the greatly changed historical circumstances of the imperialist era, but also to Marx's and Engels' failure to develop more than a very partial analysis of the national phenomenon.

History determined the three major phases of their international revolutionary strategy: up to and including 1848, 1848–71 and from 1871 to Engels' death.

The decisive stage of the future proletarian revolution was the region of bourgeois revolution and advanced capitalist development (that is, somewhere in the area of France, Britain, the German lands and conceivably the USA). Marx and Engels showed little except incidental interest in the lesser and politically not decisive 'advanced' countries, until the development of socialist movements there called for comments on their affairs. In the 1840s revolution in this zone could reasonably be expected, and did indeed take place, though, as Marx recognised,[78] it was doomed by the failure of Britain to take part in it. On the other hand, except for Britain, no real proletariat or proletarian class movement as yet existed.

In the generation after 1848 rapid industrialisation produced both growing working classes and proletarian movements, but the prospect of social revolution in the 'advanced' zone grew increasingly improbable. Capitalism was stable. During this period Marx and Engels could only hope that some combination of internal political tension and international conflict might possibly produce a situation out of which revolution might emerge, as indeed it did in France in 1870–1. However, in the final period, which was once again one of capitalist crisis on a global scale, the situation changed. In the first place, mass working-class parties — largely under Marxist influence — transformed the prospects of internal development in 'advanced' countries. In the second, a new element of social revolution emerged on the margins of developed capitalist society, in Ireland and Russia. Marx himself first became aware of both at about the same time in the late 1860s. (The first specific reference to the possibilities of a Russian revolution occurs in 1870.)[79] Though Ireland ceased to play much part in Marx's calculations after the collapse of Fenianism,[80] Russia became increasingly important: its revolution could 'give the signal for a workers' revolution in the west, so that both complement each other' (1882).[81] The major significance of a Russian revolution would, of course, lie in its transformation of the situation in the developed countries.

These changes in the perspectives of revolution determined a major change in Marx's and Engels' attitude to war. They were no more pacifist in principle than they were republican democrats or nationalists in principle. Nor, since they knew war to be

Clausewitz's 'continuation of politics by other means' did they believe in an exclusive economic causation of war, at least in their lifetime. There is no suggestion of this in their writings.[82] Briefly, in the first two phases, they expected war to advance their cause directly, and the hope of war played a major, sometimes a decisive, part in their calculations. From the late 1870s on — the turning point came in 1879–80[83] — they saw a general war as an obstacle in the short run to the advance of the movement. Moreover, in his last years Engels became increasingly convinced of the terrible character of the new and probably global war which he predicted. It would, he said prophetically, have 'only one certain result: mass butchery on a hitherto unheard-of scale, exhaustion of Europe to a hitherto unheard-of degree, and finally the collapse of the entire old system' (1886).[84] He expected such a war to end in the victory of the proletarian party but since a war was 'no longer necessary' to achieve revolution he naturally hoped that 'we shall avoid all this butchery' (1885).[85]

There were two main reasons why a war was initially an integral and necessary part of the revolutionary strategy, including Marx's and Engels'. First, it was necessary to overcome Russia, the main bulwark of European reaction, the guarantor and restorer of the conservative status quo. Russia itself was at this stage immune to internal subversion, except on its western flank in Poland, whose revolutionary movement therefore long played a major role in the Marx–Engels international strategy. Revolution would be lost unless it turned into a European war of liberation against Russia, and conversely such a war would extend the range of the revolution by disintegrating the East-European empires. 1848 had extended it to Warsaw, Debreczen and Bucharest, wrote Engels in 1851: the next revolution must extend to St Petersburg and Constantinople.[86] Such a war must inevitably involve England, the consistent adversary of Russia in the East, which must oppose a Russian predominance in Europe, and this would have the additional and crucial advantage of undermining the other great pillar of the *status quo*, a stable capitalist Britain dominating the world market — perhaps even bringing the Chartists to power.[87] The defeat of Russia was the essential international condition of progress. It may be that Marx's somewhat obsessional campaign against the British foreign minister Palmerston was coloured by his disappointment at the refusal of Britain to run the risk of a major disruption of the European balance of power by a general war. For, in the absence of a European revolution — and perhaps even in the presence of one — a major European war against Russia without England was impossible. Conversely, when a Russian revolution became probable, such a war was no longer an indispensable condition of revolution in the advanced countries, though the failure of the Russian revolution to take place in his lifetime tempted the late Engels once again to see Russia as the ultimate bulwark of reaction.

Second, such a war was the only way to unify and radicalise the European revolutions; a process for which the French Revolutionary Wars of the 1790s provided a precedent. A revolutionary France, returning to the internal and external traditions of Jacobinism, was the obvious leader of such a war-alliance against Tsarism, both because France initiated European revolution and because it would possess the most formidable revolutionary army. This hope was also disappointed in 1848, and though France continued to play a crucial role in Marx's and Engels' calculations — and indeed both fairly consistently underestimated the stability and achievements of the Second Empire and expected its imminent overthrow — from the 1860s on France could no longer play the central role in European revolution formerly assigned to it.

But if, in the 1848 period, a war was seen as the logical outcome and extension of European revolution, as well as the condition of its success, in the next twenty years it had to be seen as the most important hope of de-stabilising the status quo, and thus releasing the internal tensions within the countries. The hope that this would be achieved by economic crisis died in 1857.[88] Never thereafter did Marx or Engels seriously place similar short-term hopes in any economic crisis, not even in 1891.[89] Their calculation was correct: the wars of this period had the predicted effect, though not in the manner hoped for by Marx and Engels, for they brought about no revolution in any major European country except France, whose international role, as we have seen, had changed. Hence, as already suggested, Marx and Engels were now increasingly forced into the novel position of deciding between the international policies of existing powers, all of them bourgeois or reactionary.

This was, of course, largely academic so long as Marx and Engels remained quite unable to influence the policies of Napoleon III, Bismarck or any other statesman, and there were no socialist and labour movements whose attitude governments had to take into account. Moreover, though sometimes the 'historically progressive' policy was fairly clear — Russia was to be opposed, the North to be supported against the South in the American Civil War — the complexities of Europe left endless room for inconclusive speculation and debate. It is by no means evident that Marx and Engels were more right than Lassalle in the attitude they took towards the Italian War of 1859,[90] though in practice the attitude of neither side mattered much at the time. When there were mass socialist parties which might feel obliged to give support to one bourgeois state in conflict with another, the political implications of such debates would become more serious. Certainly one reason why the late Engels (and even the late Marx) began to turn away from calculations that international war might be an instrument of revolution, was the discovery that it would lead to 'the recrudescence of chauvinism in all countries'[91] which would serve the ruling classes and weaken the now growing movements.

If the prospects of revolution in the period after 1848 were not good, it was largely because Britain was the main bulwark of capitalist stability, as Russia was that of reaction. 'Russia and England are the two great cornerstones of the actual European system'.[92] In the long run the British would only get into movement once the country's world monopoly was at an end, and this began to happen in the 1880s and was on various occasions analysed and welcomed by Engels. As the prospect of Russian revolution undermined one cornerstone of the system, the end of Britain's world monopoly undermined the other, though even in the 1890s Engels' expectations of the British movement remained rather modest.[93] In the short run Marx hoped to 'accelerate social revolution in England', which he regarded as the most important task of the First International — and not an entirely unrealistic one, since 'it is the only country in which the material conditions for [working class] revolution have developed to a certain degree of maturity'[94] — through Ireland. Ireland split the British workers on racial lines, gave them an apparent joint interest in exploiting another people, and provided the economic base for the British landed oligarchy, whose overthrow must be the first step in Britain's advance.[95] The discovery that a national/ liberation movement in an agrarian colony could become a crucial element in revolutionising an advanced empire, anticipated Marxist developments in the era of Lenin. Nor is it an accident that in Marx's mind it was associated with that other new discovery, the potential of revolution in agrarian Russia.[96]

In the final phase of Marx's, or more precisely Engels', strategy the international situation was fundamentally transformed by the prolonged global capitalist depression, the decline in Britain's world monopoly, the continued industrial advance of Germany and the USA, and the probability of revolution in Russia. Moreover, for the first time since 1815 a world war was visibly approaching, observed and analysed with remarkable prophetic acumen and military expertise by Engels. Nevertheless, as we have seen, the international policy of the powers now played a much smaller, or rather a more negative, role in their calculations. It was considered chiefly in the light of its repercussions on the fortunes of the growing socialist parties and as an obstacle rather than as a possible aid to their advance.

In a sense Engels' interest in international politics was increasingly concentrated within the labour movement which, in his final years, was once again organised as an International. For the actions of each movement could reinforce, advance or inhibit the others. This is clear from his writings, though we need not read too much into his occasional comparison of the situation in the 1890s with that before 1848.[97] Moreover, it was natural to assume that the fortunes of socialism would be determined in Europe (in the absence of a strong movement in the USA) and on the movements in the main continental powers, now also including Russia (in the absence of a strong movement in Britain). However welcome they were, Engels did not give much thought to the movements in Scandinavia or the Low Countries, practically none to those in the Balkans, and tended to regard any movements in colonial countries as irrelevant side-shows or consequences of metropolitan developments.[98] Beyond reasserting the firm principle that 'the victorious proletariat cannot force any kind of "happiness" on any foreign people without undermining its own victory' (*ibid*. p. 358), he hardly considered the problem of colonial liberation seriously. Indeed, it is surprising how little attention he paid to these problems which, almost as soon as his ashes had been scattered, forced themselves upon the international left in the form of the great debate on imperialism. 'We have' he told Bernstein in 1882 'to work for the liberation of the west-european proletariat, and to subordinate all other aims to this purpose'.[99]

Within this central area of proletarian advance the international movement was now one of national parties and had to be so — unlike before 1848.[100] This raised the problem of co-ordinating their operations and of what to do about conflicts which arose out of particular national claims and presumptions in individual movements. Some of these could be tactfully postponed into an indefinite future by suitable formulas, for example, about eventual self-determination,[101] though socialists in Russia and Austro-Hungary were more aware than Engels, that others could not. Barely more than a year after Engels' death, Kautsky frankly admitted that 'Marx's old position' on the Poles, the Eastern Question and the Czechs, could no longer be maintained.[102] Moreover, the unequal strength and strategic importance of various movements raised minor, but troublesome, difficulties. Thus the French had traditionally assumed 'a mission as world liberators and thereby the right to stand at the head' of the international movement.[103] But France was no longer in a position to maintain this role, and the French movement, divided, confused and heavily infiltrated with petit-bourgeois radical republicanism or other distracting elements, was disappointing — and indisposed to listen to Marx and Engels.[104] Engels even suggested at one moment that the Austrian movement might replace the French as the 'avantgarde'.

Conversely, the spectacular growth of the German movement, not to mention its close association with Marx and Engels, now made it clearly into the main force for international socialist advance.[105] Though Engels did not believe in the subordination of other movements to a leading party, except possibly at the moment of immediate action,[106] it was clear that the interests of world socialism would best be served by the progress of the German movement. This view was not confined only to German socialists. It was still very much present in the early years of the history of the Third International. On the other hand the view, also expressed by Engels in the early 1890s, that in a European war the victory of Germany against a Franco-Russian alliance would be desirable[107] was not shared in other countries, though the prospect of revolution arising out of defeat, which he held out to the French and Russians, was certainly later accepted by Lenin. It is idle to speculate what Engels would have thought in 1914, had he still been alive then, and quite illegitimate to suppose that he would have held the same views as in the 1890s. It is also probable that most socialist parties would have decided to support their governments, even if the German party had been unable to appeal to the authority of Engels. Nevertheless, the heritage he left to the International on questions of international relations and especially on war and peace, was an ambiguous one.

How can we sum up the general heritage of ideas about politics which Marx and Engels left to their successors? In the first place, it stressed the subordination of politics to historical development. The victory of socialism was historically inevitable because of the process summarised by Marx in the famous passage on the historical tendency of capitalist accumulation in *Capital*, vol. I, culminating in the prophecy about the 'expropriation of the expropriators'.[108] Socialist political effort did not create 'the revolt of the working class, a class always increasing in numbers, and disciplined, united, organised, by the very mechanism of capitalist production itself'; it rested upon it. Fundamentally the prospects of socialist political effort depended on the stage which capitalist development had reached, both globally and in specific countries, and a Marxist analysis of the situation in this light therefore formed the necessary basis for socialist political strategy. Politics was embedded in history, and the Marxian analysis showed how powerless it was to achieve its ends if not so embedded; and conversely, how invincible the working-class movement, which was.

In the second place, politics was nevertheless crucial, insofar as the inevitably triumphant working class must and would be organised politically (that is, as a 'party'), must aim at the transfer of political power, which would be followed by a transitional system of state authority under the proletariat. Political action was thus the essence of the proletarian role in history. It operated *through* politics (that is, within the limits set by history) choice, decision and conscious organised action. Probably in the lifetime of Marx and Engels as well as during the Second International, the main criterion which distinguished Marxians from most other socialists, communists and anarchists (except those in the Jacobin tradition) and from 'pure' trade union or co-operative movements, was the belief in the essential role of politics before, during and after the revolution. For the post-revolutionary period, the implications of this attitude were as yet academic. For the pre-revolutionary period they necessarily involved the proletarian party in all kinds of political activity under capitalism.

In the third place, they saw such politics essentially as a class struggle within states which represented the ruling class or classes, except for certain special historical conjunctures such as those of class-balance. As Marx and Engels championed materialism against idealism in philosophy, so also they consistently criticised the view that the state stood above classes, represented the common interest of all society (except negatively, as a safeguard against its collapse), or was neutral between classes. The state was a historical phenomenon of class society, but while it existed as a state it represented class rule — though not necessarily in the agitationally simplified form of an 'executive committee of the ruling class'. This imposed limits both on the involvement of proletarian parties in the political life of the bourgeois state and on what it could be expected to concede to them. The proletarian movement thus operated both within the confines of bourgeois politics and outside them. Since power was defined as the main content of the state, it would be easy to assume (though Marx and Engels did not do so) that power was the only significant issue in politics and in the discussion of the state at all times.

Fourthly, the transitional proletarian state, whatever functions it maintained, must eliminate the separation between the people and government as a special set of governors. One would say it has to be 'democratic', if this word were not identified in common parlance with a specific institutional type of government by periodically elected assemblies of parliamentary representatives, which Marx rejected. Still, in a sense not identified with specific institutions, and reminiscent of certain aspects of Rousseau, it was 'democracy'. This has been the most difficult part of Marx's legacy for his successors, since — for reasons which go beyond the present discussion — all actual attempts to realise socialism along Marxian lines so far have found themselves strengthening an independent state apparatus (as have non-socialist regimes), while Marxists have been reluctant to abandon the aspiration so firmly regarded by Marx as an essential aspect of the development of the new society.

Finally, and to some extent deliberately, Marx and Engels left to their successors a number of empty or ambiguously filled spaces in their political thought. Since the actual forms of political and constitutional structure before the revolution were relevant to them only insofar as they facilitated, or inhibited the development of the movement, they gave little systematic attention to them, though commenting freely on a variety of concrete cases and situations. Since they refused to speculate about the details of the coming socialist society and its arrangements, or even about the details of the transitional period after the revolution, they left their successors little more than a very few general principles with which to confront it. Thus they provided no concrete guidance of practical use on such problems as the nature of the socialisation of the economy or the arrangements for planning it. Moreover, there were some subjects on which they provided no guidance, general, ambiguous or even out-of-date at all, because they never felt the need to consider them.

Yet what must be stressed is not so much what later Marxists could or could not derive in detail from the legacy of the founders, or what they would have to think out for themselves, but the extreme originality of Marx's and Engels' contribution. What they rejected, persistently, militantly and polemically, was the traditional approach of the revolutionary left of their day, including all earlier socialists,[109] an approach which has still not lost its temptations. They rejected the simple dichotomies of those who set out to replace the bad society by the good, unreason by reason, black by white. They rejected the *a priori* programmatic models of the various brands of the left, not without noting that while each brand had such a model, up to and sometimes including the most elaborate blueprints of Utopia, few of these models were in agreement with each other. They also rejected the tendency to devise fixed operational models (for example, to prescribe the exact form of the revolutionary change), declaring all others to be illegitimate, to reject or to rely exclusively on political action etc. They rejected ahistorical voluntarism.

Instead, they placed the action of the movement firmly in the context of historical development. The shape of the future and the tasks of action could be discerned only by discovering the process of social development which would lead to it, and this discovery itself became possible only at a certain stage of development. If this limited the vision of the future to a few rough structural principles, by excluding speculative forecasts, it gave to socialist hopes the certainty of historical inevitability. In terms of concrete political action, to decide what was necessary and possible (both globally and in specific regions and countries) required an analysis of both historical development and concrete situations. Thus political decision was inserted into a framework of historical change, which did not depend on political decision. Inevitably, this made the communists' tasks in politics both ambiguous and complex.

They were ambiguous, because the general principles of the Marxian analysis were too wide to provide specific policy guidance, if such were required. This applies particularly to the problems of revolution and the subsequent transition to socialism. Generations of commentators have scrutinised the texts for a clear statement of what the 'dictatorship of the proletariat' would be like and have failed, because the founders were primarily concerned to establish only the historical necessity of such a period. It was complex, because Marx and Engels' attitude to the *forms* of political action and organisation, as distinct from their *content*, and to the formal institutions among which they operated, was so largely determined by the concrete situation in which they found themselves, that they could not be reduced to any set of *permanent* rules. At any given moment and in any specific country or region, the Marxian political analysis could be formulated as a set of policy recommendations (as for instance in the *Addresses of the General Council* in 1850), but they did not, by definition, apply to situations different from the ones for which they were compiled — as Engels pointed out in his later thoughts on Marx's *Class Struggles in France*. But post-Marxian situations were inevitably different from those in Marx's lifetime, and insofar as they contained similarities, these could only be discovered by a historical analysis both of the situation Marx had faced and the one to which later Marxists sought his guidance. All this made it virtually impossible to derive from the classic writings anything like a manual of strategic and tactical instruction, and dangerous even to use them as a set of precedents; though they have nevertheless been so used. What could be learned from Marx was his method of facing the tasks of analysis and action rather than ready-made lessons to be derived from classic texts.

And this is certainly what Marx would have wished his followers to learn. Yet the translation of Marxian ideas into the inspiration of mass movements, parties and organised political groups inevitably was to bring with it what E. Lederer once called 'the well-known fore-shortened, simplifying stylisation which brutalises thought, and to which every great idea is and must be exposed, if it is to set masses into movement'.[110] A guide to action was constantly tempted to allow itself to be turned into dogma. In no part of Marxian theory has this been so damaging to both theory and movement as in the field of Marx's and Engels' political thinking. But it represents what Marxism became, perhaps inevitably, perhaps not. It represents a derivation from Marx and Engels, all the more so since the texts of the founders acquired classic or even canonical status. It does not represent what Marx and Engels thought and wrote, and only sometimes, how they acted.

Notes

1 K. Marx, *Preface to the Critique of Political Economy* in *Werke*, vol. 13, p. 8.
2 K. Marx, *Capital*, vol. III, p. 888, in *Werke*, vol. 25.
3 Admittedly the original plan of *Capital* envisaged three final books dealing with the State, Foreign Trade and the World Market (R. Rosdolsky, *Zur Entstehungsgeschichte des Marxschen Kapitals* I, Chapter 2), but the one on the State planned to deal only with 'the relation of different forms of the state to different economic structures of society.' (Marx to Kugelmann 1862, *Werke*, vol. 30, p. 639).
4 K. Marx, *German Ideology*, in *Werke*, vol. 3, p. 34; Poverty of Philosophy, in *Werke*, vol. 4, p. 182).
5 His notes have been fully analysed in L. Krader, *The Ethnological Notebooks of Karl Marx* (Assen, 1972); see also E. Lucas, *Die Rezeption Lewis H. Morgans durch Marx und Engels* (*Saeculum* XV, 1964, pp. 153–76) and the same author's, *Marx's Studien zur Frühgeschichte und Ethnologie 1880–1882* (*ibid.* pp. 327–43).
6 F. Engels to Mehring, in *Werke*, vol. 39, pp. 96ff.
7 L. Colletti, *From Rousseau to Lenin*, pp. 187–8. The tracing of the Rousseau–Marx filiation was first seriously attempted by G. della Volpe in *Rousseau e Marx* (Rome, 1957). Apart from one laudatory reference to Rousseau in Marx's *The Jewish Question*, there is little evidence in Marx's early writings of much reference to Rousseau or knowledge of other works than the *Social Contract* (which he read in 1843) and the *Essay on Political Economy*.
8 K. Marx, *German Ideology*, *Werke*, vol. 3, p. 36.
9 This is well put by L. Krader (Introduction to Marx, *Ethnological Notebooks*, p. 68):

The propertied interest is a contradictory one: on the one hand it is a relation of public obligation as a necessity, on the other it is an interest of private exception as a right. He who is with property wants a rule governing the payment of taxes or the regulation of commerce for others, a loophole for himself.

10 There is no sign that Marx ever tried to carry out the plan (late 1844) of a work on the modern state, which was also conceived in these terms, but specifically identified the origin of the modern state with the French Revolution and its abolition with the end of bourgeois society (under the heading 'Suffrage'). Draft Plan for a Work on the Modern State (*MEGA* Abt.i, vol. 5, *Marx-Engels Collected Works*, vol. 4, p. 666).
11 K. Marx, *Critique*, *Werke*, vol. I, pp. 321, 323.
12 'Poverty of Philosophy' in *Werke*, vol. 4, pp. 181–2.
13 Rezensionen aus der *Neuen Rheinischen Zeitung: Politisch-ökonomische Revue*: *Le socialisme et l'impôt, par Emile de Girardin,* in *Werke*, vol. 7, p. 288).
14 This revived interest may perhaps be traced back to Marx's discovery of the historical writings of Maurer in 1868 (Marx to Engels 14 March 1868, 25 March 1868) which opened new perspectives on primitive society, which Marx henceforth explored assiduously.
15 Mainly with L. Krader's edition of Marx's *Ethnological Notebooks*.
16 K. Marx, *German Ideology*, in *Werke*, vol. 3, pp. 33–4.

17 Cf. First Draft of Civil War in France (*Werke*, vol. 17, p. 544):

Removal of the illusion that administration and political leadership are secrets, transcendent functions which could only be confined to the hands of a trained caste... . The whole deception was swept away by a Commune which consisted predominantly of simple workers who organise the defence of Paris, wage war against the pretorians of Bonaparte, ensure the supplies of this giant city, and fill all the posts hitherto shared among government, police and prefecture.

18 F. Engels, *Anti-Dühring*, in *Werke*, vol. 20, in pp. 261–2.
19 'Origin of Family', in *Werke*, vol. 21, p. 165.
20 V.I. Lenin, *State and Revolution*, chapter III, 4.
21 In Kreuznach and Paris 1843–4.
22 See 'Holy Family', in *Werke*, vol. 2, pp. 127–31.
23 'Die moralisierende Kritik', in *Werke*, vol. 4, pp. 338–9. On the origins of this idea, cf. H. Förder, *Marx und Engels am Vorabend der Revolution* (Berlin, 1960) and W. Markov, Jacques Roux and Karl Marx (*Sitzungsberichte der deutschen Akad. d. Wissenschaften zu Berlin*, Klasse für Philos., Geschichte, Staats-, Rechts- u. Wirtschaftswissenschaften, Jg 1965 (Berlin, 1965).
24 The key references are Marx to Weydemeyer 5 March 1852, in *Werke,* vol. 28, pp. 507–8, and 'Critique of the Gotha Programme' in *Werke*, vol. 19, p. 28.
25 Cf. Wilhelm Mautner, *Zur Geschichte des Begriffes 'Diktatur des Proletariats'* (*Grünberg's Archiv*, 1920), pp. 280–3.
26 K. Marx to Nieuwenhuis 22 February 1881, in *Werke*, vol. 35, p. 161.
27 *Critical Notes on the Erfurt Programme* 1891 in *Werke*, vol. 22, p. 235.
28 K. Marx, Speech on the seventh anniversary of the IWMA, 1871, in *Werke*, vol. 17, p. 433.
29 F. Engels, Preface to K. Marx, *Civil War*, 1891, in *Werke*, vol. 22, pp. 197–8.
30 K. Marx, *Civil War*, second draft, in *Werke*, vol. 17, p. 597.
31 K. Marx, Gotha Programme, in *Werke*, vol. 19 p. 19: '*The general costs of administration, not directly belonging to production.* This part (of the social product EJH) will from the start be remarkably reduced in comparison with society today, and will diminish in proportion as the new society develops.'
32 K. Marx, Gotha Programme, *ibid*. p. 21.
33 K. Marx to Nieuwenhuis 22 February 1881, in *Werke*, vol. 35, pp. 160–1.
34 K. Marx, *Civil War* draft I, in *Werke*, vol. 17, p. 546.
35 Inaugural Address of the IWMA, in *Werke*, vol. 16, p. 11.
36 Cf. E.J. Hobsbawm, Introduction to F. Engels, *Condition of the Working Class in England in 1844* (London, 1969); K. Marx, 'Value, Price and Profit', in *Werke*, vol. 16, pp. 147–9.
37 Resolutions of the London Delegate Conference of the IWMA 1871, in *Werke*, vol. 17, pp. 421–2; Notes for Engels' speech, *ibid*. pp. 416–7.
38 To Bolte 25 November 1871 in *Werke*, vol. 33, p. 332.
39 K. Marx to Freiligrath, 1860, in *Werke*, vol. 30, pp. 490, 495.
40 *Werke*, vol. 17, p. 416.
41 To Sorge 29 November 1886, to Nieuwenhuis 11 January 1887, in *Werke*, vol. 36, pp. 579, 593.
42 To P. and L. Lafargue, in *Werke*, vol. 32, p. 671.

43 K. Marx, *Der politische Indifferentismus, in Werke*, vol. 18, p. 300.
44 K. Marx, *Civil War*, draft I, in *Werke*, vol. 17, pp. 544–46.
45 K. Marx, *Civil War*, text and draft I, in *Werke*, vol. 17, pp. 341, 549–54.
46 The point is made lucidly in G. Lichtheim, *Marxism* (London, 1964) pp. 56–7, though the author's fundamental distinction between pre- and post-1850 Marxism cannot be accepted.
47 F. Engels, *Introduction to Class Struggles in France* 1895, in *Werke*, vol. 22, pp. 513–4.
48 L. Perinix (ed.) *Karl Marx: Rivoluzione e Reazione in Francia 1848–1850*, (Torino, 1976), Introduzione LIV, perceptively analyses the differing historical references in Marx's *Class Struggles in France* and in the *18th Brumaire*.
49 Address of the Central Council in *Werke*, vol. 7, pp. 244–54.
50 Compare his attitude on the Russian peasantry (drafts and letter to Zasulich, in *Werke*, vol. 19, pp. 242–3, 384–406) with Engels' (Nachwort zu 'Soziales aus Russland', in *Werke*, vol. 22, pp. 421–35), and his extreme concern to maintain the support of peasants and middle strata after a revolution (*Civil War*, draft I, in *Werke* vol. 17, pp. 549–54) with Engels' cavalier dismissal of the danger of demagogic reactionaries capturing peasants and petty craftsmen (*Die Bauernfrage in Frankreich und Deutschland*, in *Werke* vol. 22, pp. 485–505. It is hard to conceive that the author of the *18th Brumaire* would have written, of small peasants and independent artisans unready to accept the prediction of their disappearance: 'These people belong among the Anti-Semites. Let them go to those who promise them to save their small enterprises,' (see *Werke*, vol. 22, p. 499.)
51 Bebel to Engels 24 November 1884 in W. Blumenberg (ed.) *August Bebels Briefwechsel mit Friedrich Engels* (Hague, 1965), pp. 188–9. See also L. Longinotti, 'Friedrich Engels e la "rivoluzione di maggioranza" ' (*Studi Storici*, vol. XV (4), p. 821).
52 *Konfidentielle Mitteilung*, in *Werke*, vol. 16, pp. 414–5. Here Engels' analysis went deeper. Even in 1858 his casual phrase about the 'bourgeois proletariat' created by British world monopoly (to Marx, 7 November 1858, in *Werke*, vol. 29, p. 358) already anticipated some of the main lines of his analysis in the 1880s and 1890s (cf. 'England in 1845 and 1886 in *Werke*, 21, pp. 191–7); Intro. to *Socialism, Utopian and Scientific*, in *Werke*, vol. 22, pp. 309–10.
53 To R. Fischer 8 March 1895, in *Werke*, vol. 39, pp. 424–6; Introduction, *loc. cit.* pp. 521–2; to Laura Lafargue, in *Werke*, vol. 38, p. 545.
54 Speech on the Hague Congress in *Werke*, vol. 18, p. 160. F. Engels, Preface to the English edition of *Capital*.
55 K. Marx, *Konspekt der Debatten über das Sozialistengesetz*, in *Briefe an Bebel, Liebknecht, Kautsky und andre* (Moscow–Leningrad, 1933), vol. I, p. 516; Interview with *New York Tribune* 1878, in *Werke*, vol. 34, p. 515.
56 *Critique of the Erfurt Programme* draft in *Werke*, vol. 22, pp. 227–40, esp. pp. 234–5.
57 To Bebel 1891, in *Werke*, vol. 38, p. 94) à propos of party objections to his publication of the *Critique of the Gotha Programme*.
58 Cf. The Future Italian Revolution, 1894, in *Werke*, vol. 22, pp. 440, 441: 'It is not our business directly to prepare a movement which is not precisely the movement of the class we represent'.

59 Cf. especially The Future Italian Revolution (*loc. cit.* pp. 439–42) The peasant question in France and Germany (*ibid.* pp. 483–505).

60 *Critique of Erfurt draft, loc. cit.* p. 234.

61 For Marx's attitude to Bonapartism (formulated chiefly in *The 18th Brumaire*, whose argument is continued in the *Civil War*) cf. M. Rubel, *Karl Marx devant le Bonapartisme* (Hague, 1960).

62 K. Marx, *18th Brumaire*, VII, in *Werke*, vol. 8, pp. 196–7.

63 K. Marx, *18th Brumaire*, pp. 196–7; Civil War in *Werke*, vol. 17, pp. 336–8, draft II, *ibid*.

64 To Lafargue 12 November 1866, in *Werke*, vol. 31, p. 536; for a more elaborate version, see F. Engels 'The real causes of the relative inactivity of the French proletarians last December' 1852, in *Werke*, vol. 8, pp. 224–7.

65 To Marx 13 April 1866 in *Werke*, vol. 31, p. 208.

66 'It seems to be a law of historical development that in no European country is the bourgeoisie able — at all events for a lengthy period — to capture political power in the same exclusive manner as the feudal aristocracy maintained it during the Middle Ages' (Intro. to English edition of Socialism, Utopian and Scientific, *Werke*, vol. 22, p. 307).

67 Engels to Kautsky 7 February 1882 in *Werke*, vol. 35, pp. 269.

68 Engels to Marx 15 August 1870, Marx to Engels 17 August 1870, in *Werke*, vol. 33, pp. 39–44.

69 Nachwort zu 'Soziales aus Russland', in *Werke*, vol. 22, p. 433.

70 To Bebel 13–14 September 1886, in *Werke*, vol. 36, p. 526. For the question see E. Wangermann, Introduction to *The Role of Force in History* (London, 1968).

71 Engels to Bernstein 27 August 1883, 24 March 1884, in *Werke*, vol. 36, pp. 54–5, 128. Of course Engels may have considered merely a brief phase of the future revolution itself, cf. to Bebel, 11–12 December 1884 in *Werke*, vol. 36, pp. 252–3.

72 Cf. S.F. Bloom, *The World of Nations* (New York, 1941), pp. 17ff.

73 Engels in *Neue Rheinische Zeitung*, 31 August 1848, in *Werke*, vol. 5, p. 377; see also Engels to Bernstein 24 March 1884, in *Werke*, vol. 35, p. 128.

74 Cf. Roman Rosdolsky, 'Friedrich Engels und das Problem der "Geschichtslosen Völker" ' *Archiv f. Sozialgeschichte,* vol. 4 (Hannover, 1964).

75 'Was hat die Arbeiterfrage mit Polen zu tun?', 1866, in *Werke* vol. 16, p. 157.

76 K. Marx, 'Civil War in France', in *Werke*, vol. 17, p. 341.

77 Engels to Bernstein on the Bulgarians 27 August 1882, in *Werke*, vol. 35, pp. 280–2.

78 In *Neue Rheinische Zeitung* 1 January 1849, in *Werke*, vol. 6, pp. 149–50.

79 Marx to Paul and Laura Lafargue 5 March 1870, in *Werke*, vol. 32, p. 659.

80 Engels to Bernstein 26 June 1882, in *Werke*, vol. 35, pp. 337–9.

81 Preface to the Russian edition of *Communist Manifesto*, in *Werke*, vol. 19, p. 296.

82 Cf. E.H. Carr 'The Marxist attitude to War', in *History of the Bolshevik Revolution*, vol. III (London, 1953), pp. 549–66.

83 Engels to Marx 9 September 1879, Marx to Danielson 12 September 1880, in *Werke*, vol. 34, pp. 105, 464; Engels to Bebel 16 December 1879, in *Werke*, vol. 34, p. 431; Engels to Bebel 22 December 1882, in *Werke*, vol. 35, p. 416.

264 *The History of Marxism*

84 Engels to Bebel 13 September 1886, in *Werke*, vol. 36, p. 525.
85 To Bebel 17 November 1885, in *Werke*, vol. 36, p. 391.
86 Cited in Gustav Mayer, *Friedrich Engels* (Hague, 1934), vol. II, p. 47.
87 Marx in *Neue Rheinische Zeitung* 1 January 1849, in *Collected Works*, vol. 8, pp. 213–5.
88 For their expectation of imminent revolution, Marx to Engels 26 September 1856, Engels to Marx 'not before 27 September 1856', 15 November 1857, Marx to Engels 8 September 1857, in *Werke*, vol. 29, pp. 76, 78, 212, 225.
89 Cf. On the Brussels Congress and the Situation in Europe, in *Werke*, vol. 22, p. 243.
90 The debate is summarised in Gustav Mayer, *op. cit.* vol. II, pp. 81–93.
91 Engels to Lafargue 24 March 1889, in *Werke*, vol. 37, p. 171.
92 Marx to Paul and Laura Lafargue, in *Werke*, vol. 32, p. 659.
93 Preface to English edition (1892) of 'Socialism, Utopian and Scientific', in *Werke*, vol. 22, pp. 310–1.
94 Marx to Meyer and Vogt, 9 April 1870, in *Werke*, vol. 32, pp. 667–9.
95 Marx to Kugelmann 29 November 1869, in *Werke*, vol. 32, p. 638. More fully: General Council to Federal Council of Suisse Romande 1 January 1870, in *Werke*, vol. 16, pp. 386–9.
96 Marx to P. and L. Lafargue 5 March 1870, in *Werke*, vol. 32, pp. 655ff.
97 For example to Adler 11 October 1893, in *Werke*, vol. 39, pp. 134ff.
98 To Bernstein 9 August 1882, *à propos* Egypt; to Kautsky 12 September 1882, in *Werke*, vol. 35, pp. 349, 357–8.
99 To Bernstein 22/25 February 1882, in *Werke*, vol. 35, pp. 279–280.
100 To Kautsky 7 August 1882, in *Werke*, vol. 35, pp. 269–70.
101 For example, *à propos* of Alsace and areas in dispute between Russia and Poland to Zasulich 3 April 1890, in *Werke*, vol. 37, p. 374.
102 G. Haupt, M. Lowy and C. Weill, *Les Marxistes et la Question Nationale* (Paris, 1974), p. 21.
103 Engels to Kautsky 7 February 1882, in *Werke*, vol. 35, p. 270.
104 To Adler 17 July 1894, in *Werke*, vol. 39, pp. 271ff. For the infrequency of contacts with the French, except for Lafargue, see the register of correspondence in *Marx-Engels, Verzeichnis* II, pp. 581–684.
105 To Adler 11 October 1893, in *Werke*, vol. 39, p. 136.
106 To Kautsky 7 February 1882, in *Werke*, vol. 35, p. 270.
107 To Bebel 29 September/1 October 1891, in *Werke*, vol. 38, pp. 159–63; 'Der Sozialismus in Deutschland, in *Werke*, vol. 22, p. 247.
108 K. Marx, *Capital*, vol. I, chapter 32.
109 This is particularly clearly exemplified in Engels' *Anti-Dühring* especially in the parts published separately as '*Socialism, Utopian and Scientific*'.
110 Cited in E. Weissel. *Die Ohnmacht des Sieges* (Vienna, 1976), p. 117.

9 MARX AND MARXISM
Georges Haupt

The terms 'Marxist' and 'Marxism' are universally known and currently used, sometimes without too much discernment. Some students of Marx have questioned the very legitimacy of such terms: Maximilien Rubel, for instance, has dubbed them 'illicit and unjustifiable'. In particular he accuses Engels — 'the founder' — of having 'committed the unpardonable error of giving his approval to this abscess', of 'sanctioning it with his authority', because, if he had exercised his veto, 'this universal scandal would never have seen the light of day'.[1]

This thesis, so decisively formulated, strikes me as disputable, because this way of posing the problem runs the risk of oversimplifying a much more complex process. This does not mean that Rubel's point of view deserves merely incidental consideration: on the contrary, it must be emphasised precisely because it compels us to question several commonplaces which are as misleading as they are convenient, and above all to give ourselves more thoroughly to the study of the mechanisms for the formation and spread of concepts whose ill-judged adoption defiles our political vocabulary.[2] The history of the terms 'Marxist' and 'Marxism' can be illuminating for various reasons, especially because it illustrates the complex process whereby ideologies have spread and taken root in the international workers' movement. It reveals to us the nature, transformations and metamorphoses of the revolutionary theory which has been designated with a somewhat generic term. To my mind, the problem consists not so much in an enquiry into the legitimacy and the fidelity of this notion to Marx's initial project, as in the examination of how it arose, why it took root, and of its usefulness.

The terminological confusion dates from the birth of the twin terms 'Marxist-Marxism', and continues to our own day through

Further elaboration of this essay, specially envisaged by Haupt for *The History of Marxism*, was denied us by his unexpected death. We therefore republish it in its first version, which he himself revised for *The Socialist International from the Commune to Lenin*, (Turin, 1978). We have included a few changes only, and these appear in the last revision of the manuscript.

the use and interpretation that have been made of them. They are terms involving many different meanings, and many prejudices on the part of advocates and adversaries. The content covered by the word 'Marxism' emerges as so elliptical that one may legitimately enquire what this term has meant in the various phases of its history[3] — all the more so because the advent, dissemination and successive changes that have come about in the term's meaning can to some extent give us an insight into the process that has led to the rise and spread of Marxism on a universal scale.

Part I: Marxism: a Faction or an Idea?
As has often happened in the history of great political and intellectual movements, the name did not come from within, from the partisans' ranks, but from outside, from the opposing columns. The various stages in the crystallisation of the new term were linked to those which the workers' movement passed through. From the 1840s, but especially during the process of the dissolution of the Communist League at the beginning of the 1850s, Marx's opponents spoke of a 'Marx party'.[4] Already in 1853–54, during the controversy between the followers of Weitling and Marx, there appears the designation 'Marxian' (*Marxianer*), which refers to Marx and 'his blind followers' who represent in Germany the 'kritische ökonomische Richtung'.[5]

The word 'Marxian' was to be widely disseminated in the decade following, in opposition to 'Lassallian'.[6] In the First International, Bakunin and his followers were to use the epithet 'Marxid' in their bitter struggle against Marx and the General Council.[7] The then current expression 'Marxian' (synonymous with 'dynasty of Marxids', 'Marx's law', 'authoritarian communism',) as well as the new term 'Marxists' were to serve more to accuse Marx and his adherents than to define his ideas. Yet in the use of these epithets Bakunin was doing no more than paying Marx back in his own coin: for the latter's writings abound in such terms as 'Proudhonian', 'Bakuninian', used to discount or ridicule his opponents. As Margarette Manale observes, 'the term "Marxian" first came to Bakunin by verbal analogy with "Mazzinian" ', and he ably used these polemical epithets in an attempt at cornering Marx 'within the sectarianism to which he had relegated his own opponents and critics'. On the other hand, 'the use of this terminological label, which was to undergo a series of transformations',[8] emerges as two distinct terms in Bakunin and the Jura anarchists: 'Marxians', or 'Marxian party, that of

so-called ''socialist'' democracy', which designates Marx's
adherents, his 'agents': and 'Marxist' to define their orientation
and actions.[9] The term always carries a strong polemical
resonance: thus Bakunin and his followers speak of the 'Marxist'
Hague Congress, or of 'Marxist falsifications' when referring to
the resolutions of the Hague Congress; or of 'Marxist inquisitors'
to designate the commission of enquiry nominated by that
congress. In a word, the use of the label 'Marxist' is meant to
accuse ('the Marxists do not aim at the immediate emancipation
of the proletariat') and only after a linguistic process which
remains to be clarified were the various labels finally incorporated into the infinitely more convenient word, linguistically
plausible and henceforth free of any negative connotation:
'Marxist'.[10]

Immediately after the secession which occurred at the Hague
Congress of the International Working Men's Association, the
label 'Marxist' began to gain currency. Its meaning is a good deal
different from that which Bakunin gave it. The term signifies the
fraction that remained faithful to the General Council, and is used
in contrast to 'Alliancist' or 'Bakuninist'. But it was still only one
of the many names within the wider arsenal of the internationalists. Thus, the Address of the New York socialist
revolutionary group at the 1873 International Congress in
Geneva states: 'We want union even at the price of sacrificing
some of our ideas; sacrifice some individuals, even; but let the
Romands and the Jurassians, the Federalists and the Centrists,
the Marxists and the Alliancists shake hands once more'.[11] It was
especially the hostile bourgeois press that adopted the term.[12] We
are confronted with a 'systematic confusion of terms', observed
Johann Philipp Becker, who was close to Marx's positions, in the
Journal de Genève of September 1872. His protest is characteristic of the reaction of those who were directly involved.

By planting the word 'Marxists' on the disciples of international socialism,
freeborn of the true soil cultivated by science, the bourgeois press, unless acting
in total ignorance, reveals its bad taste which is all the more irritating in that it
functions to contrast these disciples with the mindless sect of the 'Bakuninists',
who, for their part, bear this name, charged with irony and scorn, as if it were a
well-deserved punishment.[13]

The 'anti-authoritarians', like the Belgian Verrycken, equally
deplore the fact that 'the bourgeois newspapers, having seized
upon the ill-fated incident at The Hague, have made personal
attacks where what is at issue are matters of principle'.[14]

'Marxists' and 'Bakuninists' are at least agreed on one point: that 'two strands of ideas have shaken the International, and not the struggle between two leaders'.

The use of personal epithets and the personalisation of the currents of ideas that resulted from it only irritated the militant workers. A number of them rebelled against the practice. Such was the case with the Geneva internationalists, like Henri Perret, Marx's correspondent, who, in a pamphlet published on the eve of the Geneva Congress of the IWMA in September, 1873, dates the appearances of these terms from 1869, from the controversy provoked by the secessionist manoeuvres of the International Alliance of Social Democrats at Geneva: 'It is in that first dispute that the expressions "Marxists" and "Bakunists" appear'. His rejection of terms deriving from surnames is illuminating:

The fact that sections have grouped around proper names is deplorable, contrary to our principles and the interests of workers' emancipation. *Amour propre*, pride, ambition, all the human passions inherent in the personality replace the general interests of the mass. Forgotten is the slow, cold, continuous, methodical action which is essential to these interests, and the only passion is for or against this or that individuality, ever more easy to exalt or overthrow than it is to achieve progress or quash an abuse.

The workerist slant of this argument is explicit when Perret emphasises: 'These characters are rarely workers: they are uprooted members of the bourgeoisie: graduates, professors, writers, students, even at time capitalists'.

Finding fault with both the opposing camps, which he holds responsible for the crisis in the International, he concludes: '[We must] not only change the men, but also destroy the cause of the evil. Enough of Marxists and Bakuninists! [What we need is] a sincere and real alliance of the *workers*'.[15]

Should we believe that the appeal fell on sympathetic ears? It is a fact that in a short space of time — between 1874 and 1877 — those epithets tend to disappear from the socialist vocabulary. For example, the Bakuninists, who were at first uncomplaining in their acceptance of the appellation that was fastened on them, rejected it in the name of the same principles. Thus, in 1876, at the Congress of the (Federalist) IWMA, in Berne, Errico Malatesta declared that, notwithstanding the devotion and respect that linked him to Bakunin, his supporters were not 'Bakuninists', first of all because 'we do not share all Bakunin's practical and theoretical ideas', but principally 'because we follow ideas, not men: we rebel against the habit of embodying a principle in a man, a habit that is all very well for political parties, but utterly incompatible with the tendencies of modern socialism'. He went on to observe that 'Bakunin himself has aways protested against the use of this label for his friends'.[16] At the same congress, Vahlteich, the German Social Democratic deputy, who was there in a private capacity, disowned 'the attacks directed by Germany against this or that [foreign socialist] personality', declaring: 'We for our part are neither "Marxists" nor "Dühringians", and the former Lassallians, forgetting any other considerations, have united with the general movement.'[17]

This language is primarily explained by the spirit of reconciliation which spread as a result of the efforts of the Belgian internationalists to organise, in 1877, a general socialist congress in Ghent. Yet the initiative, which looked like a step forward 'on the road to a *rapprochement* of the various hostile factions',[18] ended in failure. Thenceforth hostilities were destined to resume, this time in a greatly changed context. Labels using the names of individuals reappear, and indeed are enriched with additions: side by side with 'Marxist' there now arises another neologism, 'Marxism'. They were very soon to become a closely linked pair. Who invented this term? It is a difficult question to answer. Certainly one can say that in 1882 it appeared in the title of a polemical pamphlet, *Le Marxisme dans l'Internationale*, by Paul Brousse, an ex-anti-authoritarian, 'an extremist anarchist' at the Ghent Congress, who became the leader of the possiblists in France.[19] In 1881 he was described by Engels as an excellent fellow (Kreuzbraver Kerl) but 'totally useless on the plane of theory and written expression', 'the greatest scatterbrain that I have ever known'.[20] In his writings the term 'Marxism' does not designate a theory but the practice and aims of social democracy — of the workers' parties that took their stand on the terrain of the class struggle.

'Marxism does not consist in being a partisan of Marx's ideas. In this sense, not a few of his current adversaries — the present writer in particular — would be Marxists', says Brousse, who is criticising the behaviour of a 'Marxist faction that exists in Europe', namely, 'the social democrats of the school of Marx', who would like to saddle France with their concept of the party. In a word, the term 'Marxism', used indiscriminatingly together with the adjective 'Marxist', does not indicate for Brousse a theory but the tendency of the supposed followers 'of Marx's German doctrines', the 'Marxist party', or German social democracy and its 'appendage' in France, made up of the Guesdists.[21]

The polemical ring of the two terms, notwithstanding the

persistence of the anarchists' polemical usage of them,[22] begins to die out in the early 1880s. Their meaning and their usage soon undergo remarkable changes. Such is the case, for instance, in Russia, where these terms always had a positive connotation from as early as 1881.[23] This can be explained by the precocious interest in Marx's works in populist circles, and the ready welcome they were accorded of an intense and special kind.[24] In this respect the letter dated 7th February, 1883, sent by J. Stefanovic, one of the theorists of populism, to Lev Dejc, who had been one of the founders of the first Marxist group in Russia, Liberty of Labour, appears to us to be characteristic.

There is something that I do not understand: Why contrast populism with Marxism? It may seem that its fundamental principle is not identical with that which has been adopted by contemporary political economists. Kireevsky and Dostoievsky, for instance, meant something else. We, however, are talking about present-day populism. Populism, it seems to me, consists in the application of those Marxist principles to a particular case, to the spiritual and physical profile of a given country, the level and characteristics of its civilisation, culture, etc. . . To be a Marxist as a theoretician, yet not as a member of a militant socialist party in the West, is no impediment to being a populist, while the opposite, needless to say, is not always the case.[25].

From the 1880s onwards, the terms 'Marxist' and 'Marxism' enter the international socialist vocabulary with varying senses. Most of all they serve for identification and demarcation, and there are a number of reasons for the rapid changes in their usage. In the first place there are the modifications occurring in socialist terminology, especially in the names adopted by the various currents in their eagerness to differentiate themselves from rival socialist currents. At the time of the First International, three terms defined the three principal tendencies, their aims and methods: the first, communism, indicates Marx (but is claimed by the Blanquists, too); the second, collectivism, refers to Bakunin and his tendency; finally, socialism refers to moderate tendencies, with petit bourgeois characteristics. Now, however, these three distinctions tend to disappear, or to be modified, following the dissolution of the IWMA. The noun 'social democrat' is destined to replace 'communist'[26], and indicate the orientations and the parties that take their stand on the terrain of the class struggle and the political struggle. Notwithstanding resistance by Marx and Engels, it was to meet with success.[27] The label 'anarchy'[28] was to be appropriated by a wide and heterogeneous current, which held together by virtue of its opposition to the political struggle as an instrument of socialist action. Moderate tendencies, reformist in character, were mostly known to their opponents as 'possiblist'. In the socialist vocabulary of the 1880s, the word 'Marxist' was linked to that of social democrat, almost to mark the difference from the 'possiblists'. Thus the two international congresses that met in Paris in July of 1889 were distinguished by their contemporaries as 'Marxist Congress' and 'Possiblist Congress'.[29]

In France, from that time onwards, the Parti Ouvrier Français was referred to as the 'Marxist fraction of the Socialist Party', or as the 'Marxist Workers' Party'.[30] At the same time, the Guesdist militants called themselves Marxists; thus, in 1888, Dormoy, in announcing to Guesde his intention not to offer himself as a candidate at the parliamentary elections, but to aspire instead to a seat on the Municipal Council, explained his decision in these words: 'I say to you today as I did yesterday: it is not Dormoy that has returned to the Municipal Council, but the entire Marxist party'.[31] Similarly, on 8 November of that year, in reporting the work of the Third National Congress of trades unions in Bordeaux, he wrote: 'The Marxists dominated with a solid majority, and although several were not Marxists . . . all our resolutions were unanimously adopted'.[32] Osip Zetkin, who was also a Guesdist, wrote a brief history of the socialist movement in France after the Paris Commune. Appearing in German in 1888, it was written for the militants of the German Social Democratic Party. He referred to those who were enrolled in the French party as 'Marxists', distinguishing them from the 'Blanquists' and the 'independent socialists'.[33]

At the same time the use of the words 'Marxists' and 'Marxism' was becoming clearer within the German Social Democratic Party. Instead of pejorative nicknames, they became positive indicators, and penetrated the political vocabulary with a new meaning.

This semantic evolution, which occurred in a relatively short space of time, needs to be seen in relation to the profound transformations in the working-class movement during the transitional period from the First to the Second International. The 'great depression', beginning with the crisis of 1873, hastened a reversal tendency. The abstentionist current, which had commanded a majority after the Hague Congress of the IWMA, rapidly lost ground, while the 'authoritarian' coalition which had grouped around the Federalist IWMA split in 1876. Thus the upholders of political struggle found themselves in a majority within the working-class movement. Taking their cue from the SPD, the formation of independent working-class parties accelerated, and in a decade — between 1884 and 1892 — the main European socialist parties were set up. With this process the ideological armoury changed its functions, and the forming of working-class parties created the premises for the dissemination and adoption of Marxism, which provided the foundations for their official ideologies: the principle of political struggle, means of action and self-legitimisation, and the principle of class struggle, the constitutive element in their identity and their collective consciousness.

These transformations also provoked important changes in the socialists' attitudes. The terms 'Marxist' and 'Marxism' were no longer felt as attacks upon their convictions, but on the contrary found favourable acceptance, being deliberately adopted in the interests of defining a distinct position. Moreover, the diffusion of Marxism and its increasing hold over the international working-class movements from the time of the Second International lent these words fresh substance.

Part II: The Dissemination of Marx's Ideas
What did the 'Marxians' stand for in the First International? To speak of the 'Marxists' as a current within the IWMA corresponds more to Bakunin's polemical arguments than to reality. Paradoxically, these assertions were taken over by a historiography that proclaimed itself Marxist. It gave them a positive meaning in order to construct, through a curious amalgam, a linear account of the diffusion of Marxism. To be sure, around Marx there were grouped, whether in the General Council or a certain number of sections, numerous militants who formed the 'Marx party'. But apart from a few exceptions, even those who adhered explicitly to the 'School of Marx' or those who were considered 'Marxians' did not share his ideas, or were not familiar with them.[34] His closest supporters, like Wilhelm Liebknecht, accepted his guidance, his political platform, without thereby being 'Marxists'.

Kautsky observed that in the General Council 'there was only a very frugal presence of Marx's particular orientation'. Only thanks to his intellectual supremacy and 'art of handling men' did Marx succeed in imposing his strategic lines of the IWMA.[35] It would be a mistake to confuse Marx's stature, which dominated the IWMA, with the reverberations of his theoretical ideas in the ideological milieu of the working-class movement of his day. Marx's personal authority in socialist circles was enormous. He enjoyed an extraordinary reputation, not only in the upper echelons of the International, but also among the militants. His scientific gifts, and especially the quality of his writings on economics, were recognised even amongst his most decided opponents. Bakunin went so far as to declare that Marx was 'socialism's surest, wisest and most influential support, one of the most solid defences against the penetration of bourgeois ideas and aspirations of every kind'.[36] He recognised: 'Marx is the foremost economic and socialist scientist of our age'.[37] Even in the German press the author of *Capital* was described as 'the greatest living economist, Dr Karl Marx, master of Lassalle'.[38]

The publication of volume I of *Capital* in 1867 consolidated Marx's fame, which spread beyond the confines of socialist circles. In the first place, this had repercussions on his position within the working-class movement. Thus in 1868 in Hamburg, at the General Assembly of the Allgemeiner Deutscher Arbeiter-verein, W. Bracke read a declaration dedicated to the 'work of Karl Marx', and presented a resolution, adopted without debate, which went: 'Through his work on the process of the production of capital, Karl Marx has rendered the working class an eternal service'.[39] But as far as the theses of his masterpiece were concerned, they were slow to penetrate the reality of the working-class movement, and if anything *Capital* became known through the various pamphlets that summarised and popularised it — not always written by supporters of Marx.

The dissemination of Marx's ideas during the 1860s and 1870s was mainly indebted to the basic documents of the IWMA which he edited — firstly the Inaugural Address, then the resolutions of the Congresses, and finally the Addresses to the General Council, the most important and widely circulated of which were those on the 'civil war' in France. This 'educative propaganda', Mehring observed, expressed and summed up the Marxism of the First International.[40] The programmatic documents of the IWMA were effective instruments of recruitment, and helped convert isolated militants. Their influence was first felt in Germany, particularly on the part of Eisenach. It was through reading the Inaugural Address that Bebel was induced to adopt Marx's ideas; and it was always this address that was invoked as an example and an essential argument by those who reported the problem of the programme at the Nuremberg Conference in September, 1868, when the party joined the IWMA. The German internationalists explained the influence and strength of the IWMA by the fact that it possessed a rigorous scientific programme. Thus the printworker Hillman, a follower of Eisenach, published in the journal of the association of typographers a long article on the IWMA, stressing Marx's role as author of the Address:

A *Manifesto of the Working Classes of Europe*, edited by Karl Marx, the noted social economist, was presented to the Association; the Address had to compete with a Mazzinian statutory project that was so conspiratorial it risked strangling an international association of workers at birth. It was consequently rejected, along with the Statutes (later definitively approved at the 1866 Geneva Congress). This *Manifesto* is one of the most important works from the pen of this scientific authority; it contains the bitterest criticism ever levelled at a dominant class in the whole course of human history.[41]

The Paris Commune played an important role in bringing Marx his European fame. For the press he was the head of the omnipotent International; through the identification of the IWMA with the Paris rising, the 'Marx party' and Marx personally acquired a fame that contributed appreciably to an awakening of interest in his work amidst large sections of public opinion. Marx's scientific reputation was to serve largely as a weapon for his disciples and followers in the struggle for the supremacy of his theory in the working-class movement. Thus, in the obituary that appeared in *Neue Zeit*, stress was laid on the fact that Marx, the founder of scientific socialism, was one of the most eminent scholars of his day.

By his research into the laws of historical and economic movement, Marx placed himself amongst the greatest thinkers and scientists. No one will be able or will wish to contest that [his theory] has assumed that same importance for science as Darwinian theory; just as the latter dominates the natural sciences, so the former dominates the economic and social sciences.[42]

In these words are contained the themes on which the spread of 'Marxism' was founded at the end of the nineteenth century.[43]

In the interim between the First and Second International, Marx's theory became an essential line in the ideological polyphony. Interest in the writings of Marx and Engels grew and the writings spread. All tendencies, all currents of socialist throught were determined from then on in relation to the theoretical standpoints of the founders of 'scientific socialism'. The various schools within the socialist movement, with the exception of the anarchists, recognised the importance of the work, and bowed to the uncontested authority of Marx and Engels. Socialist language underwent a prolonged transformation in the direction of Marx's vocabulary, while the quotations from his writings multiplied. But this process of assimilation took place within a dominant eclectic socialist ideology, which integrated Marx and Lassalle, Bakunin and Proudhon, Dühring and Benoît Malon. The broad lines of 'eclectic' socialism during the years 1870–80 in Germany were summed up thus by Kautsky:

In general the results of the research of Marx and Engels were accepted, but their basis was often ill digested, and the number of Marxists of consequence was small. The Gotha Programme, the influence of Dühring, the success of *The Quintessence of Socialism* by Herr Schäffle in party circles shows how far eclecticism had spread.[44]

From the beginning of the 1880s a distinction arises between the Marxist school and 'eclectic socialism', and the phenomenon occurs within the German social democratic movement. The initiative comes from Engels, with his polemic against Dühring, whose influence on the German socialists was colossal. In several ways the *Anti-Dühring* marks a crucial point in the formation of 'Marxism' as a system. There is abundant evidence of this. Kautsky, for instance, writes:

The revolution produced in our minds by *Herr Dühring's Revolution*, the way we have learned to understand Marx completely, to see him as a whole, the way it has rid us of the residues of utopian socialism, of the socialism of the professorial chair, of bourgeois-democratic modes of thought: this is something that only those who have lived through this process can measure.[45]

The Marxist nucleus that formed within German social democracy became a clearly defined current. By an incessant ideological struggle it bent itself on gaining hegemony. The destiny of the words 'Marxist' and 'Marxism', the presentation and diffusion of them in a new configuration and with a new content, occur in the midst of a long and hard theoretical and political battle, conducted by a group that defined itself from the start as 'coherently Marxist'. It aimed to bring about the triumph of 'Marxism', raising it to the official doctrine of the *Parteibewegung* (party movement). It drew theoretical support from Engels, who played an extremely important role in this process of hegemonisation, and political support from the two uncontested leaders of the party, Bebel and Liebknecht. But the christening of the school and doctrine occurred without the knowledge of either Marx or Engels, and indeed in spite of them. They granted no entrance visa to this neologism. On the contrary, they reacted to it with irritation and rejected it. Marx preferred to define his theory as 'critical materialist socialism'; Engels for his part spoke of 'critical and revolutionary socialism', (what 'distinguishes it from its predecessors is precisely this materialist base'), or else he called it 'scientific socialism', a term used in contradistinction to 'utopian socialism'.[46] Only exceptionally, and in a vaguely ironic tone, did Engels revert in the 1870s and 1880s to the already current definitions to be found in the writings of his adversaries. Thus, in 1877, with reference to the 'Dühringmania' which had spread through the SPD, he spoke of the 'assertions of the Marxians and the Dühringians'; in November, 1882, in ironic allusion to Paul Brousse's pamphlet, he made use of the terms 'Marxist' and 'Marxism' between inverted commas. In a letter of reply to Bernstein, dated 2–3 November, 1882, he wrote:

As for your repeated statement concerning the great misfortune of 'Marxism' in France, you probably have no other source that this, or else 'from Malon at second hand'. In fact, so-called 'Marxism' is a special product in France, so much so that Marx could tell Lafargue: 'What is certain is that I am not a Marxist'. But if last summer the *Citoyen* sold 25,000 copies and has gained such a position that Lissagaray staked his reputation to conquer it, this to some extent contradicts the famous misfortune.[47]

This witticism of Marx's was often repeated by Engels. Often quoted, if taken our of context it undergoes distortion.[48] Marx and Engels rebelled especially against the use of a term that they considered ridiculous, and felt to be a caricature. Such reactions are characteristic of men who were fighting in the working-class movement from the beginning of the 1870s: personal-name labels were considered a 'sectarian trade mark'. Thus in 1873 J.-P. Becker, denouncing a similar practice on the part of the press that was hostile to the IWMA, observed:

Even in the socialist camp are to be found members of a great society who, whether through fanatical pride and ignorance, or through self-interested guile, adopt the name of Lassallians and apply this sectarian label to themselves. Is not this the most merciless criticism of Lassalle's action, which is already almost completely squeezed into the straitjacket of his dogmas?[49]

Marx reacted in the same way: he too held these terms to be particularly dangerous; they were all that was needed to isolate him as the leader of a sect and encase his theories in dogmas.

Part III: Kautsky and Marxism as a Science
In spite of this, from the beginning of the 1880s the disciples closest to Marx and Engels did not share this repugnance, and considered such fears unjustified. They had grasped the changes

in the collective mentality and the socialist ideological constellation; these demanded a clear nomenclature for the various groups and tendencies. The militants no longer shrank from having recourse to a man's name to identify themselves; on the contrary they were proud of a label that tied them to the great thinker, whose fame as a scientist, as the 'founder' of scientific socialism was now consolidated.

The notions of 'Marxist' and 'Marxism' in the sense adopted by our vocabulary can be traced back to Kautsky. If in the writings of his German contemporaries and Engels' collaborators these expressions were frequently still casual, Kautsky used them from 1882 onwards in a conscious, systematic way, within a well defined context and with an ideological and political meaning that has nothing to do with mimicry or linguistic contamination.

The context is the publication, beginning in 1883, of the theoretical review *Neue Zeit*, which Kautsky had been getting ready for a year with the help of Heinrich Braun:

At the most troubled moment, in the summer of 1882 [during the time of the anti-socialist laws] I dared to propose to the publisher Dietz that he should found a monthly review. I had only just freed myself from eclectic socialism, which was then rife — a mixture of Lassallian, Rodbertussian, Langian and Dühringian elements with Marxian ones — in order to become a Marxist, joined to Bernstein with whom I had been collaborating since January, 1880. It was to the spread of this new awareness that we wished to dedicate our entire energies.[50]

Several times Kautsky stressed that *Neue Zeit*, which became a weekly ten years after its foundation, had always been 'edited as a Marxist organ', and had given itself the task of raising the low theoretical level of German social democracy, breaking up eclectic socialism and furthering the triumph of the Marxist programme.[51]

Kautsky's ambition was not confined to the sphere of Germany alone. Two years after the review's first appearance he was writing to Engels:

Perhaps my efforts to make *Neue Zeit* the fulcrum of the Marxist school will be crowned with success. I am getting the collaboration of as many Marxist forces as I am ridding myself of eclectics and Rodbertussians.[52]

From 1882, then, Kautsky and the small group around him habitually used the new terms in their correspondence, and subsequently in the review. In April, 1883, Kautsky wrote to Leo Frankel, sending him the first number of *Neue Zeit*:

I am curious to know your opinion of this venture. That it is generally useful and opportune is doubtless beyond discussion. But I myself am only too aware of what it lacks to realise our ideal. Nevertheless it seems to me that *Neue Zeit* is no worse than *Zukunft* or *Neue Gesellschaft*; it is more varied, also more attractive; and I think that Marxism, in a broad sense — and it is precisely on this ground that we all take our stand, in so far as is possible under the exceptional laws — will always visibly constitute its guiding line of thought.

Explaining his position on the Jewish question, which troubled Frankel, he ended his letter thus: 'But why do I need to say all this to an old Marxist?'[53]

The words 'Marxist' and 'Marxism' had, for Kautsky and the group around him, a programmatic value. They acted as a weapon of ideological and political struggle. Energetically, aggressively and on the attack, Kautsky (at the head of a little group around *Neue Zeit*) set out to achieve the appointed task, which consisted in carrying the Marxist school to victory. The man who thirty years afterwards was to declare himself to be only a theoretician, but a mediocre politician, gave proof at that time of great tactical ability. He was acute in his choice of target and of the terrain on which to fight: his attacks were not directed against the Lassallians but against the followers of Rodbertus. The former continued to exercise a strong influence on working-class circles, and their position on the essential problems of the class struggle and the political and party struggles was in no way removed from that of the 'Marxists'; whereas Rodbertus's theories seduced the intellectuals, towards whom Kautsky was more distanced.[54] He explicitly explained his tactical choice to Engels:

In Germany nowadays it is increasingly fashionable to play off Rodbertus against Marx; in Germany socialism has won on the scientific plane, and to block the victory of Marx the reactionary scientific rabble run and hide themselves behind Rodbertus.[55]

Thus his attacks were concentrated on C.A. Schramm, who, as an economist, a populariser of the ideas of Marx and Rodbertus, had gained a certain reputation as a theoretician amidst the ranks of the Social Democrats.[56] It was precisely in the controversy with Schramm that the terms 'Marxist' and 'Marxism' were publicly applied by *Neue Zeit* in 1883. The 'Marxist school' took up the term and made it its own to define its own programme. The terms express the idea of a polarisation into two currents, and this was the line confirmed by Kautsky in his review: 'There are two socialist schools that especially dominate minds in Germany today: Marx's and Rodbertus's.' The former recruited its followers from the workers; the latter found its expression in 'university socialism' (*Akademischer Sozialismus*).[57]

By 1883, Kautsky, the leader of the Marxist school — according to Schramm it was 'a school more Marxist than Marx' — had made his name as 'a fanatical defender of the materialist conception of history'.[58] He himself vindicated it when in May, 1884, he wrote with evident satisfaction to Engels of *Neue Zeit*:

In the eyes of the German anti-Marxist gentlemen it has for some time been the pack-saddle that rubs, because it is truly the only socialist organ in Germany that takes its stance on the terrain of Marxism.[59]

In this highly polemical intellectual climate, Kautsky's appraisals of the situation are not without exaggeration and bias; nonetheless it cannot be doubted that *Neue Zeit*'s activity and standpoint encountered strong resistance from within the SPD. This came from various sources and it tended to avoid either a direct attack on Marx or opposition to the dissemination of his doctrines. The attacks were made against the *modus operandi* of a group, a clique, the self-styled 'Marxist school', which was accused of having usurped the name of Marx to achieve its own ends. The arguments of the Rodbertussians, the Lassallians and above all the moderate wing of the party came close to those of Brousse and the French possiblists. These groups made a distinction between Marx's theoretical works and 'Marxism', in which they saw an ideology constructed by presumptuous followers. They saw Kautsky as the chief culprit, the perfidious instigator, the inventor of a dogma which he preached and raised to the level of a gospel. He was charged with having usurped Marx's authority in an attempt to impose his own doctrines on the party as its official theory. Auer spoke sarcastically to his correspondents of 'the mysteries of pure Marxism administered by Karl Kautsky and his friends',[60] while Schramm publicly attacked the 'false prophets', the Kautsky-Bernstein duo, who for years had been preaching 'the infallibility of Marxism, declaring that Marxism was the gospel' to the German Social Democrats. And he redoubled the attack, declaring: 'I do not recognise a religion of Marx, nor a programme of Marx to which I and other comrades have sworn fidelity. I recognise only a programme of the party. Kautsky preaches a religion of Marx.'[61] This image of the Church and the Gospel, not to mention that of the high priest, was to be taken up by certain circles of the SPD to cast ridicule on Kautsky's dogmas and dogmatism. By this means they were in reality attacking Marxism. Thus, at the height of the revisionist crisis, Ignaz Auer declared in the SPD sessions: 'I am not a Marxist in the sense in which this has been progressively developed by the fathers of the Church of Marxism', in other words Kautsky and Bebel.[62]

In the first years of the publication of *Neue Zeit*, one of Kautsky's best ways of repulsing these attacks and demonstrating their unfoundedness was to make sure that Engels contributed to the magazine. It saw the publication of several articles of his, as well as unpublished manuscripts by Marx himself. Thus the publication in German of *The Poverty of Philosophy* — it had originally appeared in French in 1844 — in the midst of the controversy with the Rodbertussians took on a fundamental importance for Kautsky. 'It will be a slap in the face for all the enemies of Marxism'.[63]

But what content did the 'Marxist school' that developed around *Neue Zeit* attribute to this notion? Kautsky was never casual in his use of the term, but gave it a precise connotation. 'Marxist' refers to Marx and his writings: 'To try and popularise the Marxist style of writing is, in my opinion, senseless, because Marx wrote in a fairly popular and comprehensible manner';[64] he also defines a point of principle: 'H. Braun is not a socialist of the academic variety, but takes his stand on completely Marxist terrain, the terrain of the class struggle'.[65] Here 'Marxist' refers to a certain ideological content — 'Marxist literature'. Finally the term indicates a tendency, a school: 'Braun is a diligent, conscientious member of the Marxist school'.[66] As far as the choice of the term 'Marxism' is concerned, its definition is closely related to the interpretation that Kautsky gave to Marx's theory and the systematisation of it which he undertook. In general terms the word is synonymous with 'Marx's system'. In particular, it performs a dual function. The first consists in defining the guiding principle: 'Marxism, the conception of our party as an organisation of the proletariat committed to the class struggle'.[67] The second serves to define Marx's theory as a science in general and as scientific socialism in particular. Kautsky insisted on this repeatedly. Thus, on the tenth anniversary of *Neue Zeit* he wrote: 'The term "scientific" would doubtless cover all aspects of Marxism, but at the same time it could say more, or could be felt to be more ambitious than Marxism, which by no means claims to have the last word in matters of science'. In his controversy with Bernstein he adds a further dimension: 'It is the method that arises from the application of the materialist conception of history to politics: thanks to this method, socialism has become a science . . . It is the method that is essential in Marxist socialism, not the results.'[68]

This insistence on the definition of Marxism as a science can provide us with the key to understanding the reasons why Kautsky adopted the term, as well as the interpretation he gave to 'Marx's system'. In this respect one should recall that in the 1880s Kautsky was, like all his generation, a fervent admirer of Darwin. He seems to have been inspired by the success, the resonance, the power of attraction that lay in the term 'Darwinism'. The desire to express symbolically an essential dimension of Marx's work guided the way he proceeded, and if Darwinism was synonymous with the science of nature, Marxism was synonymous with the social sciences. It should be noted that Kautsky in this respect was no innovator: the parallel between Darwin and Marx was constantly made in socialist discourse at the end of the century. It reflected the sensibility and the collective mentality of the period, saturated with scientism, dominated by monist materialism and the ideas of progress and evolution that derived from the natural sciences.

For Kautsky the essential character of Marxism as a science was the materialist conception of history. It was the definition he gave in 1883 during the course of his controversy with Schramm, when he declared that his opponent could not understand Marx 'because . . . the historical content of Marxism remains totally alien to him'; to say Marxist school is also to say 'Marxist historical school. If one may speak of the economists of the Marxist school one may also speak of its historians . . . Marx introduced materialism and economics into history, but he also introduced history into economics. In his eyes, these two constitute an indissoluble unity'.[69] Schramm retorted by casting doubt on the existence of a Marxist historical school, an assertion that even Engels found forced. Kautsky in his counterattack called *Capital* 'one of the most grandiose historical works', declaring peremptorily:

With Marx a new age of historical science begins. And all who adhere to the Marxist tendency must be historians, just as Marx was. Those who are not historians and those to whom history has remained something remote will be equally unresponsive to the Marxist conception in its totality.[70]

The Marxist historicism of the Second International dates from the same time as the emergence of the Marxist school around

Neue Zeit. The definition of Marxism that Kautsky offered in the 1880s became conceptualised in 1908 in a formula of his that has become famous: 'Marxist socialism is nothing else, in the final analysis, than the science of history with the viewpoint of the proletariat at its point of departure'.[71] Some twenty years later, on the occasion of Kautsky's seventieth birthday, the American Marxist, Louis Boudin, summarised the result of an evolutionary process that had begun in the 1880s thus: the Maxism that 'was the theory generally accepted by the socialist movement' is 'today a general theory of history and not a particular theory of revolution'.[72]

Part IV: The Revisionist Crisis and the Birth of 'Marxisms'
During the years of the first great penetration of 'Marxism' into international socialism shortly before the founding of the Second International, the initially polemical definitions underwent, as we said, a radical transformation. They acquired a theoretical and political significance and became rooted in this way in socialist usage. In the 1880s the terms in Kautsky's sense took hold and acquired so widespread an international resonance that Engels — without corroborating the usage — accepted them in a way that scarcely spelt conviction. He wrote to Laura Lafargue on 11 June, 1889, 'the anarchists . . . will be mad they gave us that name!'[73] Would he, for his part, give it his own imprimatur? Besides, was he in a position to oppose a practice that no longer depended solely on linguistic usage, but had become an outright political fact? The way these terms were applied (systematically employed by his correspondents), the meaning they assumed and the content they comprised, continued to arouse his annoyance. For example, A.M. Voden, who paid a visit to Engels in 1893, subsequently recounted in his memoirs that 'he would have preferred it if the Russians — and all the rest with them — had stopped collecting quotations from Marx and Engels, and started to think how Marx and Engels would have thought in their place. If ever such a word as 'Marxist' had the right to exist, it would only be in that sense'.[74]

Nevertheless, even if they were widespread and currently employed, these words were not officially consecrated before the revisionist crisis. In 1895 the Encyclopaedia Meyer did indeed give its blessing to the word 'Marxist', including it in the new edition of that year with a cross-reference to 'social democracy'.[75] However, in the first socialist encylopaedia, published in 1897, and edited by two members of the 'Marxist school',

Stegmann and Hugo, the expression 'Marxist socialism' was the only one to appear. They preferred to use the term in a precise manner, in relation to German Social Democracy, to indicate the most important stages and moments in the rise of Marxism.[76] Eisenach's followers were defined as 'partisans of international Marxist socialism'; Dühring was characterised by 'his hostile attitude to Marxist socialism'; *Neue Zeit* was said to be 'from the outset an organ of Marxist socialism'; and it was said of the International that 'the Brussels Congress [1891] was a complete success for Marxist socialism, whose leaders dominated the debates'; the resolutions of the Congress took up 'the two principal points in the Marxist programme': (1) The Congress 'takes its stand on the terrain of the class struggle'; (2) it recommends that 'political rights should be won through struggle, and these will enable us to acquire political power'.

The term 'Marxism' received its definitive consecration from the revisionist crisis and was used in various senses from then on:

At the turn of the century the term 'Marxism' . . . signified the thought and work of Marx, without evoking any set of problems relative to the already numerous controversies over the author's most important book. The term 'Marxist', currently used as both noun and adjective, referred to both a work by Marx and to a follower of his theories or a politcal movement which drew on them.[77]

This observation only partially recognises the multiple interpretations given to the term or to which it lent itself. As Bernstein observed in the midst of the revisionist debate: 'By the term "Marxist" is meant not only a scientific theory, but also a political doctrine'.[78] This partly explains the double use of the word in the political vocabulary from the first years of the century onwards: restrictedly, indicating by Marxism Marx's theory and scientific socialism; and more widely, covering not only Marx's theory but also his successors' contributions and the ideological armoury of the working-class parties. Thus, in the final analysis, the unlimited extension of the term assumes the form of an identification of Marxism with social democracy, and in particular with the German Social Democratic party.

On the other hand, recourse to the terms 'Marxist' and 'Marxism' was not uniform among the various protagonists and leading interpreters in this and that country. Like Kautsky, the Russian Marxists and especially Lenin adopted the practice that was already current in Russia, and made broad use of it from the 1880s onwards: they were defined in the legal press as 'Marxists';

they proposed developing 'the Marxist point of view': in the name of 'Marxism' they took up their stance against the populists, who sought to appropriate Marx to make use of him against social democracy. On the other hand, Rosa Luxemburg, at the turn of the century, was more sparing in the use of the term, preferring 'scientific socialism' and 'social democracy'. It would be a mistake to draw hasty conclusions from the frequency with which the terms were used. The subject cannot be tackled by a word count, because it is connected to the context and the intellectual and political usage, to the personal style of the writers, and also to the individual means of expression and to one's conception of ideological activity and expression. In a country like Russia, for instance, where Marxism took its place among a plurality of socialist doctrines and tendencies, all stamped by the works of Marx, its precocious frequency is explained by the desire to be characterised and qualified as a distinct political and theoretical current. But as soon as various tendencies took shape within the 'Marxist' camp, various political terms appeared — apart from 'legal Marxists' — which are no longer based on a personal name: economism, Bolshevism, Menshivism, liquidators, etc.

In Germany, where Marxism became the official ideology of the SPD, it dominated the theoretical camp of the party movement, and the differences were subsequently indicated by the names of the currents: revisionism, orthodoxy, left-wing radicalism, etc. In fact the SPD came to be taken as an example of a more general tendency: when Marxism achieved hegemony within the international working-class movement, the expressions based on surnames tended to abandon the field to generic terms that indicated the divergent currents within the Second International.

The reasons for the success of these neologisms are related to their usefulness. They proved themselves to be useful tools in a process that went beyond Marx's own perspectives while at the same time corresponding to the objectives pursued by the Marxists with the creation of the First International. As shifts in meaning became recognisable, the usefulness and advantages of employing these notions were quickly realised by those who had been thus dubbed by their enemies. The words 'Marxist' and 'Marxism', having been adopted by the 'Marxist school' and held aloft like a banner, served as a point of reference, as terms of identification and demarcation. But most of all they suggested a universal ideology and all-embracing knowledge, seen at one and the same time as a method, a world view and a programme for action.

Their vicissitudes to some extent reflect the rise of Marxism and then its internal differentiations. The terms entered the acknowledged vocabulary, and took hold in the years around 1900. Their official recognition corresponds to a precise historical moment, that of the definitive separation and break between social democracy and anarchism; of the systematisation and formation of Marx's theory as a *corpus*; of the delimitation of the Marxist school as opposed to all the other socialist currents, and of the affirmation of its political hegemony in the Second International. The conquest by Marxism of international social-democracy in its phase of ascendancy, maximum expansion but also maximum transformation ends up at the same time in the crisis provoked by Bernstein. Following the example of T. Masaryk, his contemporaries would speak of 'the crisis of Marxism' or 'the crisis in Marxism'. The revisionist crisis, for all its consequences, assured in particular the stabilisation of the usage of the two terms and their unexpected dissemination and publicity. But it also revealed the ambiguity of ideas that embraced aspirations and directions that were often contradictory. 'Marxism' split into hostile schools, and the terminology was consequently to undergo various modifications. For now on, 'Marxism' would be accompanied by some qualifying term. There were to be a whole series of labels: 'true' and 'false', 'narrow' and 'broad', 'orthodox' and 'revolutionary', 'dogmatic' and 'creative'. Yet in this way, the term changed fundamentally in meaning and ended by indicating contrasting directions and interpretations, whose sole common denominator remained a profession of faith, or a simple reference to Marx. From then on, rather than speaking of Marxism in general, it would be advisable to use the plural: Marxisms.

Notes

1 M. Rubel, 'La Légende de Marx ou Engels Fondateur', in *Marx Critique du Marxism. Essais* (Paris, 1974), pp. 20-1.

2 Cf. J. Gabel, *Idéologies* (Paris, 1974), p. 43.

3 Cf. I. Fetscher, *Karl Marx und der Marxismus. Von der Philosophie des Proletariats zur Proletarischen Weltanschauung* (Munich, 1967), pp. 61ff.

4 Cf. M. Rubel, 'La Charte de la Première Internationale', in *Marx op. cit.*, p. 26, note 2.

5 Cf. 'Republik der Arbeiter, Centralblatt der Propaganda für die Verbrüderung der Arbeiter', in *New York*, vol. V, No. 14, 1 April 1854. I owe this reference to Gian Mario Bravo, and I take this opportunity of thanking him.

6 See E. Ragionieri, *Il Marxismo e l'Internazionale. Studi di Storia del Marxismo* (Rome, 1968), p. 17, note 34, which contains some illuminating points in relation to this question.

7 But not only Bakunin's followers: Alexander Herzen too was to speak of 'Marxids'. Cf. A.I. Gercen, *Sobranie Socinenija*, vol. 30 (Moscow, 1966).

8 Cf. M. Manale, 'Aux Origines du Concept de "Marxisme" ', in *Economie et Sociétés. Cahiers de l'Isea*, Series S, October, 1974. No. 17, p. 1424.

9 Rubel's observation that from the 1840s onwards 'the use of these labels corresponded to the need to designate or denounce a group of individuals who had undergone the domination of a "leader", or a collective mentality which was linked to the teaching of this "leader" ' (*Marx*, p. 26), requires, I feel, a chronological correction: the attitude of those who appeal to 'the teaching of a leader' does not begin to crystallise until the period of transition that occurs in the 1880s.

10 Manale, *Aux Origines de Concept de 'Marxisme'*, p. 1424.

11 'Le Groupe Révolutionnaire Socialiste au Congrès International Réuni à Genève le 1er Septembre 1873, in *La Première Internationale. Recueil de Documents*, published under the editorship of Jacques Freymond. Texts established and annotated by Bert Andreas and Miklos Molnar (subsequently referred to as *Première Internationale*), vol. 4 (Geneva, 1971), p. 109.

12 See, for example, the report of the 1873 Geneva Congress of the WIA, published in *Journal des Débats Politiques et Littéraires de Paris*, in which the disputes were summarised as follows: 'The anarchists attack the authoritarians for their behaviour at the Peace Congress, and the authoritarians reply by recalling what happened at the Basle Congress, where the Bakuninists were the first to do all that they were subsequently to hold against the Marxists' (*Première Internationale*, vol. 4, p. 196).

13 J.P. Becker, 'A propos des Congrès de Genève'. These articles, reproduced *ibid.*, pp. 242ff., appeared in *Volksstaat*, 5 and 8 October, 1873.

14 'Compte Rendu du Congrès de Bruxelles, 1874 (Fédéraliste)', in *Première Internationale*, vol. 4, p. 270.

15 Brochure Génevoise (untitled), reproduced in *Première Internationale*, pp. 229-32.

16 'Congrès de Berne, 1876 (Fédéraliste)' in *Première Internationale*, p. 487.

17 *Ibid*. p. 463.

18 *Ibid*. pp. 483 and 500.

19 Rubel observes that this is 'the first text to have used the term in its title'. The hypothesis, however, is open to question, all the more as 'the term seems to have received almost official blessing'. (*Marx*, p. 27).

20 Cf. E. Bernstein, *Briefwechsel mit Friedrich Engels*, edited by H. Hirsch (Assen, 1970), p. 49; F. Engels, *Briefwechsel mit Karl Kautsky*, edited by B. Kautsky (Vienna, 1955), p. 39.

21 In this respect the letters he wrote to César De Paepe during the years 1884–8 are quite explicit. Cf. *Entre Marx et Bakounine. César De Paepe. Correspondence*, presented by B. Dandois (Paris, 1974). He privately attacks 'Marx's German doctrines', declaring that the workers' party in France has no right to profess them officially. He accuses Guesde and Lafargue of trying to impose an 'imported socialism': 'Never shall we come together in a new Marxist International' (p. 247).

22 In the anarchist vocabulary, the term always maintained its initial polemical meaning. Thus, *à propos* the 1896 London International Congress in which they were expelled from the International, they speak exclusively of 'Marxist machinations and manoeuvres'.

23 Cf. Vera Zasulic's letter to Marx, dated 16 February 1881.
24 Cf. A. Walicki, *The Controversy over Capitalism. Studies in Social Philosophy of the Russian Populists* (Oxford, 1969), pp. 132ff.
25 'Gruppa osvodozdenie truda' (Moscow-Leningrad, 1926), Collection No. 4, p. 196.
26 One of the reasons why the term 'communism' was rejected in favour of 'social democracy' may perhaps emerge from what César De Paepe said in his report at the 1874 Brussels Congress of the IWMA: 'The word communism has had the singular fortune of being rejected by the socialists as a slander, of being seen by economists as the greatest of Utopias, and finally as being, in the eyes of the bourgeoisie, a theory that consecrates theft and permanent promiscuity, hence the worst of plagues' ('Compte Rendu du Congres de Bruxelles, 1874, Fédéraliste', p. 323). De Paepe, for his part, complains about this rejection of the term, which seems to him to have a precise meaning and 'to represent a genuinely scientific idea'.
27 Rappoport was often to recall: 'I have it from Engels' own lips . . . that he and Marx did not accept the term social democracy except unwillingly, as a kind of compromise with reality; they preferred their fundamental ideas to be referred to as communism'.
28 For the origin and adaptation of the term, cf. J.M. Maitron, *Le Mouvement Anarchiste de France* (Paris, 1975), vol. I.
29 The term 'possiblist' was the Guesdists' response to the adjective 'Marxist', and it can be seen to have spread during the course of the quarrel that broke out on the eve of the Congress of Saint-Etienne in 1882 when the two currents divided. Osip Zetkin provides the following explanation: 'In 1881 Jouffrin, Brousse's right-hand man, failed in the election. Guesde and his friends thereupon asked the National Council of the Federation of Socialist Workers whether a motion of censure might be put to the vote in view of the lack of discipline Jouffrin had shown in relation to the party programme during the elections'. By 25 votes to 5, the Council refused, expressing approval of Jouffrin's behaviour. Thereupon *Egalité* attacked the National Council for this decision, and the National Council replied through its own organ, *Le Prolétaire*, accusing *Egalité's* editors of being 'authoritarians' and 'Marxists'. *Egalité* replied by coining in its turn the nickname 'possiblists'. *Le Prolétaire* had in fact written in its polemical reply that it was necessary 'somehow or other to waste no time in putting forward some of our own claims, to render them finally possible'. Cf. O. Zetkin, *Der Sozialismus in Frankreich seit der Pariser Kommune* (Berlin, 1889), pp. 25-6.
30 Letter from Fournière to Guesde, 27 March 1893; Am IISG, Archives Guesde, 224/6.
31 Am IISG, Archives Guesde, 180/3.
32 *Ibid*. 172/3.
33 O. Zetkin, *Der Sozialismus*, p. 37.
34 In reply to a letter from Lafargue, published in *Egalité* on 1 June, 1872, there is the following sentence: 'How many are there . . . at the General Council who are Marxists without having ever opened Marx's book [*Capital*]?' (*Première Internationale*, vol. 2: *Les conflits au sein de l'Internationale*, p. 315).
35 Cf. his recollections, 'Aus der Frühzeit des Marxismus', published in the form of an introduction to Engels' *Briefwechsel mit K. Kautsky*, p. 26.
36 Letter to Herzen dated 29 October 1869, in M. Bakunin, *Sozialpolitische*

Briefwechsel mit Alexander Herzen und Ogarëv (Stuttgart, 1895), pp. 174-7.

37 Letter to Ludovico Nabuzzi, dated 23 January 1872, in *Archives Bakounine*, vol. I, Part II: *Michel Bakounine et l'Italie* (Leiden, 1966), pp. 199-207.

38 *Werke*, vol. 32.

39 Quoted by H.-J. Steinberg, *Sozialismus und deutsche Sozialdemokratie. Zur Ideologie der Partei* (Hanover, 1967), p. 16.

40 *Zum Gedächtnis der Internationale*, in F. Mehring, *Gesammelte Schriften* (Berlin, 1963), vol. 4, p. 360.

41 K. Hillmann, 'Die Internationale Arbeiterassociation (1864–1871). Ihre Geschichte, Programm und Tätigkeit', extracted from *Correspondent für Deutschland Buchdrucker und Schriftgiesser*, 1871, p. 1.

42 *Neue Zeit*, I, 1883, p. 448.

43 They are appreciably different from those of the 1870s. J.-P. Becker was typical of Marx's supporters in writing: 'Very rarely have independent thinkers and researchers acted like Marx, who has never laid any absolute claim to having invented principles, but only to having discovered them or, to having scientifically proved the existence of them in the socio-economic process of evolution' (Becker, 'A propos des Congrès de Genève', p. 242).

44 K. Kautsky, 'Darwinismus und Marxismus', in *Neue Zeit*, XIII, vol. I, 1894–5, p. 715.

45 *Ibid.*

46 *Werke*, vol. 34, p. 403.

47 Bernstein, *Briefwechsel mit F. Engels*, p. 154.

48 Kautsky refers to it in such a way, distorting its meaning. He speaks of Lafargue as if he, with Kautsky himself, were the only one to have 'declared himself at a very early stage for the materialist conception of history and to have made use of it in his research'. But he stresses the paradox that 'at times made Marx despair', and adds: 'It is to him that Marx's witticism refers, so often quoted, for the most part in a distorted form: "If this is Marxism, I am not a Marxist" ' (Engels, *Briefwechsel mit K. Kautsky*, p. 90).

49 Becker, *A propos des Congrès de Genève*, p. 242.

50 K. Kautsky. 'Zum 70. Geburtstag Heinrich Dietz', in *Neue Zeit*, XXXII, 1914, pp. 1-8.

51 These declarations of intent have been critically analysed by Ragionieri (*Il Marxismo e l'Internazionale*, pp. 57-8, 63 and 81), who expounds *Neue Zeit's* viewpoint and aims. The publication of *Neue Zeit* was deemed by its contemporaries to be a 'turning-point' in the theoretical history of German social democracy'.

52 Kautsky's letter to Engels, dated 9 January 1885, in Engels, *Briefwechsel mit K. Kautsky*, p. 163.

53 Am IISG, Kautsky Fund (in preparation *Kautsky et les Socialistes des Balkans. Correspondance*).

54 In his correspondence of 1883–5, Kautsky systematically identifies the opponents of the Marxist school with the intellectuals both inside and outside social democracy. Cf. Steinberg, *Sozialismus*.

55 Letter dated 14 February, 1884, in Engels, *Briefwechsel mit K. Kautsky*, p. 98. Three months later he is insisting: 'Amongst our intellectuals there reigns a veritable hatred of Marx and Marxism, and they seize greedily on any non-Marxist socialist they can find, from Louis Blanc to Rodbertus, in order to play him off against Marx' (p. 118).

56 On this controversy see Steinberg, *op. cit.* and Ragionieri, *op. cit.*

57 'Marx generally finds his support among the working classes . . . whereas

Rodbertus has become the revered guide of university socialism' (K. Kautsky, *'Das Kapital'*, in *Neue Zeit*, II, 1884, p. 337).

58 The words are those of C.A. Schramm, 'Kautsky und Rodbertus', in *Neue Zeit*, II, 1884, pp. 484 and 488.

59 In October 1884, he writes in the same vein to Bebel: 'I wish to continue with *Neue Zeit*; I hold with it because it is the only publication in Germany that takes its stance fully and utterly on Marxist ground' (A. Bebel, *Briefwechsel mit K. Kautsky*, edited by K. Kautsky Jr. (Assen, 1971), p. 21).

60 'Quoted by Steinberg, *Sozialismus*, p. 39, note 81.

61 *Ibid*. p. 37.

62 *Protokoll über die Verhandlungen des Parteitages der SPD, abgehalten zu Hannover vom 9-14.10.1899*, p. 208.

63 Engels, *Briefwechsel mit K. Kautsky*, p. 108.

64 *Ibid*. p. 92.

65 *Ibid*. p. 60, letter dated 6 September 1882. For the use of this term, what Kautsky wrote to Bebel on 14 February 1885 is significant: 'We must treat the German events from *our* point of view, from the Marxist point of view, not from that of petit bourgeois and Philistine socialism' (Bebel, *Briefwechsel mit K. Kautsky*, p. 27).

66 Bebel, *Briefwechsel mit K. Kautsky*, p. 24, letter to Bebel dated 8 November 1884.

67 K. Kautsky, *Bernstein und das sozialdemokratische Programm* (Stuttgart, 1899), p. 17.

68 Recounting to Bebel, in his letter of 14 February 1885, the difficulties that *Neue Zeit* was finding and the tensions with its publisher, he returned to the same idea: *'Neue Zeit* must . . . be a resolutely Marxist organ, an organ situated on the terrain of *The Communist Manifesto*, on the terrain of the conception of history developed in that work' (Bebel, *Briefwechsel mit K. Kautsky*, p. 27).

69 K. Kautsky, *Neue Zeit*, I, 1883.

70 K. Kautsky, 'Eine Replik', in *Neue Zeit*, II, 1884, p. 496.

71 K. Kautsky, *Die historische Leistung von K. Marx* (Stuttgart, 1908), p. 30. He had already given expression to the idea in 1866, when he formulated the thesis that, thanks to the materialist conception of history, 'Marx has achieved the union of socialism with the working-class movement, showing that the goal of socialism . . . will be naturally and necessarily attained through the development of the modern mode of production and the class struggle, and it will not be understood except through the study of this mode of production, its influence and its origin' (Das Elend der Philosophie und das Kapital', in *Neue Zeit*, IV, 1886, p. 15).

72 L.B. Boudin, 'Theorien der Revolution', in *Die Gesellschaft, Karl Kautsky zum 70. Geburtstag*, p. 38.

73 Frederick Engels, Paul and Laura Lafargue, *Correspondence*, vol. 2 (Moscow, 1960), p. 277.

74 *Colloqui con Marx e Engels. Testimonianze sulla vita di Marx e Engels*, collected by H.M. Enzensberger (Turin, 1977), p. 525.

75 Manale, *Aux Origines du Concept de 'Marxisme'*, pp. 1400-1.

76 C. Stegmann and C. Hugo, *Handbuch des Sozialismus* (Zurich, 1897), pp. 166, 164, 640 and 387.

77 Manale, *Aux Origines du Concept de 'Marxisme'*, p. 1401.

78 E. Bernstein, Preface to the French edition of *Voraussetzungen des Sozialismus* (Paris, 1902).

10 ENGELS AND THE HISTORY OF MARXISM
Gareth Stedman Jones

Since his death in London in 1895, it has proved peculiarly difficult to arrive at a fair and historically balanced assessment of Engels' place in the history of Marxism, both within the Marxist tradition and outside it. Engels was both the acknowledged co-founder of historical materialism and the first and most influential interpreter and philosopher of Marxism. Yet, since at least the breakup of the Second International, he has been persistently treated, either simply as Marx's loyal lieutenant, or else as the misguided falsifier of true Marxist doctrine. The continued prevalence of these rather stale alternatives cannot be attributed to the lack of an adequate scholarly basis on which Engels' career could more imaginatively be judged. On the contrary, Engels was magnificently served by one of the best of twentieth-century scholarly biographies, that of Gustav Mayer, the product of over three decades research and a scarcely rivalled knowledge of nineteenth-century German labour and socialist history.[1] But Mayer's work has remained little studied, indeed virtually unknown until its republication in the last decade. Because Mayer was not a Marxist, his research went virtually unacknowledged by communist writers, even though he deliberately confined himself to a painstaking descriptive reconstruction of Engels' life and work, and ventured few judgements of his own. He was also unlucky in the timing of his biography. The first volume appeared in 1918 at a time when the attention of German socialists was deflected by the end of the war and the splits of the November revolution. The second volume appeared at the end of 1932 and was almost immediately suppressed by the incoming Nazis. Even in the German speaking world the book almost immediately became a bibliographic rarity, and it was never translated, except in an extremely truncated version. It thus remained the restricted possession of a few specialised scholars in the post-war period.

But the one-sidedness of most modern treatment of Engels was not solely or even principally the consequence of the mishaps of Mayer's book. For, from at least the end of World War I, assessment of Engels' particular contribution to Marxism had become a highly charged political question. After a period of unrivalled prestige, between the 1880s and 1914, Engels' reputation suffered first in the revolutionary leftist critique of the failings of the Second International and subsequently in the non-communist or anti-communist critique of the excesses of the Third.

It was Lukacs and to a lesser extent Korsch, in the revolutionary period following the Russian Revolution who drove the first effective wedge between the theory of Marx and that of Engels.[2] In a respectful but ominous critique of Engels' *Anti-Dühring*, Lukacs from a radical Hegelian standpoint attacked Engels' preoccupation with a uniform dialectic linking human and natural history, and in particular his distinction between 'metaphysical' and 'dialectical' science, on the grounds that it obscured the truly revolutionary dialectic within Marx: that between subject and object within human history. This criticism was not merely epistemological. For in Lukacs' eyes, the prestige of Darwin and evolutionary science within the Second International was intimately bound up with an undialectical separation of theory and practice, and hence the immobilism and reformism of its politics. Although Lukacs' critique had little immediate impact, and he himself later retracted it, it was a prefiguration of the form taken by many later attacks. Dialectical materialism — Plekhanov's term for a Marxist philosophy and a general view of the world — was largely constructed from Engels' later writings, and once this philosophy received the official *imprimatur* of the Soviet Union, it became difficult to differentiate an attitude to Engels from an attitude to the communist positions of the Stalinist era. On the one hand, the publication of Engels' unfinished manuscript, *The Dialectics of Nature*, in 1927, became associated with Stalin's attempt to impose a dialectical materialist orthodoxy upon natural scientists. On the other hand, it was the social democrats, Landshut and Meyer who first published a version of Marx's *1844 Manuscripts* in an effort to pit an ethical humanist Marx against a Leninist interpretation of Marxism. The alleged rift between the theories of Marx and Engels, first implied by Lukacs, was further widened, no longer as an attack upon social democracy, but in defence of it.

In the post-war period, if Cold War commentators were happy to lump together Marx and Engels as the twin architects of a determinist and totalitarian system, the official spokesmen of the Communist Parties were equally insistent upon the seamless unity of the work of the two men and intensely suspicious of any attempt to distinguish their individual contributions. Alternative interpretations of the Marxist legacy were largely developed by those who felt uncomfortable with either of these poles — a mixed bag of dissident communist theorists, Second International social democrats, radical Christian theologians and existentialist or neo-Hegelian philosophers. Their efforts, either to construct a Marx which challenged the authorised version, or to appropriate him to a pre-existing philosophical tradition, generally took the form of heaping on to Engels all the unwanted components of Soviet Marxism, from which they were so anxious to distance themselves.

The one-sidedness and distortions of the twentieth-century treatment of Engels are really only a measure of the immense and lasting influence that he exerted on the definition of Marxist socialism at the point at which it first began seriously to be adopted by the European socialist movement. This effectively happened, neither in the 1840s, nor in the 1860s, but in the 1880s and the immense burden of work and responsibility that this involved was virtually shouldered by Engels alone. Already in the last years of the First International, the brunt of the battle against Proudhonism and Bakuninism had fallen on Engels, and in the last ten years of his life, Marx produced little of immediate public consequence. His answers to the queries of Russian revolutionaries on the relevance of *Capital* to the character of a future Russian revolution were hesitant and open-ended. They were not sufficiently decisive to be used by Russian social democrats in their struggle against the Narodniks and were thus left unpublished until the 1920s.[3] Similarly, Marx's *Critique of the Gotha Programme* was an unwanted contribution to the unity negotiations between Eisenach and Lassallean wings of German social democracy in 1875. Little heed was taken of it even by the professed friends and followers of Marx in the social democratic leadership, and it was only made public by Engels during the negotiations over a new party programme fifteen years later. The last joint attempt of Marx and Engels directly to challenge the running of the German Social Democratic Party, the so-called *drei Sterne affair* of 1879 — an angry critique of the leadership's toleration of an attempt from within the party to dilute the proletarian character of the SPD — ended in an equally bitter blow to their pride. Their threat of public dissociation from the party evoked little response, and thereafter it became clear that direct and overt attempts at political intervention would be self-defeating, and that the London exiles would have to accept their honoured but remote role as founding theorists or have their political powerlessness publicly exposed.

But if the late 1870s marked the nadir of Marx and Engels' personal influence upon the policy of the German party, it also marked the effective point of origin of the Marxism of the Second International. For the world-wide diffusion of Marxism in the guise of a systematic and scientific socialism began neither with the *Communist Manifesto*, nor with *Capital* but with the publication of Engels' *Anti-Dühring*.

'Judging by the influence that Anti-Dühring had upon me', wrote Kautsky, 'no other book can have contributed so much to the understanding of Marxism. Marx's *Capital* is the more powerful work, certainly. But it was only through *Anti-Dühring* that we learnt to understand *Capital* and read it properly'.[4] This was the formative book of the most influential leaders of the Second International — Bebel, Bernstein, Kautsky, Plekhanov, Axelrod and Labriola. Nor was its influence confined to party leaders and theorists. *Socialism: Utopian and Scientific*, an excerpt from it, shorn of all reference to Dühring published in 1882 became the most popular introduction to Marxism apart from the *Manifesto*. Not only was it widely read in the social democratic parties of the German speaking world, but it paved the way to an understanding of Marxism in areas of traditional resistance to Marx's and Engels' positions, especially France. The difference in atmosphere between the late 1870s and the late 1880s was evident in Engels' *Ludwig Feuerbach* of 1888. *Anti-Dühring* was in origin a reluctant local intervention into the confused socialism of early German social democracy. 'It was a year before I could make up my mind to neglect other work and get my teeth into this sour apple',[5] wrote Engels of his polemic which had been published serially in Vorwärts between 1877 and 1878 (Liebknecht had in fact been urging him to combat Dühring's influence since at least 1874). *Feuerbach*, however, was written in a quite different spirit. 'The Marxist world outlook has found representatives far beyond the boundaries of Germany and Europe and in all the literary languages of the world',[6] wrote Engels in the Preface. Popular conceptions of orthodox Marxism today still date back to Engels' work of systematisation and popularisation in that crucial decade.

It is this fact which has tended to dominate all subsequent assessments of Engels' achievement. Engels, the prophet of dialectical materialism has wholly overshadowed Engels, the co-founder and elaborator of historical materialism. Little attention has been paid to his early life and work. Criticism or appreciation of Engels has overwhelmingly focussed on his later writings. Those who have defended an orthodox Marxist tradition, particularly when filtered through a Bolshevik perspective, have given equal authority to historical materialism and to Engels' generalisation of the dialectic, as if they formed part of one seamless web. Conversely, in the eyes of his western critics, Engels has loosely been associated with positivism and evolutionism and with the passivity of Second International politics, as if the differences between his outlook and that of Kautsky and Plekhanov were simply one of degree, and as if the positions adopted by Marx would have been substantially different from his own. In the light of the subsequent development of Marxism, preoccupations with dialectical materialism or the failures of the Second International has not been surprising. But they have led to a consistent imbalance in the historical treatment of Engels. In the orthodox view, Engels' individuality as a thinker all but disappears. In the conventional western views, his credentials as a Marxist are seriously impugned.

At a simple level of historical fact, the second view is easier to dispose of than the first. It is an elementary failure of historical interpretation not to make any distinction between the constituents of Engels' own outlook, and the way in which he was read by a generation of intellectuals nurtured on Buckle and Comte. Again to quote Kautsky, 'they had started from Hegel, I started from Darwin'.[7] It is highly unlikely that Engels conceived his *Dialectics of Nature*, as an all-encompassing genetic theory of development, of which *Capital* was to form the final social-historical part. His concern was rather to redefine materialism in terms which took account of scientific development in the nineteenth century. It was to combat the physiologically based vulgar materialism of Vogt and Büchner so popular in the liberal-dominated *Arbeiterbildungsvereine* of the 1850s, that Engels had first begun to take an interest in developments in the natural sciences. After the publication of the *Origin of the Species*, he was in no doubt that the historical materialist conception of a mode of production clearly distinguished human history from the Darwinian struggle for existence, and wryly commented upon the fact that the bourgeoisie first projected its social theory (from Hobbes to Malthus) into the world of nature and then of the basis of Darwin's researches, accepted it back again as an adequate portrayal of human society. Against the later positivist-evolutionist stress upon natural laws of development whose effects were conceived in terms of a simple transitive causality and which proceeded unilinearly from the natural through the economic/technological to the political and ideological, Engels, on the basis of historical materialism was more concerned to demonstrate the effect of human practice on nature through science and production, and in later years particularly, the relative autonomy of politics and ideology from any simple determination by the economic. It was in relation to the spread of positivist and economic determinist ideas, that he wrote to Conrad Schmidt in 1890:

What these gentlemen all lack is dialectics. They always see only here cause, there effect. That this is a hollow abstraction, that such metaphysical polar opposites exist in the real world only during crises, while the whole vast process goes on in the form of interaction — though of very unequal forces, the economic movement being by far the strongest, most primordial, most decisive — that here everything is relative and nothing absolute — this they never begin to see. As far as they are concerned Hegel never existed.[8]

What was problematic in Engels' attempts to theorise the sciences of nature and history, was not the few dubiously positivist formulations to be found there, but his confident resort to a Hegel whom he and Marx had 'inverted'. Here, however, one should beware of any simple juxtaposition between Marx's and Engels' thought. In the years after Marx's death, Engels had neither the desire, the confidence nor the time to develop new positions of his own. His arguments in *Feuerbach* on the relationship between historical materialism and the natural sciences and upon the dialectical nature of reality, whether natural or historical had been developing from at least the end of the 1850s and had frequently been raised in his correspondence with Marx.[9] It is well known that Marx contributed some of the economic chapters of the *Anti-Dühring* and that he was acquainted with the work as a whole. It should also be mentioned that there are comments in Marx's handwriting on parts of the unfinished manuscript of Engels' *Dialectics of Nature*. Similarly, although it has been convincingly demonstrated that historical materialism is not an inversion of Hegel's dialectic and that such an inversion is not to be found in the theoretical structure of *Capital*, that should not obscure the fact that this was how both Marx and Engels tried to theorise its achievement.[10] In this sense Engels' explanations in *Feuerbach* do not significantly depart from Marx's brief statement in the Preface to *Capital*, or from

Engels' own unfinished review of Marx's *Critique of Political Economy*, published in *Das Volk* in 1859. Thus, if there was an inadequacy in Engels' later explanation of the relationship between Marxism and the Hegelian dialectic, it was an inadequacy fully sanctioned by Marx.

But simply to emphasise the congruence of outlook between Marx and Engels is not adequate either. Its effect has been to render invisible the considerable independent contribution that Engels made to the development of Marxist theory and to diminish his own individuality as a thinker. Engels' own very modest assessments of his contribution have been the principle obstacle here, and later commentators have generally been content to follow his judgement. In *Feuerbach*, he wrote:

I cannot deny that both before and during my forty years collaboration with Marx I had a certain independent share in laying the foundations of the theory, and more particularly in its elaboration. But the greater part of its leading basic principles, especially in the realm of economics and history, and above all their final trenchant formulation, belong to Marx. What I contributed — at any rate with the exception of my work in a few special fields — Marx could very well have done without me. What Marx accomplished I would not have achieved. Marx stood higher, saw further, and took a wider and quicker view than all the rest of us. Marx was a genius; we others were at best talented.[11]

It would clearly be pointless to contest Marx's theoretical superiority nor need there be any doubt that Engels could neither have given historical materialism the logical coherence and explanatory breadth with which Marx imbued it. Indeed, on his own, he would probably never have arrived at the theory of historical materialism at all. The division of labour between the two collaborators was established almost from the beginning. In one of his earliest letters to Marx (17 March 1845), concerning their respective plans to write critiques of Frederick List's *System of National Economy*, Engels wrote that he would deal with the practical consequences of List's theory, 'while I presume in view of . . . your personal inclinations you will go into the *premisses* rather than his conclusions.[12]

Most subsequent commentators have left the matter there, assigning to Engels a vaguely auxillary role in the formation of the theory. They miss the centrality of Engels' contribution because they look for it in the wrong place. For theoretical ability, even when possessed in as exceptional a degree as Marx, is a necessary but not sufficient condition of a theoretical revolution: especially in the social domain. For such revolutions to occur, disturbing phenomena are also necessary, which not only point to the inadequacy of the existing theoretical problematic, but are suggestive of the raw components of a new theoretical structure. It was Engels in his writings of 1844 and 1845 who provided these decisive new components — even if in a raw and unsatisfactory theorised practical state. Before, however, making clear what these components were, it is first necessary to say something of Engels himself, so that the importance and limitations of his contribution become easier to understand.

Engels was two years younger than Marx, born in Barmen in 1820, the eldest son of one of the principal manufacturers in the town. [13] In the backward and non-industrialised state of Germany in the Restoration period, Barmen and its sister town of Elberfeld, as manufacturing towns dependent on the world market were exceptional. Travelling journalists *literateurs* in the 1830s and 1840s were apt to refer to the region as the German Manchester, although the German Coventry would have been a more apt description, since its principal trade was ribbon-making and its workers generally worked together with their families in their homes for putting-out merchants who controlled the purchase of raw materials and the sale of finished goods. Elberfeld-Barmen was also exceptional in another respect. Although, subject like the rest of the Rhineland to the Napoleonic conquest and the benefits of the Code Napoleon, the population was Calvinist or Lutheran rather than Catholic, and thus much more amenable to Prussian rule after 1815 than the Rhineland itself.

These two features markedly differentiated Engels' family and cultural background from that of Marx. Living in the Francophile zone, and the son of a nominally Protestant Jewish lawyer with liberal enlightenment beliefs, Marx appears to have experienced little early conflict with his father's political or cultural outlook. At least until the end of the 1830s, the local Trier middle class continued to resent the Prussian occupation, the nostalgia for Napoleon remained strong, and the educated population were receptive to French ideas, both liberal and, in the 1830s, Saint-Simonian. The adolescent Marx appears to have been little moved by the political and cultural stirrings of German nationalism and to have felt a much deeper affinity with the outlook of the German *Aufklärung* with its humanist adulation of classical civilisation. It is therefore not surprising that when after a period in Bonn he arrived as a graduate student in Berlin, he should have felt drawn to a liberal tinged version of Hegel's notion of the state as the guiding principle of his reflection, rather than the emotive principle of the nation. Until his friend and mentor, Bruno Bauer was sacked from Bonn University, he appeared destined for an academic career, and his move to the political left and finally to communism was of a much more gradual and measured kind than that of the young Engels.

Engels' formation was quite different. The pietist Protestantism of the Barmen merchants was fiercely opposed to the pagan associations of the *Aufklärung*, to any rationalist dilution of Biblical interpretation and to the ambiguously protestant philosophy of Hegel. The value placed on education was strictly practical. The gymnasium at Elberfeld to which Engels went, enjoyed an excellent reputation, particularly in languages, so important for the Barmen merchant's profession. But schooling stopped at the end of the secondary level and was followed by a commercial apprenticeship in the firm of a business colleague. It was in this way that the young Engels was sent to the Bremen import–export firm of Heinrich Leopold in 1838. Within the close society of Barmen merchants, creative literature was suspect, Goethe prone to dismissal as 'a godless man' and the theatre regarded as immoral. Although grateful for some of the Napoleonic legal reforms, the prevalent attitude to French ideas was hostile. Family prayers and reading of the Bible, meditation on devotional literature, an ethic of dedication and hard work and a sectarian theology communicated through the terrifying pulpit oratory of preachers like Krummacher were the principle components of the merchant-family culture of Engels' youth (though lightened somewhat by a love of music, both choral and instrumental). The outlook of the merchant manufacturers was strongly patriarchal, in their attitude to their families, to their workers and to their religion. The world of the merchants was closely tied to the world of the preachers. As social equals, it was normal for merchants' sons to marry priests' daughters, and vice versa. Engels' mother, the daughter of a protestant pastor in Hamm was typical of this pattern.

There are early signs of Engels' adolescent striving to escape the narrow imaginative horizons of his family and of Wuppertal society. His father was shocked to discover his 13-year-old son secretly reading a French medieval romance — '*ein schmutziges Buch*'. But it is important not to over-individualise or overpsychologise Engels' revolt against his father.[14] He was not an unloved, cruelly treated or neglected child. On the contrary, as the intended heir to the family business, he appears to have been subject to the constant worried solicitude of his parents. However perennial generational conflict might be, it is only in particular historical circumstances that it acquires social and political significance. In the Wuppertal in the late 1830s and 1840s a generational divide in religious and social attitudes was not confined to the Engels household, but present, if in a milder degree, among other of his contemporaries. To understand why this was a social rather than an individual phenomenon, it is necessary to realise that the social and religious world of the old merchant families had by the later 1830s begun to disintegrate. The sober Calvinism of the older generation had been deeply ingrained because it provided a satisfactory ordering of social experience. The merchant élite had made no distinction between the church and municipal government of the town, and the patriarchalism of their religion had been an appropriate articulation of their face-to-face government of the workforce whose cottages clustered round their chapels and their warehouses.

But from the Napoleonic period onwards, Barmen's trade entered a period of prolonged crisis resulting from its dependence on an English-dominated world market. In social terms, the population was threatened by dearth, declining living standards and intensification of work punctuated by frequent spells of unemployment. In religious terms, the result was a break-up of stable church government. Small domestic masters and their apprentices increasingly engulfed by 'pauperism', were attracted to breakaway revivalist and millenarian sects, while many relapsed into a state of semi-despair exacerbated by a dramatic increase in cheap schnapps consumption. While preaching became more revivalist and emotional, the traditional merchant élite began to withdraw from active church government. It was against this background that the 19-year-old Engels made his first pseudonymous attack upon the philistinism of the pietism of the Wuppertal.

The dissidence of the young Engels and his circle in Barmen took the initial form of aesthetic revolt against the narrowness of the merchant world and juvenile attempts to emulate the current literary *avant garde*. Engels' denunciation of the Wuppertal was not that of an embryo socialist, but that of the aspirant poet and representative of modern literary ideas. He particularly identified himself with the poet, Ferdinand Freiligrath, who had come to the Wuppertal to work as a commercial clerk. The image of a double life — a merchant by occupation and a writer by vocation — remained attractive until he managed to escape the family profession in 1845 — and it reappeared in various guises in later life.

But by the end of the 1830s, the pre-occupations of literary political and religious debate were too intertwined to allow meaningful separation. Pietism, romantic conservatism and the absolution of the Christian Prussian state were all sharply opposed to the various strands of liberalism, rationalism and post-Hegelian biblical criticism. Since the debate was so polarised, to be a writer or poet necessitated a conscious choice between progress and reaction, and there was little doubt which direction Engels would follow. Unlike Marx, Engels' first political attitudes were strongly shaped by the liberal nationalist literary movement of the 1830s. His earliest heroes had been drawn from teutonic mythology and in Bremen the legend of Siegfried remained important to him as a symbol of the courageous qualities of young German manhood in struggle against the petty servile Germany of the princes. Soon after he began work in Bremen he became an enthusiastic disciple of *Young Germany*, a short-lived literary group which had arisen in the wake of the 1830 revolution, and modelled its style and stance upon the exiled Jews, Heine and Börne. Engels was at first an admirer of Karl Gutzkow, the editor of the *Telegraph für Deutschland*, who published his *Letters from the Wuppertal*. But by the end of 1839, Engels' enthusiasm had began to shift towards Gutzkow's former mentor, Börne whose radical republican denunciations of German princes and aristocrats, combined with his polemic against the Francophobe tendencies of German nationalism appealed to Engels' combative enthusiasm for the 'ideas of the century'.

But for Engels at this time, the problem of religious belief was uppermost. Despite his discontent with the outlook of his family, the strength of his religious upbringing was not easily shaken off. The intensity of his religious longings can be testified by a pietist poem he wrote at the time of his confirmation. The stages by which he moved away from orthodox Christianity — from a liberal Christianity through Schleiermacher to Strauss — can be traced in detail in his letters from Bremen to his schoolfriends, the Graeber brothers. One thing is clear. He could not simply move away from belief. He could only abandon one belief when he had found another. His first criticisms of Wuppertal pietism were written from the viewpoint of liberal Christianity. But through his reading of Gutzkow's essays, he came across Strauss, and by October 1839, he could write, 'I am now an enthusiastic Straussian'. Strauss was a bridge to Hegel, and the first impact made upon him by Hegel was akin to a religious conversion. In a real or imaginary voyage across the North Sea in July 1840, he stood at the bowsprit of the ship looking out over the 'distant green surface of the sea, where the foaming crests of the waves spring up in eternal unrest' and reflected:

I have had only one impression that could compare with this; when for the first time the divine idea of the last of the philosophers, this most colossal creation of the thought of the nineteenth century, dawned upon me, I experienced the same blissful thrill, it was like a breath of fresh sea air blowing down upon me from the purest sky; the depths of speculation lay before me like the unfathomable sea from which one cannot turn one's eyes straining to see the ground below; in God we live, move and have our being! We become conscious of that when we are on the sea; we feel that God breathes through all around us and through us ourselves; we feel such kinship with the whole of nature, the waves beckon to us so intimately, the sky stretches so lovingly over the earth, and the sun shines with such indescribable radiance that one feels one could grasp it with the hand.[15]

It was this difference in intensity of emotional need which is one of the features which distinguished Engels' relationship with Hegel from that of Marx. Engels had no academic education in philosophy, he found Hegel in his search for a secure resting place to replace the awesome contours of the Wuppertal faith which had been so deeply imprinted on his childhood imagination. He never subjected Hegel to the rigorous dissection which Marx undertook in his *Critique of Hegel's Philosophy of Right* or his *Critique of the Hegelian Dialectic and Philosophy as a whole* in 1843 and 1844, and thus when in later years in reaction to vulgar materialism and positivism, he resorted once more to Hegel, he tended to reproduce elements of his own pre-Marxist relationship with the German idealist tradition.

Already an enthusiastic Young Hegelian when he left Bremen for his year's military service in Berlin in 1841, he rapidly replaced the pantheist Hegel by the 'secret atheist' Hegel, and soon became one of the most apocalyptic members of 'the free'. Within weeks in Berlin, he was launching polemics against Schelling, who had been summoned to the chair of philosophy there in order to combat the dangerous tendency of Hegelianism. He did not appreciate the incompatibility between Bruno Bauer's left Hegelian concept of 'self-consciousness', and Feuerbach's *Man* which through the method of inversion, effectively annulled the Hegelian dialectic altogether. In all his references to German philosophical radicalism up to the *Holy Family*, he bracketed Bauer and Feuerbach together as part of a single line of thought. Years later in *Ludwig Feuerbach*, he wrote of the *Essence of Christianity* 'one must himself have experienced the liberating effect of this book to get an idea of it; enthusiasm was general. We all became at once Feuerbachians'.[16] This was much truer of himself than of other members of the group. For what captured his attention and his enthusiasm, both in the *Essence of Christianity* and in the later *Provisional Theses for the Reform of Philosophy*, was not Feuerbach's criticism of Hegel, but his conversion of theology into anthropology, his humanist religion. In all his writings up to his meeting with Marx in Paris in the late summer of 1844, he remained methodologically a Hegelian, all his more ambitious essays taking the form of a dialectical juxta-position of the development of one-sided principles, whose contradiction was transcended in a higher unity represented by the postulates of communist humanism.

Perhaps another reason why Engels never felt impelled to subject Hegel to a searching critique, was that unlike some of the other Young Hegelians, he never seems to have taken Hegel's theory of the state very seriously. This appeared to him part of Hegel's conservative 'system' rather than to his 'revolutionary method', and unlike the rest of the circle Engels had already become a revolutionary republican democrat before he became a Hegelian. Thus in Berlin, he still believed he could combine a Hegelian philosophy of history with Börne's republican view of politics. In a comic Young Hegelian mock epic which he wrote with Edgar Bauer in the summer of 1842, he referred to himself as:

... *Oswald* the Montagnard
A radical is he, dyed in the wool, and hard.
Day in, day out, he plays upon the guillotine a
Single, solitary tune and that's a cavatina,
The same old devil-song; he bellows the refrain:
Formez vos bataillons! Aux armes, citoyens![17]

His political position remained Jacobin until he met Moses Hess at the *Rheinische Zeitung* offices at Köln, while preparing to go to England, and was converted to Hess's philosophical com-munism. It is probably because he had participated so fully in the bohemian anti-Christian excesses of 'the free', and was at one with Edgar Bauer in his frequent denunciations of the politics of a *juste milieu*, that his meeting with Marx in Köln around the same time, was so cool.

But Engels' weaknesses were also his strengths. If he did not possess the intellectual persistence and deductive power to be a rigorous original theorist, if his attempts to theorise were more remarkable for their boldness than their finality, his great virtues were his relative openness to new impressions, the persistent radicalism of his temperament, an astonishing quickness of perception, and comprehension, a daring intuition and an omnivorous curiosity about his surroundings. He was and remained marked by his merchant upbringing and training. It was to be seen in his methodical dealing with his correspondence, his careful ordering of his affairs, his ability to use every hour of the day, his irritation at the bohemianism of a Liebknecht and his complete antipathy to the generous flourishes of a disorderly aristocrat like Bakunin. He was by all accounts a good businessman and the acumen with which he represented the family firm in Manchester in the early 1850s greatly helped to ease the tensions caused by the deep rift with his father which had come to its head in 1848. It was the desire to get outside and beyond this background that made him more personally adventurous than Marx, more willing to flout convention, and at the same time more abrasive to those outside his circle. It would be difficult to imagine Marx living with a working-class Irish woman, exploring the slums of Manchester of his own accord, scribbling comic drawings over the manuscript of the *German Ideology*, roving the French countryside in late 1848 and extolling the charms of the peasant girls, fighting a military campaign in 1849, and back in England, riding to hounds, keeping a pet parrot and boasting of his wine cellar. *Spiessburger* was one of Engels' favourite terms of abuse, and there was nothing of the petit-bourgeois in Engels' make-up. He never concealed his background and was no diplomatist. Working men were probably justified in their intermittent complaints of his arrogance,[18] though it shouldn't be forgotten that this was accompanied by a genuine personal modesty, a candid avowal of his own limitations, and a warm loyalty to old friends. If, as he wrote, he was no genius, he was certainly a man of exceptional talents. He possessed a fluent and lucid prose and wrote with unusual speed. Not only was he a superb exponent of the application of historical materialism, once it was in his possession, but he was also surely one of the most gifted journalists of the nineteenth century and one of its best historians. It was this unusual combination of attributes that enabled him to make his particular contribution to the formation of historical materialism.

Engels left for England at the end of November 1842, ostensibly to continue his commercial training at the firm of Ermen and Engels in Manchester, and he remained there for 21 months.

Looking back to this first stay in England forty years later, Engels wrote:

While I was in Manchester, it was tangibly brought home to me that the economic facts, which have so far played no role or only a contemptible one in the writing of history, are at least in the modern world, a decisive historical force; that they form the basis of the origination of the present day class antagonisms in the countries where they have become fully developed, thanks to large scale industry, hence especially in England, are in their turn the basis of the formation of political parties, and of party struggles and thus of all political history.[19]

From the evidence of the writing he produced at the time, the process by which he came to those conclusions, was by no means as simple and clearcut as his later retrospect implied. For he not only had to use his eyes and ears, to open himself to new impressions, but also to frame questions against the grain of some of the basic presuppositions of the German philosophical communism which he now brought with him to England. The beginnings of a break with these presuppositions did not really appear until the second year of his visit, were not manifest until *The Condition of the Working Class in England* which he wrote up in Barmen after his return home between September 1844 and March 1845, and not completed until the time which he and Marx spent defining their position in opposition to *German Ideology* in Brussels in 1845 and 1846.

The first signs of his growing preoccupation with the importance of 'economic facts' are to be found from the end of 1843 in an ambitious series of essays on political economy, Carlyle's *Past and Present* and the condition of England, which were in part published in the *Deutsch-Französische Jahrbücher* and continued in *Vorwärts*. A reading of Fourier, but in particular of Carlyle, led him to 'the condition of England': 'the "national wealth" of the English is very great and yet they are the poorest people under the sun'.[20] Or as Carlyle put it: 'in the midst of plethoric plenty, the people perish; with gold walls and full barns, no man feels himself safe or satisfied'.[21] A reading of Proudhon's *What is Property* and some of the works of Owen, stimulated him to connect this condition with the consequences of private property. In late 1843, he wrote of Proudhon: 'The right of private property, the consequences of this institution, competition, immorality, misery, are here developed with a power of intellect, and real scientific research which I never found united in a single volume'.[22] However, Engels in his 'Outlines of a Critique of

Political Economy', published in the *Deutsch-Französische Jahrbücher* went considerably further than Proudhon. He did not simply contrast the miserable economic reality with the statements of political economists, but attempted to show that the contradictions of political economy were necessary results of the contradictions engendered by private property. He was the first of the German philosophical left to shift discussion towards political economy and to highlight the connections between private property, political economy and modern social conditions in the transition to communism. Political economy, he defined as 'a science of enrichment', 'a developed system of licensed fraud' resulting from the expansion of trade and 'born of the merchants' mutual envy and greed'.[23] For trade was based on competition engendered by private property, which opposed individual interests to one another, and thus produced the division between land, labour and capital, the confrontation between the labourer and his product in the form of a wage, the conversion of man into a commodity, the invention of machinery and the factory, the dissolution of family and nationality and of all other bonds into a mere cash-nexus, the polarisation of society into millionaires and paupers and the universalisation of 'the war of all against all'. The 'science of enrichment' which accompanied this process was seen to be trapped in irresolvable antinomies, and its practitioners to be guilty of ever greater hypocrisy and immorality. For the defenders of free trade and liberal economics from Adam Smith onwards, despite their attacks on monopoly and professions of peaceful progress through free trade, refused to question the greatest monopoly of all, private property, productive, under the name of competition, of the most bloodthirsty and general war of all against all.

It is known that this essay strongly influenced Marx's own first reflections on political economy in the 1844 manuscripts, and was still regarded by him in 1859 as a 'brilliant sketch on the criticism of economic categories'.[24] Nevertheless, it would be quite wrong to regard the *Outlines* as evidence of a break with his philosophical communism under the impact of English conditions or of an anticipation of historical materialism as it was to be conceived in 1845. Not only was the stress placed upon private property and competition rather than mode of production and the struggle between classes, but private property itself was made dependent on 'the unconscious condition of mankind'.[25] The stance from which Engels made his critique was 'human' (that is, anthropological rather than theological), and Carlyle was praised

because his book showed 'traces of a human point of view'.[26]
Engels fully accepted Carlyle's definition of the condition of
England, but he ascribed Carlyle's contempt for democracy and
ignoring of socialism, not to his class position, but to his
'pantheism' which still placed a supernatural power above man.
Carlyle's solution was a new religion based on the gospel of work.
But for Engels, religion, far from being an answer to the
immorality and hypocrisy of the present, was in fact the root of
the present evil. The solution was:

the giving back to man the substance he has lost through religion; not as divine
but as human substance, and this whole process of giving back is no more than
simply the awakening of self-consciousness . . . . The root of all untruth and
lying is the pretension of the human and the natural to be superhuman and
supernatural. For that reason we have once and for all declared war on religion
and religious ideas.[27]

It was for this reason that trade crises could be defined as 'a
natural law based on the unconsciousness of the participants',
that Adam Smith could be described as 'the *economic Luther*'
who put 'Protestant hypocrisy' in place of 'Catholic candour',
and the Malthusian population theory be seen as 'the pinnacle of
Christian economics'.[28] It was for similar reasons, evidently
reinforced by a reading of Marx's essay on *The Jewish Question*,
that a few months later, Engels attempted to develop a theory of
the English constitutional monarchy as an expression of 'man's
fear of himself'.[29]

Furthermore, if the standpoint of Engels' critique was
humanist, its method of critique remained Hegelian. As he wrote,
with some consternation a few days after his arrival in England in
November 1842:

there is one thing that is self-evident in Germany, but which the obsti.ate Briton
cannot be made to understand, namely that the so-called material interests can
never operate in history as independent guiding aims, but always consciously or
unconsciously serve a principle which controls the threads of historical
progress.[30]

Writing a year later on political economy, he remained equally
confident that 'once a principle is set in motion it works by its own
impetus through all its consequences whether the economists like
it or not'.[31] His method of analysing political economy was to
'examine the basic categories, uncover the contradiction
introduced by the free trade system and bring out the
consequences of both sides of the contradiction'.[32]

Engels came to England in full agreement with Hess's prophecy that England would be the bearer of a social revolution which would consummate and transcend the religious-philosophical revolution in Germany and the political revolution in France.[33] But from the beginning, he was forced to admit that 'among the parties which are now contending for power, among the whigs and tories, people know nothing of struggles over principles and are concerned only with conflicts of material interests'.[34] The problem therefore was to discover how in England principle had realised itself through the apparent domination of material interests and pure practice. His solution to this problem appeared a year later in an unfinished series on the *Condition of England*, written in the first few months of 1844. 'The concern of history from the beginning', he wrote, was 'the antithesis of substance and subject, nature and mind, necessity and freedom'. World history up to the end of the eighteenth century had only set these antitheses ever more sharply against one another. 'The Germans, the nation of Christian spiritualism, experienced a philosophical revolution; the French, the nation of classical materialism and hence of politics, had to go through a political revolution'.[35] But: 'The English, a nation that is a mixture of German and French elements, who therefore embody both sides of the antithesis and are for that reason more universal than either of the two factors taken separately, were for that reason drawn into a more universal, a social revolution'. The English embodied these antitheses in their sharpest form and it was their inability to resolve them that explained 'the everlasting restlessness of the English'. 'The conclusion of all English philosophising is the despair of reason, the confessed inability to solve the contradictions with which one is ultimately faced, and consequently on the one hand a relapse into faith and on the other devotion to pure practice'.[36] This explained the religious bigotry of the English middle class combined with its empiricism but at the same time 'this sense of contradiction was the source of colonisation, seafaring, industry and the immense practical activity of the English in general'.[37] Thus only England had a social history:

Only in England have individuals as such, without consciously standing for universal principles, furthered national development and brought it near to its conclusion. Only here have the masses acted as masses, for the sake of their interests as individuals; only here have principles been turned into interests before they were able to influence history.[38]

We have stressed the philosophical problematic within which

Engels attempted to come to terms with England between 1842 and 1844, not to contradict his statement about his growing awareness of the importance of 'economic facts', but to show how great was the intellectual and imaginative effort that had to be made before he could write *The Condition of the Working Class in England* — a book, which is by no means solely an achievement of observant reportage, but which also embodies a profound shift in his political and theoretical position. The distance he had to travel and the extent to which he had to unlearn, not only the presuppositions of radical German idealism, but also virtually all the available varieties of socialism of the time, can be highlighted by his changing view of the revolution the working class and modern industry.

Engels came to England just after the Chartist general strike, confident of Hess's prophecy of imminent social revolution and the realisation of communism. Communism, in Hess's scenario, it should be stressed, represented the triumph of the principles of community and 'unity' over egoism and fragmentation.[39] It was not the outcome of a battle between classes, nor was its realisation located in the destiny of any particular class. Hess repeatedly rejected Lorenz von Stein's identification of communism with a proletariat spurred on by a greedy and selfish desire for equality derived from the needs of the stomach.[40] Thus Engels acted quite consistently in January 1843 when he turned down the invitation of Bauer, Schapper and Moll in London to join the League of the Just. He refused the communism of the German artisans since, as he later confessed, 'I still owned, as against their narrow-minded equalitarian communism, a goodly dose of just as narrow-minded philosophical arrogance'.[41] As he described the creed of the German philosophical communists, among whom he counted himself, later that year,[42] 'a *Social* revolution based upon common property, was the only state of mankind agreeing with their abstract principles'. Thus Germans were bound for communism since: 'The Germans are a philosophical nation, and will not, cannot abandon communism, as soon as it is founded upon sound philosophical principles: chiefly if it is derived as an unavoidable conclusion from their own philosophy. And this is the part we have to perform now'.

Since socialism concerned humanity and not the interests of a particular class, it is not surprising to find that for most of his stay in England, Engels should ascribe much more importance to the Owenites than the Chartists. 'As to the particular doctrines of our party', he wrote in 1843, 'we agree much more with the English socialists than with any other party. Their system like ours, is based upon philosophical principle'.[43] He was very impressed by how far ahead the English were in the practice of socialism and his only disagreement with them was that: 'The Socialists are still Englishmen, when they ought to be simply men, of philosophical developments on the Continent they are only acquainted with materialism but not with German philosophy, that is their only real shortcoming'.[44] His distance from the outlook of the Chartists was further reinforced by their concentration on overcoming solely a form of the state rather than the state itself. For, as he wrote, 'Democracy is, as I take all forms of government to be, a contradiction in itself, an untruth, nothing but hypocrisy (theology, as we Germans call it), at the bottom'.[45] He clearly admired the combativity and spirit of the Chartists from the start and he regarded their victory as inevitable, but his sights were set firmly beyond the transitory triumph of democracy. The socialists, he wrote in January 1844, 'are the only party in England which has a future, relatively weak though they may be. Democracy, Chartism must soon be victorious, and then the mass of the English workers will have the choice only between starvation and socialism'.[46]

Given these positions however, his early impressions of England were somewhat disconcerting. On his arrival, he was surprised to discover that, 'when people here speak of Chartists and Radicals, they almost always have in mind the lower strata of society, the mass of proletarians, and it is true that the party's few educated spokesmen are lost among the masses'.[47] He was even more astonished to find that the appeal of socialism was likewise virtually confined to the lower end of society and that the works of Strauss, Rousseau, Holbach, Byron and Shelley were read by workers, but virtually unmentionable in middle class and 'educated' circles. Carlyle helped him to understand why the middle class should be so sunk in 'mammonism' and bigotry, but he could find no better reason why enlightenment should be confined to the lower classes, than that the situation was analogous to what had occurred at the beginnings of Christianity.[48]

From around the beginning of 1844 however, a shift in his perceptions is detectable. Philosophical humanism and Hegelian method remained dominant, but the weight attached to different elements within this framework changed. Particularly noticeable is the new and primordial importance attached to the Industrial Revolution. After a detailed description of changes in industry,

Engels stated:

This revolution through which British industry has passed is the foundation of every aspect of modern English life, the driving force behind all social development. Its first consequence was . . . the elevation of self-interest to a position of dominance over man. Self-interest seized the newly created industrial powers and exploited them for its own purposes; these powers which by right belong to mankind became, owing to the influence of private property, the monopoly of a few rich capitalists and the means to the enslavement of the masses. Commerce absorbed industry into itself, and thereby became omnipotent, it became the nexus of mankind.[49]

His attention, in other words, had shifted from explaining competition as a consequence of merchant's greed and the political economists' 'science of enrichment' to the real forces which had universalised competition. He had also begun to discern how industrialisation had transformed the class system. The most important fact about eighteenth-century England had been the creation of the proletariat, a wholly new class; while in the same process, the middle class had become aristocratic. But this crystallisation of England into three distinct classes — landed aristocracy, monied aristocracy and working-class democracy — had in turn undermined the state. In an analysis of the English constitution and the legal system written in March 1844, he came to the conclusion that the famed balance of powers inscribed in the constitution was 'one big lie'.[50] Contrasting the theory and practice of the Constitution, he wrote: 'on the one hand the trinity of the legislature — on the other the tyranny of the middle class'. Neither Queen, Lords or Commons ruled England. 'Who then actually rules in England? Property rules'.[51] The power of the aristocracy did not derive from its constitutional position but from its vast estates. Thus, to the extent that the power both of the aristocracy and the middle class derived from their property and to the extent that 'the influence conferred by property' constituted 'the essence of the middle class' . . . 'to that extent the middle class does indeed rule'.[52]

But if the constitution were found to be a mere shell concealing the rule of property, and if other English 'birthrights' — freedom of the press, freedom of assembly, *Habeus Corpus* and the Jury system — were likewise found to be privileges of the rich and denied to the poor, then what had at first seemed so mysterious to Engels — the unreasoning opposition of the middle class to democracy and socialism — now became much clearer. Socialism remained his guiding aim, and 'democratic equality' remained a 'chimera'. But if the battle against the undemocratic state was in reality, not a political battle, but a social battle against the rule of property, then Chartism assumed a quite different significance. For what sort of democracy would a Chartist victory entail?

Not that of the French Revolution whose antithesis was the monarchy and feudalism, but *the* democracy whose antithesis is the middle class and property . . . . The middle class and property are dominant; the poor man has no rights, is oppressed and fleeced, the Constitution repudiates him and the law mistreats him; the struggle of democracy against the aristocracy in England is the struggle of the poor against the rich. The democracy towards which England is moving is a *social* democracy.[53]

Around the beginning of September 1844, Engels stayed with Marx in Paris on his way back to Barmen. Continuing his retrospect on his discovery in Manchester, of the decisive importance of 'economic facts' as the basis of 'present day class antagonisms' Engels wrote in 1885:

Marx had not only arrived at the same view, but had already in the *German-French Annals* (1844) generalised it to the effect, that speaking generally, it is not the state which conditions and regulates civil society, but civil society which conditions and regulates the state, and consequently, that policy and its history are to be explained from the economic relations and their development, and not vice versa.[54]

This statement is only partly true. For on the evidence of Marx's extant writings up to his meeting with Engels, he had not arrived 'at the same view' in at least two important respects. Firstly, while Marx had established the determination of the state by civil society Engels had established — though not in theoretically generalised form — an equally important proposition, the class character of the state. In his *Critical Notes on the Article, 'The King of Prussia and Social Reform' by a Prussian*, written a few weeks before Engels' arrival, Marx's basic definition of the state was that: 'The state is based on the contradiction between *public* and *private* life, on the contradiction between *general interests* and *private interests*'.[55] In this article, there was no conception of a ruling class in a later Marxist sense. The theme was rather the incapacity of political administration in the face of the domination of civil society from whose contradictory character, the illusion of the political realm was itself to be explained. Engels on the other hand, had defined the English state as an instrument used by the propertied ruling class in its struggle against the working class.[56]

Secondly, Engels' allusion to the type of class struggle engendered by modern industry, pertained primarily to himself.

Until his unfinished essay on List, written early in 1845, Marx's references to modern industry had been cursory and descriptive. The decisive concept around which the new theory of historical materialism was to crystallise between 1845 and 1847 was that of the mode of production, and the lynchpin of that concept was the emphasis that it placed upon *means of production*. Theoretically, it would eventually enable Marx and Engels to understand class struggle as the revolt of the forces of production against the relations of production. Politically, it would enable them to declare war on capital, while stressing the progressive tendency of modern industry. The crucial change effected by the industrial revolution had been its transformation of the relationship between the labourer and the means of production. It was this transformation that had produced the unprecedented form assumed by modern class struggle.

Although Engels in 1844 had begun to sense with increasing sureness the revolutionary significance of modern industry through its creation of a new form of class struggle, he was nowhere near to producing the theory of historical materialism. He was simply concerned with the particular path that England appeared to be taking to social revolution, and he clung inconsequentially to a blend of Hegel and Feuerbach writings to explain it. But embodied in the space created by that inconsequentiality were precisely the raw elements which would be the catalyst of the new theory. Marx, on the other hand in the 1844 *Manuscripts*, precisely because of his theoretical rigour, remained essentially within an artisanal framework. Following with greater consistency the technique of Feuerbachian inversion, the crucial relationship emphasised was not that between labourer and means of production, but between the labourer and his product, and his vision was that of man's pauperisation, both materially and anthropologically — a world of alienation and private property unmediated by the progressive revolutionary possibilities of the new form of production. Marx's particular impact upon Engels in the summer of 1844 was that of a brilliant humanist theorist, bolder and more original in his application and extension of the logic of inversion to the state and political economy, and clearsighted about the incompatibility between Feuerbach and Hegel.

The Condition of the Working Class in England represents the final phase of Engels' thinking before he joined Marx in Brussels. The narrowing of his theme to modern industry, the working class and the development of class struggle is itself indicative of a change in his priorities. Like Marx, who later planned to write a book on dialectics, Engels never found time to write his social history of England, of which *The Condition of the Working Class* was intended to form a part. The Hegelian categorisation of English prehistory which had formed such a prominent part of his preceding essays, is absent from the book, no doubt as a result of his conversations with Marx. But so also, despite his continuing belief that communism stood above the battle of classes, is the preoccupation with theology and Feuerbach. Engels had contributed some of the most ecstatic passages on Feuerbach in the *Holy Family*, but already by November 1844, a reading of Stirner's, *Ego and His Own* had convinced him that:

Feuerbach's 'man' is derived from God . . . and therefore his 'man' is still possessed of a theological halo of abstractions. The true path for arriving at 'man' is the opposite one . . . . We must start out from empiricism and materialism, if our thoughts and in particular our 'man' are to be something real. We must deduce the general from the particular and not from itself or out of thin air à la Hegel.[57]

Marx evidently disapproved of this programme, in particular its concession to Stirner, and in his next letter, Engels deferred to Marx's judgement.[58] Nevertheless, the negative impact of Stirner remained. For the results of Engels' irritation with 'theological chatter' about 'man' and 'theology' and his new concern with 'real, living things, with historical developments and their results' were clearly to be seen in his book.

The starting point of *The Condition of the Working Class* was not competition or private property, but the historically specific changes in manufacture from the middle of the eighteenth century. His explanation of this shift was uninformative,[59] but its rationale can be deduced from the general structure of his argument. Competition in itself could only describe a negative process of dissolution, an ever more brutish struggle between individuals, whose only chance of salvation could arise from a renewed consciousness of their humanity, awakened from outside by philosophy. 'Manufacture' on the other hand, could provide the starting point of a more complex and contradictory process — a process which contained the potentiality of liberation within itself: 'Manufacture, on a small scale, created the middle class; on a large scale it created the working class, and raised the elect of the middle class to the throne, but only to overthrow them more surely when the time comes'.[60] 'Manufacture' under free competition could not only explain 'the war of all against all', but also the growth of a labour movement united in an effort to overthrow the competitive system. The English socialists were no longer praised for their adherence to a 'philosophical principle, but criticised for being 'abstract' and acknowledging 'no historic development':

While bemoaning the demoralisation of the lower classes, they are blind to the element of progress in this dissolution of the old social order . . . . In its present form, socialism can never become the common creed of the working class; it must condescend to return for a moment to the Chartist standpoint.[61]

Competition only implied the abstract alternative of community, but 'manufacture' was a historic process which by concentrating population into large units of production and large cities had itself created the material possibility of combination between workers:

If the centralisation of population stimulates and develops the property-holding class, it forces the development of the workers yet more rapidly. The workers begin to feel as a class, as a whole; they begin to perceive that, though feeble as individuals they form a power united; their separation from the bourgeoisie, the development of views peculiar to the workers and corresponding to their position in life, if fostered, the consciousness of opposition awakens, and the workers attain social and political importance. The great cities are the birth-places of labour movements; in them the workers first began to reflect upon their own condition, and to struggle against it; in them the opposition between proletariat and bourgeoisie first made itself manifest; from them proceeded the trade unions, Chartism and socialism. The great cities have transformed the disease of the social body which appears in chronic form in the country, into an acute one, and so made manifest its real nature and the means of curing it.[62]

In his *Outlines of a Critique of Political Economy*, Engels had defined competition as an affliction of humanity; 'In this discord of identical interests resulting precisely from this identity is constituted the immorality of mankind's condition hitherto; and this consummation is competition'.[63] Now, on the contrary, competition was the nodal point of the class struggle between the bourgeoisie and the working class. The productiveness of each hand raised to the highest pitch by competition among the workers themselves, by division of labour and machinery generated 'the unemployed reserve army of workers' and deprived 'a multitude of workers of bread'. Competition among workers was 'the sharpest weapon against the proletariat in the hands of the bourgeoisie'.[64] Moreover competition constituted not only the practice, but the whole theory of the bourgeoisie: 'Supply and demand are the formulas according to which the logic of the English bourgeois judges all human life'. Even the state was reduced to the minimum necessary to 'hold the . . . indispensable proletariat in check'.[65]

Conversely, the constant thread in the growth of the working class movement through Luddism and trade unionism to Chartism had been the battle to abolish competition among the workers. The split between bourgeois 'political' democrats and working class 'social' democrats after 1842 had revolved around free trade:

Free competition has caused the workers suffering enough to be hated by them; its apostles, the bourgeoisie, are their declared enemies. The working man has only disadvantages to await from the complete freedom of competition. The demands hitherto made by him, the Ten Hours' Bill, protection of the workers against the capitalist, good wages, a guaranteed position, repeal of the New Poor Law, all of the things which belong to Chartism, quite as essentially as the 'Six Points', are directly opposed to free competition and Free Trade.[66]

'This question', wrote Engels, 'is precisely the point at which the proletariat separates from the bourgeoisie, Chartism from Radicalism'. Chartism was 'of an essentially social nature, a class movement'. But because Chartism was a social movement, and because socialism represented the only ultimate alternative to competition, a unification of the Chartists and the socialists in a 'true proletarian socialism' was soon to be expected, and in that form it must 'play a weighty part in the development of the English people'.

How then should we characterise Engels' contribution to Marxism? How essential was his presence to the birth of historical materialism?

There are no signs that Engels on his own would have produced a new general theory which broke decisively with its various philosophical antecedents. A historical materialist theory could not have been constructed from 'materialism and empricism' or from a progression from the 'particular' to the 'general', in the way that Engels had proposed in the late autumn of 1844. A new-found enthusiasm for the empirical produced many of the enduring strengths of his book on the working class, but it could not have produced the positions outlined in the *German Ideology* from 1845. England was still treated by him as a special case. It was still possible for him to imagine that France's path to communism would be political, and that of Germany, philosophical. Despite signs that in the light of his English experience, his expectations of Germany were becoming less naïve, the distance between his position at the time of the writing of *The Condition of the Working Class* and the position he was to reach at the time of his collaboration on the *German Ideology*, remained profound. It can be measured by comparing two reports he wrote in Germany, the first in December 1844, the second in September 1845:

Up to the present time our stronghold is the middle class, a fact which will perhaps astonish the English reader, if he does not know that this class is far more disinterested, impartial and intelligent, than in England, and for the very simple reason that it is poorer.[67]

It is true there are among our middle classes a considerable number of republicans and even communists . . . who, if a general outbreak occurred now, would be very useful in the movement, but these men are 'bourgeois', profit-mongers, manufacturers by profession; and who will guarantee us they will not be demoralised by their trade, by their social position, which forces them to live on the toil of other people, to grow fat by being the leeches, the 'exploiteurs' of the working classes? . . . . Fortunately we do not count on the middle class at all.[68]

Nevertheless, without Engels' work on England, the formulation of a Marxist theory, would at the very least, have been much slower than it actually was. The *Condition of the Working Class in England* provided an extraordinarily lucid account of how the development of modern industry had by the same token generated proletarian class struggle and the possibility of ultimate liberation. He provided a systematic explanation of the development of a proletarian political economy and of the social character of working-class political demands. It was the process itself rather than the intervention of the philosophers which had awakened workers to a consciousness of their class position, and which he hoped would lead to the emergence of a 'proletarian socialism'. Moreover his Hegelian formation, for all its limitations, had helped him to avoid two important theoretical obstructions which inhibited advances in the English working-class movement itself. While learning from English socialism the liberating potential of modern industry, through his assumption of a rational kernel to historical development, he could come to avoid their negative evaluation of the antagonism between middle and working class. On the other hand he could come to share the Chartist's belief in the necessity of an independent working-class politics, without having to base its legitimacy on a labour theory of value derived from a theory of natural right.[69] Thus, distanced by his nationality from some of the more sectarian aspects of the working-class movement, he was able to give a remarkable assessment of the significance of their struggle as a whole.

The importance of this assessment needs to be stressed. For, simply from a comparison of the extant texts, it is clear that a number of basic and enduring Marxist propositions first surface in Engels' rather than Marx's early writings: the shifting of focus from competition to production, the revolutionary novelty of modern industry marked by its crises of overproduction and its constant reproduction of a reserve army of labour, the embryo at least of the argument that the bourgeoisie produces its own gravediggers and that communism represents, not a philosophical principle, but 'the *real* movement which abolishes the present state of things', the historical delineation of the formation of the proletariat into a class, the differentiation between 'proletarian socialism' and small master or lower-middle-class radicalism, and the characterisation of the state as an instrument of oppression in the hands of the ruling propertied class.

All these were to become basic propositions in the theory of Marx and Engels, but it is of course true that they only became 'Marxist' by virtue of the historical materialist logic which was to connect and underpin them. It was Marx who constructed that logic and conceived the historical causality and new concepts, of which these propositions could be the result. As he wrote to Weydemeyer in 1852, 'what I did that was new was to prove . . . that the existence of classes is only bound up with particular historical phases in the development of production'.[70]

It is thus possible to agree with Engels that 'the materialist theory of history . . . which revolutionised the science of history is essentially the work of Marx', but at the same time to dispute his claim to have had 'only a very insignificant share' in its gestation.[71] For what Engels had provided, were the raw components which dramatised the inadequacies of the previous theory and formed a large part of the nucleus of the propositions to which the new theory was addressed. Engels' disclaimer becomes more understandable if it is realised that some of the most important of these propositions were not in any sense original to Engels himself. Take, for instance, the definition of the modern state, set out in the *German Ideology*:

To this modern private property corresponds the modern state, which, purchased gradually by the owners of property by means of taxation, has fallen entirely into their hands through the national debt, and its existence has become wholly dependent on the commercial credit which the owners of property, the bourgeois extend to it, as reflected in the rise and fall of government securities on the stock exchange.[72]

Such statements or less sophisticated variants of them had been commonplaces of the unstamped press and Chartist politics. So had much of the case against Malthus, the condemnation of overproduction as a result of concentration upon the world market and the notion of the reserve army of labour. The importance of Engels' contribution derived less from his moments of theoretical originality than from his ability to transmit elements of thinking and practice developed within the working-class movement itself in a form in which it could become an intrinsic part of the architecture of the new theory.

The importance of this moment in the beginnings of Marxism is generally ignored. In the standard account, first formulated by Kautsky and subsequently given enormous prestige through its partial adoption by Lenin in *What is to be Done*, the process of the connection between socialism and the labour movement is wholly one way. Socialist theory is developed outside the working class by bourgeois intellectuals then communicated to the most far-seeing of the working class and finally filters down to the working-class movement. The working class plays a wholly passive role in the process, a picture resembling Marx's view of 1843 in which the proletariat lends its force of arms to the philosopher and is given in return a consciousness of what it is and what its struggle means. It is in accordance with this position to view Marxism's own theoretical break as *sui generis* — a motor fuelled solely by theoretical introspection. It is only after the theory has been formed, that a juncture is made with the proletarian movement, which then propagates the new ideas.

Against this interpretation it should be stressed that while the concepts and structure of the new theory are certainly irreducible to experience and can only be the result of theoretical work, the changing questions which provoked the new theory had their source by definition outside the pre-existing theoretical discourse. Both in Engels' and in Marx's case, the form of their questioning changed, as their knowledge and experience of the working-class movement increased. It is known that Marx attended meetings of Parisian artisans in 1844 and that this experience made an evident impression on his work.[73] But the effect was even more striking in Engels' case. For Paris was not as strategic a place as Manchester to assimilate the connections between modern industry and the modern labour movement.

What distinguished Engels from many of his contemporaries was a deep-rooted discontent with his own background and milieu. It made him willing not merely to learn *about*, but also *from* workers, not merely to read the available sources but also to make personal contact, and consider himself part of their movement. How he spent his time in Manchester, is stated by Engels in the Preface to his book, 'I forsook the company and the dinner parties, the port wine and the champagne of the middle classes, and devoted my leisure hours almost exclusively to the intercourse with plain working men; I am glad and proud of having done so'.[74] It is known that in Manchester, he became acquainted with the Burns sisters, that he argued with John Watts of the Owenites, that he attended the Halls of Science, witnessed Chartist interventions against the Anti-Corn Law League, met James Leach, a factory worker prominent in the National Charter Association and in the autumn of 1843 introduced himself to Harney at the *Northern Star* offices at Leeds. The effect of this experience is clear from his book, but part of what he learnt, he tells us explicitly in the Preface, 'Having . . . ample opportunity to watch the middle classes, your opponents, I soon came to the conclusion that you are right, perfectly right in expecting no support whatever from them'.[75]

Of course, as we have tried to show, there was no simple capitulation of theory in the face of experience between 1842 and 1845, either on Marx's or on Engels' part. The process was necessarily much more complex, since a theory, however ultimately inappropriate, is more likely to be stretched and forced to take account of new phenomena than to be abandoned — at least, until the possibility or beginnings of another can be discerned. It was Marx who accomplished this theoretical transformation. But it was Engels who had preceded him, in providing so many of the elements of what was to be the object of that theory, though only in a practical state and posed unsatisfactorily within an inappropriate philosophical problematic. If Engels was a less consistent thinker than Marx, that was a crucial virtue in the formative period that led up to the break-through to historical materialism. For what it ensured was that the juncture between a materialist theory of history and the practical assumptions of working class struggle — an event which in the orthodox account took place in 1847 when Marx and Engels joined the Communist League — was already there as part of the new theory at its moment of formation in Brussels in 1845.

Because it has been necessary to argue at some length the inportance of Engels' initial contribution to Marxism, it has not been possible to do justice to the many other contributions he made to its subsequent development. There has been no space to deal with his work in the Communist League and in the preparation of the *Communist Manifesto*. It has been impossible to deal with his work as a correspondent on European affairs and his handling of the vexed problem of nationality in the *Neue Rheinische Zeitung* in 1848, his growing expertise on military strategy and theory from the early 1850s, his masterly analyses of Germany, developed in the *Peasants' War* and *Revolution and Counter-revolution in Germany* and continued in his writings on Bismarck and the new unified German state. Nor has it been possible to consider his later work on natural science, the family, or the origins of the state, nor, in the more immediately political realm, his reflections on Ireland, his many lucid analyses of the situation and strategy of the various working class movements in Europe and America, his battles against Proudhonism and anarchism, his close relations with the leadership of German social democracy nor his growing anxiety about the maintenance of a European peace from the foundation of the Second International. All that can be done in conclusion is to suggest a certain consistency in his strengths and limitations from the beginning through to the end of his long career as a Marxist.

From 1845 onwards, the relationship between Marx and Engels was a remarkably constant one. What Engels wrote in 1887 had applied throughout their working relationship:

As a consequence of the division of labour that existed between Marx and myself, it fell to me to present our opinions in the periodical press, that is to say, particularly in the fight against opposing views, in order that Marx should have time for the elaboration of his great basic work.[76]

Such a relationship could never have lasted, had it simply been one between master and disciple, creator and populariser. It worked because the initial theory was the joint property of both of them, so that both could be equally committed to its enlargement through the development of a specific theory of the capitalist mode of production. Engels never entertained any doubts that Marx rather than he was best fitted for this task. It would therefore be quite wrong to extend sympathy to Engels for his long years' support of Marx during the preparation of *Capital*. He would not have asked for such sympathy and indeed regarded *Capital* as much a vindication of himself as of Marx. There are no real signs of strain on Engels' side, except at the time of Marx's unfeeling response to the death of Mary Burns. As might be expected, the tension was felt more by the Marx family, the well-born Mrs Marx in particular resenting the humiliating dependence of her family for their subsistence on the charity of her husband's friend. For Engels himself, however tiresome the long years of office work in Manchester, the relationship fulfilled a deep-felt need for intellectual certainty and a firm basis from which he could develop his much more diverse talents. Engels did not possess the certainty of self to be a great original theorist; he therefore sought this quality in others. Apart from Marx, the only other thinker who satisfied this desire for intellectual security was Hegel.

The initial conception of historical materialism developed in Marx and Engels' work between the *German Ideology* and the *Communist Manifesto* was far from unproblematic. Its tendency was to reduce the status of ideology to a mere reflex of the real movement, and the development of the real movement itself to a reflex of the development of the forces of production. Specific countries were allotted their particular roles in the coming revolution according to a scale of development, and there was little space within the theory to enable a distinction between the specific character of the capitalist crisis of the 1840s and an ultimate crisis of capitalism as a whole. The 1848 revolutions did not take their predicted course. Chartism and 'proletarian socialism' did not triumph in England, Germany did not accomplish its bourgeois revolution, the French Revolution miscarried, producing the 'farce' of the Second Empire, and the 'history-less peoples' of Eastern Europe demonstrated in practice the existence of a more complex and uneven historical logic than the initial theory had envisaged.

Nevertheless, the failures of 1848 did not lead to any fundamental recasting of the basic theory. Indeed, after a more detailed analysis of the trade cycle and a recognition of further room for the development of productive forces within capitalism, it appeared to Marx and Engels that the character of the revolutions had only served to confirm the correctness of their position. The theory of the capitalist mode of production was infinitely deepened in *Capital*, but the general conception of the relationship between the economic, political and ideological realms remained in essentials unchanged. It was reaffirmed in their 1872 Preface to the *Communist Manifesto*, and it was not until the 1880s in reaction to the growth of a positivist-tinged vulgar Marxism that Engels began to stress the complex and indirect character of economic determination and the importance of the political sphere. Even this, however, remained a qualification rather than a development of the theory, since Engels was unprepared to rethink the character of determination within the terms of the theory itself. It is in fact unlikely that Engels would have conceded the necessity of such a substantial reformulation. For his basic vision of the theory remained remarkably constant. He remained imperturbably convinced of a historical process leading to capitalist downfall, but unlike most of the Second International Zusammenbruch theorists, saw the development of class struggle as an integral part of the process of collapse. Similarly, he remained true to his initial conviction derived from Chartism that the struggle for democracy in capitalist countries was a social struggle and thus part of the struggle for socialism, and this explains his and Marx's continuing enthusiasm for universal suffrage and their belief that the achievement of socialism in certain countries might be a peaceful one. Moreover, for all the sophistication of Engels' analyses of Germany in which he developed his important conceptions of absolutism, of the 'buonapartism' of the bourgeoisie and of the 'revolution from above', or again of his theory connecting the character of the English labour movement to English domination of the world market, the political point of his interventions remained that which he and Marx had developed in the 1840s — to encourage the formation of independent working-class parties based on class struggle, to make alliances with other progressive forces only on the basis of this independence and to combat all sectarian obstacles to such development.

Engels remained clearly marked by his early English experience. His judgement was always at its most incisive, his intuition most sure in the handling of working-class movements in industrial countries. He retained his youthful conviction of the 'idiocy of rural life' and found it difficult to regard peasants except as barbarian survivals or future proletarians.[77] His sense of proportion went awry in the manner of his dealing with the Bakuninists in Spain and Italy. He never really forgave the Southern Slavs and the Czechs for their anti-teutonic and anti-magyar activities in 1848 and he refused to treat nationalism as a serious phenomenon, except where consciously or unconsciously it aided the cause of the revolution. Both the strength and the weakness of his thinking was contained in the absolute priority he accorded to those situations which apparently offered the best chances of socialist advance, and this sometimes made him insensitive to parallel conflicts of an inconvenient but equally material character.

Such calculations consistently dominated his changing views on international relations. In the 1850s and 1860s, he and Marx hopefully scanned the political horizon for any possibility of a European war which might provoke a progressive alliance against Tzardom, radicalise the citizenry and topple the reactionary autocracies. Once Bismarck had annexed Alsace-Lorraine however, he became increasingly insistent upon the necessity of peace. Since the future of socialism now depended on the future of Germany and the unobstructed development of the SPD, a Franco-Russian alliance must at all costs be prevented and the restitution of France's lost provinces left until after socialist victory. There can be no doubt that this German-oriented position was based on socialist criteria, and not upon any particular national predilections — Bebel and Bernstein were shocked to discover among his papers a plan for the defence of Paris against the Prussians in 1870, and destroyed it for fear of the reaction at home.[78] Nevertheless this unilateral emphasis on the prospects of German socialist success produced problems in the Second International. French socialists were intensely irritated in 1891, by an attack by Engels upon French chauvinism and the necessity of German socialists supporting a defensive war if attacked, without any mention of what French socialists should do in the case of an offensive attack by Germany.[79] Engels' preoccupation with a Russian menace and the necessity of peace for the building of socialism in Germany, somewhat blinded him to the case of France, and one result was that the SPD were not wholly unjustified in claiming his authority in its justification of its support of war credits in August 1914.[80]

Both the strengths and weaknesses of Engels' Marxism derived from an intense and enduring sense of the onward march of a historical dialectic, of the concomitant advance of modern industry and the proletarian movement. It was this that explained his lasting attraction to Hegel, and his recurrent resort to Hegel when faced with problems to which Marxism provided no apparent solution. It was to Hegel's concept of 'historic nations' that he turned when confronted with the nationalisms of 1848. It was to Hegel's Natural Philosophy that he looked for guidance in seeking to develop an alternative to the mechanical materialism of the late 1850s; and it was to Hegel's notion of dialectical interaction that he returned when he wanted to oppose vulgar Marxist conceptions of economic or technological determination in the 1880s and 1890s.

But Hegel was not the only loyalty he retained from his early years. Despite his insistence upon placing socialism upon a scientific foundation, he remained in many respects a true disciple of the great utopians of his youth. He thought, not only of the immediate strategy of the various socialist parties of his time, but also of the abolition of the distinction between town and country, the liberation of women, the freeing of sexual and social relations from the trammels of property and wage slavery, and of the disappearance of the state. He remained an admirer of Owen, and above all of Fourier. The strength of his hatred of property, government and the miseries of 'civilisation' came out to the full in his *Origins of the Family Private Property and the State*. And who but someone who had once tasted and not forgotten the vision of a socialist Utopia, could write:

Man's own social organisation, hitherto confronting him as a necessity imposed by Nature and history, now becomes the results of his own free action. The extraneous objective forces that have hitherto governed history pass under the control of man himself. Only from that time will man himself more and more consciously, make his own history — only from that time will the social causes set in movement by him have, in the main and in a constantly growing measure, the results intended by him. It is the ascent of man from the kingdom of necessity to the kingdom of freedom.[81]

Notes

1 G. Mayer, *Friedrich Engels, Eine Biographie* (Köln, 1969); among other biographical studies of Engels, see A. Cornu, *Karl Marx et Friedrich Engels, leur vie et leur oeuvre* (Paris, 1954); H. Ullrich, *Der junge Engels* (Berlin, 1961); S.E.D., *Friedrich Engels, Eine Biographie* (Berlin, 1970); H. Hirsch, *Engels* (Hamburg, 1968); H. Pelger (ed.), *Friedrich Engels 1820–1970: Referate, Diskussionen, Dokumente* (Hannover, 1971); W. Henderson, *Frederick Engels* (London, 1976).
2 G. Lukacs, *History and Class Consciousness* (London, 1971); Karl Korsch, *Marxism and Philosophy* (London, 1970).
3 See D. Rjazanov, 'Briefwechsel zwischen Vera Zasulic und Marx', *Marx-Engels Archiv* (Frankfurt/M, 1928), vol. 1, pp. 309–45.
4 *F. Engels' Briefwechsel mit K. Kautsky* (Vienna, 1955), pp. 4, 77.
5 F. Engels, *Anti-Dühring* (Moscow, 1969), pp. 9–10.
6 F. Engels, *Ludwig Feuerbach and the End of German Classical Philosophy*, in K. Marx and F. Engels, *Selected Works* (Moscow, 1969), vol. 3, p. 335.
7 Cited in G. Mayer, *op. cit.* vol. 2, p. 448.
8 Engels to Schmidt, 27 October 1890, *Selected Works*, vol. 3, p. 495.
9 See for instance, Engels to Marx, 14 July 1858, in *Werke*, vol. 29, pp. 337–39.
10 On the problem of the possibility of inverting Hegel, see L. Althusser, 'Contradiction and Overdetermination' in *For Marx* (London, 1970); for the relationship between Engels' later theory and Hegel, see G. Stedman Jones, 'Engels and the End of Classical German Philosophy', *New Left Review*, No. 79, 1973; for other discussions of Engels and 'dialectical materialism' see L. Colletti, *Marxism and Hegel* (London, 1973); S. Timpanaro, *On Materialism* (London, 1975).

11 *Selected Works*, vol. 3, p. 361.
12 *Werke*, vol. 27, p. 26.
13 On the social history of nineteenth-century Wuppertal, see in particular, W. Köllman, *Sozialgeschichte der Stadt Barmen im 19 Jahrhundert* (Tubingen, 1960).
14 For an interesting attempt at a psychoanalytical interpretation of the young Engels, see S. Marcus, *Engels, Manchester and the Working Class* (London, 1974).
15 K. Marx and F. Engels, *Collected Works* (London, 1975), vol. 2, p. 99.
16 *Ibid.* vol. 3, p. 344.
17 *Ibid.* vol. 2, p. 335.
18 See for instance, S. Born, *Erinnerungen eines Achtundvierzigers* (Leipzig, 1898).
19 F. Engels, 'On the History of the Communist League', *Selected Works*, vol. 3, p. 178.
20 F. Engels, 'Outlines of a Critique of Political Economy', *Collected Works*, vol. 3, p. 421.
21 F. Engels, 'The Condition of England. *Past and Present* by Carlyle', *Collected Works*, vol. 3, p. 449.
22 F. Engels, 'Progress of Social Reform on the Continent', *Collected Works*, vol. 3, p. 399.
23 F. Engels, 'Outlines', *Collected Works*, vol. 3, p. 422–3.
24 K. Marx, 'Preface to *A Contribution to the Critique of Political Economy*' *Selected Works*, vol. 1, p. 504.
25 F. Engels, 'Outlines', *Collected Works*, vol. 3, p. 433.
26 F. Engels, 'Condition of England: Carlyle', *Collected Works*, vol. 3, p. 444.
27 *Ibid.* p. 463.
28 F. Engels, 'Outlines', *Collected Works*, vol. 3, pp. 422, 439.
29 F. Engels, 'The Condition of England: The English Constitution', *Collected Works*, vol. 3, p. 491.
30 F. Engels. 'The Internal Crises', *Collected Works*, vol. 2, p. 371.
31 F. Engels, 'Outlines', *Collected Works*, vol. 3, p. 424.
32 *Ibid.* p. 424.
33 See M. Hess, *Die europaische Triarchie* (Leipzig, 1841).
34 F. Engels, 'The Internal Crises', *Collected Works*, vol. 2, p. 371.
35 F. Engels, 'The Condition of England', *Collected Works*, vol. 3, p. 471.
36 *Ibid.* p. 472.
37 *Ibid.*
38 *Ibid.* p. 474.
39 See M. Hess, 'Philosophie der Tat', in T. Zlocisti (ed.), *Moses Hess: Sozialistische Aufsätze* (Berlin, 1921), pp. 62–3.
40 L. von Stein, *Der Sozialismus und Kommunismus des heutigen Frankreich* (Leipzig, 1842).
41 F. Engels, 'On History of the Communist League', *Selected Works*, vol. 3, p. 175.
42 F. Engels, 'Progress of Social Reform on the Continent', *Collected Works*, vol. 3, p. 406.
43 *Ibid.* p. 407.
44 F. Engels, 'Condition of England: Carlyle', *Collected Works*, vol. 3, p. 467.
45 F. Engels, 'Progress of Social Reform', *Collected Works*, vol. 3, p. 393.
46 F. Engels, 'Carlyle', *Collected Works*, vol. 3, p. 467.

47 'The English View of the Internal Crises', *Collected Works*, vol. 2, p. 368.
48 'Letters from London', *Collected Works*, vol. 3, p. 380.
49 F. Engels, 'The Condition of England: The 18th Century', *Collected Works*, vol. 3, p. 485.
50 F. Engels, 'The Condition of England, The English Constitution', *Collected Works*, vol. 3, p. 498.
51 *Ibid*.
52 *Ibid*.
53 *Ibid*. p. 513.
54 F. Engels, 'On the History of the Communist League', *Selected Works*, vol. 3, p. 178.
55 K. Marx, 'Critical Marginal Notes on the Article "The King of Prussia and Social Reform. By a Prussian" ', *Collected Works*, vol. 3, p. 198.
56 The discrepancy between Marx and Engels' early views on the state, is brought out, though not adequately explained in R. Hunt, *The Political Ideas of Marx and Engels* (Pittsburg, 1974), vol. I.
57 Engels to Marx, 19 November 1844, in *Werke*, vol. 27, p. 12.
58 Engels to Marx, 20 January 1845, in *Werke*, vol. 27, p. 14.
59 F. Engels, 'The Condition of the Working Class in England', *Collected Works*, vol. 4, p. 325.
60 *Ibid*.
61 *Ibid*. p. 526.
62 *Ibid*. p. 418.
63 F. Engels, 'Outlines', *Collected Works*, vol. 3, p. 432.
64 F. Engels, 'Conditions of the Working Class', *Collected Works*, vol. 4, p. 376.
65 *Ibid*. pp. 563, 564.
66 *Ibid*. p. 523.
67 'The Rapid Progress of Communism in Germany', *Collected Works*, vol. 4, p. 230.
68 'The Late Butchery at Leipzig', *Collected Works*, vol. 4, p. 647.
69 On this subject, see the forthcoming article, G. Stedman Jones, 'The Limitation of Proletarian Theory in England before 1850', *History Workshop*, No. 5 (Oxford, 1978).
70 *Werke*, vol. 28, p. 508.
71 *Selected Works*, vol. 3, p. 179.
72 K. Marx and F. Engels, *The German Ideology*, in *Collected Works*, vol. 5, p. 90.
73 For a good account of Marx's changing attitude to the working class in this period, see M. Lowy, *La Théorie de la Révolution chez le jeune Marx* (Paris, 1970).
74 *Collected Works*, vol. 4, p. 297.
75 *Ibid*. p. 298.
76 F. Engels, 'The Housing Question', *Selected Works*, vol. 2, p. 297.
77 Although, see his impressive *Of The Peasant Question in France and Germany*, *Selected Works*, vol. 3, pp. 457–77.
78 G. Mayer, *op. cit.* vol. 2, p. 196.
79 *Ibid*. pp. 508–9.
80 See Engels to Bebel, 13 October 1891, *August Bebel Briefwechsel mit Friedrich Engels*, edited by W. Blumenberg (Hague, 1965), pp. 450–3.
81 F. Engels, 'Socialism: Utopian and Scientific', *Selected Works*, vol. 3, pp. 149–50.

11 THE FORTUNES OF MARX'S AND ENGELS' WRITINGS
Eric J. Hobsbawm

The writings of Marx and Engels have acquired the status of 'classics' in the socialist and communist parties deriving their inspiration from them, including, since 1917, a growing number of states in which they have become the basis of official ideology, or even of a secular equivalent of theology. A great deal of Marxist discussion since the death of Engels — indeed, probably most of it — has taken the form of textual exegesis speculation and interpretation, or of debates about the acceptability of, or the desirability for the revision of, the views of Marx and Engels as contained in the texts of their writings. Yet these writings did not, initially, form a complete published corpus of the works of the two classics. Indeed, no attempt to publish a complete edition of their work was made before the 1920s, when the celebrated *Gesamtausgabe* (usually known as *MEGA*)[1] was initiated in Moscow under the editorship of Ryazanov. It remained incomplete in the original German, though the work was continued in Russian, but in a less complete form than originally intended. Independent attempts to publish an edition intended to be complete were made elsewhere at the same time, notably in France by Alfred Costes (*Editeur*). A full, but not by any means complete edition of the works of Marx and Engels (usually known and cited as *Werke*) was published in the German Democratic Republic from 1956, and provided the basis for various similar editions in other languages, many of which are still in progress at the time of writing (1977). In the 1970s a new *Gesamtausgabe* (the new *MEGA*) in something like 100 volumes was begun by the Institutes of Marxism-Leninism of the USSR and the GDR in collaboration, of which at the time of writing only a few volumes have actually been published. For most of the history of Marxism, debate has therefore been based on a varying selection of Marx's and Engels' writings. To understand that history, a brief and necessarily cursory survey of the fortunes of these writings is therefore required.

Part I
If we omit a great body of journalistic work, mainly in the 1840s

327

and 1850s, the actual body of writing published by Marx and Engels in Marx's lifetime was relatively modest. Before the 1848 Revolution it comprises, *grosso modo*, various important essays by Marx (and to a lesser extent Engels) before the start of their systematic collaboration (for example, in the *Deutsch-Französische Jahrbücher*), Engels' *Condition of the Working Class in England* (1845), Marx and Engels' *Die Heilige Familie* (1845), Marx's polemic with Proudhon *Misère de la Philosophie* (1847), the *Communist Manifesto* (1848) and some lectures and articles of the later 1840s. Except for the *Communist Manifesto*, none of these were republished in Marx's lifetime in a form accessible to a wider public. In the aftermath of the defeat of 1848–9 Marx published the now celebrated analyses of the revolution and its aftermath in emigré reviews of sadly restricted circulation (that is, the works now known as *Class Struggles in France*), and — under that original title — *The Eighteenth Brumaire of Louis Bonaparte*. The latter work he reprinted in 1869. Engels' own work on the *German Peasant War* (1850), which also appeared in the emigré press — unlike the articles now known as *Revolution and Counter-revolution* in Germany which appeared under Marx's name in the *New York Tribune* — was also reprinted in Marx's lifetime. Marx's own published works thereafter, omitting current journalism and political polemics, are virtually confined to the *Critique of Political Economy* (1859), not reprinted, *Capital* (vol. 1, 1867), whose history will be briefly referred to, and a number of works written for the International Workingmen's Association, of which the *Inaugural Address* (1864) and *The Civil War in France* (1871) are the most famous. The latter work was reprinted on several occasions. Engels published various pamphlets mainly on military-political questions, but in the 1870s began, with his *Herr Eugen Dührings Umwälzung der Wissenschaft* (1878) (*Anti-Dühring*), the series of writings through which, in effect, the international socialist movement was to become familiar with Marx's thought on questions other than political economy. Most of these, however, belong to the period after Marx's death.

In, say, 1875, the known and available corpus of Marx's and Engels' work was therefore exiguous, since much of the early writing had long gone out of print. It consisted essentially of the *Communist Manifesto*, which began to be better known from the early 1870s on — in 1871–3 at least nine editions appeared in six languages, as many as in the twenty-two previous years — of *Capital*, which was soon translated into Russian and French —

and *The Civil War in France*, which gave Marx a good deal of publicity. Nevertheless, between 1867 and 1875 we can say that *a* corpus of work by Marx for the first time became available.

The period between Marx's and Engels' death saw a double transformation. In the first place interest in Marx's and Engels' work quickened with the rise of the international socialist movement. In these twelve years, according to Andréas,[2] no less than seventy-five editions of the *Communist Manifesto* appeared in fifteen languages. It is interesting that the editions in the languages of the Tsarist Empire already outnumbered those in the original German. Secondly, a large corpus of the work of the classics was now published systematically in the original language, mainly by Engels. This comprised:

(a)   republications (generally with new introductions) of works long out-of-print whose permanent significance Engels thus wished to underline;
(b)   new publication of works left unpublished or incomplete by Marx; and
(c)   new writings by Engels, sometimes incorporating important unpublished texts by Marx such as the *Theses on Feuerbach*, in which he attempted to provide a coherent and rounded picture of the Marxian doctrine.

Thus under (a) Engels republished as a pamphlet Marx's articles on *Wage Labour and Capital of 1847* (1884), *The Poverty of Philosophy of 1847* (1885), the *Eighteenth Brumaire* (1885), *The Civil War in France* (1891) and finally (1895) the *Class Struggles in France*, as well as his own *Condition of the Working Class* and reprints of various writings of his from the 1870s. The main works made available under (b) were the second and third volume of *Capital* and the *Critique of the Gotha Programme* (1891). The main works under (c) were, in addition to the *Anti-Dühring* and the even more frequently reprinted *Socialism, Utopian and Scientific* adapted from the larger work, *The Origin of the Family, Private Property and the State* (1884) and *Ludwig Feuerbach* (1888), as well as numerous contributions to current political debate. These works were, perhaps with the exception of *Socialism, Utopian and Scientific*, not published in large editions. Nevertheless, they were, and henceforth remained, permanently available. They form the bulk of what Engels considered the corpus of his and Marx's writings, though, had he lived, he might have added some further texts — for example, the

Theories on Surplus Value, which eventually appeared under Kautsky's editorship and a revised version of the *Peasant War*, which he himself had hoped to bring out.

With some exceptions, such as writings originally published in English (some of which was reissued by Eleanor Marx shortly after Engels' death), this was the material available for the international Marxist movement at the end of the nineteenth century, including for foreign translation. It consisted of a selection, and to some extent a compilation, made by Engels. Thus *Capital* has come down to us not as Marx intended it to, but as Engels thought he would have intended it to. The last three volumes, as is well known, were put together by Engels — and later Kautsky — from Marx's incomplete drafts. However, the first volume is also a text finalised by Engels and not by Marx, for the standard version (the German fourth edition of 1890) was modified by Engels in the light of the last (second) edition revised by Marx, the further changes made by Marx for the French edition of 1872–5, some manuscript notes, and minor technical considerations. (Indeed, Marx's own second edition of 1872 included substantial rewriting of sections of the first edition of 1867). This, then, was the main corpus of the classic texts on which the Marxism of the Second International would have been built, had not many of its theoreticians and leaders, especially in Germany, had direct personal contact with the late Engels, both in conversation and through the bulky correspondence which was not published until after World War I. The point to note is that it *was* a corpus of 'finished' theoretical writings, and intended as such by Engels, whose own writings attempted to fill the gaps left by Marx and to bring earlier publications up-to-date. Thus the object of his editorial labours on *Capital* was (naturally enough) not to reconstruct the flow and development of Marx's own economic thought, still in progress at the time of his death. Such a historical reconstruction of the genesis and development of *Capital* (including the changes between editions of the published volume) was only undertaken seriously after World War II, and is even now not complete. Engels' object was to produce a 'final' text of his friend's major work, which would make the earlier drafts superfluous.

His own brief compendia of Marxism, and notably the very successful *Socialism, Utopian and Scientific* were intended to make the contents of this corpus of theory accessible to the members of the new mass socialist parties. And indeed during this period a good deal of the attention of the theorists and leaders of socialist movements was devoted to making such popular compendia of Marx's doctrine. Thus in France Deville, in Italy Cafiero, in Britain Aveling, produced compendia of *Capital*, while Kautsky published his *Economic Doctrines of Karl Marx*. These are only some of the works of this type. Indeed, the main educational and propagandist effort of the new socialist movements appears to have concentrated on the production and diffusion of works of this kind, rather than those of Marx and Engels themselves. In Germany, for instance, the average number of copies printed per edition of the *Communist Manifesto* before 1905 was a mere 2,000 or at most 3,000 copies, though thereafter the size of the editions increased.[3] For a comparison, Kautsky's *Social Revolution* (Part I) was printed in an edition of 7,000 in 1903 and 21,500 in 1905, Bebel's *Christenthum und Socialismus* had sold 37,000 copies between 1898 and 1902, followed by another edition of 20,000 in 1903, and the party's *Erfurt Programme* (1891) was distributed in 120,000 copies.[4]

This does not mean that the now available corpus of classic writings was not read by socialists of a theoretical bent. It was certainly translated rapidly into various languages. Thus in Italy, admittedly a country with an unusually lively interest in Marxism among intellectuals during the 1890s, virtually the whole corpus as selected by Engels was available by 1900 (except for the later volumes of *Capital*) and the *Scritti* of Marx, Engels and Lassalle edited by Ciccotti (from 1899) also included a number of further works.[5] Until the middle 1930s very little was added in the English language to the body of classic writings which had been translated by 1913 — albeit often rather badly — mainly by the firm of Charles H. Kerr in Chicago.

Among those with theoretical interests — that is to say among intellectuals in central and eastern Europe, and also partly in Italy, to whom Marxism made a great appeal — a demand for the rest of Marx's and Engels' writings was naturally lively. The German Social Democratic Party, which owned the literary *Nachlass* of the founders, made no attempt to publish their complete works, and may indeed have considered it inexpedient to publish or to republish some of their more tactless or offensive remarks as well as political writings of purely temporary interest. Nevertheless Marxist scholars, notably in Germany Kautsky and Franz Mehring, in Russia D. Ryazanov, set about publishing a more complete body of Marx's and Engels' *published* writings than Engels had evidently considered immediately necessary. Thus Mehring's *Aus dem literarischen Nachlass von Marx und*

Engels (1902) republished writings of the 1840s, and Ryazanov, works between 1852 and 1862,[7] both in several volumes. Before 1914 at least one major breakthrough into the unpublished material was achieved with the publication of the correspondence between Marx and Engels in 1913.[8] Kautsky had already (from time to time) published selected manuscript material in the *Neue Zeit*, the SPD's theoretical review, notably (in 1902) Marx's letters to Dr Kugelmann and (in 1903) a few fragments from what is now known as the *Grundrisse*, such as the incomplete Introduction to the *Critique of Political Economy*. Writings by Marx and Engels addressed to correspondents in specific countries, or published in the languages of those countries, or having special reference to them, were also published from time to time locally, though at the time they were rarely translated into other languages. The availability of the classic writings in 1914 is perhaps best indicated in the bibliography attached by Lenin to his encyclopedia article on Karl Marx, written in that year. If a text of Marx and Engels was not known to the Russian Marxists, the most assiduous students of the classic works, then it may be assumed that it was not effectively available to the international movement.

Part II
The Russian Revolution transformed the publication and popularisation of the classic works in several ways. First, it transferred the centre of Marxian textual scholarship to a generation of editors who no longer had had personal contacts with Marx, or more usually, with the old Engels — men such as Bernstein, Kautsky and Mehring. This new group was therefore no longer directly influenced either by Engels' personal judgements on the classic writings or by the questions of tact and expediency — both in relation to persons and contemporary politics — which had so obviously influenced Marx's and Engels' immediate literary executors. The fact that the main centre of Marxian publication was now the communist movement under-lined this break, for communist (and especially Russian) editors tended — sometimes quite correctly — to interpret the omissions and modifications of earlier texts by German social democracy as 'opportunist' distortions. Second, and partly for this reason, the aim of the Bolshevik marxists (who now possessed the resources of the Soviet state) was the publication of the *entire* body of the classic writings — in short a *Gesamtausgabe*. This raised a number of technical problems, of which two may be mentioned.

Marx's — and to a lesser extent Engels' — writings ranged from finished works published with varying degrees of care, through drafts of varying degrees of incompleteness and provisionality to mere reading notes and marginalia. The line between 'works' and preliminary notes and drafts was not easy to draw. The newly formed Marx-Engels Institute, under the direction of that formidable Marx-scholar, Ryazanov, excluded some writings from the actual 'works', though it set out to publish them in a parallel miscellaneous periodical, the *Marx-Engels Archiv*. They were not to be included in a collection of *all* writings until the new *MEGA* of the 1970s. Furthermore, while the bulk of the actual drafts was available in the Marx-Engels *Nachlass*, in the possession of the SPD (and after 1933 transferred to the International Institute of Social History in Amsterdam), the correspondence of the classics was widely dispersed, and a collected edition was therefore impossible, if only because the whereabouts of much of it was not known. In fact, a series of Marx/Engels letters were published separately, sometimes by the recipients or their literary executors, from *ca.* 1920 on, but so large and important a corpus as the correspondence with Lafargue was not published until the 1950s.[9]

Since *MEGA* was never completed, these problems soon lost their urgency, but they ought to be noted. So also should the continued publication of Marxiana based on the surviving older centres of Marxian material, notably the SPD archives. For if the Moscow Institute sought to acquire all possible writings of the classics for their complete edition — the only one in preparation — in fact it was able to acquire only photocopies of the overwhelmingly largest archival collection, the originals remaining in the west.

The 1920s therefore saw a remarkable spurt in the publication of the classic writings. For the first time two classes of material became generally available: unpublished manuscripts and the correspondence of Marx and Engels with third parties. However, political events soon put obstacles in the way of both publication and interpretation, such as had not been thought of before 1914. The triumph of the Nazis in 1933 disrupted the western (German) centre of Marxian studies, and largely postponed the repercussion of the interpretations based on them. To take merely one example, Gustav Mayer's monumental Engels-biography, a work of remarkable scholarship, had to appear in 1934 in a Dutch emigré edition, and remained virtually unknown to younger Marxists in post-1945 West Germany until well into the 1970s.

Many of the new publications of Marxian texts were not merely, to quote the title of a series published in the 1920s 'Marxist rarities',[10] but inevitably *became* rarities. In Russia the rise of Stalin disrupted the Marx-Engels Institute, particularly after the dismissal of its director Ryazanov, and put an end to the publication of *MEGA* in German, though not — in spite of the tragic impact of the purges — to further editorial work. Furthermore, and in some ways more seriously, the growth of what might be called an orthodox Stalinist interpretation of Marxism, officially promulgated in the *History of the CPSU (b): Short Course* of 1938, made some of Marx's own writings appear heterodox, and therefore caused problems with regard to their publication. This was notably the case with the writings of the early 1840s.[11] Finally, the war reached Russia itself, with serious results for Marx's works. The splendid edition of the *Grundrisse*, published in Moscow in 1939–41, remained virtually unknown (though one or two copies reached the USA) until the East Berlin reprint of 1953.

The third way in which the publication of the classic writings was transformed after 1917 concerns their popularisation. As has been suggested, the mass social democratic parties before 1914 made no serious attempt to get their members to read Marx and Engels themselves, with the possible exception of *Socialism, Utopian and Scientific*, and perhaps the *Manifesto. Capital* vol. I was indeed frequently reprinted — in Germany ten times between 1903 and 1922 — but it may be doubted whether it lent itself to wide popular reading. Many of those who bought it were probably content to have it on their shelf as a living proof that Marx had proved the inevitability of socialism scientifically. Small parties, whether composed of intellectuals, cadres or those unusually devoted militants who like to gather together in Marxist sects, certainly made greater demands on their members. Thus between 1848 and 1918 thirty-four editions of the *Manifesto* were published in English for the relatively minuscule Marxist groups and parties of the Anglo-Saxon world, as against twenty-six in French and fifty-five for the enormous parties of the German-speaking countries.[12]

The international communist movement, on the other hand, paid enormous attention to the Marxist education of its members, and no longer relied primarily on doctrinal compendia for this purpose. Hence the selection and popularisation of the actual classic texts became a matter of major concern. The increasing tendency to back political argument by textual authority, which had long marked some parts of the Marxist tradition — notably in Russia — encouraged the diffusion of classic texts, though naturally within the communist movement in the course of time the textual appeals to Lenin and Stalin were considerably more frequent than those to Marx and Engels. The wide availability of such texts undoubtedly transformed the situation of those who wished to study Marxism everywhere they were allowed to appear — though the area in which Marx and Engels could be published, contracted sharply between 1933 and 1944.

Of the major hitherto unpublished manuscripts, those of the 1840s began to make their impact before 1939. Both the *German Ideology* and the *Economic-Political Manuscripts of 1844* were published in 1932, though slow to be translated *in extenso*. This is not the place to discuss their significance. We merely note in passing that a great deal of Marxist discussion since 1945 turns on the interpretation of these early writings, and conversely, that most Marxist discussion before 1932 proceeded in ignorance of these works. The second large body of unpublished manuscripts concerned the preliminary work for *Capital*. One large body of writing, the *Grundrisse* of 1857–8 remained, as we have seen, unknown for even longer, since its first effective publication occurred in 1953 and its first (unsatisfactory) translations into foreign languages were only published in the late 1960s. It did not become a major basis for international Marxist debate until the 1960s, and even then initially not as a whole, but chiefly in relation to the historical section of the manuscript, which was separately republished under the title *Formen, die der kapitalistischen Produktion vorhergehen* (Berlin, 1952) and translated within a few years (into Italian 1956, into English 1964). Once again the appearance of this text forced upon the majority of Marxists who had hitherto been ignorant of it, a major reconsideration of Marx's writings. Of the substantial body of Marx's drafts in connection with the writing of *Capital* which were not included in the final published versions, sections have filtered into circulation even later and more gradually (for example, the projected Part VII of vol. I (*Resultate des unmittelbaren Produktionsprozesses*) which, though published in the *Arkhiv K. Marksa i F. Engelsa* in 1933, did not come to be seriously discussed until the late 1960s or was translated, at all events into English, until 1976. Some of this material remains unpublished.)

The third major unpublished manuscript, Engels' *Dialectics of Nature*, was first issued somewhat earlier, together with other Engels drafts, in the *Arkhiv K. Marksa i F. Engelsa* (1925). That it was not included in, or perhaps destined for, publication in the *Gesamtausgabe* was probably due to the fact, noted by Ryazanov, that much of Engels' discussion of the natural sciences, written in the 1870s, had become factually obsolete. Nevertheless, the work fitted into the 'scientist' orientation of Marxism which, long popular in Russia, was reinforced in the Stalin era. The *Dialectics of Nature* were therefore quite rapidly diffused in the 1930s — they were published in English in 1940 — and indeed cited by Stalin in the *Short Course* of 1938.[13] The text had some influence among the then rapidly growing number of Marxist natural scientists, the English edition being introduced by J.B.S. Haldane.

Of the Marx–Engels correspondence with third parties, which constituted probably the largest single body of unpublished Marxian material other than notes, relatively little had been published before 1914, partly in periodicals, partly as collections or selections of letters to individual correspondents, such as the *Briefe und Auszüge aus Briefen von Joh. Phil. Becker, Jos. Dietzgen, Friedrich Engels, Karl Marx u.A. und F.A. Sorge und Andere* (Stuttgart, 1906). A number of similar collections were published after 1917 — notably those to Bernstein (in Russian 1924, in German 1925),[14] and those to Bebel, Liebknecht, Kautsky and others (Russian 1932, German, Leningrad 1933), but no complete collection was published before the Russian edition (*Sochineniya* XXV–XXIX) of 1934–46, or in the original German, the *Werke* of 1956–68. As already noted, some highly important collections did not become available until the late 1950s, and the correspondence can still not be considered complete. Nevertheless, the collection available to the Moscow Institute by 1933 included a very substantial body of letters, which were popularised mainly through foreign translations and adaptations of the *Selected Correspondence* from the early 1930s.

However, a note about the 'official' publication of these letters is necessary. They were seen not so much as a correspondence (except for the exchanges between Marx and Engels), but rather as part of the classic writings. The letters of Marx's and Engels' correspondents were therefore not usually included in the official communist collections, though some editions of special collections, mainly produced by Marx's and Engels' correspondents or their executors (for example, Kautsky, Victor Adler) did contain both sides of the exchange. The Engels-Lafargue correspondence (1956–9) was perhaps the first issued under communist auspices, which included both sides, thus opening a new phase in the study of this aspect of the Marx–Engels texts. Moreover, the practice of keeping the Marx–Engels letters and their correspondence with third parties separate in the various collected editions of their works until the 1970s, still made a strictly chronological study of the letters relatively inconvenient.

Part III

As we have seen, the publication and translation of the corpus of Marx's and Engels' works in a far more complete form than before, made substantial progress after World War II, and especially in the post-Stalin era. By the early 1970s it could be said that, barring further discoveries of drafts and letters, the great bulk of the known works were in print in the original language, though not necessarily widely available. This increasingly included the highly incomplete preparatory material — reading notes, marginalia, etc. — which it became increasingly customary to treat as 'works' and to publish accordingly. What is perhaps more to the point, the attempt to analyse and interpret such materials with a view to discovering the lines of Marx's own thinking — especially on subjects about which he did not publish even drafts of texts — was increasingly made, as in the edition of Marx's *Ethnological Notebooks*. This may be regarded as the beginning of a new and promising phase in Marxian textual scholarship. The same applies to the study of Marxian drafts and variants, such as the preparatory drafts for the *Civil War in France* and the famous letter to Vera Zasulic of 1881. Indeed, such a development was inevitable, since several of the more important new texts, such as the *Grundrisse*, were themselves drafts, not intended for publication in the surviving form. However, the study of textual variants also advanced substantially with the republication in Japan, of the original first chapter of *Capital* vol. I (1867 edition) which had been substantially rewritten by Marx for subsequent editions.[15]

One might say that, particularly since the 1960s, Marxian scholarship has increasingly tended to seek in Marx and Engels not a definitive and 'final' set of texts expounding the Marxist theory, but a *process* of developing thought. It has also increasingly tended to abandon the view that the works of Marx and Engels are substantially indistinguishable components of the corpus of Marxism, and investigated the differences and sometimes divergences between the two lifelong partners. That this has led to sometimes exaggerated interpretations of these differences does not concern us here. The gradual decline of

Marxism as a formal dogmatic system since the mid-1950s has naturally encouraged these new tendencies in Marxian textual scholarship, though it has also led to the search for textual authority for alternative and sometimes dogmatic versions of 'Marxism' in the recently published or popularised and less familiar Marxian writings.

Part IV

The decline in dogmatic Marxism after 1956 produced a growing divergence between the countries under Marxist government, with their more-or-less monolithic official Marxist doctrines, and the rest of the world, in which a plurality of Marxist parties, groups and tendencies co-existed. Such a divergence had hardly existed before 1956. The Marxist parties of the pre-1914 Second International, though tending to develop an orthodox interpretation of doctrine as against 'revisionist' challengers on the right and anarcho-syndicalist ones on the left, accepted a plurality of interpretations, and were hardly in a position to prevent it, had they wished. Nobody in the German SPD thought it odd that the arch-revisionist Eduard Bernstein should edit the correspondence of Marx and Engels in 1913, though Lenin detected 'opportunism' in his editorial judgements. Social-democratic and communist Marxism co-existed in the 1920s, yet with the foundation of the Marx-Engels Institute the centre of publication for the classic texts passed increasingly into the communist side. It may be observed in passing that it still remains there. In spite of attempts, from the 1960s, to publish rival editions of the classic works (for example, by M. Rubel in France, H.J. Lieber and Benedikt Kautsky in Germany), the standard editions — without which none of the others, including numerous translations, would be conceivable — remain those based on Moscow (and since 1945 East Berlin), the first and second *MEGA* and the *Werke*. After 1933 for practical purposes the vast majority of orthodox Marxists in and outside the USSR were associated with the communist parties, for the various schismatics and heretics of the communist movement gained no numerically significant body of supporters. Marxism in the social democratic parties — even if we leave aside the virtual destruction of the German and Austrian ones after 1933–4 — grew increasingly attenuated and openly critical of classic orthodoxy, insofar as it had not already been so. After 1945, with few exceptions, these parties no longer considered themselves Marxist, except perhaps in a historical sense. It is only in retrospect, and in the light of the Marxist pluralism of the 1960s and 1970s, that the plural character of the Marxist literature between the wars was recognised, and systematic efforts were made, notably in Germany since the middle 1960s, to publish or reprint the writings of that period.

For something like a quarter of a century, therefore, there was no substantial difference between the Marxism of communist parties abroad (which meant most of Marxism in quantitative terms) and that of the USSR; at least no such difference was allowed to emerge into the open. This situation changed gradually, but with increasing speed, after 1956. Not merely was one doctrinal orthodoxy replaced by at least two, with the split between the USSR and China, but the non-governmental communist parties increasingly faced competition from rival Marxist groups with more substantial support, at least among intellectuals (that is, readers of Marxian texts), while within several western communist parties a considerable freedom of internal theoretical discussion developed, at least on matters of Marxian doctrine. There was thus a marked divergence between the countries in which Marxism remained official doctrine, closely associated with government, and, at any given moment, with a single binding version of 'what Marxism teaches' on any and every subject; and those in which this was no longer the case. A convenient measure of this divergence is the treatment of the actual biography of the founders. In the first group of countries this remained, if not totally hagiographic, then at all events restricted by a reluctance to deal with aspects of their lives and activities which did not show them in a favourable light. (This tradition was not new: it is very noticeable in the first phase of orthodox Marx-biography in Germany before 1914, as exemplified in Mehring's quasi-official life, published in 1918 and perhaps even more in the omissions from the original Marx–Engels correspondence.) In the second group of countries Marxists and Marx-biographers have publicly come to terms with the facts of the founders' lives, even when they do not show their subjects in an attractive light. Divergences of this kind have been increasingly characteristic of the history of Marxism, including the Marxian tests, since 1956.

It remains to survey briefly the diffusion of the works of the classics. Here again it is important to note the major significance of the period of 'monolithic' communist orthodoxy, which was also that of the systematic popularisation of actual texts by the founders.

This popularisation took four forms: the publication of separate works by Marx and Engels, generally in a series of short and one of longer writings, the publication of selected or collected works, the publication of anthologies on special topics, and finally, the compilation of compendia of Marxist theory based on, and containing quotations from, the classics. It need hardly be said that during this period 'the classics' included Lenin and later Stalin as well as Marx and Engels. However, with the exception of Plekhanov, no other Marxist writer maintained himself internationally in the company of the 'classics', at least after the 1920s.

Works published separately in the more modest series, under some such title as *les Elements du Communisme* or *Piccola Biblioteca Marxista* (probably on the model of the *Elementarbücher des Kommunismus* pioneered in Germany before 1933), included such works as the *Manifesto*, *Socialism, Utopian and Scientific*, *Value, Price and Profit*, *Wage Labour and Capital*, the *Civil War in France*, and suitable topical selections (for example, in the 1930s Marx and Engels' polemics with anarchists). The longer works were also usually published in a standard format, under some such title as the *Marxist-Leninist Library* or *Classici del Marxismo*. The catalogue of this library in Britain on the eve of the war may illustrate the content of such a series. It included (omitting works not by Marx and Engels), *Anti-Dühring*, *Feuerbach*, the *Letters to Kugelmann*, *Class Struggles in France*, *Civil War in France*, *Germany, Revolution and Counter-revolution*, Engels' *The Housing Question*, *The Poverty of Philosophy*, the *Selected Correspondence* of Marx and Engels, the *Critique of the Gotha Programme*, Engels' *Essays on 'Capital'* and a shortened edition of the *German Ideology*. *Capital* vol. I was not usually published *in extenso*, and not in such abbreviated or digested forms as had been popular in the social-democratic era. Until the end of the 1930s no attempt seems to have been made to issue *Selected Works* of Marx and Engels, but Moscow produced such a selection in two — later three — volumes which was distributed in various languages mainly after the war. No communist attempt to produce a *Collected Works* in languages other than Russian appears to have been made after the end of *MEGA*, until the appearance of the *Werke* (1956–68). The French edition did not get under way until the 1960s, the Italian edition until 1972, the English edition until 1975, doubtless because the task of translation was vast and difficult. The significance of the diffusion of Marxist texts is indicated by the fact that the leader of the C.P., Palmiro Togliatti, himself figures as the translator of several of the Italian versions of these works.

Anthologies of Marxist texts on various themes seem to have become popular, both in Russian-based and locally based selections, during the 1930s: Marx and Engels on Britain, Marx and Engels on Art and Literature, on India, China, Spain etc. Of the compendia the most authoritative by far was Section 2 of Chapter 4 of the *History of the CPSU (b): Short Course*, associated with Stalin himself. This work became influential, especially in countries with few vernacular editions of the classics, not only because of the pressure on communists to study it, but also because its simple and lucid presentation made it a brilliantly effective teaching-manual. Its impact on the generation of Marxists between 1938 and 1956, and perhaps especially in Eastern Europe after 1945, cannot be exaggerated.

In the 1960s, particularly with the rise of a large body of students and other intellectuals interested in Marxism, and of various Marxist or Marxisant movements outside the communist parties, the diffusion of the classic texts ceased to be something like a monopoly of the USSR and the communist parties associated with it. Increasingly commercial publishers entered this market, with or without urging from Marxists or sympathisers on their staffs. The number and variety of left and 'progressive' publishers also multiplied. To some extent, of course, this was a reflection of the general acceptance of Marx as a 'classic' in the general rather than the political sense — as someone about whom the normally educated and cultured reader should know something, irrespective of his or her ideological views. It was for this reason that he was published in the *Pleiade* collection of French classics, as *Capital* had long since been published in the British 'Everyman's Library'. The new interest in Marxism was no longer confined to the traditional corpus of popular works. Thus in the 1960s such works as the *Critique of Hegel's Philosophy of Law*, the *Holy Family*, Marx's doctoral dissertation, the *1844 Manuscripts* and the *German Ideology* were available in countries not hitherto in the forefront of Marxian studies, such as Spain. Certain of these works were no longer primarily translated under communist auspices, (for example, the French, Spanish and English translations of the *Grundrisse* — 1967-8, 1973, 1973 respectively; the Italian translation appeared in 1968-70).

Finally a few words about the geographical distribution of the Marxian classics. Some elementary texts were widely translated even before the October Revolution. Thus between 1848 and 1918 the *Communist Manifesto* appeared in something like thirty languages, including even three Japanese and one Chinese edition — though in practice Kautsky's *Economic Doctrines of Karl Marx* remained the main basis for Chinese Marxism. They included the major languages of western Europe (but only marginally those of the Iberian peninsula, with a single Portuguese edition and six Spanish editions, including those issued in Latin America). The languages of Tsarist Russia were well represented, though overshadowed by the seventy Russian editions (eleven Polish, five Ukrainian, six Finnish, seven Yiddish, four Georgian, two Armenian), but those of northern Europe only moderately, considering the degree of literacy in those countries (six Danish, five Swedish, two Norwegian). East Central and Southeastern Europe were represented in varying degrees, ranging from the nine Hungarian, eight Czech and seven Bulgarian editions to the single Slovak and Slovene edition, but the Eastern Mediterranean remained a void, except for a single Ladino translation, presumably published in Salonica. At the other extreme, *Capital* vol. I had been translated into most major literary languages of Europe before the death of Engels, though only incompletely into Spanish (German, Russian, French, Danish, Italian, English, Dutch, Polish). Before the October Revolution it was also translated into Bulgarian (1910), Czech (1913–5), Estonian (1910–4), Finnish (1913) and Yiddish (1917).

In western Europe a few stragglers brought up the rear much later: Norwegian (presumably because of familiarity with Danish as a literary language) in 1930–1, and the first incomplete Portuguese edition in 1962. Between the wars *Capital* penetrated southeastern Europe, though incompletely, with Hungarian (1921), Greek (1927) and Serbian (1933–4) editions. No major attempt seems to have been made to translate it into the languages of the USSR, except for Ukrainian (1925). A local version was published in independent Latvia (1920), a late echo of the major development of Marxism in the Tsarist empire. However, in this period for the first time *Capital* penetrated the non-European world (outside the USA) with editions in Argentina (1918), in Japanese (1920), Chinese (1930–3), Arabic (1939) and (in part) Marathi (1943). It is safe to say that this penetration was closely connected with the effects of the Russian Revolution.

The period since 1945 has seen a large-scale translation of *Capital* into the languages of countries under communist government (Romanian in 1947, Macedonian in 1953, Slovak in

1955, Korean in 1955–6, Slovene in 1961, Vietnamese in 1961–2, Spanish (Cuba) in 1962). Curiously enough the systematic effort to translate this work into the languages of the USSR did not occur until 1952 and thereafter (Byelorussian, Armenian, Georgian, Uzbek, Azerbaijani, Lithuanian, Ugrian, Turkmen and Kazakh). The only other major linguistic extension of *Capital* occurred in independent India, with editions in Hindi, Bengali and Malayalam in the 1950s and 1960s.[16] However, the wide range of certain international languages (Spanish in Latin America, Arabic in the Islamic world and English or French), conceals the actual geographic spread of Marxian texts. Nevertheless, it may be suggested that even in the late 1970s the writings of Marx and Engels were not available in the spoken languages of a very substantial part of the non-socialist world outside Europe, with the exception of Latin America. How accessible or widely diffused the available texts were, cannot be investigated here, though it may be suggested that (where not prohibited by governments) they were probably more widely available in schools and universities and for the educated public, than ever before, in all parts of the world. How far they were read or even bought outside these circles, is unclear. To answer this question would require very considerable research, which has not at present been undertaken.

Notes

1 K. Marx and F. Engels, *Gesamtausgabe* (Frankfurt-Moscow, 1927–1933), 12 volumes published.
2 B. Andréas, *Le Manifeste Communiste de Marx et Engels. Histoire et Bibliographie* (Milan, 1963).
3 Data from Social Democratic Party of Germany, Annual Conferences (*Parteitage*) 1895, 1898, 1901, 1903, 1904, 1906, 1907, 1908, 1910. Editions after 1906 became very much greater.
4 *Loc. cit.* for the relevant years.
5 R. Michels, 'Die Italienische Literatur über den Marxismus', *Archiv für Sozialwissenschaft*, vol. 25 (2), (1907), pp. 525–72.
6 F. Mehring (ed.) *Aus dem literarischen Nachlass von Karl Marx, Friedrich Engels und Ferdinand Lassalle*, 4 vols. (Stuttgart, 1902).
7 N. Rjasanoff (ed.) *Gesammelte Schriften von Marx und Engels 1852–1862*, 2 vols. (Stuttgart, 1917).
8 A. Bebel and E. Bernstein (eds.) *Der Briefwechsel zwischen Friedrich Engels und Karl Marx*, 4 vols. (Stuttgart, 1913).
9 F. Engels, *Paul et Laura Lafargue, Correspondence*, edited by E. Bottigelli, 3 vols (Paris, 1956–9).
10 *Neudrucke marxistischer Seltenheiten*, Verlag Rudolf Liebing (Leipzig, 1926).
11 As late as the 1960s the GDR edition of the *Werke*, while not actually

refraining from publishing these works, issued them separately from the main series and not as numbered volumes of the works.

12 B. Andréas, *op. cit.*

13 The following works of Marx and Engels were textually cited in that, inevitably influential, work: *Anti-Dühring, Capital*, the *Communist Manifesto*, the *Critique of Political Economy* (preface), *Dialectics of Nature, Feuerbach, Zur Kritik der Hegelschen Rechtsphilosophie, Poverty of Philosophy, Socialism, Utopian and Scientific, Wage Labour and Capital*, and one or two letters and prefaces by Engels.

14 *Briefe von Friedrich Engels an Eduard Bernstein* (Berlin, 1925).

15 K. Marx, *Das Kapital, Erster Band* (Hamburg, 1867), photographic reprint, (Tokyo, Aoki-Shoten, 1958).

16 *Marxistische Blätter* (Frankfurt a. Main) Sonderheft 2/1967: *Karl Marx. Das Kapital 1867–1967*. Indian friends have kindly corrected and added to the data on Indian languages.

INDEX

345